D0319625

Ding! Ding!

THE ★ BAG ★ OF ★ SLUGS

An open gash dripping with the moip of issues 100-105

Floating like Spam butterflies: Alex Collier, Simon Donald, Graham Dury, Wayne Gamble, Stevie Glover, Davey Jones, Ian McKie, Danny Sanderson, Sheila Thompson & Simon Thorp.

Stinging like NSU: Simon Ecob, John Fardell, Carl Hollingsworth, Kieron McCaffrey, Jamie McMorrow, Graham Murdoch, Mike Shaw, Lew Stringer & Brian Walker.

ISBN No. 0-75 2215-06-X

**Published in Great Britain by
IFG
9 Dallington Street (DSS welcome)
London EC1V 0BQ**

This edition published 2002 for Index Books Ltd

First Printing August or September 2002, something like that

Printed in Great Britain

To subscribe to new 10-times-a-year "monthly" Viz, call **01454 642459** or do it securely on the "internet", by "clicking" your "browser" onto **www.viz.co.uk** and blasting your credit card details into cyberspace.

Letterbocks

It's the page that wears a silver suit, goes to work in a hover-car and eats a small pill instead of a three course dinner.

Star Letter

❑ Nothing really. I was just testing the new e-mail service on my mobile and your address was handy. Sorry.

D. Falk
e-mail

Congratulations D. Falk. There's a Profanisaurus mug and a £100 Star Letter prize winging its way to you.

❑ In issue 6 you asked your dyslexic readers to write in and spell the word 'fuck'. As a dyslexic, I find this personally insulting, and having just finished the article I thought I should voice my concern.

R. Baker
Cheshire

A bit of the udder

❑ Have any of your readers been disturbed, like my wife, by what could be the first lesbian zoophiliac adverts on British telly? I mean the one where a great big horny cow, udders swinging, chases the woman around, shamelessly after a bit of 'cross-species carpet munching'. What's going on there?

Dean Wright
Staffordshire

*Have **you** got something to tell us? Maybe you committed some dreadful murder many years ago and the guilt is eating away at you. Or maybe you've just heard your grandson say something innocently amusing. Whatever it is, write and tell us at Letterbocks. There's a Roger's Profanisaurus Mug for every letter and Top Tip we publish.*

Letterbocks
Viz Comic
PO Box 1PT
Newcastle upon Tyne
NE99 1PT
Faxophone: 0191 2414244
electro-mail viz.comic@virgin.net

Bottle of Becks

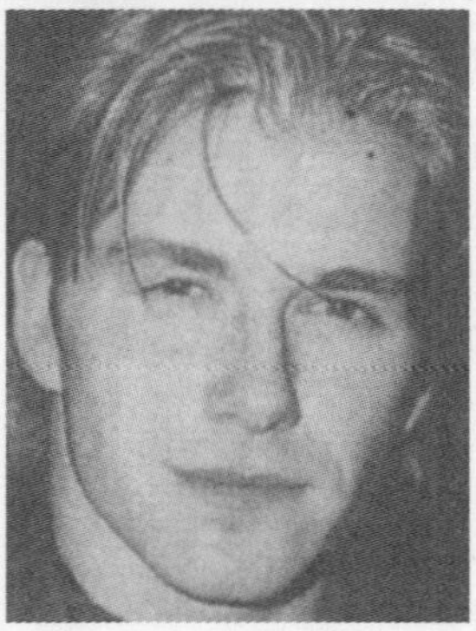

❑ Father of the Millennium award must surely go to David Beckham. Unlike many fathers, he is prepared to endure excruciating pain to have his son's name tattooed in fancy Old English capitals across the top of his arse. I doubt many of his critics would show a similar love for their children.

J. Vance
Cardiff

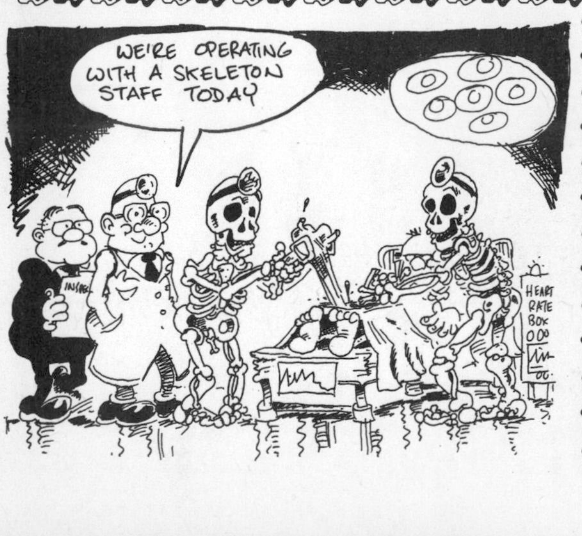

WE'RE OPERATING WITH A SKELETON STAFF TODAY
HEART RATE BOX

Don't try this at home

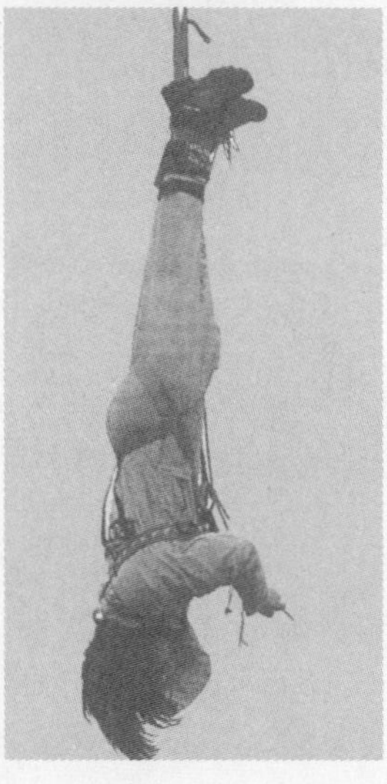

❑ Davina McCall says that dangling off a helicopter over the Grand Canyon on a 700 foot bungee rope was the most terrifying and dangerous thing she has ever done. She must be forgetting that she went out with Stan Collymore.

M. Duckworth
Poole

Organ music

❑ A good heart these days is hard to find, sang 80's popster Fergal Sharkey. How true. My husband has been waiting on the hospital transplant list for 7 months.

Big Vicky
e-mail

❑ Coming home from London on a GNER train last week, the steward announced over the tannoy that the buffet was open for the sale of tea, coffee, sandwiches and home made cakes and pastries. I'd like to know in what way they are home made? Did the driver's mum bake them that morning and send him to work with them in a tin?

J. Bristol
Cursitor

❑ Christmas seems to come earlier every year. My next door neighbours have already got a Christmas tree growing in their garden- *in February.* It's absolutely ridiculous.

J. Bishop
Oslo

❑ As a mincing homosexual, I am utterly sickened by the fact that the perfectly good word 'gay' is being hijacked as a socially acceptable term for 'happy' by retired, purple-faced army Majors who read the Daily Telegraph. I for one will not allow these tweed-clad buffers with their handlebar moustaches to stop me using the word in its proper context, meaning 'on the other bus'.

J. Wilson
London

It's good to stalk

❑ Psychologists tell us that it is practically unheard of for stalkers to attack the objects of their obsession. This must be some comfort to the 50% of The Beatles who haven't been shot or stabbed.

J. Van der Lande
Den Haag

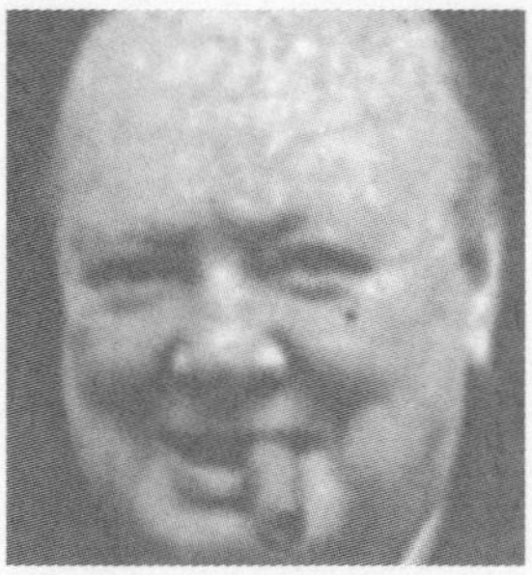

❑ "We shall fight them on the beaches, we shall fight them in the fields and on the landing grounds," said Churchill in 1939. Unusual use of the word 'we'. I was on Omaha Beach having my leg shot off and I can't remember seeing Winnie anywhere. Perhaps I missed the bit where he said "We shall fight them 50 feet underground in a reinforced concrete bunker."

S. Whiting
Carlisle

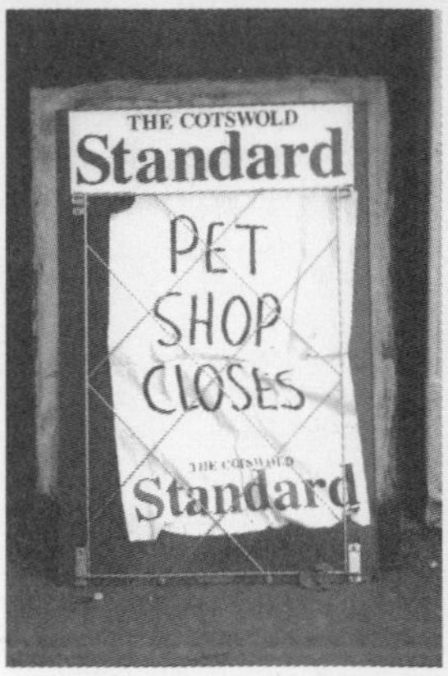

THE COTSWOLD
Standard
PET SHOP CLOSES
Standard

❑ Thought you might like to know what goes on in the Cotswolds.

Pete Coulton
Heaton

❑ I smoke 80 a day, but I am unable to take any comfort from from the statistics that say I am just as likely to be ran over by a bus as I am do die of lung cancer. That's because I live on Sark.

R. Le Feuvre
Sark

❑ So Sting is able to shag his wife for five hours without going off. I know how he feels. My wife is no oil painting either.

J. Leonard
Hull

Really useless engines

❑ After the Paddington Rail crash, it was impossible to get away from anyone who ever caught a train calling for John Prescott to resign. Well my kids watch Thomas the Tank Engine reguarly, and their trains crash more often than a Sinclair ZX81. Why then does no one go on TV calling for the Fat Controller to resign? I for one would travel by road if I ever visited the Isle of Sodor.

Oz
Huddersfield

❑ I don't know what Roy Castle is complaining about. I got cancer of the ears from listening to trumpet records in a fag factory.

T. Evans
Pitlochrie

❑ Around lunchtime last Sunday, I saw *four* bald men erecting a greenhouse. Surely this must be some kind of record.

N. Brown
Newton Hill

Is this a record, or do you know different? Perhaps you've seen six slapsters building a shed, or maybe you witnessed five men with alopaecia putting up a lean-to. Write and tell us at the usual address and we'll give a prize to the best letter we receive. Mark your envelope 'Garden Building Baldies' and enclose a £5 judging fee. The winner will receive the first thing we can lay our hands on in the stationery cupboard.

False economy

❑ They say that artificial Christmas trees are every bit as good as the real ones. Nonsense. We spent a fortune on a high quality imitation Norweigan Spruce last year. It looked nice enough and dropped no needles. But come January it took 5 hours and six hacksaw blades to chop it up, and the branches stank of burning plastic when we put them on the fire.

C. Donkin
Northumberland

❑ With reference to your search for the most miserable sod at work. I came across this sorry looking individual in the catalogue for 'Kee Klamps pipes and fittings'. I mean, would you *really* want this man promoting your business?

K. Hunt
Poole

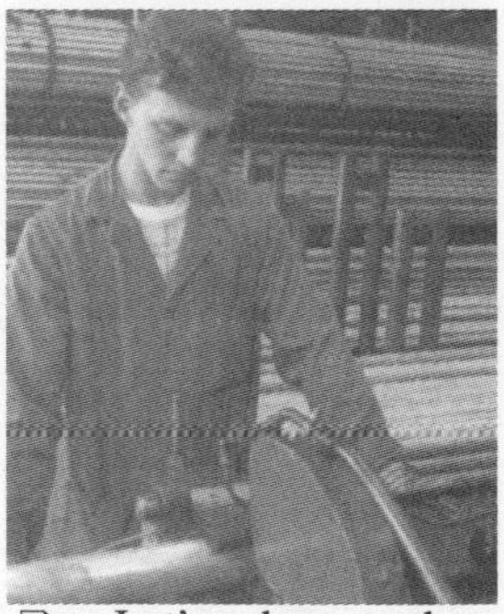

❑ Let's hope that 'Heartbeat' manages another 8 series or so. I for one can't wait for the hilarious day the first punk rocker turns up in Aidensfield.

Spud
Luton

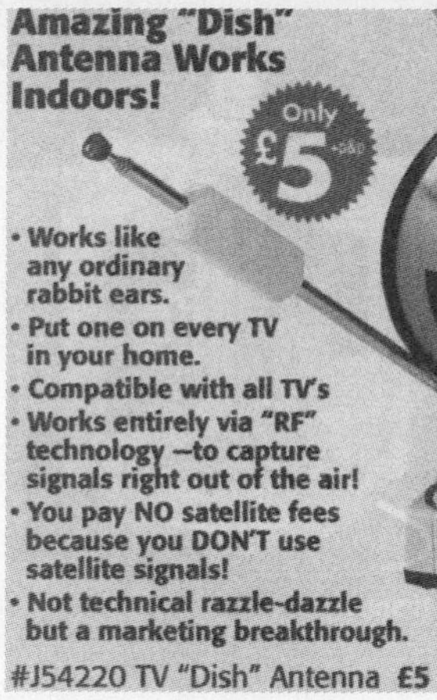

Amazing "Dish" Antenna Works Indoors!
Only £5
• Works like any ordinary rabbit ears.
• Put one on every TV in your home.
• Compatible with all TV's
• Works entirely via "RF" technology --to capture signals right out of the air!
• You pay NO satellite fees because you DON'T use satellite signals!
• Not technical razzle-dazzle but a marketing breakthrough.
#J54220 TV "Dish" Antenna £5

❑ Please find enclosed one of the cheekiest unsolicited adverts for a crap product ever to fall out of a newspaper. "Marketing breakthrough"- too right, because if they shift just one of these to anyone who has even one of their marbles left, then they're the king of salesmen.

Stuart Edwards
Hertfordshire

❑ With reference to the above letter. I think it's very sad how cynical people are in this day and age. I think the Amazing Indoor TV Dish Antenna, costing £5 and promising to get you terrestrial channels plus all satellite channels free of charge *really will work*.

J. Booth
Wednesbury

Royal flush

❑ I want it known that I have sat on the same toilet seat as the Queen, hubby Phil, son Charles and his late wife Di. I was a copper here in Perth and one of the crappier jobs in my career was to babysit Government House. When the Governor General was away we had free range of the place and never missed a chance to sit on the shitter in the Royal Suite and wonder what went through those great minds as they sat and strained. Not much judging by the lack of wall poetry. Have any of your other readers crimped off a length in such hallowed halls?

P. Buzz
West Australia

❑ Do any of your readers have Carol Vorderman's telephone number? I'm on 'Who Wants to be a Millionaire?' next week and all my mates are as thick as pigshit. There's a bag of sand and a shag in it for her if I win the big one.

S. Bunny
Rochdale

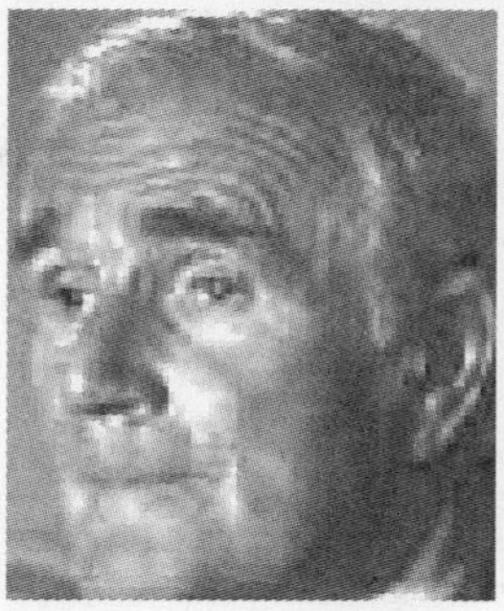

❑ All this wank about the Millennium Bug. Britain spends £85 billion, and the only thing that crashes is Q out of the Bond films.

T. Hall
Tewksebury

❑ On the subject of Bond film boffin actor Desmond Llewellyn, he was always telling 007 to 'pay attention'. Perhaps if he practised what he preached and paid attention to the road he'd now be happily 'Q'-ing for his pension instead of being dead. And if he'd had his wits about him he could have used his ejector seat or something.

Louise
Leytonstone

❑ Having studied the facsimile of Viz number one, included with your 20th anniversary issue, I wish to express my incredulity that there was ever an issue two.

Martin Bradley
Middlesex

In the frame

❑ My favourite 'You've Been Framed' clip is the one when that bloke is waving cheerily to all those people from his car, completely unaware that he's about to be shot in the head. *The look on his wife's face!*

Chuck Wanker Jnr.
Des Moines

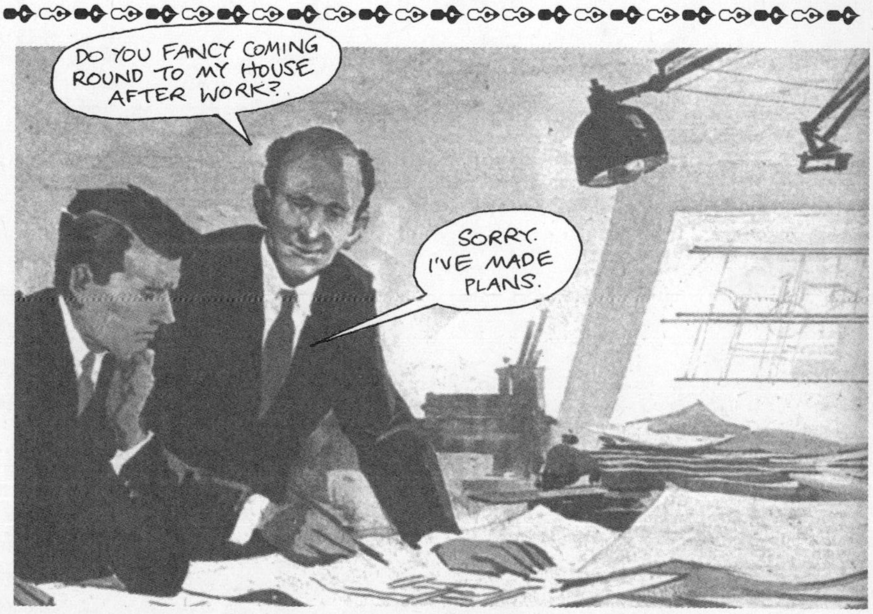

DO YOU FANCY COMING ROUND TO MY HOUSE AFTER WORK?
SORRY. I'VE MADE PLANS.

TOP TIPS

FOOL your friends into thinking you are insane by inviting them round for dinner and greet them at the door naked with 'HELP ME' cut into your chest with a razor blade, eating shit out of an ice-cream container. Watch them laugh when you reveal it was a joke.

Lachlan, e-mail

DON'T throw away those disposable razors until I think of something amusing to do with them.

Peter Busby, Perth

DESIGNERS of internet porn sites. Ease congestion of the net and decrease downloading time by putting the pictures upside down with the minge at the top.

Peter Bushby again, Perth

MAKE people think you have your very own RoboCop by walking a few yards behind a policeman on the beat, pointing a remote control at his back, twiddling the knobs everytime he turns a corner, scratches himself or bashes somebody.

B. Pushby, Perth

MALE readers. Add vital extra inches to your penis by swopping the traditional 'up and down' method of masturbating for a rolling motion similar to that used when making a plasticine sausage.

Rob Baker, Crewe

CREATE your own sauna by climbing naked into a wardrobe with a couple of strangers, occasionally throwing water over a one-bar electric heater.

Marc Blake, e-mail

SMOKERS. Save money by rolling up the net curtains in any good pub and lighting the end. Hey Presto! A fag with about 20 years worth of smoke in one go.

Ross & Keith, Lincoln

CONVINCE neighbours opposite that you have a PC by staring into the corner of your bedroom whilst tapping on an oblong piece of wood, pausing occasionally to masturbate furiously.

P. Watson, Gateshead

GREENGROCERS. Pre-tend you are a QVC telly presenter by talking to your customers about onions in a patronising way for 3 hours.

J. Mingewater, Feltham

GENTLEMEN. Tempt the ladies to gobble you off by marinating the old man in Bailey's before you hit the town.

M. Partridge, e-mail

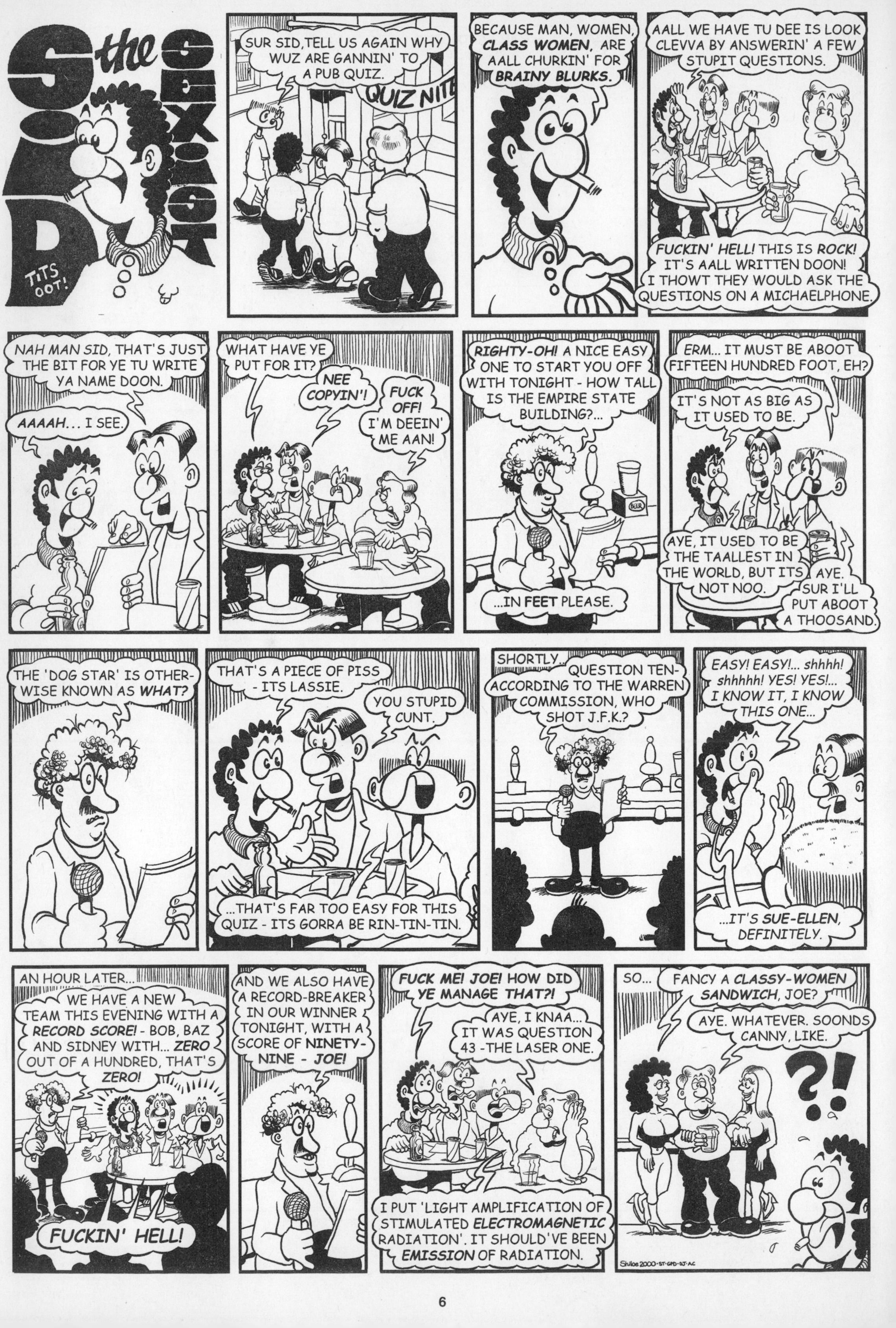
SID the SEXIST
TITS OOT!
SUR SID, TELL US AGAIN WHY WUZ ARE GANNIN' TO A PUB QUIZ.
QUIZ NITE
BECAUSE MAN, WOMEN, CLASS WOMEN, ARE AALL CHURKIN' FOR BRAINY BLURKS.
AALL WE HAVE TU DEE IS LOOK CLEVVA BY ANSWERIN' A FEW STUPIT QUESTIONS.
FUCKIN' HELL! THIS IS ROCK! IT'S AALL WRITTEN DOON! I THOWT THEY WOULD ASK THE QUESTIONS ON A MICHAELPHONE.
NAH MAN SID, THAT'S JUST THE BIT FOR YE TU WRITE YA NAME DOON.
AAAAH... I SEE.
WHAT HAVE YE PUT FOR IT?
NEE COPYIN'!
FUCK OFF! I'M DEEIN' ME AAN!
RIGHTY-OH! A NICE EASY ONE TO START YOU OFF WITH TONIGHT - HOW TALL IS THE EMPIRE STATE BUILDING?...
BEER
...IN FEET PLEASE.
ERM... IT MUST BE ABOOT FIFTEEN HUNDRED FOOT, EH?
IT'S NOT AS BIG AS IT USED TO BE.
AYE, IT USED TO BE THE TAALLEST IN THE WORLD, BUT ITS NOT NOO.
AYE. SUR I'LL PUT ABOOT A THOOSAND.
THE 'DOG STAR' IS OTHERWISE KNOWN AS WHAT?
THAT'S A PIECE OF PISS - ITS LASSIE.
YOU STUPID CUNT.
...THAT'S FAR TOO EASY FOR THIS QUIZ - ITS GORRA BE RIN-TIN-TIN.
SHORTLY...
QUESTION TEN- ACCORDING TO THE WARREN COMMISSION, WHO SHOT J.F.K.?
EASY! EASY!... shhhh! shhhhh! YES! YES!... I KNOW IT, I KNOW THIS ONE...
...IT'S SUE-ELLEN, DEFINITELY.
AN HOUR LATER...
WE HAVE A NEW TEAM THIS EVENING WITH A RECORD SCORE! - BOB, BAZ AND SIDNEY WITH... ZERO OUT OF A HUNDRED, THAT'S ZERO!
FUCKIN' HELL!
AND WE ALSO HAVE A RECORD-BREAKER IN OUR WINNER TONIGHT, WITH A SCORE OF NINETY-NINE - JOE!
FUCK ME! JOE! HOW DID YE MANAGE THAT?!
AYE, I KNAA... IT WAS QUESTION 43 -THE LASER ONE.
I PUT 'LIGHT AMPLIFICATION OF STIMULATED ELECTROMAGNETIC RADIATION'. IT SHOULD'VE BEEN EMISSION OF RADIATION.
SO...
FANCY A CLASSY-WOMEN SANDWICH, JOE?
AYE. WHATEVER. SOONDS CANNY, LIKE.
?!

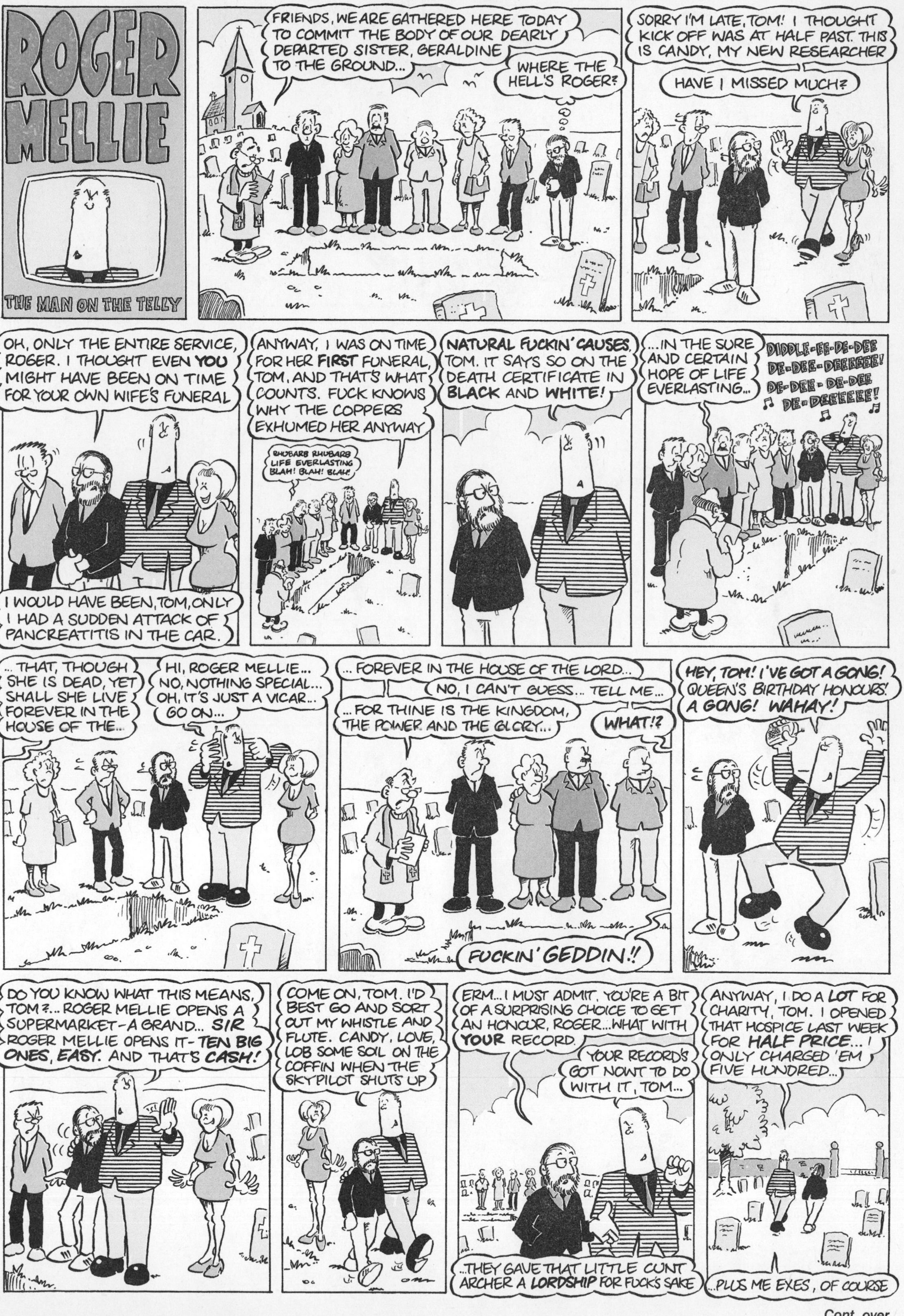

ROGER MELLIE
THE MAN ON THE TELLY
FRIENDS, WE ARE GATHERED HERE TODAY TO COMMIT THE BODY OF OUR DEARLY DEPARTED SISTER, GERALDINE TO THE GROUND...
WHERE THE HELL'S ROGER?
SORRY I'M LATE, TOM! I THOUGHT KICK OFF WAS AT HALF PAST. THIS IS CANDY, MY NEW RESEARCHER
HAVE I MISSED MUCH?
OH, ONLY THE ENTIRE SERVICE, ROGER. I THOUGHT EVEN YOU MIGHT HAVE BEEN ON TIME FOR YOUR OWN WIFE'S FUNERAL
I WOULD HAVE BEEN, TOM, ONLY I HAD A SUDDEN ATTACK OF PANCREATITIS IN THE CAR.
ANYWAY, I WAS ON TIME FOR HER FIRST FUNERAL, TOM, AND THAT'S WHAT COUNTS. FUCK KNOWS WHY THE COPPERS EXHUMED HER ANYWAY
RHUBARB RHUBARB LIFE EVERLASTING BLAH! BLAH! BLAH!
NATURAL FUCKIN' CAUSES, TOM. IT SAYS SO ON THE DEATH CERTIFICATE IN BLACK AND WHITE!
...IN THE SURE AND CERTAIN HOPE OF LIFE EVERLASTING...
DIDDLE-EE-DE-DEE DE-DEE-DEEEEEE! DE-DEE-DE-DEE DE-DEEEEEE!
...THAT, THOUGH SHE IS DEAD, YET SHALL SHE LIVE FOREVER IN THE HOUSE OF THE...
HI, ROGER MELLIE... NO, NOTHING SPECIAL... OH, IT'S JUST A VICAR... GO ON...
...FOREVER IN THE HOUSE OF THE LORD...
NO, I CAN'T GUESS... TELL ME...
...FOR THINE IS THE KINGDOM, THE POWER AND THE GLORY...
WHAT!?
FUCKIN' GEDDIN!!
HEY, TOM! I'VE GOT A GONG! QUEEN'S BIRTHDAY HONOURS! A GONG! WAHAY!
DO YOU KNOW WHAT THIS MEANS, TOM?... ROGER MELLIE OPENS A SUPERMARKET - A GRAND... SIR ROGER MELLIE OPENS IT - TEN BIG ONES, EASY. AND THAT'S CASH!
COME ON, TOM. I'D BEST GO AND SORT OUT MY WHISTLE AND FLUTE. CANDY, LOVE, LOB SOME SOIL ON THE COFFIN WHEN THE SKYPILOT SHUTS UP
ERM... I MUST ADMIT, YOU'RE A BIT OF A SURPRISING CHOICE TO GET AN HONOUR, ROGER... WHAT WITH YOUR RECORD.
YOUR RECORD'S GOT NOWT TO DO WITH IT, TOM...
...THEY GAVE THAT LITTLE CUNT ARCHER A LORDSHIP FOR FUCK'S SAKE
ANYWAY, I DO A LOT FOR CHARITY, TOM. I OPENED THAT HOSPICE LAST WEEK FOR HALF PRICE... I ONLY CHARGED 'EM FIVE HUNDRED...
...PLUS ME EXES, OF COURSE

Cont. over

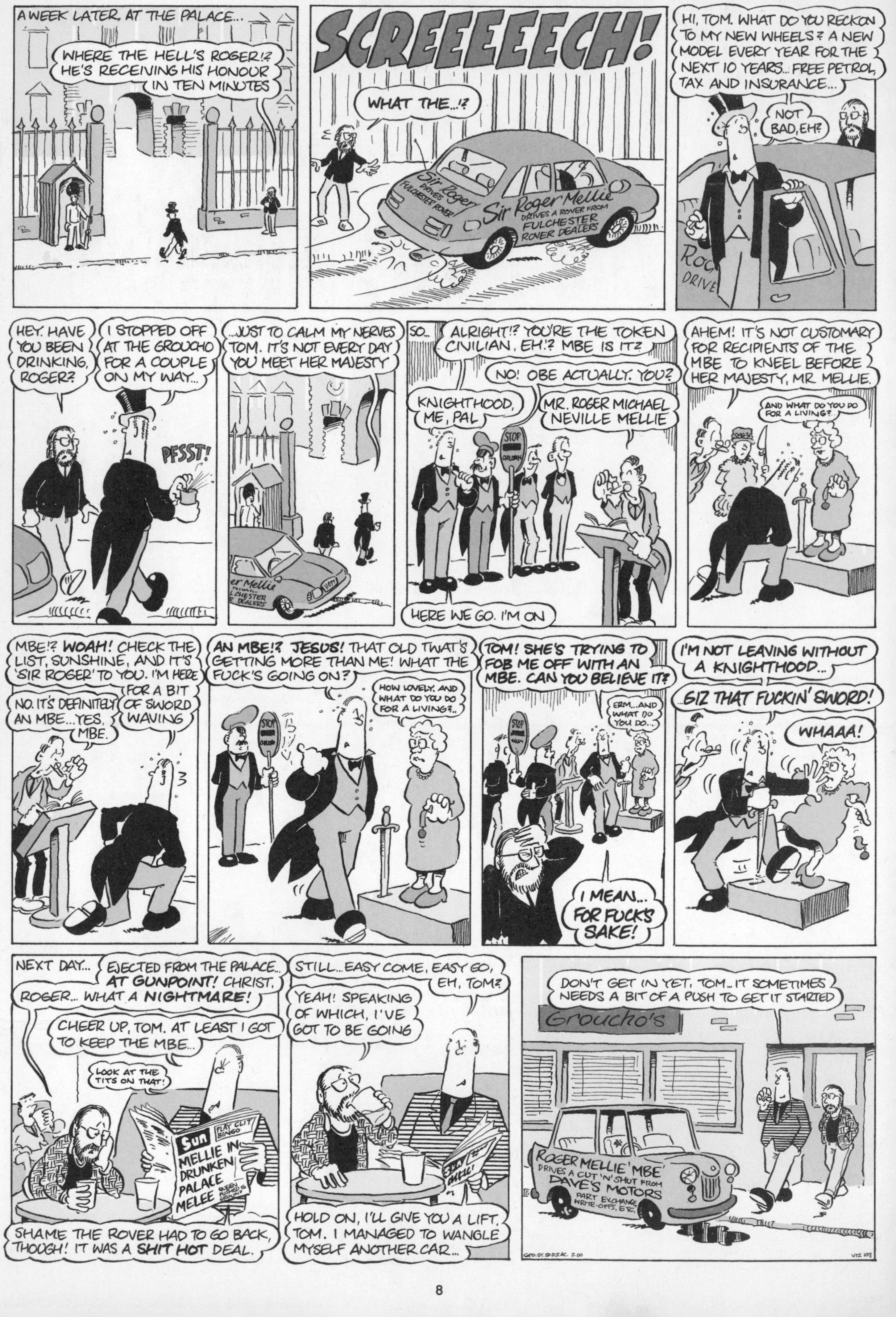

A WEEK LATER, AT THE PALACE...
WHERE THE HELL'S ROGER!? HE'S RECEIVING HIS HONOUR IN TEN MINUTES
SCREEEEEECH!
WHAT THE...!?
Sir Roger DRIVES FULCHESTER ROVER!
Sir Roger Mellie DRIVES A ROVER FROM FULCHESTER ROVER DEALERS
HI, TOM. WHAT DO YOU RECKON TO MY NEW WHEELS? A NEW MODEL EVERY YEAR FOR THE NEXT 10 YEARS... FREE PETROL, TAX AND INSURANCE...
NOT BAD, EH?
HEY. HAVE YOU BEEN DRINKING, ROGER?
I STOPPED OFF AT THE GROUCHO FOR A COUPLE ON MY WAY...
PFSSST!
...JUST TO CALM MY NERVES TOM. IT'S NOT EVERY DAY YOU MEET HER MAJESTY
SO..
ALRIGHT!? YOU'RE THE TOKEN CIVILIAN, EH!? MBE IS IT?
NO! OBE ACTUALLY. YOU?
KNIGHTHOOD, ME, PAL
MR. ROGER MICHAEL NEVILLE MELLIE
STOP
HERE WE GO. I'M ON
AHEM! IT'S NOT CUSTOMARY FOR RECIPIENTS OF THE MBE TO KNEEL BEFORE HER MAJESTY, MR MELLIE.
AND WHAT DO YOU DO FOR A LIVING?..
MBE!? WOAH! CHECK THE LIST, SUNSHINE, AND IT'S 'SIR ROGER' TO YOU. I'M HERE FOR A BIT OF SWORD WAVING
NO. IT'S DEFINITELY AN MBE... YES, MBE.
AN MBE!? JESUS! THAT OLD TWAT'S GETTING MORE THAN ME! WHAT THE FUCK'S GOING ON?
HOW LOVELY. AND WHAT DO YOU DO FOR A LIVING?..
TOM! SHE'S TRYING TO FOB ME OFF WITH AN MBE. CAN YOU BELIEVE IT?
ERM... AND WHAT DO YOU DO...
I MEAN... FOR FUCK'S SAKE!
I'M NOT LEAVING WITHOUT A KNIGHTHOOD...
...GIZ THAT FUCKIN' SWORD!
WHAAA!
NEXT DAY...
EJECTED FROM THE PALACE... AT GUNPOINT! CHRIST, ROGER... WHAT A NIGHTMARE!
CHEER UP, TOM. AT LEAST I GOT TO KEEP THE MBE...
LOOK AT THE TITS ON THAT!
Sun
FLAT CLIT BINGO
MELLIE IN DRUNKEN PALACE MELEE
SHAME THE ROVER HAD TO GO BACK, THOUGH! IT WAS A SHIT HOT DEAL.
STILL... EASY COME, EASY GO, EH, TOM?
YEAH! SPEAKING OF WHICH, I'VE GOT TO BE GOING
HOLD ON, I'LL GIVE YOU A LIFT, TOM. I MANAGED TO WANGLE MYSELF ANOTHER CAR...
DON'T GET IN YET, TOM... IT SOMETIMES NEEDS A BIT OF A PUSH TO GET IT STARTED
Groucho's
ROGER MELLIE 'MBE' DRIVES A CUT 'N' SHUT FROM DAVE'S MOTORS
PART EXCHANGE WRITE-OFFS, ETC.

HE THINKS IT'S NOT OVER...

Another load of bollocks from our Sports Correspondent

Stan PIESHOP

A JAPANESE National footballer, unaware that the 1966 World Cup has been over for nearly 34 years, has been discovered in a changing room at Wembley Stadium.

IT IS NOW!

Demolition men were surprised to discover 60-year-old centre forward Satoru Nakajima hiding behind some towels, where he had been living since his country's first round match against Portugal in June 1966.

trick

Nakajima refused to accept the workmen's assurances that the game had ended over three decades ago, insisting that they were part of a Portuguese trick.

uni

And it was not until the 1966 Japanese squad manager, Mr. Iwao Takamoto, 102, was brought to the stadium to confirm the news, that Nakajima came out from behind his towels.

poly

During the world cup match, Nakajima had been told to limber up in the dressing room as he was to be brought on for the last ten minutes.

sukki

However, Portugal scored three times in the second half, and the demoralised manager forgot all about him.

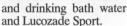

Nakajima (above, circled) in the 1966 squad, and (right) as he appeared yesterday.

Nakajima spent the next 34 years waiting for the call from the bench, eating discarded orange peel and drinking bath water and Lucozade Sport.

The NEWS in BRIEFS with RICHARD BAKER

- *Britain's oldest mayfly, Harold Cooper of Leeds has died at the age of 25 hours 16 minutes. This now means that Gladys Sanderson of Blackpool is the oldest living mayfly, at 24 hours 47 minutes. The oldest mayfly in the world is believed to be Xiao tse Deng of Kiangsi, China, who claims to be 28 hours 33 minutes old.*

- Former World champion racing driver Damon Hill has never passed his driving test! According to a new biography published this week, the F1 ace has to get his dad, the late Graham Hill, to sit beside him whenever he ventures onto public streets.

- *38-year-old Crawford McBinnie couldn't believe his eyes when he opened up a disused barn on his late grandfather's farm in Auchtermuchty, Fife, and discovered the Nazi war machine under a tarpaulin. Virtually unrecognisable under a thick layer of dust and chicken droppings, the infamous contraption is to be restored and put on permanent display at Flamingoland, North Yorkshire.*

- Leather-clad 70's glam-rocker Alvin Stardust was last night helping Mansfield police with their enquiries after a jammed toaster which he had taken to Currys to be repaired was found to contain several slices of obscene toast. Stardust's solicitor emphasised that the singer - real name Shane Fenton and the Fentones - had gone to the station voluntarily and had not yet been arrested or charged with any offence.

- *13th century Neapolitan theologian St Thomas Aquinas has been voted the most influential figure of the Millennium in a poll of 1000 leading European academics. Second choice was 16th century heretical astronomer, mathematician and physicist Galileo Galilei, whose observations of the phases of Venus proved that the Earth actually orbited the Sun. In third place was Robbie Williams.*

OH, LORDY!
IT'S... THE FAT SLAGS
I'VE JUST SEEN THE DOCTOR OUT, SAN. WHAT DID HE SAY?
IT'S THE 'FLU
SNIFF!
A R AL BAD CASE! HE SAID I'VE GOT TO STAY IN BED FOR AT LEAST A WEEK
WORRA SHAME! IT'S BAZ'S BIRTHDAY TODAY, AN' ALL. WE'RE GOIN' DOWN THE DOG AN' HAMMER
AYE!..
SNIFF!
LATER...
TRAY, PUSH US TO THE BOGS, WILL YA? I'M BUSTIN' FORRA PISS. SNIFF!

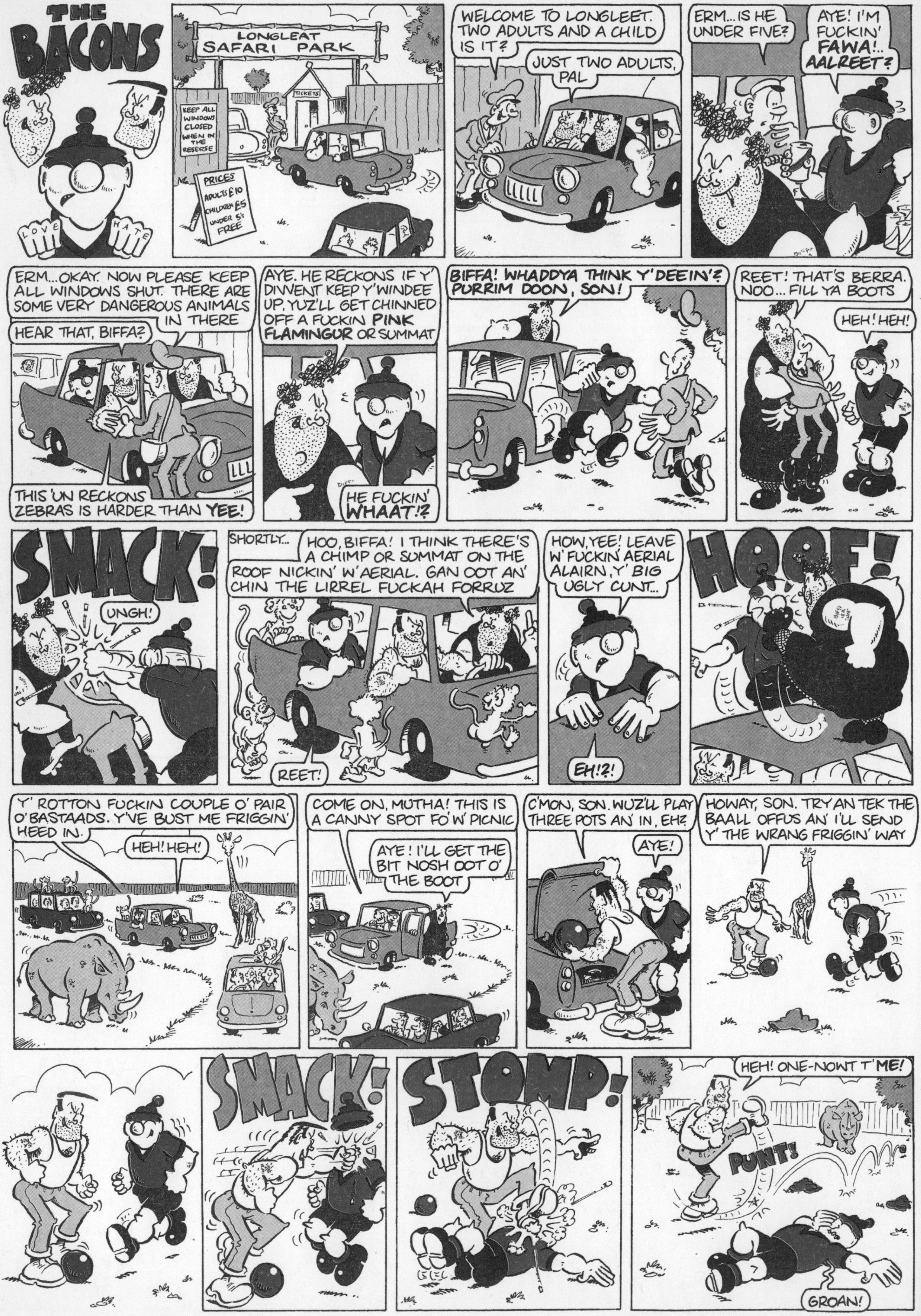
THE BACONS
LOVE
HATE
LONGLEAT SAFARI PARK
TICKETS
KEEP ALL WINDOWS CLOSED WHEN IN THE RESERVE
PRICES ADULTS £10 CHILDREN £5 UNDER 5's FREE
WELCOME TO LONGLEET. TWO ADULTS AND A CHILD IS IT?
JUST TWO ADULTS, PAL
ERM... IS HE UNDER FIVE?
AYE! I'M FUCKIN' FAWA!.. AALREET?
ERM... OKAY. NOW PLEASE KEEP ALL WINDOWS SHUT. THERE ARE SOME VERY DANGEROUS ANIMALS IN THERE
HEAR THAT, BIFFA?
THIS 'UN RECKONS ZEBRAS IS HARDER THAN YEE!
AYE. HE RECKONS IF Y' DIVVENT KEEP Y'WINDEE UP, YUZ'LL GET CHINNED OFF A FUCKIN PINK FLAMINGUR OR SUMMAT
HE FUCKIN' WHAAT!?
BIFFA! WHADDYA THINK Y'DEEIN'? PURRIM DOON, SON!
REET! THAT'S BERRA. NOO... FILL YA BOOTS
HEH! HEH!
SMACK!
UNGH!
SHORTLY...
HOO, BIFFA! I THINK THERE'S A CHIMP OR SUMMAT ON THE ROOF NICKIN' W'AERIAL. GAN OOT AN' CHIN THE LIRREL FUCKAH FORRUZ
REET!
HOW, YEE! LEAVE W' FUCKIN' AERIAL ALAIRN, Y' BIG UGLY CUNT...
EH!?!
HOOF!
Y' ROTTON FUCKIN COUPLE O' PAIR O'BASTAADS. Y'VE BUST ME FRIGGIN' HEED IN.
HEH! HEH!
COME ON, MUTHA! THIS IS A CANNY SPOT FO' W' PICNIC
AYE! I'LL GET THE BIT NOSH OOT O' THE BOOT
C'MON, SON. WUZ'LL PLAY THREE POTS AN' IN, EH?
AYE!
HOWAY, SON. TRY AN TEK THE BAALL OFFUS AN' I'LL SEND Y' THE WRANG FRIGGIN' WAY
SMACK!
STOMP!
HEH! ONE-NOWT T' ME!
PUNT!
GROAN!

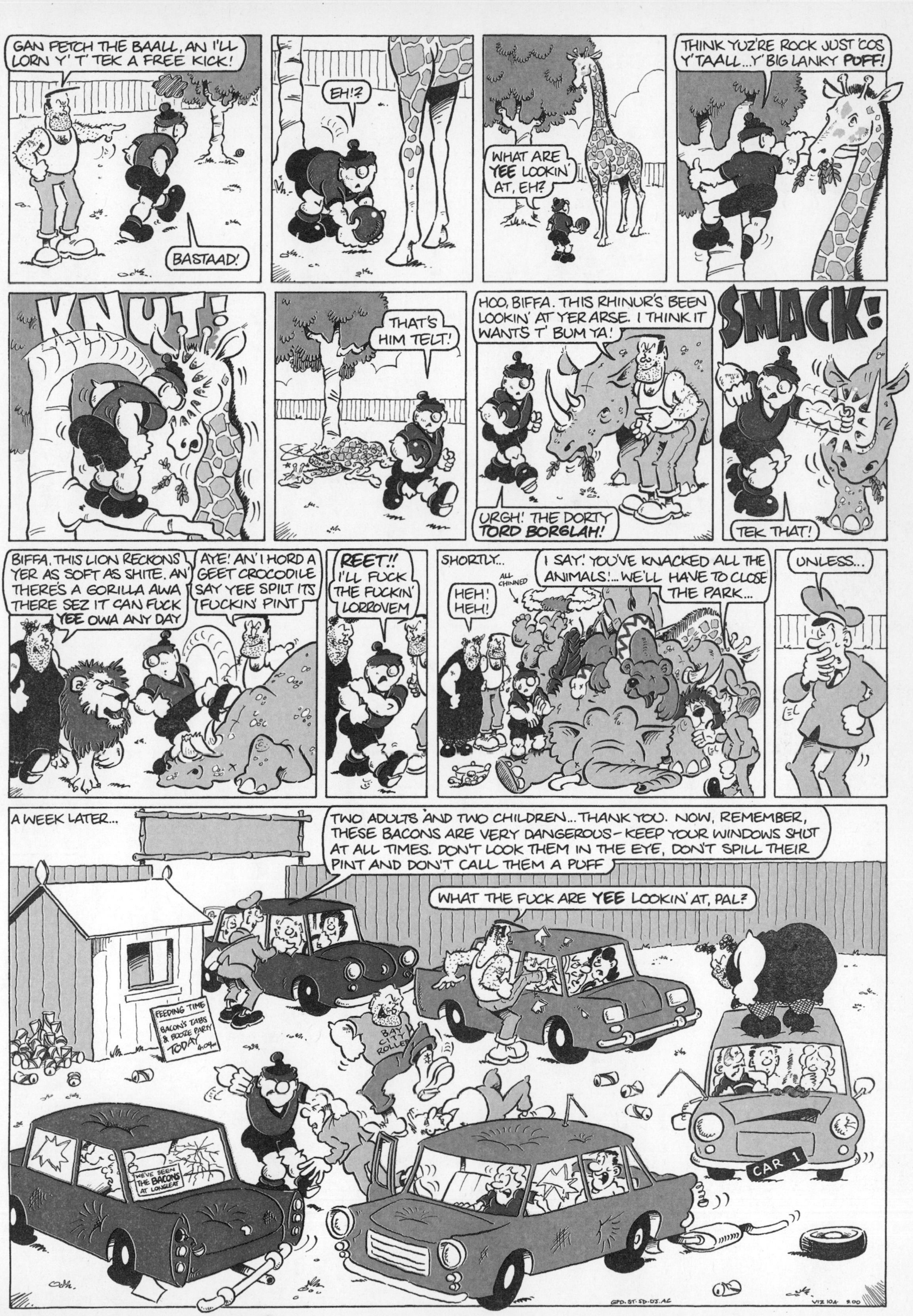

GAN FETCH THE BAALL, AN I'LL LORN Y' T' TEK A FREE KICK!
BASTAAD!
EH!?
WHAT ARE YEE LOOKIN' AT, EH?
THINK YUZ'RE ROCK JUST 'COS Y' TAALL... Y' BIG LANKY PUFF!
KNUT!
THAT'S HIM TELT!
HOO, BIFFA. THIS RHINUR'S BEEN LOOKIN' AT YER ARSE. I THINK IT WANTS T' BUM YA!
URGH! THE DORTY TORD BORGLAH!
SMACK!
TEK THAT!
BIFFA. THIS LION RECKONS YER AS SOFT AS SHITE. AN' THERE'S A GORILLA AWA THERE SEZ IT CAN FUCK YEE OWA ANY DAY
AYE! AN' I HORD A GEET CROCODILE SAY YEE SPILT ITS FUCKIN' PINT
REET!! I'LL FUCK THE FUCKIN' LORROVEM
SHORTLY...
HEH! HEH!
ALL CHINNED
I SAY! YOU'VE KNACKED ALL THE ANIMALS!... WE'LL HAVE TO CLOSE THE PARK...
UNLESS...
A WEEK LATER...
TWO ADULTS AND TWO CHILDREN... THANK YOU. NOW, REMEMBER, THESE BACONS ARE VERY DANGEROUS - KEEP YOUR WINDOWS SHUT AT ALL TIMES. DON'T LOOK THEM IN THE EYE, DON'T SPILL THEIR PINT AND DON'T CALL THEM A PUFF
WHAT THE FUCK ARE YEE LOOKIN' AT, PAL?
FEEDING TIME BACON'S TABS & BOOZE PARTY TODAY
BAY CITY ROLLER
WE'VE SEEN THE BACONS AT LONGLEAT
CAR 1

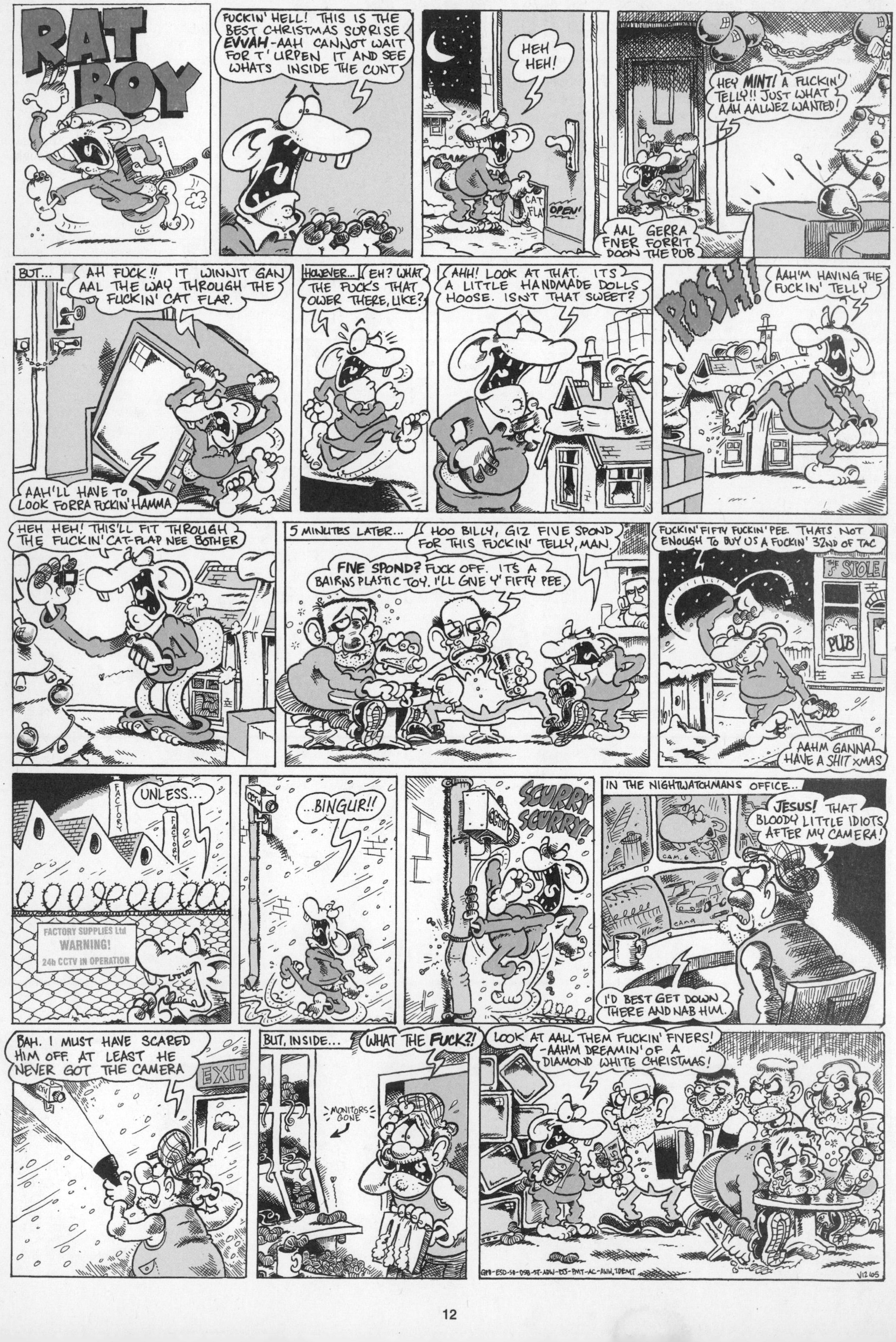

RAT BOY
FUCKIN' HELL! THIS IS THE BEST CHRISTMAS SURPRISE EVVAH - AAH CANNOT WAIT FOR T' URPEN IT AND SEE WHATS INSIDE THE CUNT
HEH HEH!
CAT FLAP
OPEN!
HEY MINT! A FUCKIN' TELLY!! JUST WHAT AAH AALWEZ WANTED!
AAL GERRA FIVER FORRIT DOON THE PUB
BUT...
AH FUCK!! IT WINNIT GAN AAL THE WAY THROUGH THE FUCKIN' CAT FLAP.
AAH'LL HAVE TO LOOK FORRA FUCKIN' HAMMA
HOWEVER...
EH? WHAT THE FUCK'S THAT OWER THERE, LIKE?
AHH! LOOK AT THAT. ITS A LITTLE HANDMADE DOLLS HOOSE. ISN'T THAT SWEET?
POSH!
AAH'M HAVING THE FUCKIN' TELLY
HEH HEH! THIS'LL FIT THROUGH THE FUCKIN' CAT-FLAP NEE BOTHER
5 MINUTES LATER...
HOO BILLY, GIZ FIVE SPOND FOR THIS FUCKIN' TELLY, MAN.
FIVE SPOND? FUCK OFF. IT'S A BAIRNS PLASTIC TOY. I'LL GIVE Y' FIFTY PEE.
FUCKIN' FIFTY FUCKIN' PEE. THATS NOT ENOUGH TO BUY US A FUCKIN' 32nd OF TAC
THE STOLE
PUB
AAHM GANNA HAVE A SHIT XMAS
FACTORY
UNLESS...
FACTORY SUPPLIES Ltd
WARNING!
24h CCTV IN OPERATION
CCTV
...BINGUR!!
CCTV
SCURRY SCURRY!
IN THE NIGHTWATCHMANS OFFICE...
JESUS! THAT BLOODY LITTLE IDIOTS AFTER MY CAMERA!
CAM. 6
I'D BEST GET DOWN THERE AND NAB HIM.
BAH. I MUST HAVE SCARED HIM OFF. AT LEAST HE NEVER GOT THE CAMERA
EXIT
BUT, INSIDE...
WHAT THE FUCK?!
MONITORS GONE
LOOK AT AALL THEM FUCKIN' FIVERS! - AAH'M DREAMIN' OF A DIAMOND WHITE CHRISTMAS!

Council in Rat Row

A WAKEFIELD man whose house is over-run with love-rats yesterday slammed penny-pinching council chiefs who have refused to act to sort out the problem.

EXCLUSIVE

Unemployed bus driver Eric Fletcher, 58, first discovered evidence of love-rat infestation at his Crofton home last August.

face

He told us: "I came down one morning to find my wife sitting in the kitchen with an unusual expression on her face. On closer inspection, I realised that her breasts had been nibbled by a love-rat."

richard

Thinking he could deal with the problem himself, Mr Fletcher bought a trap which he baited with his wife.

"About 2 in the morning, I heard the trap go off and ran downstairs. I put the kitchen light on and I found womanising Defence Minister Alan Clark limping round in circles, squeaking. I finished him off with a spade and threw him over the hedge."

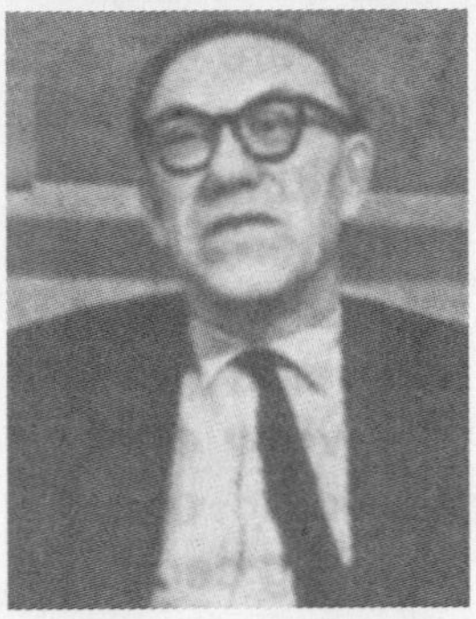

Fletcher - furious

Mr Fletcher then went back to bed and thought no more about it.

thorburn

However, later that night there was evidence that love-rats were still getting into the house.

"I was awoken by a loud scrabbling sound coming from my wife's side of the bed," he said. "When I turned on the lamp, I was amazed to see three enormous love-rats - London mayoral candidate Steven Norris, royal cad James Hewitt and Coronation Street's Mike Baldwin - having sex with my wife."

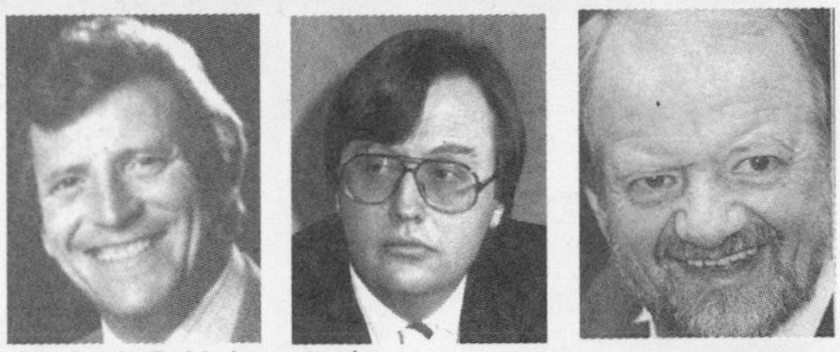

Rat Pack: Baldwin yesterday, Mellor last week and Cook on May 4th 1998 yesterday

michelmore

As soon as they saw Mr Fletcher, they scampered for cover.

"Frankly, they were a bloody nuisance," recalls Eric.

hanger

"They got cheeky. Foreign Secretary Robin Cook would come out in broad daylight and scuttle the wife while she was making my dinner. I even found a tunnel behind the bath where former Heritage Minister David Mellor was getting in and chewing her fanny.

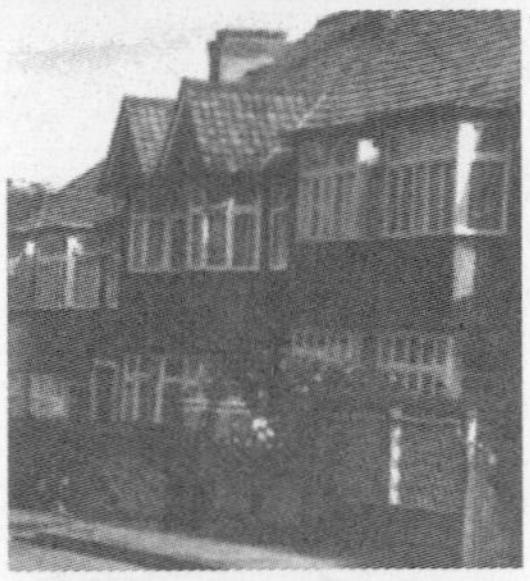

The love-rat infested house in Turd Road, Crofton

hook

"After a couple of weeks of it, I called in the council. That was six months ago, and they've never even phoned me back."

Wakefield Council spokesman Terry Sands told us: "We are aware of Mr Fletcher's problem, but following an exceptionally mild Summer there has been a particular love-rat problem throughout the borough.

d'Azur

"The local authority has to prioritise its resources, and unfortunately we are legally bound to deal with infestations in public areas - such as seedy motels and secluded bistros - first."

And he had this advice for anyone wishing to avoid love-rat infestation:

* *MAKE sure that her underwear is cleared away. A washing line of your wife's pants and bras is an open invitation to love-rats.*

* *DON'T leave your wife lying around unattended. Keep her out of harm's way in a locked room.*

* *KEEP your eyes peeled for tell-tale droppings, such as discarded election rosettes or pin-stripe trousers on the bedroom floor.*

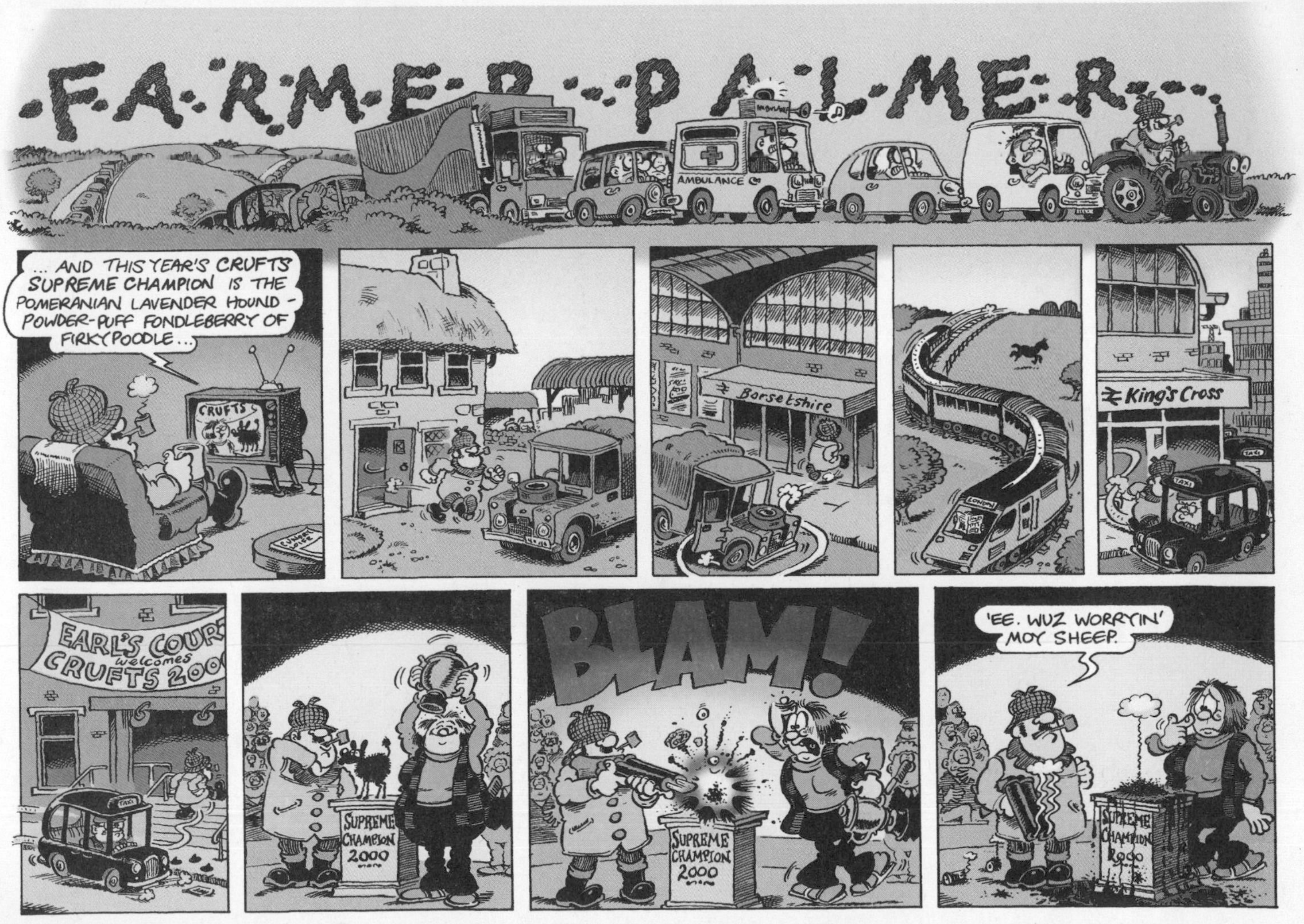
F·A·R·M·E·R P·A·L·M·E·R
AMBULANCE
... AND THIS YEAR'S CRUFTS SUPREME CHAMPION IS THE POMERANIAN LAVENDER HOUND - POWDER-PUFF FONDLEBERRY OF FIRKYPOODLE...
CRUFTS
Borsetshire
King's Cross
EARL'S COURT welcomes CRUFTS 200
SUPREME CHAMPION 2000
BLAM!
SUPREME CHAMPION 2000
'EE. WUZ WORRYIN' MOY SHEEP.
SUPREME CHAMPION 2000

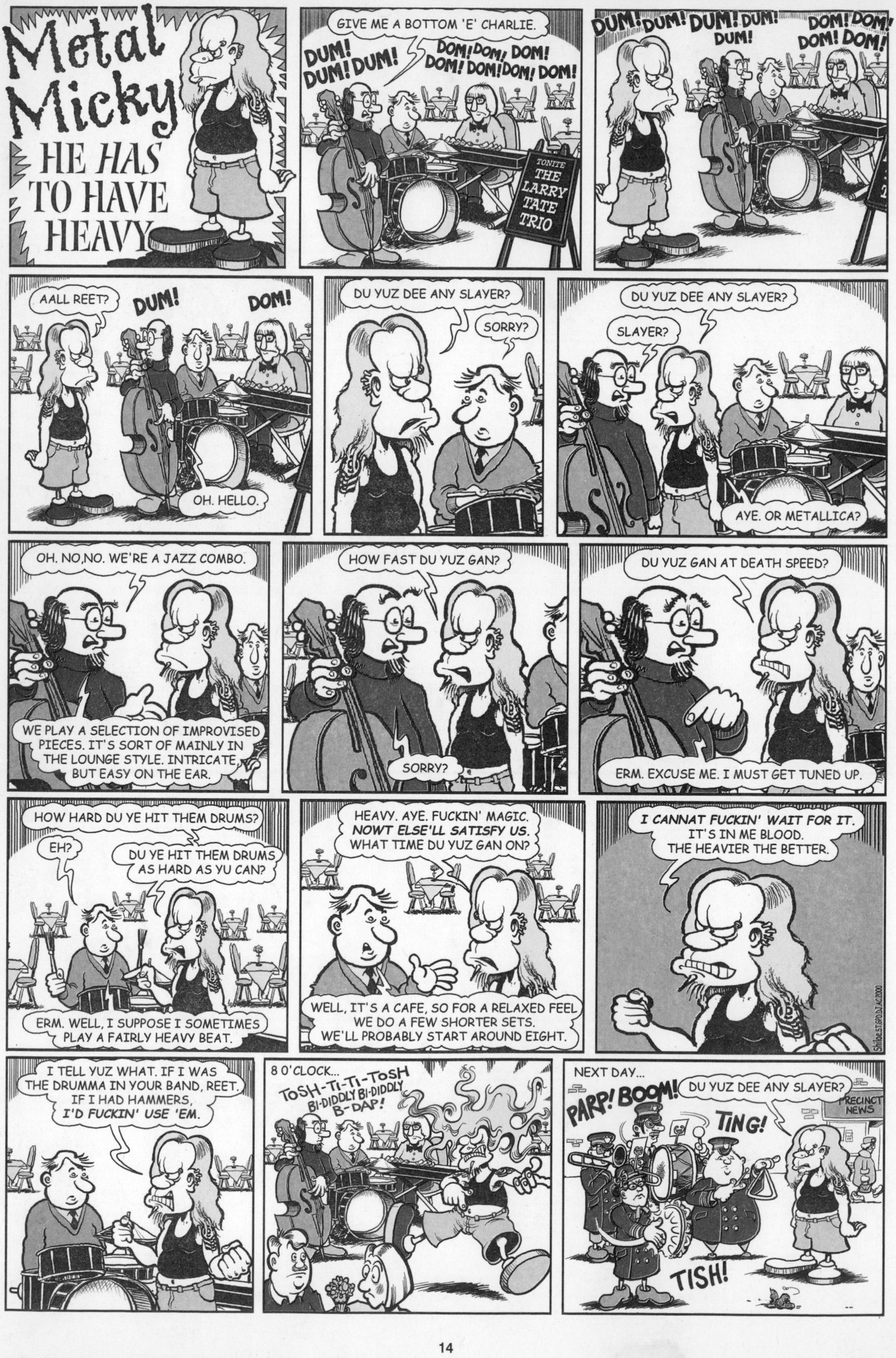
Metal Micky
HE HAS TO HAVE HEAVY
GIVE ME A BOTTOM 'E' CHARLIE.
DUM! DUM! DUM!
DOM! DOM! DOM! DOM! DOM! DOM! DOM!
TONITE THE LARRY TATE TRIO
DUM! DUM! DUM! DUM! DUM!
DOM! DOM! DOM! DOM!
AALL REET?
DUM!
DOM!
OH. HELLO.
DU YUZ DEE ANY SLAYER?
SORRY?
DU YUZ DEE ANY SLAYER?
SLAYER?
AYE. OR METALLICA?
OH. NO,NO. WE'RE A JAZZ COMBO.
WE PLAY A SELECTION OF IMPROVISED PIECES. IT'S SORT OF MAINLY IN THE LOUNGE STYLE. INTRICATE, BUT EASY ON THE EAR.
HOW FAST DU YUZ GAN?
SORRY?
DU YUZ GAN AT DEATH SPEED?
ERM. EXCUSE ME. I MUST GET TUNED UP.
HOW HARD DU YE HIT THEM DRUMS?
EH?
DU YE HIT THEM DRUMS AS HARD AS YU CAN?
ERM. WELL, I SUPPOSE I SOMETIMES PLAY A FAIRLY HEAVY BEAT.
HEAVY. AYE. FUCKIN' MAGIC. NOWT ELSE'LL SATISFY US. WHAT TIME DU YUZ GAN ON?
WELL, IT'S A CAFE, SO FOR A RELAXED FEEL WE DO A FEW SHORTER SETS. WE'LL PROBABLY START AROUND EIGHT.
I CANNAT FUCKIN' WAIT FOR IT. IT'S IN ME BLOOD. THE HEAVIER THE BETTER.
I TELL YUZ WHAT. IF I WAS THE DRUMMA IN YOUR BAND, REET. IF I HAD HAMMERS, I'D FUCKIN' USE 'EM.
8 O'CLOCK...
TOSH-TI-TI-TOSH BI-DIDDLY BI-DIDDLY B-DAP!
NEXT DAY...
PARP! BOOM!
DU YUZ DEE ANY SLAYER?
PRECINCT NEWS
TING!
TISH!

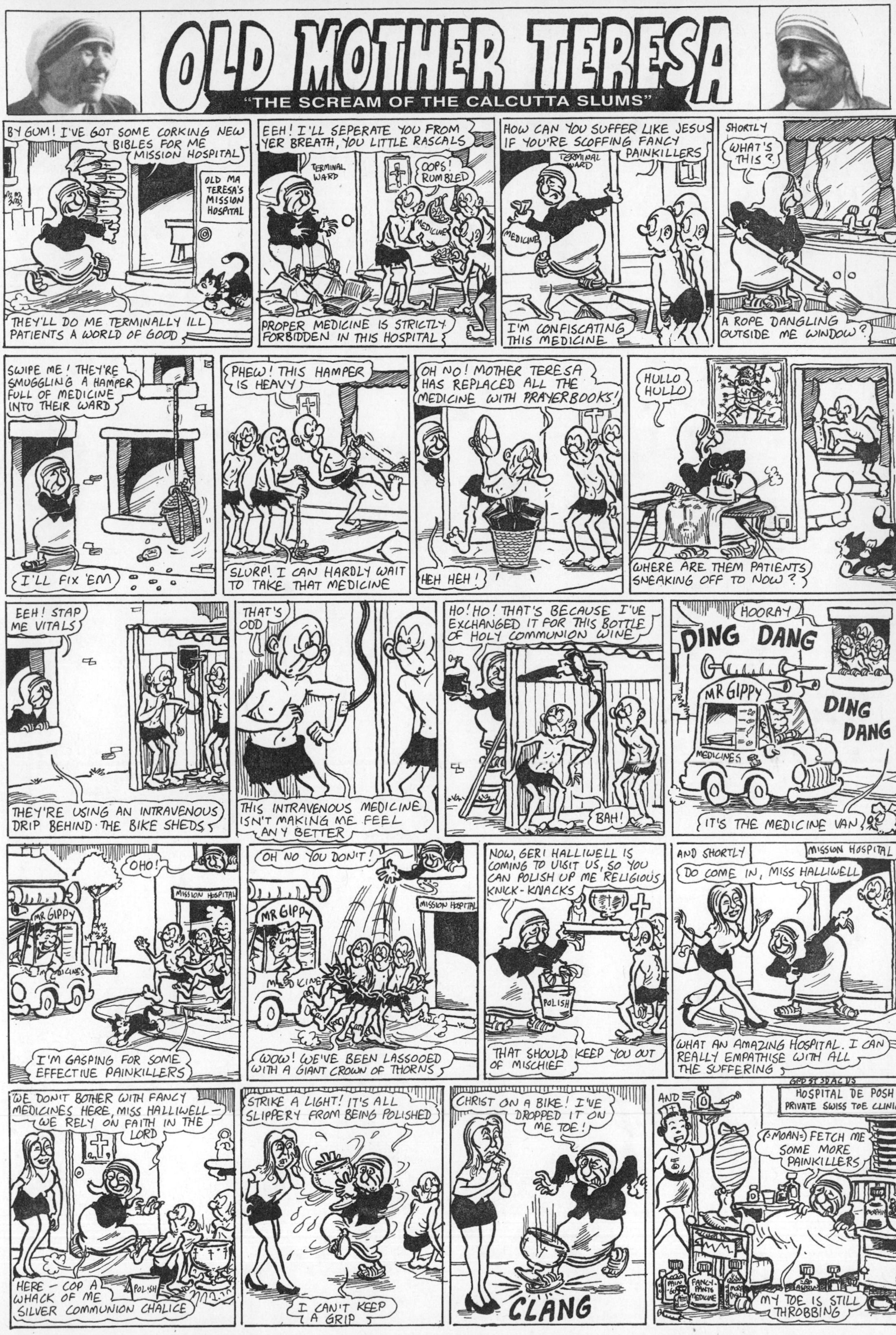
OLD MOTHER TERESA
"THE SCREAM OF THE CALCUTTA SLUMS"
BY GUM! I'VE GOT SOME CORKING NEW BIBLES FOR ME MISSION HOSPITAL
OLD MA TERESA'S MISSION HOSPITAL
THEY'LL DO ME TERMINALLY ILL PATIENTS A WORLD OF GOOD
EEH! I'LL SEPERATE YOU FROM YER BREATH, YOU LITTLE RASCALS
TERMINAL WARD
OOPS! RUMBLED
MEDICINE
PROPER MEDICINE IS STRICTLY FORBIDDEN IN THIS HOSPITAL
HOW CAN YOU SUFFER LIKE JESUS IF YOU'RE SCOFFING FANCY PAINKILLERS
TERMINAL WARD
MEDICINE
I'M CONFISCATING THIS MEDICINE
SHORTLY
WHAT'S THIS?
A ROPE DANGLING OUTSIDE ME WINDOW?
SWIPE ME! THEY'RE SMUGGLING A HAMPER FULL OF MEDICINE INTO THEIR WARD
I'LL FIX 'EM
PHEW! THIS HAMPER IS HEAVY
SLURP! I CAN HARDLY WAIT TO TAKE THAT MEDICINE
OH NO! MOTHER TERESA HAS REPLACED ALL THE MEDICINE WITH PRAYERBOOKS!
HEH HEH!
HULLO HULLO
WHERE ARE THEM PATIENTS SNEAKING OFF TO NOW?
EEH! STAP ME VITALS
THEY'RE USING AN INTRAVENOUS DRIP BEHIND THE BIKE SHEDS
THAT'S ODD
THIS INTRAVENOUS MEDICINE ISN'T MAKING ME FEEL ANY BETTER
HO! HO! THAT'S BECAUSE I'VE EXCHANGED IT FOR THIS BOTTLE OF HOLY COMMUNION WINE
BAH!
HOORAY
DING DANG
MR GIPPY
MEDICINES
DING DANG
IT'S THE MEDICINE VAN
OHO!
MISSION HOSPITAL
MR GIPPY
MEDICINES
I'M GASPING FOR SOME EFFECTIVE PAINKILLERS
OH NO YOU DON'T!
MR GIPPY
MISSION HOSPITAL
MEDICINE
WOW! WE'VE BEEN LASSOOED WITH A GIANT CROWN OF THORNS
NOW, GERI HALLIWELL IS COMING TO VISIT US, SO YOU CAN POLISH UP ME RELIGIOUS KNICK-KNACKS
POLISH
THAT SHOULD KEEP YOU OUT OF MISCHIEF
AND SHORTLY
MISSION HOSPITAL
DO COME IN, MISS HALLIWELL
WHAT AN AMAZING HOSPITAL. I CAN REALLY EMPATHISE WITH ALL THE SUFFERING
WE DON'T BOTHER WITH FANCY MEDICINES HERE, MISS HALLIWELL - WE RELY ON FAITH IN THE LORD
POLISH
HERE - COP A WHACK OF ME SILVER COMMUNION CHALICE
STRIKE A LIGHT! IT'S ALL SLIPPERY FROM BEING POLISHED
I CAN'T KEEP A GRIP
CHRIST ON A BIKE! I'VE DROPPED IT ON ME TOE!
CLANG
AND
HOSPITAL DE POSH
PRIVATE SWISS TOE CLINIC
(=MOAN=) FETCH ME SOME MORE PAINKILLERS
FANCY-PANTS MEDICINE
MY TOE IS STILL THROBBING

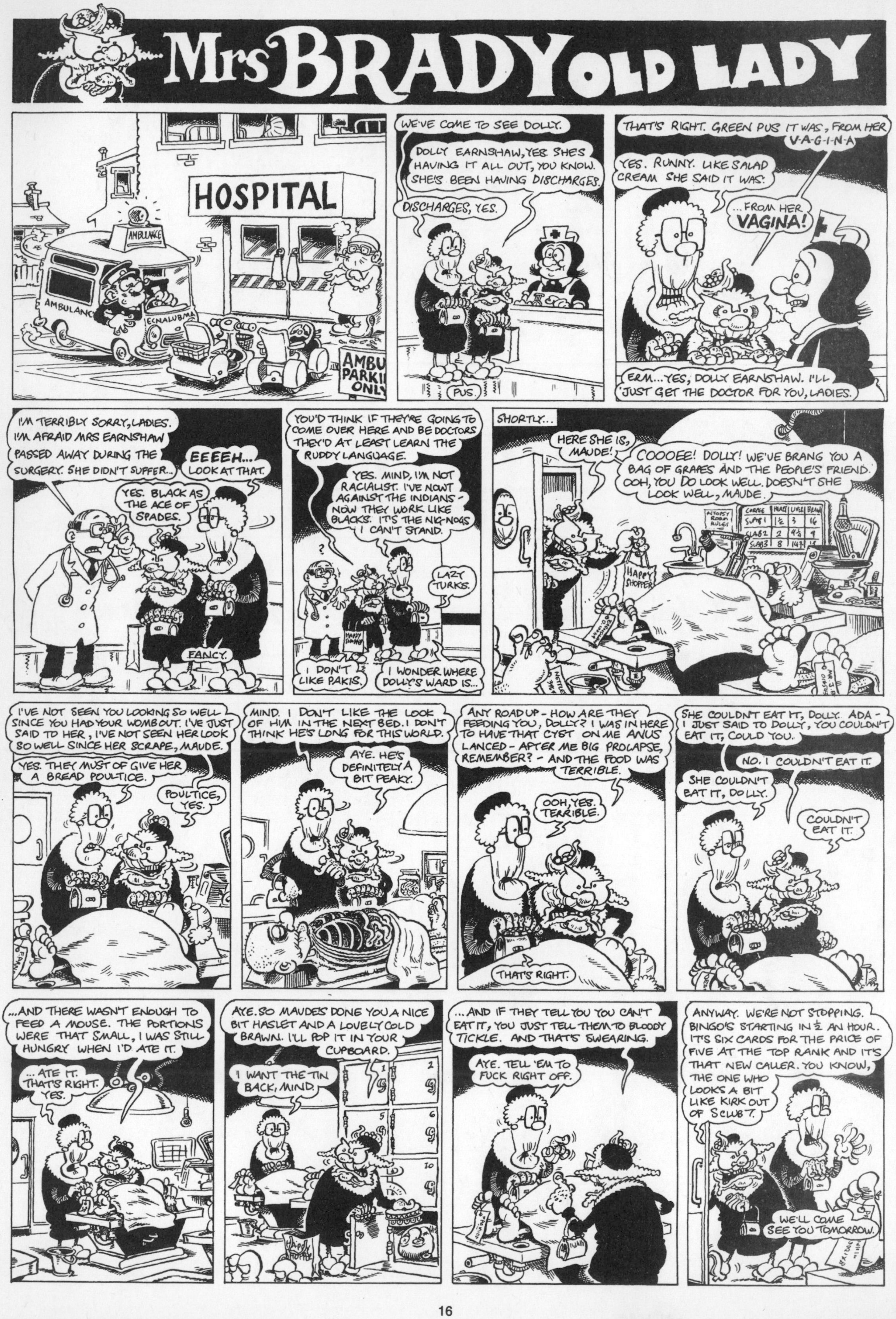
Mrs BRADY OLD LADY
HOSPITAL
AMBULANCE
AMBULANCE
ECNALUBMA
AMBU PARKI ONLY
WE'VE COME TO SEE DOLLY.
DOLLY EARNSHAW, YES. SHE'S HAVING IT ALL OUT, YOU KNOW. SHE'S BEEN HAVING DISCHARGES.
DISCHARGES, YES.
PUS.
THAT'S RIGHT. GREEN PUS IT WAS, FROM HER V-A-G-I-N-A
YES. RUNNY. LIKE SALAD CREAM SHE SAID IT WAS.
...FROM HER VAGINA!
ERM... YES, DOLLY EARNSHAW. I'LL JUST GET THE DOCTOR FOR YOU, LADIES.
I'M TERRIBLY SORRY, LADIES. I'M AFRAID MRS EARNSHAW PASSED AWAY DURING THE SURGERY. SHE DIDN'T SUFFER...
EEEEH... LOOK AT THAT.
YES. BLACK AS THE ACE OF SPADES.
FANCY.
YOU'D THINK IF THEY'RE GOING TO COME OVER HERE AND BE DOCTORS THEY'D AT LEAST LEARN THE RUDDY LANGUAGE.
YES. MIND, I'M NOT RACIALIST. I'VE NOWT AGAINST THE INDIANS - NOW THEY WORK LIKE BLACKS. IT'S THE NIG-NOGS I CAN'T STAND.
?
LAZY TURKS.
I DON'T LIKE PAKIS.
I WONDER WHERE DOLLY'S WARD IS...
SHORTLY...
HERE SHE IS, MAUDE!
COOOEE! DOLLY! WE'VE BRANG YOU A BAG OF GRAPES AND THE PEOPLE'S FRIEND. OOH, YOU DO LOOK WELL. DOESN'T SHE LOOK WELL, MAUDE.
HAPPY SHOPPER
I'VE NOT SEEN YOU LOOKING SO WELL SINCE YOU HAD YOUR WOMB OUT. I'VE JUST SAID TO HER, I'VE NOT SEEN HER LOOK SO WELL SINCE HER SCRAPE, MAUDE.
YES. THEY MUST OF GIVE HER A BREAD POULTICE.
POULTICE, YES.
MIND. I DON'T LIKE THE LOOK OF HIM IN THE NEXT BED. I DON'T THINK HE'S LONG FOR THIS WORLD.
AYE. HE'S DEFINITELY A BIT PEAKY.
ANY ROAD UP - HOW ARE THEY FEEDING YOU, DOLLY? I WAS IN HERE TO HAVE THAT CYST ON ME ANUS LANCED - AFTER ME BIG PROLAPSE, REMEMBER? - AND THE FOOD WAS TERRIBLE.
OOH, YES. TERRIBLE.
THAT'S RIGHT.
SHE COULDN'T EAT IT, DOLLY. ADA - I JUST SAID TO DOLLY, YOU COULDN'T EAT IT, COULD YOU.
NO. I COULDN'T EAT IT.
SHE COULDN'T EAT IT, DOLLY.
COULDN'T EAT IT.
...AND THERE WASN'T ENOUGH TO FEED A MOUSE. THE PORTIONS WERE THAT SMALL, I WAS STILL HUNGRY WHEN I'D ATE IT.
... ATE IT. THAT'S RIGHT. YES.
AYE. SO MAUDE'S DONE YOU A NICE BIT HASLET AND A LOVELY COLD BRAWN. I'LL POP IT IN YOUR CUPBOARD.
I WANT THE TIN BACK, MIND.
Happy Shopper
...AND IF THEY TELL YOU YOU CAN'T EAT IT, YOU JUST TELL THEM TO BLOODY TICKLE. AND THAT'S SWEARING.
AYE. TELL 'EM TO FUCK RIGHT OFF.
ANYWAY. WE'RE NOT STOPPING. BINGO'S STARTING IN ½ AN HOUR. IT'S SIX CARDS FOR THE PRICE OF FIVE AT THE TOP RANK AND IT'S THAT NEW CALLER. YOU KNOW, THE ONE WHO LOOKS A BIT LIKE KIRK OUT OF S CLUB 7.
WE'LL COME SEE YOU TOMORROW.

NEXT DAY...
COOOEE! DOLLY! IT'S ONLY US AGAIN. WE'VE BROUGHT EVERYONE FROM BINGO TO SEE YOU.
SEE YOU, YES.
I'VE GOT YOU A NICE OX TONGUE GOLD DISH AND HALF A BRISKET.
...EEH. I DON'T LIKE THESE NEW FIVE PEES...
...AND I'VE MADE YOU A CLARTY DICK. EEH, YOU DO LOOK WELL, DOLLY.
YES. I WAS IN SERVICE WHEN I WAS FOURTEEN
...AND WE NEVER HAD A FRIDGE IN THEM DAYS...
FOURTEEN.
EXCUSE ME, SONNY JIM...
I'M 96 AND I NEED THE TOILET.
DOCTOR. WHILE I'M HERE WILL YOU HAVE A LOOK AT ME HYMEN?

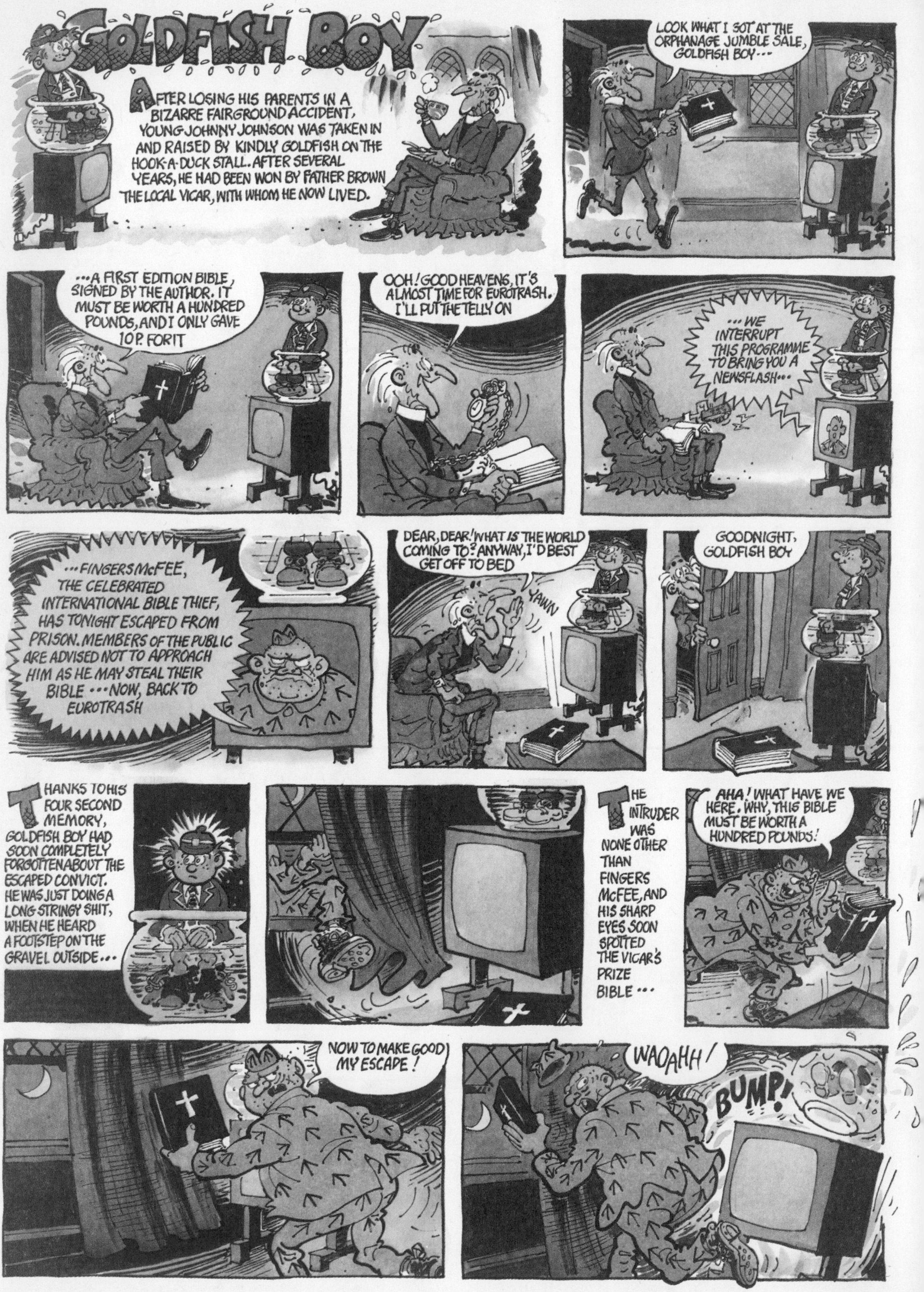
GOLDFISH BOY
AFTER LOSING HIS PARENTS IN A BIZARRE FAIRGROUND ACCIDENT, YOUNG JOHNNY JOHNSON WAS TAKEN IN AND RAISED BY KINDLY GOLDFISH ON THE HOOK-A-DUCK STALL. AFTER SEVERAL YEARS, HE HAD BEEN WON BY FATHER BROWN THE LOCAL VICAR, WITH WHOM HE NOW LIVED.
LOOK WHAT I GOT AT THE ORPHANAGE JUMBLE SALE, GOLDFISH BOY...
...A FIRST EDITION BIBLE, SIGNED BY THE AUTHOR. IT MUST BE WORTH A HUNDRED POUNDS, AND I ONLY GAVE 10P. FOR IT
OOH! GOOD HEAVENS, IT'S ALMOST TIME FOR EUROTRASH. I'LL PUT THE TELLY ON
...WE INTERRUPT THIS PROGRAMME TO BRING YOU A NEWSFLASH...
...FINGERS McFEE, THE CELEBRATED INTERNATIONAL BIBLE THIEF, HAS TONIGHT ESCAPED FROM PRISON. MEMBERS OF THE PUBLIC ARE ADVISED NOT TO APPROACH HIM AS HE MAY STEAL THEIR BIBLE ... NOW, BACK TO EUROTRASH
DEAR, DEAR! WHAT IS THE WORLD COMING TO? ANYWAY, I'D BEST GET OFF TO BED
YAWN
GOODNIGHT, GOLDFISH BOY
THANKS TO HIS FOUR SECOND MEMORY, GOLDFISH BOY HAD SOON COMPLETELY FORGOTTEN ABOUT THE ESCAPED CONVICT. HE WAS JUST DOING A LONG STRINGY SHIT, WHEN HE HEARD A FOOTSTEP ON THE GRAVEL OUTSIDE...
THE INTRUDER WAS NONE OTHER THAN FINGERS McFEE, AND HIS SHARP EYES SOON SPOTTED THE VICAR'S PRIZE BIBLE...
AHA! WHAT HAVE WE HERE. WHY, THIS BIBLE MUST BE WORTH A HUNDRED POUNDS!
NOW TO MAKE GOOD MY ESCAPE!
WAOAHH!
BUMP!

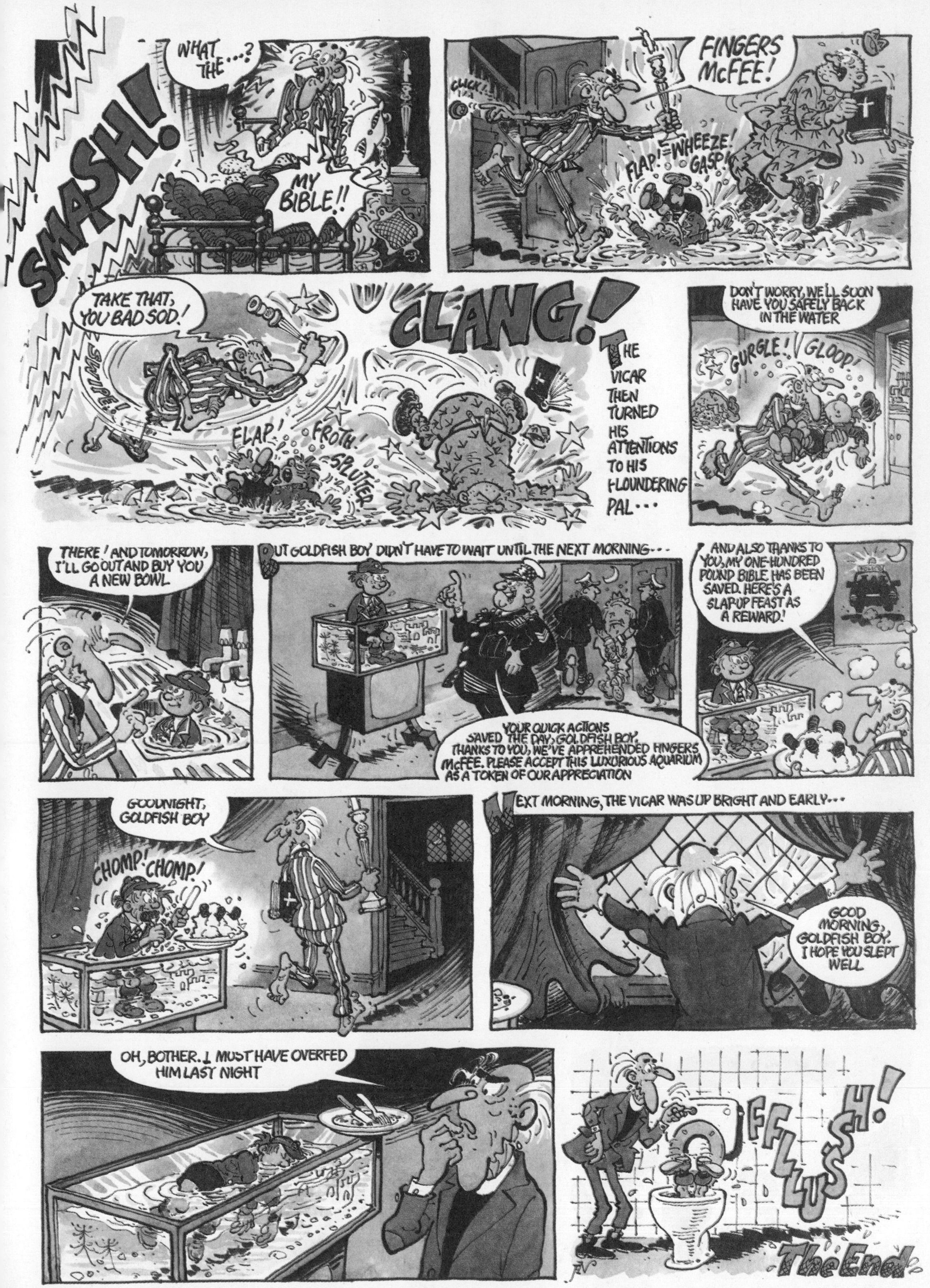
WHAT THE...?
SMASH!
MY BIBLE!!
CLICK!
FINGERS McFEE!
FLAP! WHEEZE! GASP!
TAKE THAT, YOU BAD SOD!
SWIPE!
CLANG!
FLAP! FROTH! SPLUTTER
THE VICAR THEN TURNED HIS ATTENTIONS TO HIS FLOUNDERING PAL...
DON'T WORRY, WE'LL SOON HAVE YOU SAFELY BACK IN THE WATER
GURGLE! GLOOP!
THERE! AND TOMORROW, I'LL GO OUT AND BUY YOU A NEW BOWL
BUT GOLDFISH BOY DIDN'T HAVE TO WAIT UNTIL THE NEXT MORNING...
YOUR QUICK ACTIONS SAVED THE DAY, GOLDFISH BOY, THANKS TO YOU, WE'VE APPREHENDED FINGERS McFEE. PLEASE ACCEPT THIS LUXURIOUS AQUARIUM AS A TOKEN OF OUR APPRECIATION
AND ALSO THANKS TO YOU, MY ONE-HUNDRED POUND BIBLE HAS BEEN SAVED. HERE'S A SLAP-UP FEAST AS A REWARD!
GOODNIGHT, GOLDFISH BOY
CHOMP! CHOMP!
NEXT MORNING, THE VICAR WAS UP BRIGHT AND EARLY...
GOOD MORNING, GOLDFISH BOY. I HOPE YOU SLEPT WELL
OH, BOTHER. I MUST HAVE OVERFED HIM LAST NIGHT
FFLUSSH!
The End

Letterbocks

It's the page you have to break up with a stick because it won't flush away

Star Letter

Letterbocks
Viz comic
PO Box 1PT
Newcastle upon Tyne
NE99 1PT

Fax: 0191 241 4244
e-mail viz.comic@virgin.net

❒ You clearly state on the letterbocks page of the last issue that a '£100 Star Letter prize' is winging its way to me. Where is it? I haven't got it yet.

D. Falk
e-mail

* *Congratulations, D. Falk. Your second Star Letter in a row. A £200 Star Letter prize is in the post.*

Sick note

❒ I visited my local GP last week complaining of a sore throat and stiff neck. Imagine my surprise on being told I had absentmindedly swallowed a flute.

Danny Keough
Exeter

❒ Since the 29th of February is put there to keep our calendarial system in tune with the heavens by creating an extra day out of all the missing bits from each of the days over the previous four years, surely $2/7$ of those bits are from Saturdays and Sundays, and we should all get to go home at 3 o'clock.

Steve Gaw
e-mail

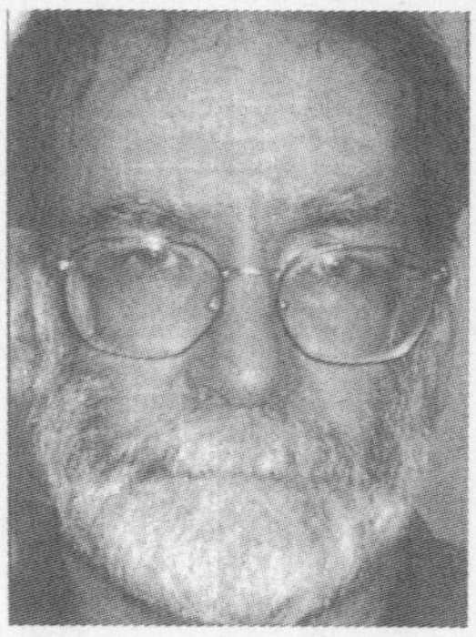

❒ To call Dr. Harold Shipman 'Britain's Worst Serial Killer' is utter nonsense. With more confirmed kills to his name than any other UK-based murderer, surely Dr. Shipman is 'Britain's *Best* Serial Killer'. Someone like Colin Stagg who, not only was arrested in connection with only one killing, but then turned out not to have done it in the first place, would qualify at the country's 'Worst Mass Murderer'.

Danny King
Balham

*Have **you** got something to tell us? Maybe you've got an anal cyst, or perhaps a burning question about kangaroos. Or maybe your wife has got one mudflap bigger than the other.*
Drop us a line at the above address. There's a Roger's Profanisaurus mug for every letter or tip we print.

Parcel of crap

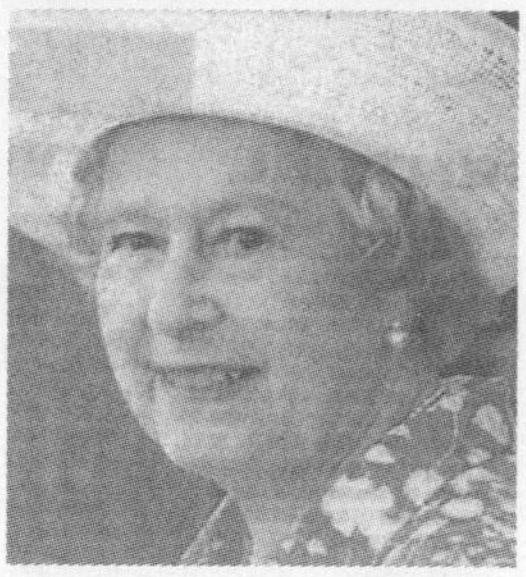

❒ I heard recently that on average, Her Majesty the Queen receives two turds in the post each week. What I want to know is, who's sending the other one?

F. Jacks
Hartlepool

❒ With the recent hospital slip ups, I can understand how a doctor amputates the wrong arm or leg, or removes the wrong organ. As arms and legs come in pairs, and are therefore easy to confuse, perhaps the nurses could put a glove or a sock on the limb to be removed. As for internal organs, well we will just have to take our chances.

P.M. Maiello
Llanelli

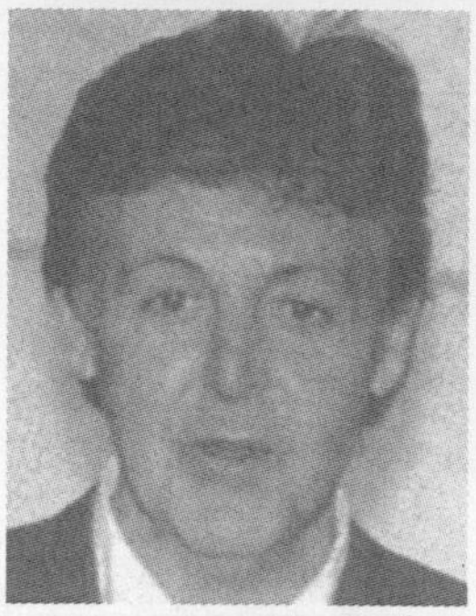

❒ What a complete hypocrite Paul McCartney is. He won't eat sausages, but he's quite prepared to have ivory on his piano keyboard, oh lord. Does he really expect us to believe that if they made pianos out of sausages, he'd suddenly start eating elephants again? Frankly, I think not.

Brigadier Sir J. Lewthwait
Cumberland

Sued's corner

❒ The magazine I work for in Canada recently got sued for $60,000 of our Canadian dollars (about 30,000 quid) for calling some local politician an incompetent twat. During the trial, the bastard dragged his senile mum down to the courthouse to parade in front of all the photographers, and I reckon she's the spitting image of Mrs. Brady. Do I win £5? We really need the money.

C. Sullivan
Canada

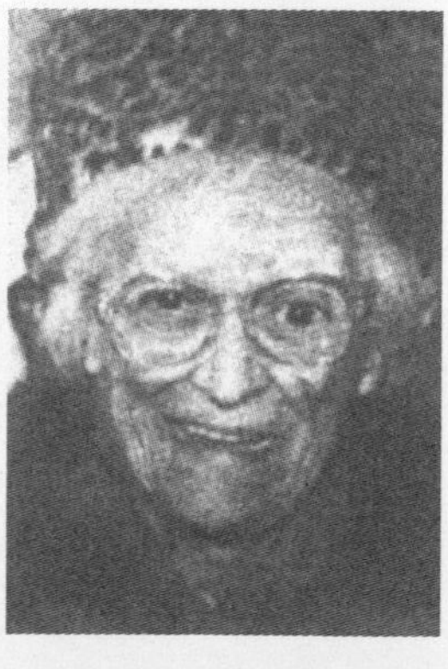

❒ If there is one thing that makes me incandescent with fury, it is transport authorities who wilfully refuse to apply an apostrophe before the word "bus" on 'bus stop signs. As anyone knows, 'bus is a contraction of the word "omnibus" and therefore requires the apostrophe in all circumstances. Whenever I phone the transport agencies to remonstrate I am invariably treated with disdain.

Stephen Fry
The Groucho Club

Grinning Twat

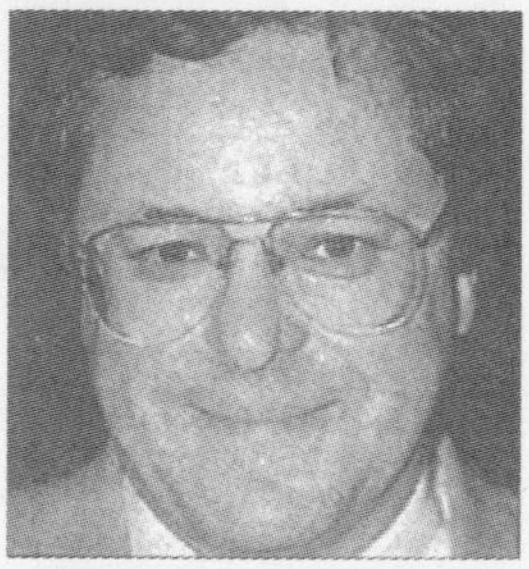

❒ So Richard Whiteley reckons he has appeared on British telly more times than anyone else over the last thirty-five years. You'd think by now he would actually be able to do it, wouldn't you?

A. Mitchell
Grimsby

❒ Now that our education system is funded entirely by tokens off the back of crisp packets, we can expect to see the best National Curriculum results coming from schools full of fat, Monster Munch-scoffing bloaters on 500 packets of cheese n' onion a day. Young kids who looks after themselves by eating a healthy diet are going to fall way behind academically. Let's reward other more wholesome pastimes and put tokens on apples, running shoes and flesh mags.

P. Bratley
e-mail

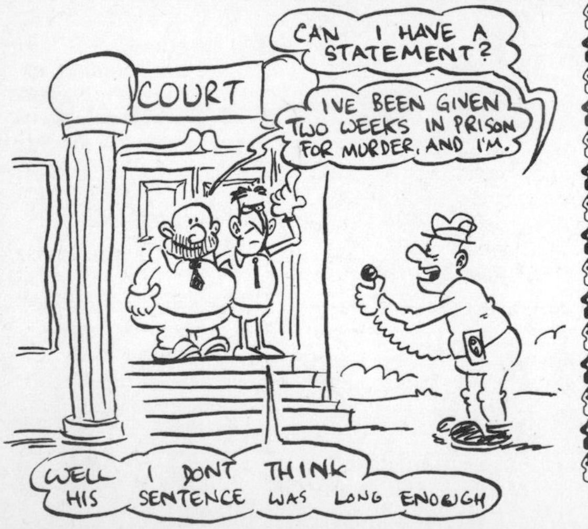
COURT
CAN I HAVE A STATEMENT?
I'VE BEEN GIVEN TWO WEEKS IN PRISON FOR MURDER, AND I'M.
WELL I DONT THINK HIS SENTENCE WAS LONG ENOUGH

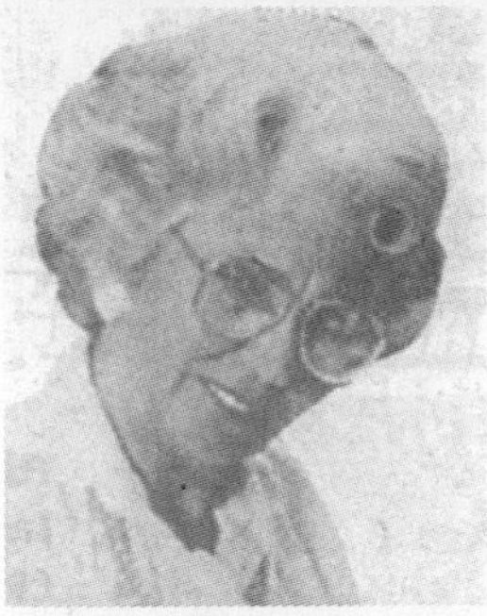

❒ I am regularly mistaken for retired televisual decency campaigner Mary Whitehouse, due to our having similar names. This annoys me greatly, as I am all for sex, violence and swearing on the box. Plus, I am a rodent.

Hairy Whitemouse
Skirting Board Hole

❒ We are constantly having to see 'clammy bottoms' on nappy adverts these days, so how about seeing some of those fine young models on the Tampax adverts actually sticking their products up their minges. I for one would much prefer to see some second-rate actress's biff close up than have to see a baby's piss-soaked arse while I'm eating my cornflakes first thing in the morning.

Rhydian Lewis
Porthcawl

Clever bard

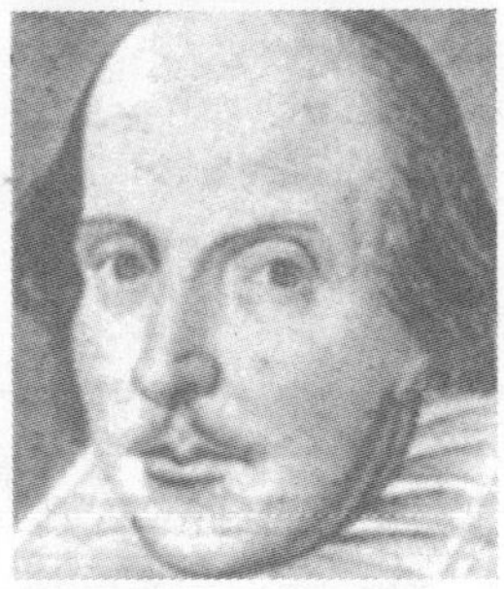

❒ I recently read that William Shakespeare died on the same day that he was born, 23rd of April. No wonder he was known as a fucking genius if he wrote 37 plays and all them sonnets in one day.

Bruce Goodman
Colchester

❒ Has anyone seen those stupid red and white tents over man-hole covers recently?

Jim Gearbox
Lamesville

❒ I see the BBC have organised a talent search for budding new writers. My idea for a sitcom would be three old cunts in the Yorkshire Dales who keep falling off their bikes and waving their legs in the air.

Steven Boltano
White City

Local angle

❒ I saw a sign in a fish-monger's window the other day that read "Local Fish". How did he know? They might have just been passing by.

Davy Lynn
e-mail

❒ I write to express my profoundest regret and shame over my failure to place correctly an apostrophe before the contracted word "phone" in my previous letter (this issuc). I havc lct everybody down. I feel I must get away for a short time to mull over the consequences of my foolish behaviour. Please do not try to find me.

Stephen Fry
Belgium

❒ Bearing in mind the large amount of pornography available on the internet and the forthcoming free internet access, now would be a prudent time to invest in shares in tissue manufacturers and companies that make sore-knob cream.

John Hunt
Edinburgh

❒ In the Lloyds TSB advert, they ask "What can we do to make you feel good?" How about having one lovely bank teller go down on me, whilst another one sits on my face, and all their female colleagues shower me with money?

A. Riley
London

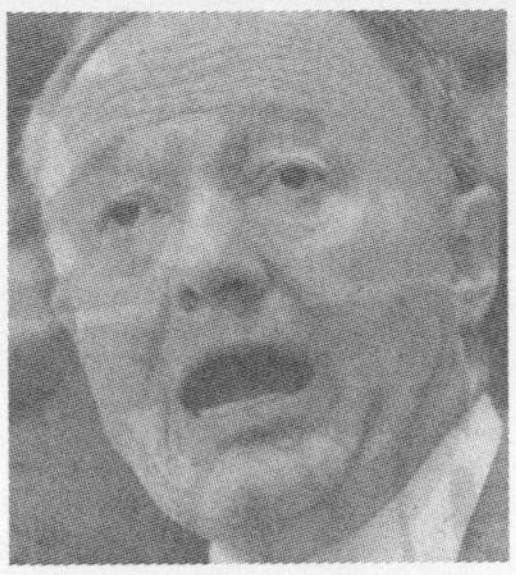

❒ Once a loony leftie, always a loony leftie I say. If the people of London are foolish enough to elect Ken 'Red' Livingstone as their Lord Mayor, they will have no one to blame but themselves when the lesbians and the IRA are winning all the sandcastle and snowmen competions in the park.

M. Compton
Bristol

Crap jokes

❒ What ever happened to jokes about white dog shit? You used to see loads of jokes about white dog shit, and now you never see any at all.

M. Speaker
e-mail

❒ Mariah Carey used to believe that the right side of her face was the better side, and that her left was in some way unattractive. It is nice to know that she has recently got over this psychological insecurity, and now believes that both sides of her face are equally attractive. I wouldn't know. I've only ever looked at her tits.

Tony Fisher
Ipswich

Cyril Fletcher's Photo Corner

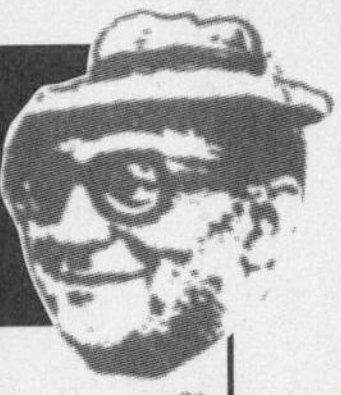

This week's Guest Presenters- PJ and Duncan out of TV's 'Ant and Dec'

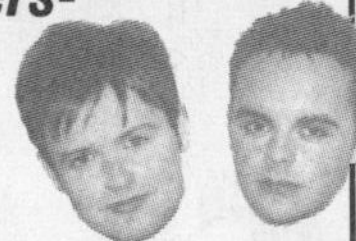

PJ: Hi, there! Now, this week's bad news is that Cyril Fletcher is unable to host this column, as he is canny worried as to whether he is dead or not, and it's affecting his health.

Duncan: *Whye, aye, Ant. We all wish him a speedy recovery, if he's alive.*

Dec: That's right, Dunc. But every cloud has a silver lining, and it means that PJ and myself have been asked to select this week's crop of hilarious photographs sent in by you, the eagle-eyed Viz readers.

Ant: *Yes. And the first one has been sent in by **Mark Gipps of Hertfordshire**.*

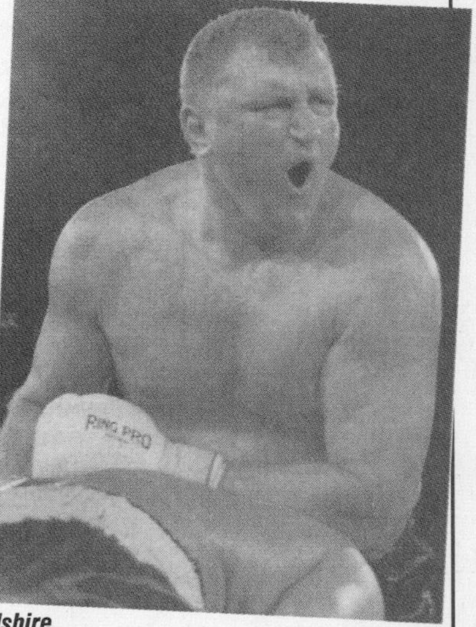
RING PRO

"I always thought Joe Bugner was a cunt," Mark writes, "but I was surprised to see that he has one".

Dec: Well spotted, Mark. It certainly does look like the old slugger has got a woman's fanny. It's a real dandy picture.

Duncan: *Speaking of dandy pictures, what about this frame from the "Growing Paynes" cartoon in the March 18th issue of my favouirite comic, The Dandy.*

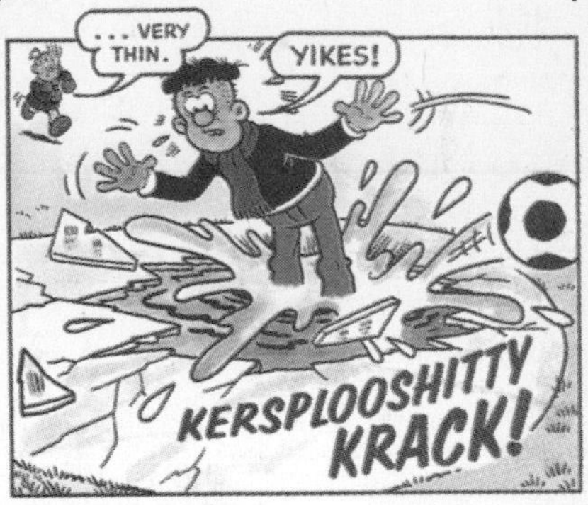

... VERY THIN.
YIKES!
KERSPLOOSHITTY KRACK!

Ant: Well, I've got satellite telly, Dunc, so I'm used to seeing lots of shitty cracks on the German porn channels, but Viz reader **Roland Gill**, aged 8, got quite a surprise when he saw this one.

PJ. *Why aye! Well that's all from us for this week. Don't forget to watch us on 'Live and Kicking' every Saturday morning on BBC1.*

Dec: Byeeeeee!

TOP TIPS

LOCAL councils. Instead of wasting money putting speed humps all over the place, simply make anyone convicted of speeding put egg-shaped wheels on their cars.
Paddy O'Faggot, e-mail

MRS TOM JONES. Prevent your husband from bursting on a hot day by pricking him several times with a fork.
E. Hoover, Leeds

OLD biddies. Easter will neither be 'very late' nor 'very early' this year. So that's one less interminable conversation you can have with each other.
D. Stuttard, Warrington

MOUNTAIN bikers. Stop that irritating squeal from your brakes and reduce wear on them by oiling the rims of your wheels before taking on that tricky descent.
SS, Bunny

GAME show enthusiasts. By taking a potato waffle, standing it on its side and placing an insect in each hole, you can recreate your own miniature Celebrity Squares. It would probably be more exciting than the show itself.
E. Grant, Newcastle

SAFARI park visitors. Prevent monkeys from climbing on your car by gluing broken glass all over the roof and bonnet.
H. Freerson Widmerpool

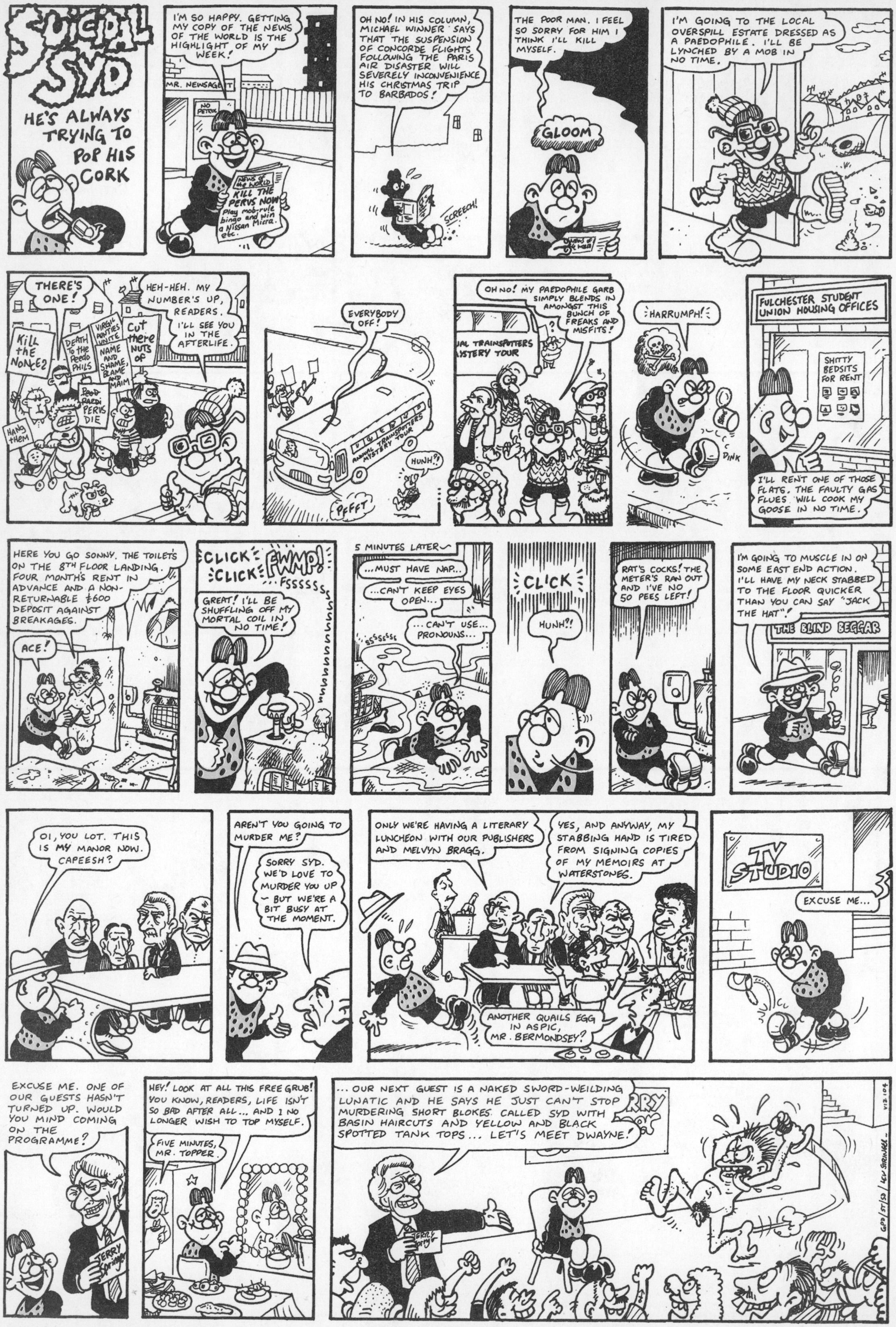
SUICIDAL SYD
HE'S ALWAYS TRYING TO POP HIS CORK
I'M SO HAPPY. GETTING MY COPY OF THE NEWS OF THE WORLD IS THE HIGHLIGHT OF MY WEEK!
MR. NEWSAGENT
NO PETROL
NEWS OF THE WORLD KILL THE PERVS NOW! Play mob-rule bingo and win a Nissan Micra etc.
OH NO! IN HIS COLUMN, MICHAEL WINNER SAYS THAT THE SUSPENSION OF CONCORDE FLIGHTS FOLLOWING THE PARIS AIR DISASTER WILL SEVERELY INCONVENIENCE HIS CHRISTMAS TRIP TO BARBADOS!
SCREECH!
THE POOR MAN. I FEEL SO SORRY FOR HIM I THINK I'LL KILL MYSELF.
GLOOM
I'M GOING TO THE LOCAL OVERSPILL ESTATE DRESSED AS A PAEDOPHILE. I'LL BE LYNCHED BY A MOB IN NO TIME.
THERE'S ONE!
HEH-HEH. MY NUMBER'S UP, READERS. I'LL SEE YOU IN THE AFTERLIFE.
Kill the NONCE?
DEATH to the Peedo PHILS
VIRGIL PUNTIES UNITE NAME AND SHAME, BLAME AND MAIM
Cut there NUTS of
Peed Paedi PERVS DIE
Hang them
EVERYBODY OFF!
ANNUAL TRAINSPOTTERS MYSTERY TOUR
HUNH?!
PFFFT
OH NO! MY PAEDOPHILE GARB SIMPLY BLENDS IN AMONGST THIS BUNCH OF FREAKS AND MISFITS!
HARRUMPH!
DINK
FULCHESTER STUDENT UNION HOUSING OFFICES
SHITTY BEDSITS FOR RENT
I'LL RENT ONE OF THOSE FLATS. THE FAULTY GAS FLUES WILL COOK MY GOOSE IN NO TIME.
HERE YOU GO SONNY. THE TOILET'S ON THE 8TH FLOOR LANDING. FOUR MONTH'S RENT IN ADVANCE AND A NON-RETURNABLE £600 DEPOSIT AGAINST BREAKAGES.
ACE!
CLICK CLICK FWMP! FSSSSSS
GREAT! I'LL BE SHUFFLING OFF MY MORTAL COIL IN NO TIME!
5 MINUTES LATER
...MUST HAVE NAP...
...CAN'T KEEP EYES OPEN...
...CAN'T USE... PRONOUNS...
CLICK
HUNH?!
RAT'S COCKS! THE METER'S RAN OUT AND I'VE NO 50 PEES LEFT!
I'M GOING TO MUSCLE IN ON SOME EAST END ACTION. I'LL HAVE MY NECK STABBED TO THE FLOOR QUICKER THAN YOU CAN SAY "JACK THE HAT".
THE BLIND BEGGAR
OI, YOU LOT. THIS IS MY MANOR NOW. CAPEESH?
AREN'T YOU GOING TO MURDER ME?
SORRY SYD. WE'D LOVE TO MURDER YOU UP - BUT WE'RE A BIT BUSY AT THE MOMENT.
ONLY WE'RE HAVING A LITERARY LUNCHEON WITH OUR PUBLISHERS AND MELVYN BRAGG.
YES, AND ANYWAY, MY STABBING HAND IS TIRED FROM SIGNING COPIES OF MY MEMOIRS AT WATERSTONES.
ANOTHER QUAILS EGG IN ASPIC, MR. BERMONDSEY?
TV STUDIO
EXCUSE ME...
EXCUSE ME. ONE OF OUR GUESTS HASN'T TURNED UP. WOULD YOU MIND COMING ON THE PROGRAMME?
JERRY Springer
HEY! LOOK AT ALL THIS FREE GRUB! YOU KNOW, READERS, LIFE ISN'T SO BAD AFTER ALL... AND I NO LONGER WISH TO TOP MYSELF.
FIVE MINUTES, MR. TOPPER.
... OUR NEXT GUEST IS A NAKED SWORD-WEILDING LUNATIC AND HE SAYS HE JUST CAN'T STOP MURDERING SHORT BLOKES CALLED SYD WITH BASIN HAIRCUTS AND YELLOW AND BLACK SPOTTED TANK TOPS... LET'S MEET DWAYNE!
JERRY Springer

Countdown to Armageddon!

A Brief History of Professor's trip

By our Defence Correspondent
BOBBY CRUSH

RED-FACED Pentagon officials were yesterday reviewing their launch procedures after a simple computer error threatened to spark off World War III.

A glitch in the NATO Computerised Defence System caused Cambridge physicist Professor Stephen Hawking to be launched towards Moscow.

the mission

Military staff looked on as technicians battled to abort the unplanned mission. Although able to follow the hapless boffin's progress, they were forced to stand powerlessly by as he hurtled at speeds of up to 4mph from his Cambridge home towards the Russian capital.

death cult

After six anxious hours, relieved defence staff were able to get Hawking back under control, and he was finally brought to a safe halt in a ploughed field near Thetford.

sisters of mercy

A spokesman for the Pentagon attempted to play down the significance of yesterday's incident. "The was never any danger that Professor Hawking was going to reach Moscow and explode. We were aware of his position all the time and absolutely confident we could turn him back," said Pentagon spokesman General Silas T. Oysterburger.

dollar

"In a worst case scenario he would simply have fallen harmlessly off the end of Felixstowe pier."

bucks fizz

Professor Hawking was yesterday recovering at

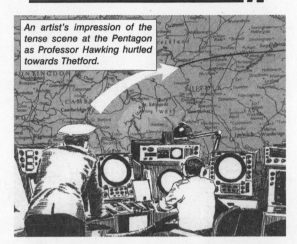

An artist's impression of the tense scene at the Pentagon as Professor Hawking hurtled towards Thetford.

home after his ordeal. "Stephen is doing some really difficult sums at the moment, but it's safe to say he won't be *Russian* about much in the foreseeable future," his wife Mrs Professor Hawking quipped to waiting reporters.

New Year's Honour's List 2000

KNIGHT OF THE BRITISH EMPIRE

***Norman Wisdom**, Actor.* *For services to avoiding tax by living in the Isle of Man, falling off a ladder in a suit that's too small, and shouting 'Mr Grimsdale.'*

***Richard Branson**, Grinning Ladyboy Entrepreneur.* *For services to customs fraud, being allergic to fanny batter and snapping his banjo whilst watching 'Barberella'.*

***Sean Connery**, Actor.* *For services to avoiding tax by living in Spain, not being able to do accents and hitting his wife with an open hand.*

Henry Cooper, Boxer. For services to getting chinned of Cassius Clay and Lloyds of London, doing roofing felt adverts and getting bitten on the arse by a snake.

DAME OF THE BRITISH EMPIRE

Elizabeth Taylor, Boozy, Fat actress. *For services to avoiding tax by living in America, getting married loads of times and being the only grown up prepared to be Michael Jackson's friend except for Dianna Ross.*

Julie Andrews, Nanny actress. *For services to avoiding tax by living in America and flashing her knockers once in her career in a suspiciously engineered tit-prop garment.*

LORD KNIGHT COMMENDER OF THE ORDER OF THE DUCHY OF CORNWALL

Lord Sir Richard Ffitch-Ffitch Chipchase Strothers de Montifiore-Ffitch, KG, GCMG, GCVO, Earl of Cumbernauld, Baron Glenlivvit *For services to making a hat for the Queen mum.*

CBE

Keith Armitage, Air-Sea Rescue Helicopter Winchman. *For 27 years service to the Naval Rescue Unit, but specifically this year because he was seen doing it on a BBC documentary.*

Hilda Cretis, Lolipop lady. *Token award to provide patronising 'common touch' photo opportunity for the Prime Minister.*

...and Twat's a fact! with TV Twat Giles Brandreth

Did you know that there are no elephants WHATSOEVER in Japan, except for the ones in zoos and safari parks.

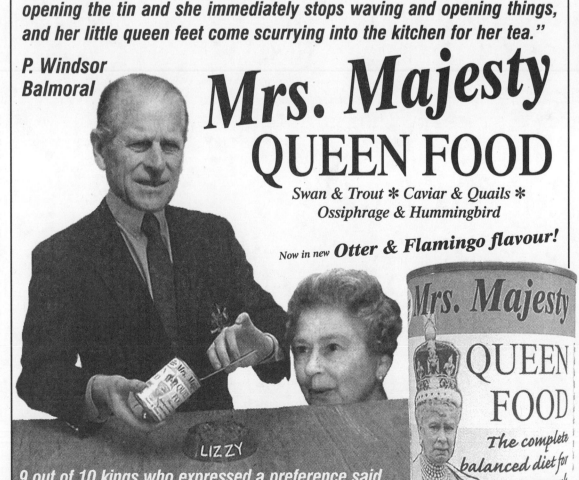

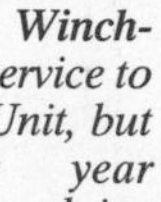

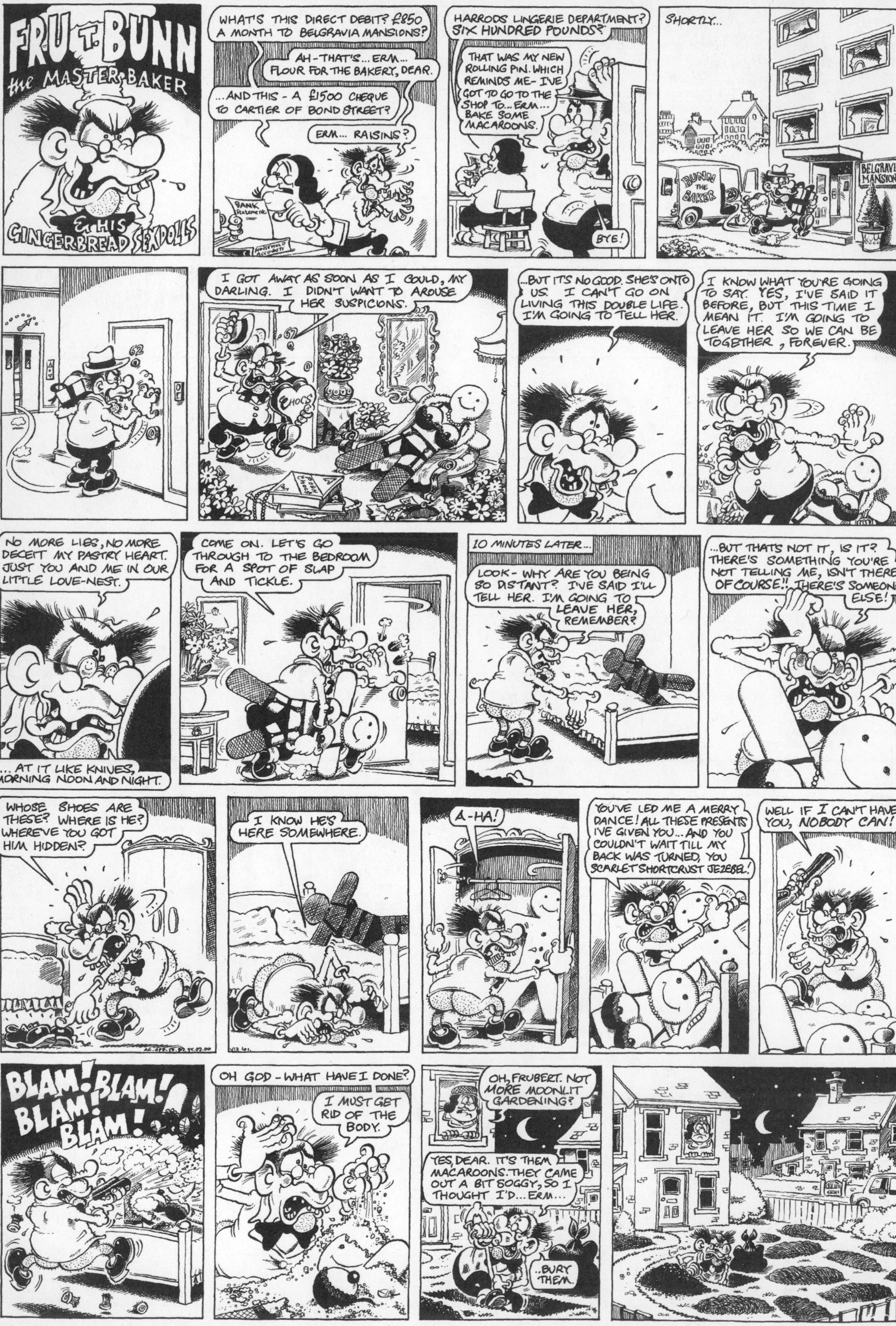
FRU T. BUNN
the MASTER BAKER
& HIS GINGERBREAD SEXDOLLS
WHAT'S THIS DIRECT DEBIT? £850 A MONTH TO BELGRAVIA MANSIONS?
AH - THAT'S... ERM... FLOUR FOR THE BAKERY, DEAR.
...AND THIS - A £1500 CHEQUE TO CARTIER OF BOND STREET?
ERM... RAISINS?
HARRODS LINGERIE DEPARTMENT? SIX HUNDRED POUNDS?
THAT WAS MY NEW ROLLING PIN. WHICH REMINDS ME - I'VE GOT TO GO TO THE SHOP TO... ERM... BAKE SOME MACAROONS.
BYE!
SHORTLY...
BUNN THE BAKER
BELGRAVIA MANSIONS
I GOT AWAY AS SOON AS I COULD, MY DARLING. I DIDN'T WANT TO AROUSE HER SUSPICIONS.
...BUT IT'S NO GOOD. SHE'S ONTO US. I CAN'T GO ON LIVING THIS DOUBLE LIFE. I'M GOING TO TELL HER.
I KNOW WHAT YOU'RE GOING TO SAY. YES, I'VE SAID IT BEFORE, BUT THIS TIME I MEAN IT. I'M GOING TO LEAVE HER SO WE CAN BE TOGETHER, FOREVER.
NO MORE LIES, NO MORE DECEIT MY PASTRY HEART. JUST YOU AND ME IN OUR LITTLE LOVE-NEST.
... AT IT LIKE KNIVES, MORNING NOON AND NIGHT.
COME ON. LET'S GO THROUGH TO THE BEDROOM FOR A SPOT OF SLAP AND TICKLE.
10 MINUTES LATER...
LOOK - WHY ARE YOU BEING SO DISTANT? I'VE SAID I'LL TELL HER. I'M GOING TO LEAVE HER, REMEMBER?
...BUT THAT'S NOT IT, IS IT? THERE'S SOMETHING YOU'RE NOT TELLING ME, ISN'T THERE. OF COURSE!! THERE'S SOMEONE ELSE!
WHOSE SHOES ARE THESE? WHERE IS HE? WHEREVE YOU GOT HIM HIDDEN?
I KNOW HE'S HERE SOMEWHERE.
A-HA!
YOU'VE LED ME A MERRY DANCE! ALL THESE PRESENTS I'VE GIVEN YOU... AND YOU COULDN'T WAIT TILL MY BACK WAS TURNED, YOU SCARLET SHORTCRUST JEZEBEL!
WELL IF I CAN'T HAVE YOU, NOBODY CAN!
BLAM! BLAM! BLAM! BLAM!
OH GOD - WHAT HAVE I DONE?
I MUST GET RID OF THE BODY.
OH, FRUBERT. NOT MORE MOONLIT GARDENING?
YES, DEAR. IT'S THEM MACAROONS. THEY CAME OUT A BIT SOGGY, SO I THOUGHT I'D... ERM...
..BURY THEM.

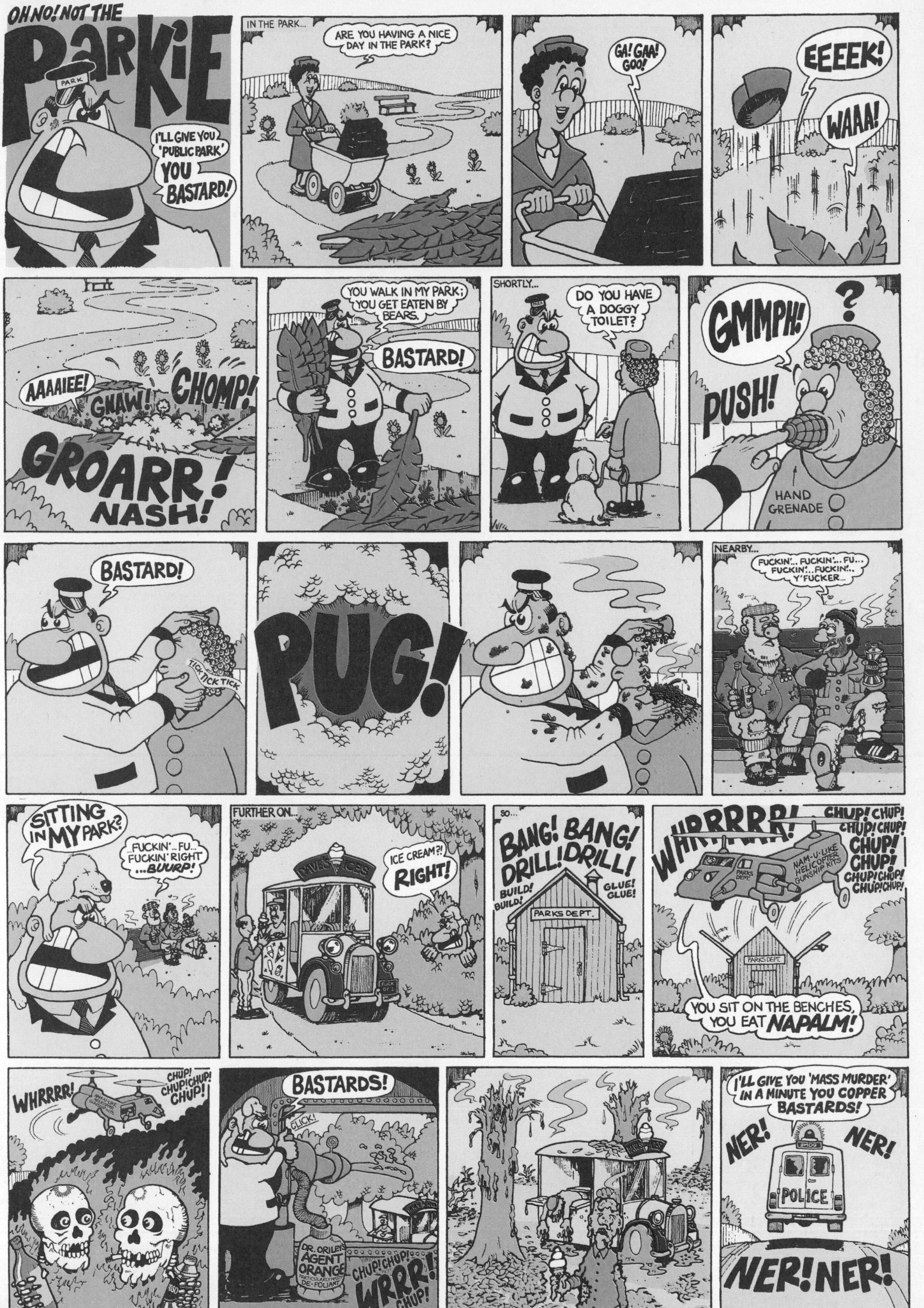
OH NO! NOT THE
PARKIE
PARK
I'LL GIVE YOU 'PUBLIC PARK' YOU BASTARD!
IN THE PARK...
ARE YOU HAVING A NICE DAY IN THE PARK?
GA! GAA! GOO!
EEEEK!
WAAA!
AAAAIEE!
GNAW!
CHOMP!
GROARR!
NASH!
YOU WALK IN MY PARK; YOU GET EATEN BY BEARS.
BASTARD!
SHORTLY...
DO YOU HAVE A DOGGY TOILET?
GMMPH!
?
PUSH!
HAND GRENADE
BASTARD!
TICK TICK TICK
PUG!
NEARBY...
FUCKIN'.. FUCKIN'... FU... FUCKIN'... FUCKIN'... Y'FUCKER...
SITTING IN MY PARK?
...FUCKIN'... FU... FUCKIN' RIGHT ...BUURP!
FURTHER ON...
DAVE'S ICES
ICE CREAM?! RIGHT!
SO...
BANG! BANG! DRILL! DRILL!
BUILD! BUILD!
GLUE! GLUE!
PARKS DEPT.
WHRRRRR!
CHUP! CHUP! CHUP! CHUP! CHUP! CHUP! CHUP! CHUP! CHUP! CHUP!
NAM-U-LIKE HELICOPTER GUNSHIP KITS
PARKS DEPT.
YOU SIT ON THE BENCHES, YOU EAT NAPALM!
WHRRRR!
CHUP! CHUP! CHUP! CHUP!
BASTARDS!
CLICK!
DR. ORILEY'S AGENT ORANGE DE-FOLIANT
CHUP! CHUP! WRRR! CHUP!
I'LL GIVE YOU 'MASS MURDER' IN A MINUTE YOU COPPER BASTARDS!
NER! NER!
POLICE
NER! NER!

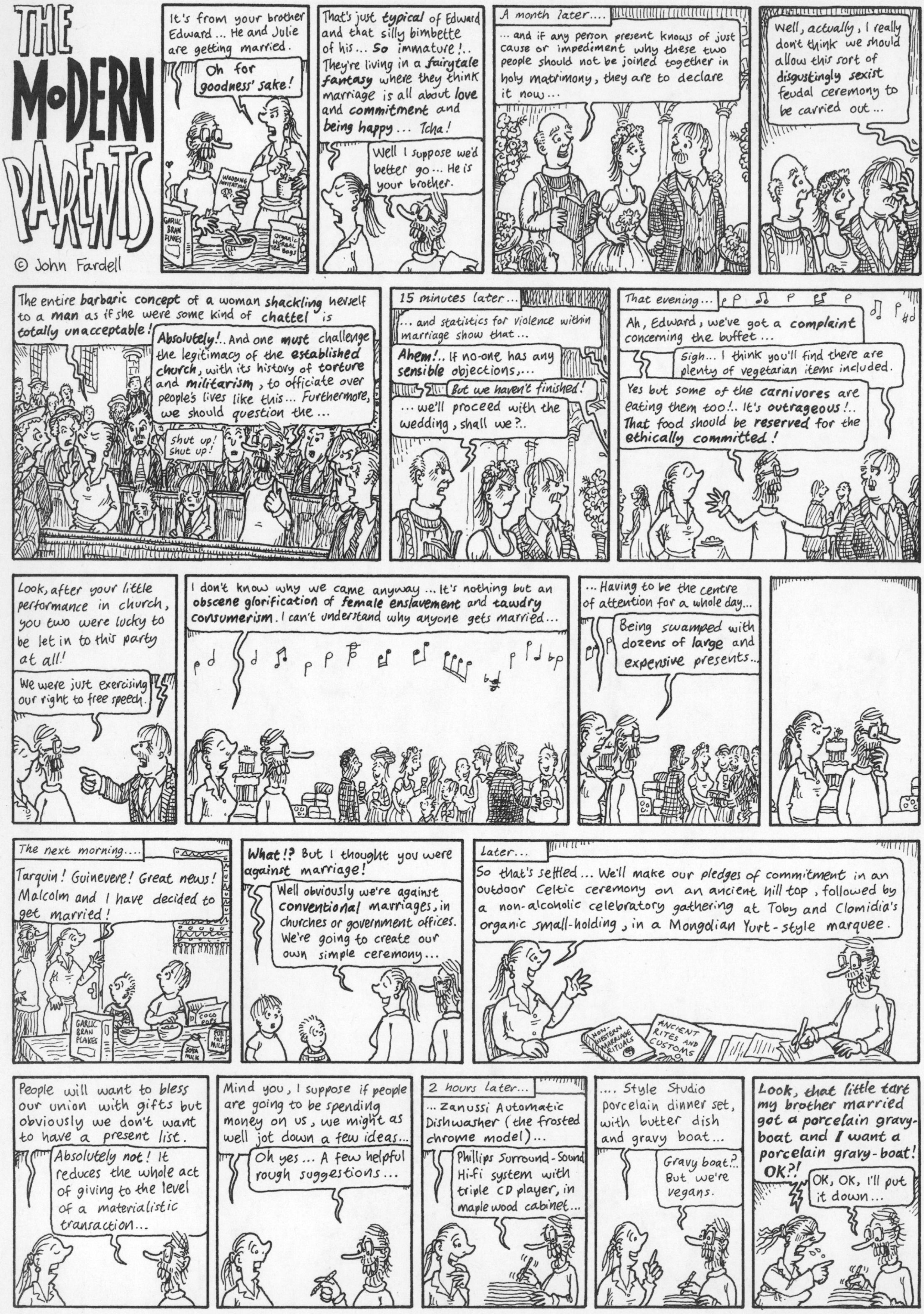
THE MODERN PARENTS
© John Fardell
It's from your brother Edward ... He and Julie are getting married.
Oh for goodness' sake!
WEDDING INVITATION
GARLIC BRAN FLAKES
ORGANIC HERBAL TEA BAGS
That's just typical of Edward and that silly bimbette of his ... So immature!.. They're living in a fairytale fantasy where they think marriage is all about love and commitment and being happy ... Tcha!
Well I suppose we'd better go ... He is your brother.
A month later....
... and if any person present knows of just cause or impediment why these two people should not be joined together in holy matrimony, they are to declare it now ...
Well, actually, I really don't think we should allow this sort of disgustingly sexist feudal ceremony to be carried out ...
The entire barbaric concept of a woman shackling herself to a man as if she were some kind of chattel is totally unacceptable!
Absolutely!.. And one must challenge the legitimacy of the established church, with its history of torture and militarism, to officiate over people's lives like this ... Furthermore, we should question the ...
Shut up! Shut up!
15 minutes later ...
... and statistics for violence within marriage show that ...
Ahem!.. If no-one has any sensible objections, ...
But we haven't finished!
... we'll proceed with the wedding, shall we?..
That evening ...
Ah, Edward, we've got a complaint concerning the buffet ...
Sigh ... I think you'll find there are plenty of vegetarian items included.
Yes but some of the carnivores are eating them too!.. It's outrageous!.. That food should be reserved for the ethically committed!
Look, after your little performance in church, you two were lucky to be let in to this party at all!
We were just exercising our right to free speech.
I don't know why we came anyway ... It's nothing but an obscene glorification of female enslavement and tawdry consumerism. I can't understand why anyone gets married ...
... Having to be the centre of attention for a whole day ...
Being swamped with dozens of large and expensive presents ...
The next morning....
Tarquin! Guinevere! Great news! Malcolm and I have decided to get married!
GARLIC BRAN FLAKES
COCO POPS
FULL FAT MILK
SOYA MILK
What!? But I thought you were against marriage!
Well obviously we're against conventional marriages, in churches or government offices. We're going to create our own simple ceremony ...
Later ...
So that's settled ... We'll make our pledges of commitment in an outdoor Celtic ceremony on an ancient hill top, followed by a non-alcoholic celebratory gathering at Toby and Clomidia's organic small-holding, in a Mongolian Yurt-style marquee.
NON-WESTERN MARRIAGE RITUALS
ANCIENT RITES AND CUSTOMS
People will want to bless our union with gifts but obviously we don't want to have a present list.
Absolutely not! It reduces the whole act of giving to the level of a materialistic transaction ...
Mind you, I suppose if people are going to be spending money on us, we might as well jot down a few ideas ...
Oh yes ... A few helpful rough suggestions ...
2 hours later ...
... Zanussi Automatic Dishwasher (the frosted chrome model) ...
Phillips Surround-Sound Hi-fi system with triple CD player, in maple wood cabinet ...
.... Style Studio porcelain dinner set, with butter dish and gravy boat ...
Gravy boat?.. But we're vegans.
Look, that little tart my brother married got a porcelain gravy-boat and I want a porcelain gravy-boat! OK?!
OK, OK, I'll put it down ...

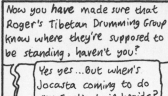
A month later....
Well, here we are... The big day! I'm so glad we've planned everything so simply...

Oh yes... Most people get totally stressed out by all the crap that usually goes with weddings...

Now you *have* made sure that Roger's Tibetan Drumming Group know where they're supposed to be standing, haven't you?

Yes yes...But when's Jocasta coming to do my Gaelic hair braids? I want to look radiant.

Don't worry...She'll be here soon. And Tarquin and Guinevere's *Floral Attendant* outfits look really effective.

There is *no way* we're wearing these flowers and *dresses*.

Tarquin, they're robes... We researched them at the Cornish Folklore Archive... You should be proud of your Celtic heritage.

Shortly....

Do you, Cressida Wright and Malcolm Pratt, **commit** to each other, sexually and emotionally (whilst acknowledging the right of all women to total sexual freedom, the inherent inability of all men to fully commit to anything and the inevitable stresses placed on relationships by our consumerist Western culture), for as long as you both shall find acceptable and convenient?

I do.   I do.

That was *so* spiritual... In a non-religious way of course.
Did I look *radiant*?
Oh *yes!*
You looked ridiculous.

Malcolm and I will get down to the Yurt to make sure everything's ready, if you could clear up here and bring everyone down.

Well, everything seems to be sorted... Let's have a quick peek at our presents before the guests arrive.

This one's from Ashley and Cordelia...

There's a note: "We knew you'd prefer something hand-made and special."

Oh...er...Well, that's really lovely.

10 minutes later....
Hmm... Another hand-made garlic rack... No-one's given us anything from our list at all.
There's one more here... It's from Andromeda, our Tai-Chi teacher...

Excellent! She's given me a personal stereo.

What do you mean, given *you*?

Well obviously it's for me. Andromeda knows how I like to listen to my whalesong tapes when I'm doing my breathing exercises.
Nonsense!...It's clearly a woman-to-woman gift to help me find my inner-space.

So, did you enjoy the ceremony, Edward?
Oh..um.. it was alright... I prefer something a bit more traditional myself.

But a non-establishment wedding like this really reflects the true meaning of love — The caring, the sharing.... The selfless giving...

IT'S MINE, YOU STUPID BITCH!! GIVE IT HERE!!
LET GO, YOU BASTARD!! IT'S MINE!! MINE MINE MINE!!

27

SPAWNY GET
BAH! I'M OFF FOR A WALK IN THE PARK BUT MY FEET ARE KILLING ME. I WISH I HAD A CAR, BUT I'VE ONLY GOT £10.
TO THE PARK 38 MILES
WOW! MY LUCK'S IN! A TOP OF THE RANGE ROLLER FOR A TENNER.
HONEST BERT'S CARS
£10
I'LL TAKE IT!
DONE!
SLAP!
OH NO! THAT'S THE CAR I'VE BOUGHT.
ARF ARF!
LEE-1
CARDBOARD FAKE CARS LTD
CRUMP!
EXCUSE ME...
I'M LOTTERY VERMINILLIONAIRE LEE BRIAN. THAT NUMBER PLATE IS JUST THE THING THAT I STUPIDLY WANT. HERE'S ONE MILLION POUND.
YOU SPAWNY GET!
LEE-1
ARF ARF!
Shortly...
IT'S THE LIFE OF RILEY FOR ME, READERS. I'M GOING TO SIT IN THE PARK AND SMOKE THIS CIGAR FOR THE REST OF MY LIFE!
NEWSAGEN
WE SELL FAGS TO KIDS
LEW STRINGER/GPD
EXCUSE ME, WOULD YOU HOLD MY CIGAR WHILE I SNIP THE END OFF?
CERTAINLY SONNY.
SNIP!
AAARGH!
OOER.
LOOK AT THAT, YOU BLITHERING OAF! YOU'VE CHOPPED MY HANDS OFF, AND I'M A MANUAL LABOURER. YOU'RE GOING TO HAVE TO DO MY JOB FOR ME – IS THAT CLEAR?
ER... YES.
HEH HEH! THIS BLOKE'S JOB WAS CHECKING SEXY BRA MODELS FOR BREAST IMPLANTS BEFORE THEY GET ON A PLANE!
AIRPORT
CHECK IN
HURRY UP, SPAWNSWORTH. TWO HUNDRED MORE SEXY BRA MODELS HAVE JUST ARRIVED. YOU'VE GOT TO FEEL ALL THEIR TITS BEFORE LUNCHTIME.
OOH, YOU SPAWNY GET!

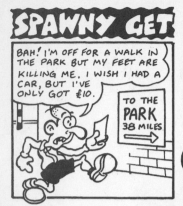

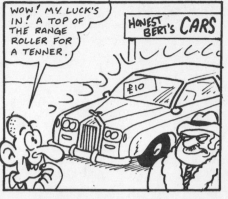

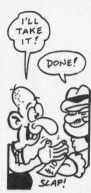

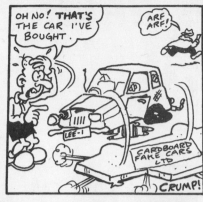

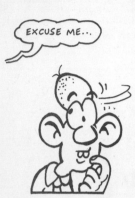

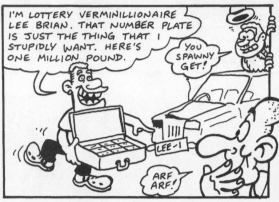

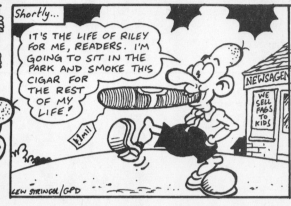

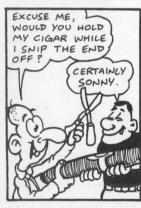

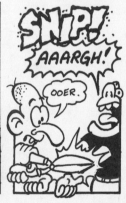

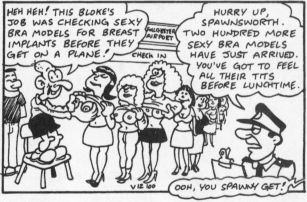

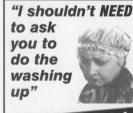

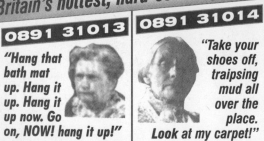

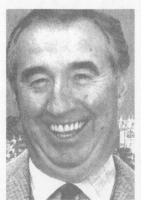

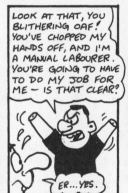

Wattle he do?

by our Rumours Editor HARRY BOLLOCKS

Growth of concern over Turkey magnate's chin

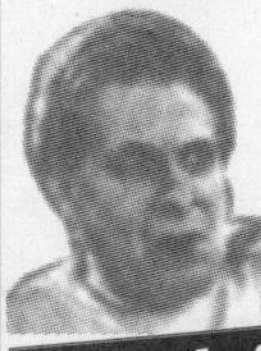

FEARS were growing last night that poultry by-products supremo Sir Bernard Matthews may have grown a turkey's wattle.

Rumours were fuelled by the fact that in his latest advert, the publicity hungry Norfolk billionaire is seen from one side only in a mysterious half light, as if to disguise the growth of a fleshy excrescence dangling from his chin.

dinosaur

A spokesman for Matthews' Turkey Dinosaur empire added to the uncertainty by remaining non committal when questioned by reporters: "No. Sir Bernard is not growing a turkey's wattle. I repeat, he is NOT growing a turkey's wattle," she said.

dyno-rod

A statement issued by the Boy Scouts Association, who have appeared in many of Bernard Matthews' adverts on account of their small hands making his turkey drummers look bigger, yesterday added to the mystery. "Bob a job, mister? Wash your car for 50p?" said a spokesman.

Matthews - in happier pre-wattle rumour days yesterday.

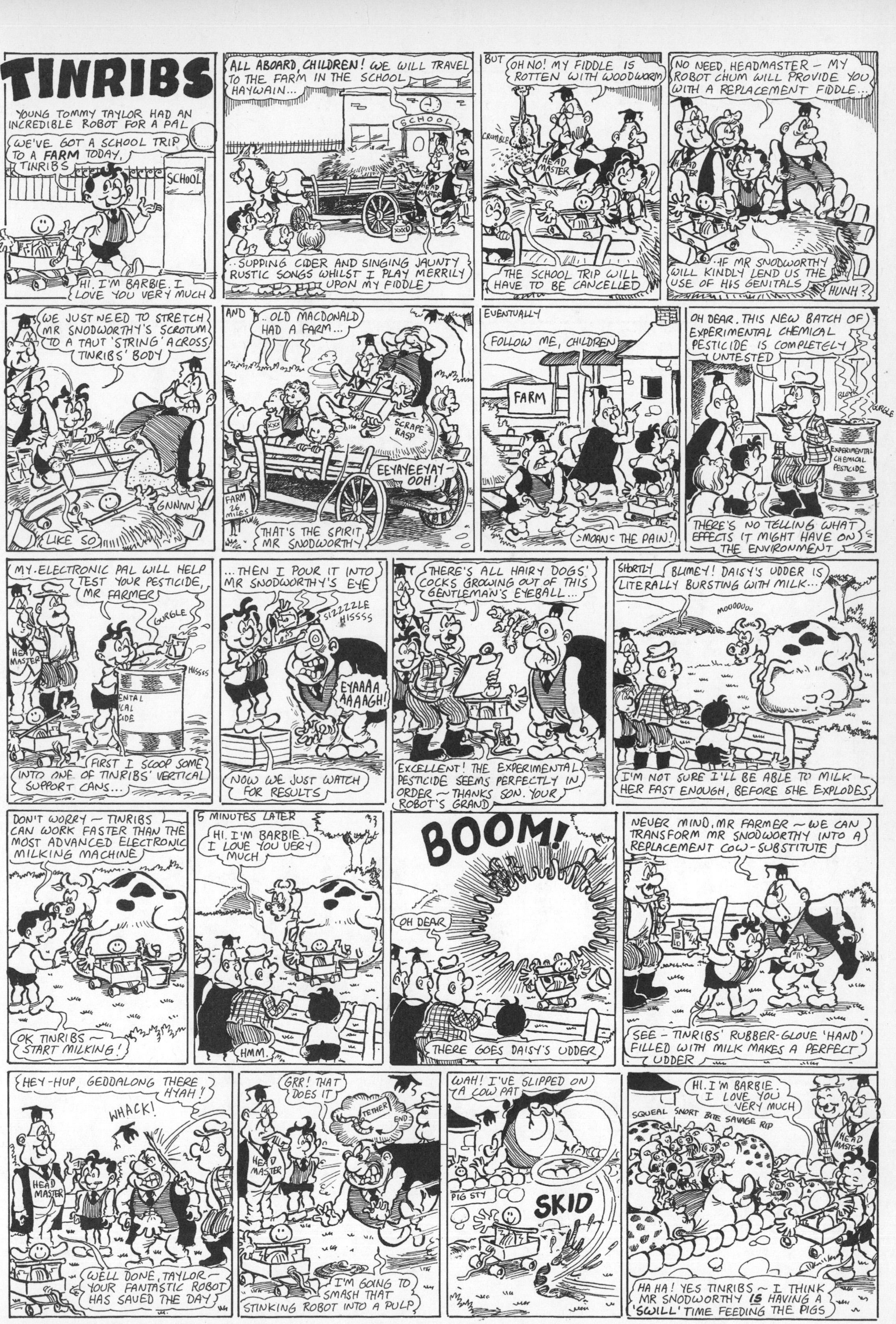
TINRIBS
YOUNG TOMMY TAYLOR HAD AN INCREDIBLE ROBOT FOR A PAL
WE'VE GOT A SCHOOL TRIP TO A FARM TODAY, TINRIBS
SCHOOL
HI. I'M BARBIE. I LOVE YOU VERY MUCH
ALL ABOARD, CHILDREN! WE WILL TRAVEL TO THE FARM IN THE SCHOOL HAYWAIN...
SCHOOL
HEAD MASTER
XXX
...SUPPING CIDER AND SINGING JAUNTY RUSTIC SONGS WHILST I PLAY MERRILY UPON MY FIDDLE
BUT
OH NO! MY FIDDLE IS ROTTEN WITH WOODWORM
CRUMBLE
HEAD MASTER
THE SCHOOL TRIP WILL HAVE TO BE CANCELLED
NO NEED, HEADMASTER – MY ROBOT CHUM WILL PROVIDE YOU WITH A REPLACEMENT FIDDLE...
...IF MR SNODWORTHY WILL KINDLY LEND US THE USE OF HIS GENITALS
HUNH?
WE JUST NEED TO STRETCH MR SNODWORTHY'S SCROTUM TO A TAUT 'STRING' ACROSS TINRIBS' BODY
GNNNN
LIKE SO
AND ...OLD MACDONALD HAD A FARM...
XXX
SCRAPE RASP
EEYAYEEYAY-OOH!
FARM 26 MILES
THAT'S THE SPIRIT, MR SNODWORTHY
EVENTUALLY
FOLLOW ME, CHILDREN
FARM
>MOAN< THE PAIN!
OH DEAR. THIS NEW BATCH OF EXPERIMENTAL CHEMICAL PESTICIDE IS COMPLETELY UNTESTED
BLOTH
GURGLE
EXPERIMENTAL CHEMICAL PESTICIDE
THERE'S NO TELLING WHAT EFFECTS IT MIGHT HAVE ON THE ENVIRONMENT
MY ELECTRONIC PAL WILL HELP TEST YOUR PESTICIDE, MR FARMER
GURGLE
HISSSS
HEAD MASTER
FIRST I SCOOP SOME INTO ONE OF TINRIBS' VERTICAL SUPPORT CANS...
...THEN I POUR IT INTO MR SNODWORTHY'S EYE
SIZZZZLE HISSSS
EYAAAA AAAAGH!
NOW WE JUST WATCH FOR RESULTS
THERE'S ALL HAIRY DOGS' COCKS GROWING OUT OF THIS GENTLEMAN'S EYEBALL...
EXCELLENT! THE EXPERIMENTAL PESTICIDE SEEMS PERFECTLY IN ORDER ~ THANKS SON. YOUR ROBOT'S GRAND
SHORTLY
BLIMEY! DAISY'S UDDER IS LITERALLY BURSTING WITH MILK...
MOOOOUUU
I'M NOT SURE I'LL BE ABLE TO MILK HER FAST ENOUGH, BEFORE SHE EXPLODES
DON'T WORRY – TINRIBS CAN WORK FASTER THAN THE MOST ADVANCED ELECTRONIC MILKING MACHINE
OK TINRIBS – START MILKING!
5 MINUTES LATER
HI. I'M BARBIE. I LOVE YOU VERY MUCH
HMM.
BOOM!
OH DEAR
THERE GOES DAISY'S UDDER
NEVER MIND, MR FARMER ~ WE CAN TRANSFORM MR SNODWORTHY INTO A REPLACEMENT COW-SUBSTITUTE
SEE – TINRIBS' RUBBER-GLOVE 'HAND' FILLED WITH MILK MAKES A PERFECT UDDER
HEY-HUP, GEDDALONG THERE HYAH!
WHACK!
HEAD MASTER
WELL DONE, TAYLOR – YOUR FANTASTIC ROBOT HAS SAVED THE DAY
GRR! THAT DOES IT
TETHER END
HEAD MASTER
I'M GOING TO SMASH THAT STINKING ROBOT INTO A PULP
WAH! I'VE SLIPPED ON A COW PAT
PIG STY
SKID
HI. I'M BARBIE. I LOVE YOU VERY MUCH
SQUEAL SNORT BITE SAVAGE RIP
HEAD MASTER
HA HA! YES TINRIBS ~ I THINK MR SNODWORTHY IS HAVING A 'SWILL' TIME FEEDING THE PIGS

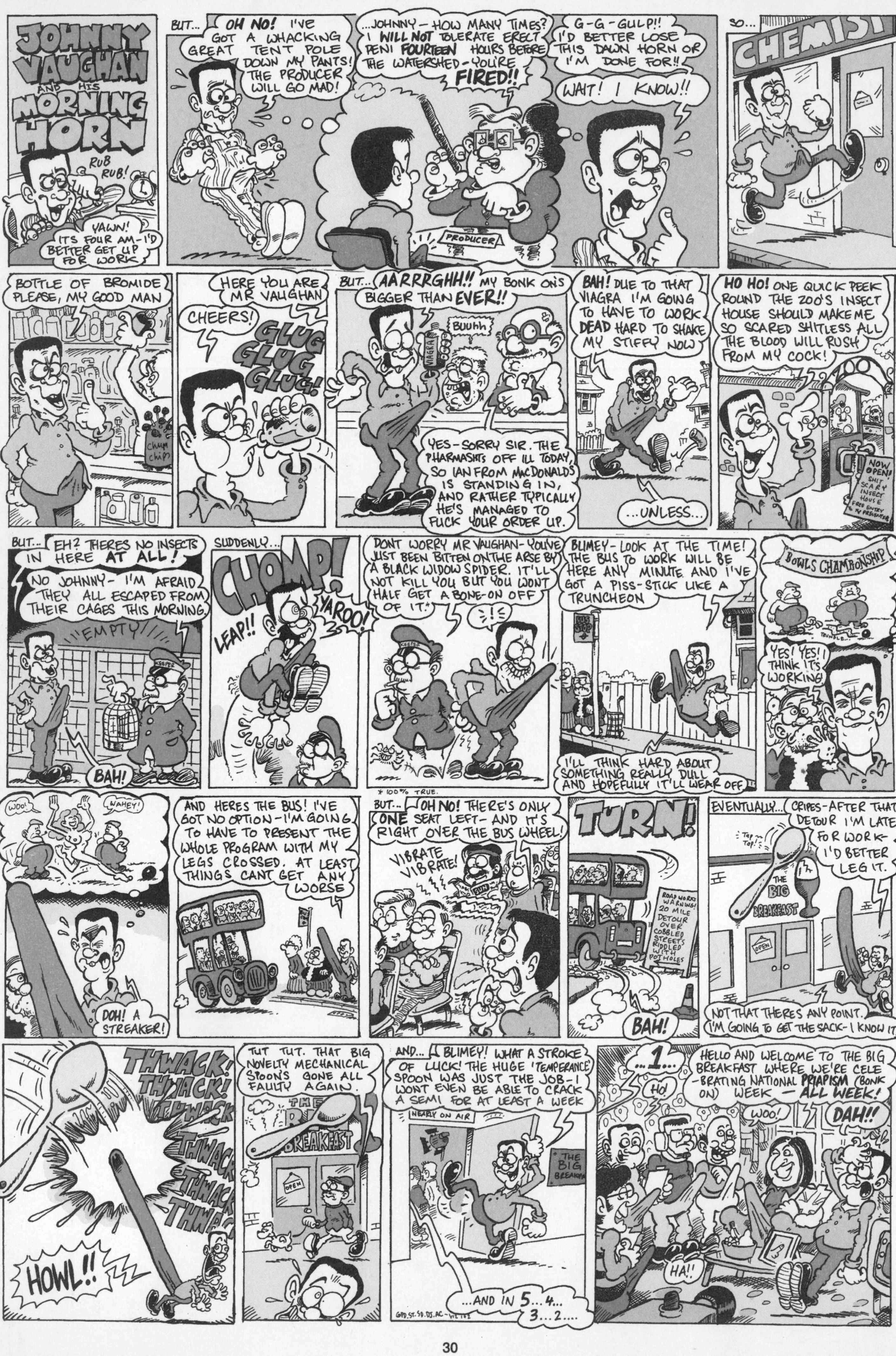
JOHNNY VAUGHAN AND HIS MORNING HORN
RUB RUB!
YAWN! ITS FOUR AM - I'D BETTER GET UP FOR WORK
BUT...
OH NO! I'VE GOT A WHACKING GREAT TENT POLE DOWN MY PANTS! THE PRODUCER WILL GO MAD!
...JOHNNY - HOW MANY TIMES? I WILL NOT TOLERATE ERECT PENI FOURTEEN HOURS BEFORE THE WATERSHED - YOU'RE FIRED!!
PRODUCER
G-G-GULP!! I'D BETTER LOSE THIS DAWN HORN OR I'M DONE FOR!!
WAIT! I KNOW!!
SO...
CHEMIST
BOTTLE OF BROMIDE PLEASE, MY GOOD MAN
CHUM CHIPS
HERE YOU ARE MR VAUGHAN
CHEERS!
GLUG GLUG GLUG!
BUT...
AARRRGHH!! MY BONK ON'S BIGGER THAN EVER!!
VIAGRA
BUUHH
YES - SORRY SIR. THE PHARMASHTS OFF ILL TODAY, SO IAN FROM MACDONALDS IS STANDING IN, AND RATHER TYPICALLY HE'S MANAGED TO FUCK YOUR ORDER UP.
BAH! DUE TO THAT VIAGRA I'M GOING TO HAVE TO WORK DEAD HARD TO SHAKE MY STIFFY NOW
...UNLESS...
HO HO! ONE QUICK PEEK ROUND THE ZOO'S INSECT HOUSE SHOULD MAKE ME SO SCARED SHITLESS ALL THE BLOOD WILL RUSH FROM MY COCK!
NOW OPEN! SHIT SCARY INSECT HOUSE
BUT...
EH? THERES NO INSECTS IN HERE AT ALL!
NO JOHNNY - I'M AFRAID THEY ALL ESCAPED FROM THEIR CAGES THIS MORNING.
EMPTY
KEEPER
BAH!
SUDDENLY...
CHOMP!
YAROO!
LEAP!!
DONT WORRY MR VAUGHAN - YOU'VE JUST BEEN BITTEN ON THE ARSE BY A BLACK WIDOW SPIDER. IT'LL NOT KILL YOU BUT YOU WONT HALF GET A BONE-ON OFF OF IT.*
!
KEEPER
* 100% TRUE.
BLIMEY - LOOK AT THE TIME! THE BUS TO WORK WILL BE HERE ANY MINUTE AND I'VE GOT A PISS-STICK LIKE A TRUNCHEON
BUS STOP
I'LL THINK HARD ABOUT SOMETHING REALLY DULL AND HOPEFULLY IT'LL WEAR OFF
BOWLS CHAMPIONSHIP
TRUNDLE...
YES! YES! I THINK IT'S WORKING
WOO!
WAHEY!
DOH! A STREAKER!
AND HERES THE BUS! I'VE GOT NO OPTION - I'M GOING TO HAVE TO PRESENT THE WHOLE PROGRAM WITH MY LEGS CROSSED. AT LEAST THINGS CANT GET ANY WORSE
BUT...
OH NO! THERE'S ONLY ONE SEAT LEFT - AND IT'S RIGHT OVER THE BUS WHEEL!
VIBRATE VIBRATE!
SUN
TURN!
ROAD WORKS WARNING! 20 MILE DETOUR OVER COBBLED STREETS RIDDLED WITH POTHOLES
BAH!
EVENTUALLY...
CRIPES - AFTER THAT DETOUR I'M LATE FOR WORK - I'D BETTER LEG IT.
TAP TAP!
THE BIG BREAKFAST
OPEN
NOT THAT THERES ANY POINT. I'M GOING TO GET THE SACK - I KNOW IT!
THWACK! THWACK! THWACK! THWACK THWACK THWACK
HOWL!!
TUT TUT. THAT BIG NOVELTY MECHANICAL SPOON'S GONE ALL FAULTY AGAIN.
BREAKFAST
OPEN
AND...
BLIMEY! WHAT A STROKE OF LUCK! THE HUGE 'TEMPERANCE' SPOON WAS JUST THE JOB - I WONT EVEN BE ABLE TO CRACK A SEMI FOR AT LEAST A WEEK
NEARLY ON AIR
THE BIG BREAKFAST
...AND IN 5...4... 3...2...
...1...
HO!
HELLO AND WELCOME TO THE BIG BREAKFAST WHERE WE'RE CELEBRATING NATIONAL PRIAPISM (BONK ON) WEEK - ALL WEEK!
WOO!
DAH!!
HA!!

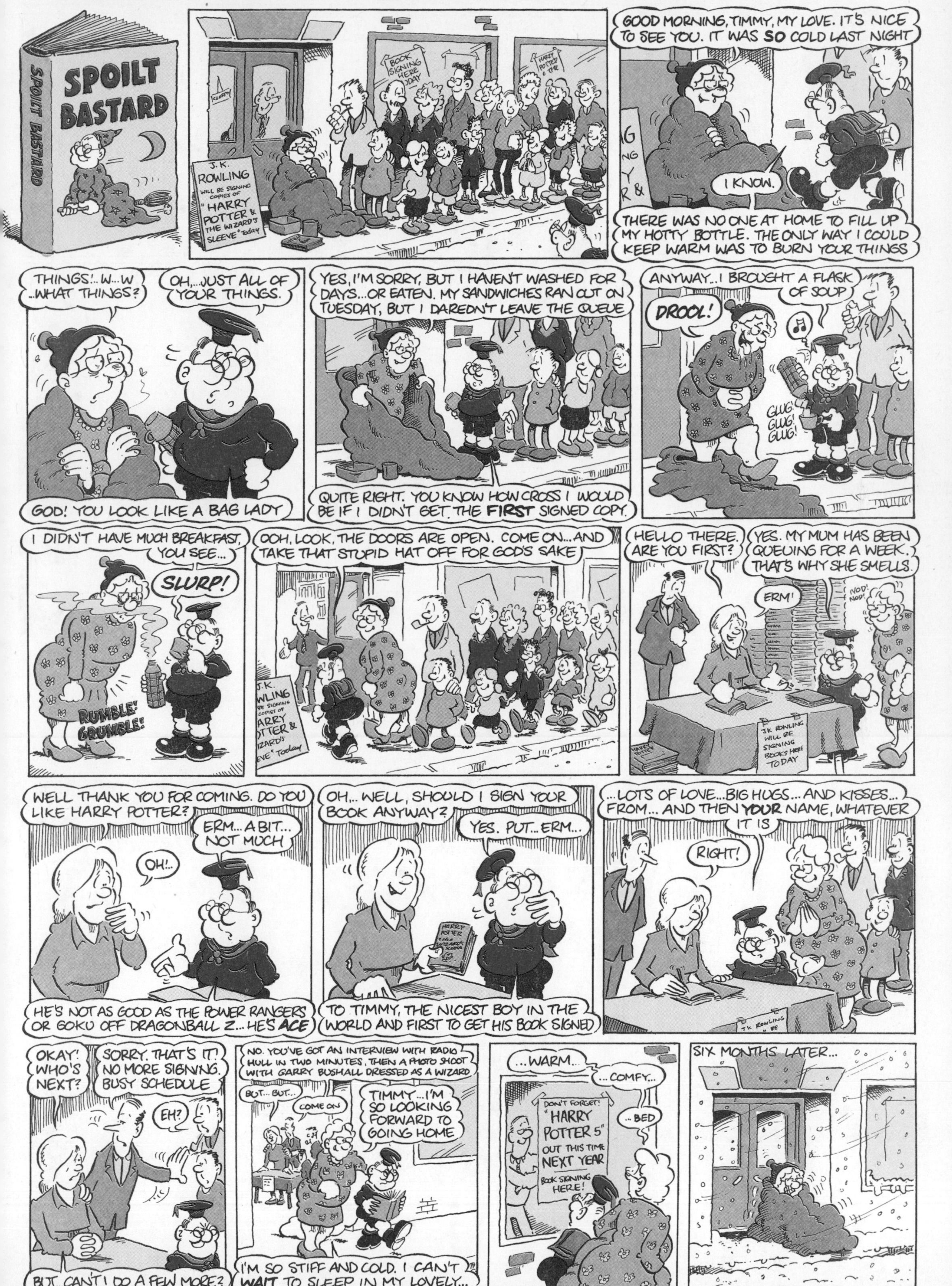
SPOILT BASTARD
J.K. ROWLING WILL BE SIGNING COPIES OF "HARRY POTTER & THE WIZARD'S SLEEVE" Today
BOOK SIGNING HERE TODAY
GOOD MORNING, TIMMY, MY LOVE. IT'S NICE TO SEE YOU. IT WAS SO COLD LAST NIGHT
I KNOW.
THERE WAS NO ONE AT HOME TO FILL UP MY HOTTY BOTTLE. THE ONLY WAY I COULD KEEP WARM WAS TO BURN YOUR THINGS
THINGS!.. W...W ..WHAT THINGS?
OH,...JUST ALL OF YOUR THINGS.
GOD! YOU LOOK LIKE A BAG LADY
YES, I'M SORRY, BUT I HAVEN'T WASHED FOR DAYS...OR EATEN. MY SANDWICHES RAN OUT ON TUESDAY, BUT I DAREDN'T LEAVE THE QUEUE
QUITE RIGHT. YOU KNOW HOW CROSS I WOULD BE IF I DIDN'T GET THE FIRST SIGNED COPY.
ANYWAY...I BROUGHT A FLASK OF SOUP
DROOL!
GLUG! GLUG! GLUG!
I DIDN'T HAVE MUCH BREAKFAST, YOU SEE...
SLURP!
RUMBLE! GRUMBLE!
OOH, LOOK, THE DOORS ARE OPEN. COME ON...AND TAKE THAT STUPID HAT OFF FOR GOD'S SAKE
HELLO THERE. ARE YOU FIRST?
YES. MY MUM HAS BEEN QUEUING FOR A WEEK. THAT'S WHY SHE SMELLS.
ERM!
NOD! NOD!
JK ROWLING WILL BE SIGNING BOOKS HERE TODAY
WELL THANK YOU FOR COMING. DO YOU LIKE HARRY POTTER?
ERM... A BIT... NOT MUCH
OH!..
HE'S NOT AS GOOD AS THE POWER RANGERS OR GOKU OFF DRAGONBALL Z... HE'S ACE
OH,... WELL, SHOULD I SIGN YOUR BOOK ANYWAY?
YES. PUT...ERM...
TO TIMMY, THE NICEST BOY IN THE WORLD AND FIRST TO GET HIS BOOK SIGNED
...LOTS OF LOVE...BIG HUGS... AND KISSES... FROM... AND THEN YOUR NAME, WHATEVER IT IS
RIGHT!
OKAY! WHO'S NEXT?
SORRY. THAT'S IT! NO MORE SIGNING. BUSY SCHEDULE
EH?
BUT...CAN'T I DO A FEW MORE?
NO. YOU'VE GOT AN INTERVIEW WITH RADIO HULL IN TWO MINUTES, THEN A PHOTO SHOOT WITH GARRY BUSHALL DRESSED AS A WIZARD
BUT... BUT...
COME ON
TIMMY...I'M SO LOOKING FORWARD TO GOING HOME
I'M SO STIFF AND COLD. I CAN'T WAIT TO SLEEP IN MY LOVELY...
...WARM...
...COMFY...
...BED
DON'T FORGET! "HARRY POTTER 5" OUT THIS TIME NEXT YEAR
BOOK SIGNING HERE!
SIX MONTHS LATER...

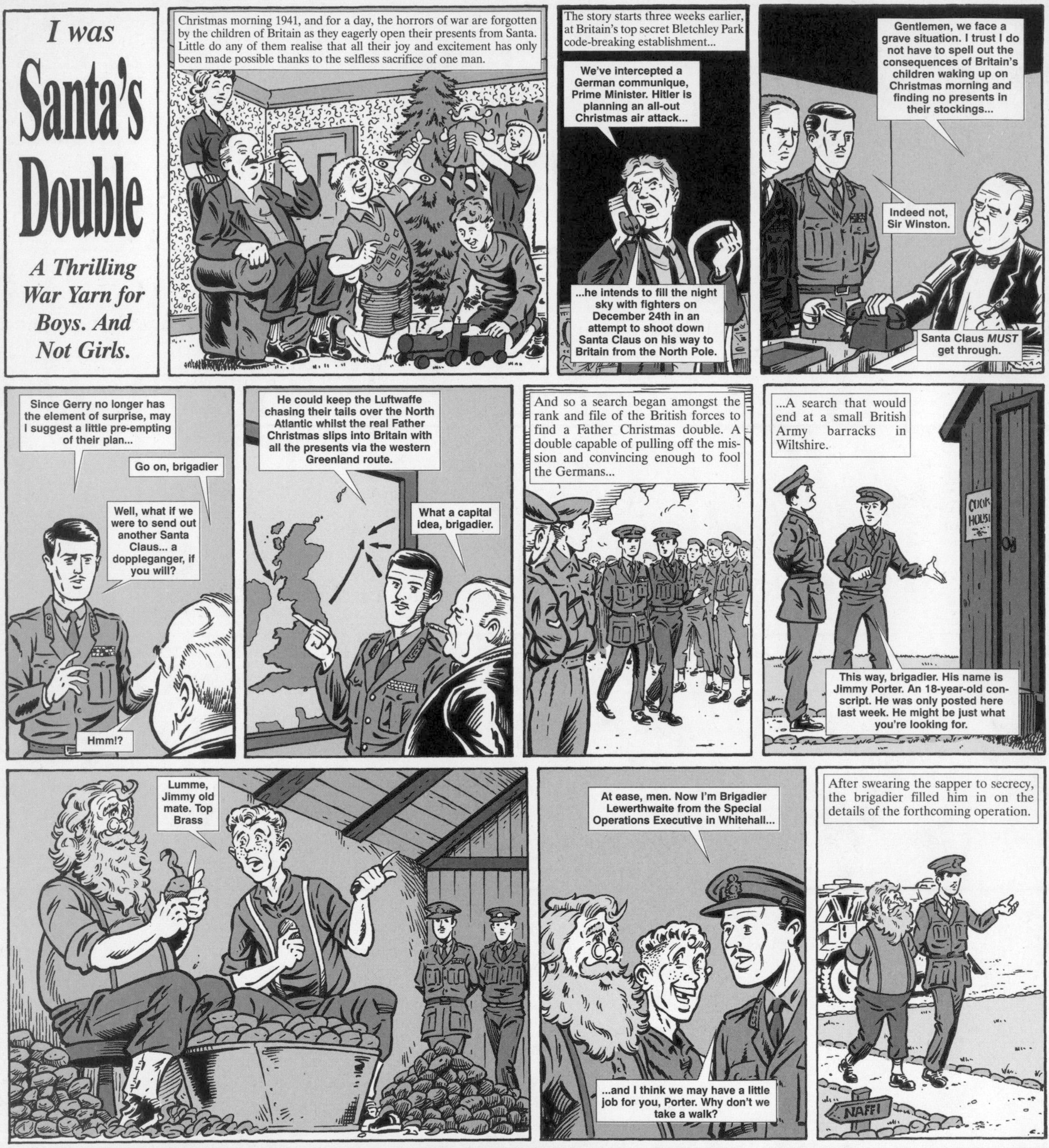

I was
Santa's Double
A Thrilling War Yarn for Boys. And Not Girls.
Christmas morning 1941, and for a day, the horrors of war are forgotten by the children of Britain as they eagerly open their presents from Santa. Little do any of them realise that all their joy and excitement has only been made possible thanks to the selfless sacrifice of one man.
The story starts three weeks earlier, at Britain's top secret Bletchley Park code-breaking establishment...
We've intercepted a German communique, Prime Minister. Hitler is planning an all-out Christmas air attack...
...he intends to fill the night sky with fighters on December 24th in an attempt to shoot down Santa Claus on his way to Britain from the North Pole.
Gentlemen, we face a grave situation. I trust I do not have to spell out the consequences of Britain's children waking up on Christmas morning and finding no presents in their stockings...
Indeed not, Sir Winston.
Santa Claus *MUST* get through.
Since Gerry no longer has the element of surprise, may I suggest a little pre-empting of their plan...
Go on, brigadier
Well, what if we were to send out another Santa Claus... a doppleganger, if you will?
Hmm!?
He could keep the Luftwaffe chasing their tails over the North Atlantic whilst the real Father Christmas slips into Britain with all the presents via the western Greenland route.
What a capital idea, brigadier.
And so a search began amongst the rank and file of the British forces to find a Father Christmas double. A double capable of pulling off the mission and convincing enough to fool the Germans...
...A search that would end at a small British Army barracks in Wiltshire.
COOK HOUSE
This way, brigadier. His name is Jimmy Porter. An 18-year-old conscript. He was only posted here last week. He might be just what you're looking for.
Lumme, Jimmy old mate. Top Brass
At ease, men. Now I'm Brigadier Lewerthwaite from the Special Operations Executive in Whitehall...
...and I think we may have a little job for you, Porter. Why don't we take a walk?
After swearing the sapper to secrecy, the brigadier filled him in on the details of the forthcoming operation.
NAAFI
The following morning, and every morning for the following three weeks, the decoy Santa was put through a rigorous training exercise at a secret location...
Come on, Man! Get into that chimney! Faster, faster! We haven't got all day!
Puff! Pant!
Come on, come ON! In a week's time you'll have to be able to eat 11 million of these in a single night...
cough! choke!
And what do you want for Christmas, sonny?
And what do you want for Christmas, sonny?
That's it! Again.
...until finally, he was ready.
Ho! Ho! Ho! *Merrrrrrrry* Christmas!
It's uncanny... *fantastic!*

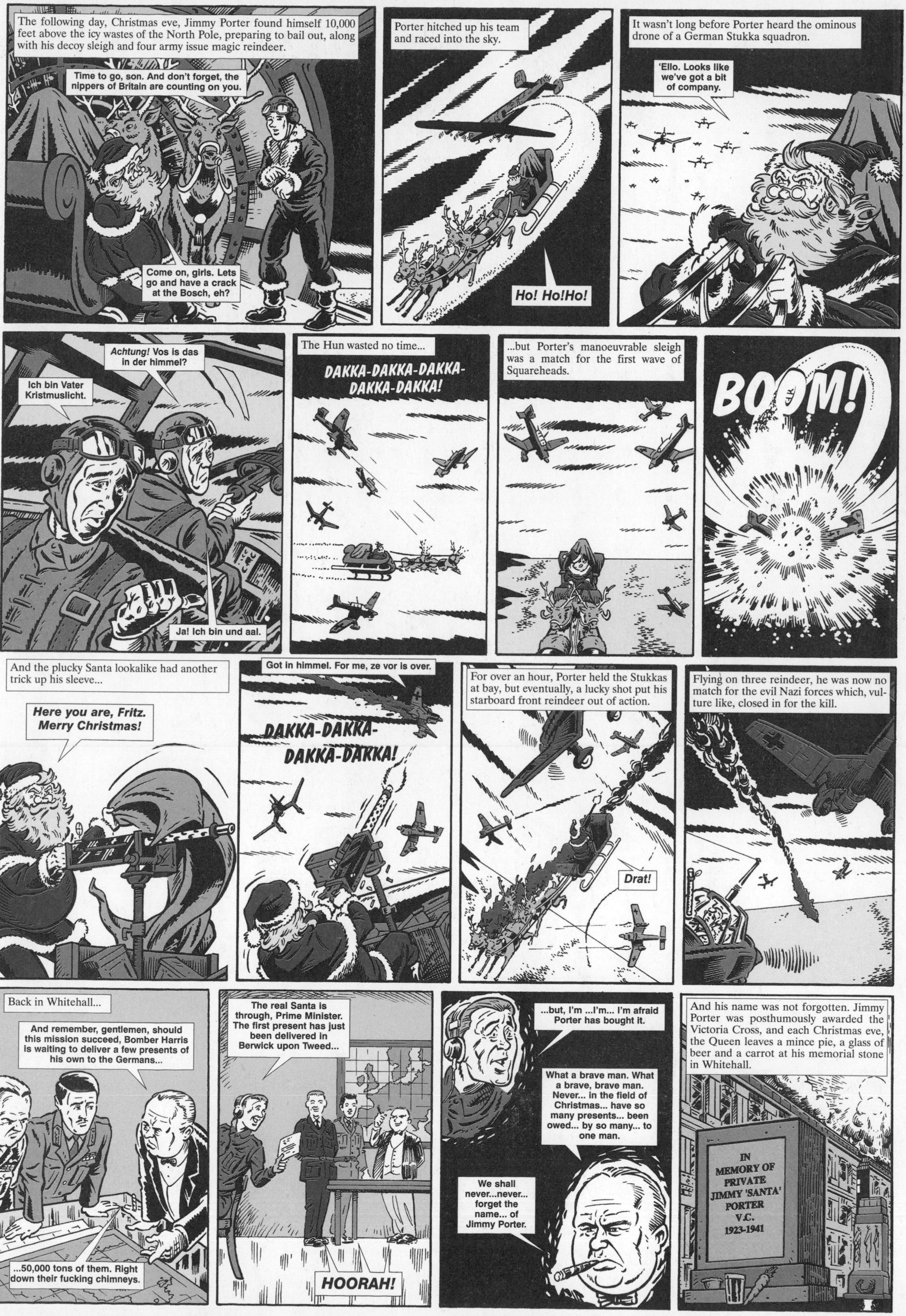

The following day, Christmas eve, Jimmy Porter found himself 10,000 feet above the icy wastes of the North Pole, preparing to bail out, along with his decoy sleigh and four army issue magic reindeer.
Time to go, son. And don't forget, the nippers of Britain are counting on you.
Come on, girls. Lets go and have a crack at the Bosch, eh?
Porter hitched up his team and raced into the sky.
Ho! Ho!Ho!
It wasn't long before Porter heard the ominous drone of a German Stukka squadron.
'Ello. Looks like we've got a bit of company.
Achtung! Vos is das in der himmel?
Ich bin Vater Kristmuslicht.
Ja! Ich bin und aal.
The Hun wasted no time...
DAKKA-DAKKA-DAKKA-DAKKA-DAKKA!
...but Porter's manoeuvrable sleigh was a match for the first wave of Squareheads.
BOOM!
And the plucky Santa lookalike had another trick up his sleeve...
Here you are, Fritz. Merry Christmas!
Got in himmel. For me, ze vor is over.
DAKKA-DAKKA-DAKKA-DAKKA!
For over an hour, Porter held the Stukkas at bay, but eventually, a lucky shot put his starboard front reindeer out of action.
Drat!
Flying on three reindeer, he was now no match for the evil Nazi forces which, vulture like, closed in for the kill.
Back in Whitehall...
And remember, gentlemen, should this mission succeed, Bomber Harris is waiting to deliver a few presents of his own to the Germans...
...50,000 tons of them. Right down their fucking chimneys.
The real Santa is through, Prime Minister. The first present has just been delivered in Berwick upon Tweed...
HOORAH!
...but, I'm ...I'm... I'm afraid Porter has bought it.
What a brave man. What a brave, brave man. Never... in the field of Christmas... have so many presents... been owed... by so many... to one man.
We shall never...never... forget the name... of Jimmy Porter.
And his name was not forgotten. Jimmy Porter was posthumously awarded the Victoria Cross, and each Christmas eve, the Queen leaves a mince pie, a glass of beer and a carrot at his memorial stone in Whitehall.
IN MEMORY OF PRIVATE JIMMY 'SANTA' PORTER V.C. 1923-1941

THE END

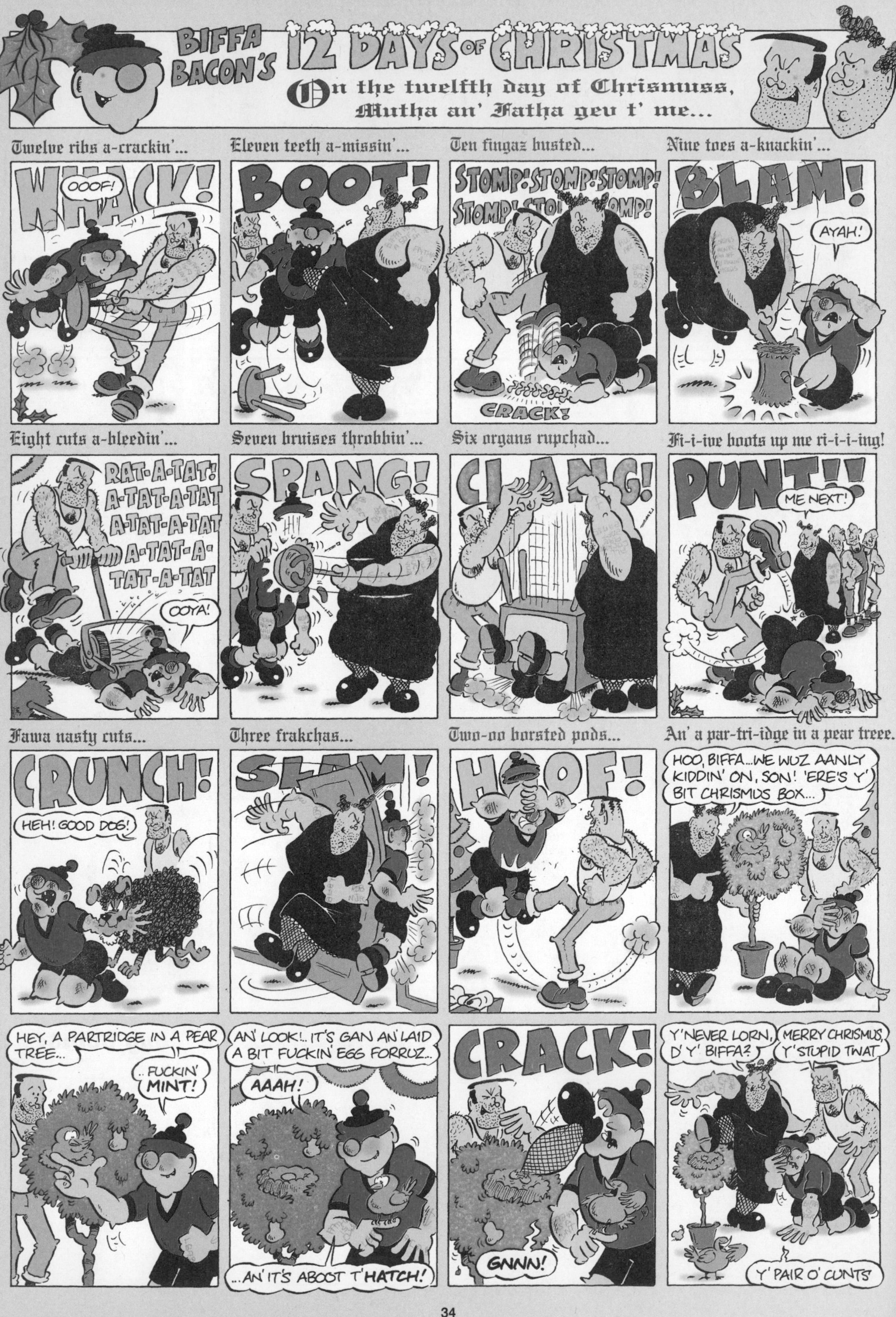

BIFFA BACON'S 12 DAYS OF CHRISTMAS
On the twelfth day of Chrismuss, Mutha an' Fatha geu t' me...
Twelve ribs a-crackin'...
WHACK!
OOOF!
Eleven teeth a-missin'...
BOOT!
Ten fingaz busted...
STOMP! STOMP! STOMP! STOMP! STOMP! STOMP!
CRACK!
Nine toes a-knackin'...
BLAM!
AYAH!
Eight cuts a-bleedin'...
RAT-A-TAT! A-TAT-A-TAT A-TAT-A-TAT A-TAT-A- TAT-A-TAT
OOYA!
Seven bruises throbbin'...
SPANG!
Six organs rupchad...
CLANG!
Fi-i-ive boots up me ri-i-i-ing!
PUNT!!
ME NEXT!
Fawa nasty cuts...
CRUNCH!
HEH! GOOD DOG!
Three frakchas...
SLAM!
Two-oo borsted pods...
HOOF!
An' a par-tri-idge in a pear treee.
HOO, BIFFA...WE WUZ AANLY KIDDIN' ON, SON! 'ERE'S Y' BIT CHRISMUS BOX...
HEY, A PARTRIDGE IN A PEAR TREE...
..FUCKIN' MINT!
AN' LOOK!..IT'S GAN AN' LAID A BIT FUCKIN' EGG FORRUZ..
AAAH!
...AN' IT'S ABOOT T' HATCH!
CRACK!
GNNN!
Y'NEVER LORN, D'Y' BIFFA?
MERRY CHRISMUS, Y'STUPID TWAT
Y' PAIR O' CUNTS

NORMAN the DOORMAN
NORMAN'S GOT A NEW JOB...
HOTEL de POSH
GOOD MORNING, SIR. WOULD YOU LIKE ME TO GET A TAXI FOR YOU?
YES PLEASE.
PHEEP!
SORRY, PAL. YOU'RE NOT GETTING IN THAT TAXI.
EH?
TAXI
SORRY. THAT BRIEFCASE IS CASUAL.
DON'T BE SO RIDICULOUS! NOW LET ME IN. I'VE GOT AN IMPORTANT MEETING IN TEN MINUTES.
HAVE YOU, NOW? WELL I'LL FUCKING "MEETING" YOU, PAL.
GET ME THE MANAGER! I WANT TO SEE THE MANAGER!
HURGH!
GROAN

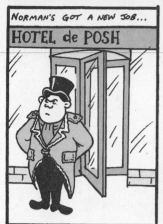

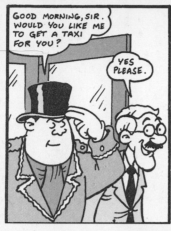

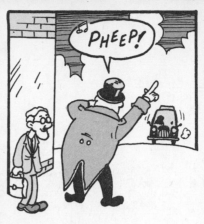

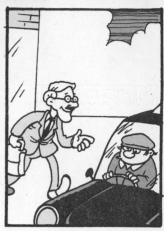

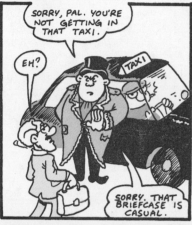

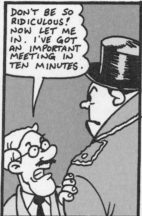

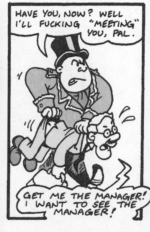

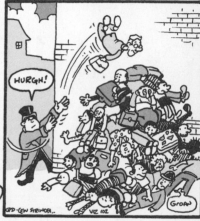

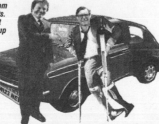

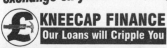

Fanny's Batter bits

*Gravel-voiced '48 Hours' actor **Nick Nolte** has been fined $200 by Hollywood magistrates after pleading guilty to building a mermaid. The bizarre woman/fish hybrid - made out of the bottom half of a dolphin and the top half of **Mary Tyler-Moore** is presently being cared for in the veterinary centre at Seaworld, California.*

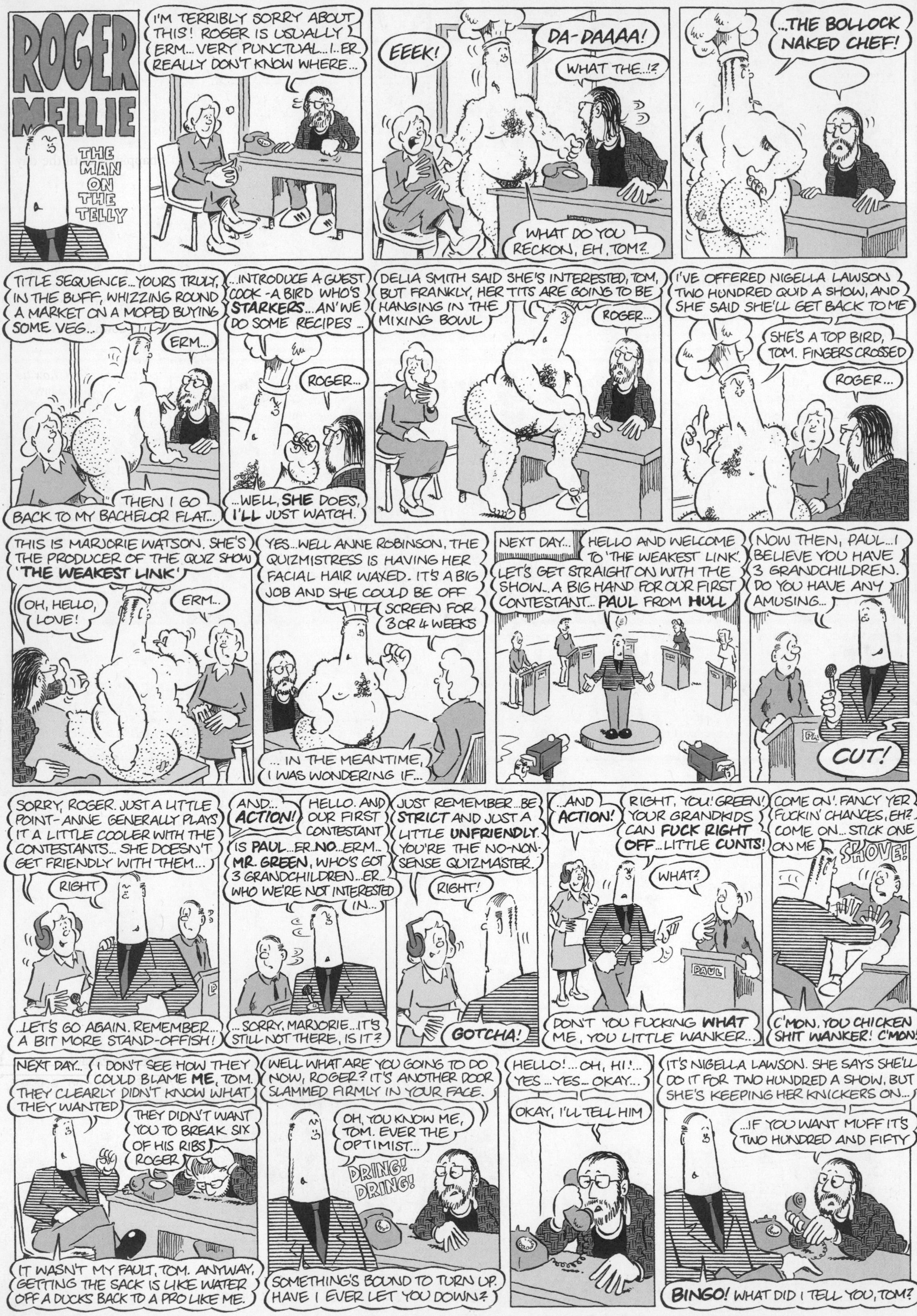
ROGER MELLIE
THE MAN ON THE TELLY
I'M TERRIBLY SORRY ABOUT THIS! ROGER IS USUALLY ERM... VERY PUNCTUAL... I.. ER.. REALLY DON'T KNOW WHERE...
EEEK!
DA-DAAAA!
WHAT THE...!?
WHAT DO YOU RECKON, EH, TOM?
...THE BOLLOCK NAKED CHEF!
TITLE SEQUENCE... YOURS TRULY, IN THE BUFF, WHIZZING ROUND A MARKET ON A MOPED BUYING SOME VEG...
ERM...
THEN I GO BACK TO MY BACHELOR FLAT...
...INTRODUCE A GUEST COOK - A BIRD WHO'S STARKERS... AN' WE DO SOME RECIPES...
ROGER...
...WELL, SHE DOES, I'LL JUST WATCH.
DELIA SMITH SAID SHE'S INTERESTED, TOM, BUT FRANKLY, HER TITS ARE GOING TO BE HANGING IN THE MIXING BOWL
ROGER...
I'VE OFFERED NIGELLA LAWSON TWO HUNDRED QUID A SHOW, AND SHE SAID SHE'LL GET BACK TO ME
SHE'S A TOP BIRD, TOM. FINGERS CROSSED
ROGER...
THIS IS MARJORIE WATSON. SHE'S THE PRODUCER OF THE QUIZ SHOW 'THE WEAKEST LINK'
OH, HELLO, LOVE!
ERM...
YES... WELL ANNE ROBINSON, THE QUIZMISTRESS IS HAVING HER FACIAL HAIR WAXED. IT'S A BIG JOB AND SHE COULD BE OFF SCREEN FOR 3 OR 4 WEEKS
... IN THE MEANTIME, I WAS WONDERING IF...
NEXT DAY...
HELLO AND WELCOME TO 'THE WEAKEST LINK'.
LET'S GET STRAIGHT ON WITH THE SHOW... A BIG HAND FOR OUR FIRST CONTESTANT... PAUL FROM HULL
NOW THEN, PAUL... I BELIEVE YOU HAVE 3 GRANDCHILDREN. DO YOU HAVE ANY AMUSING...
CUT!
SORRY, ROGER. JUST A LITTLE POINT - ANNE GENERALLY PLAYS IT A LITTLE COOLER WITH THE CONTESTANTS... SHE DOESN'T GET FRIENDLY WITH THEM...
RIGHT
...LET'S GO AGAIN. REMEMBER... A BIT MORE STAND-OFFISH!
AND... ACTION!
HELLO. AND OUR FIRST CONTESTANT IS PAUL... ER.. NO... ERM.. MR. GREEN, WHO'S GOT 3 GRANDCHILDREN... ER... WHO WE'RE NOT INTERESTED IN...
... SORRY, MARJORIE... IT'S STILL NOT THERE, IS IT?
JUST REMEMBER... BE STRICT AND JUST A LITTLE UNFRIENDLY. YOU'RE THE NO-NON-SENSE QUIZMASTER.
RIGHT!
GOTCHA!
...AND ACTION!
RIGHT, YOU! GREEN! YOUR GRANDKIDS CAN FUCK RIGHT OFF... LITTLE CUNTS!
WHAT?
DON'T YOU FUCKING WHAT ME, YOU LITTLE WANKER...
COME ON! FANCY YER FUCKIN' CHANCES, EH? COME ON... STICK ONE ON ME
SHOVE!
C'MON, YOU CHICKEN SHIT WANKER! C'MON!
NEXT DAY...
I DON'T SEE HOW THEY COULD BLAME ME, TOM. THEY CLEARLY DIDN'T KNOW WHAT THEY WANTED
THEY DIDN'T WANT YOU TO BREAK SIX OF HIS RIBS ROGER
IT WASN'T MY FAULT, TOM. ANYWAY, GETTING THE SACK IS LIKE WATER OFF A DUCKS BACK TO A PRO LIKE ME.
WELL WHAT ARE YOU GOING TO DO NOW, ROGER? IT'S ANOTHER DOOR SLAMMED FIRMLY IN YOUR FACE.
OH, YOU KNOW ME, TOM. EVER THE OPTIMIST...
DRING! DRING!
SOMETHING'S BOUND TO TURN UP. HAVE I EVER LET YOU DOWN?
HELLO! ... OH, HI!... YES ... YES... OKAY...
OKAY, I'LL TELL HIM
IT'S NIGELLA LAWSON. SHE SAYS SHE'LL DO IT FOR TWO HUNDRED A SHOW, BUT SHE'S KEEPING HER KNICKERS ON...
...IF YOU WANT MUFF IT'S TWO HUNDRED AND FIFTY
BINGO! WHAT DID I TELL YOU, TOM?

Carole 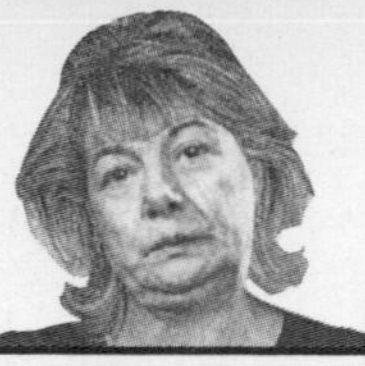 MALONE

Shame upon you, Sir Paul

So Sir Paul McCartney has found love again, with blonde model Heather Mills. Well pardon me if I don't start jumping for joy.

It's less than two years since the death of his wife Linda brought their thirty year fairy-tale marriage to an end. We all recall his tears at her memorial service.

Those tears rang a little hollow when I saw the pictures of him in this week's papers - grinning from ear to ear as though nothing had happened. And with a woman half his age on his arm. Behind his dead wife's back.

When Paul and Linda married all those years ago, they made a vow. A vow to stay together 'till death us do part'. Linda kept *her* promise. Can the same be said of her husband?

It seems not. When I heard the news I was physically sick. Don't get me wrong, I think Sir Paul deserves happiness. And I'm sure Linda would want him to be happy too.

But I believe he should have to be substantially more miserable for quite a while longer before he's allowed to be happy again. At least another 3 years. And that's if he's going to have an affair with a woman his own age. For someone of Miss Mills' age, perhaps a wait of 5 or 6 years would be more acceptable.

Anyway, I won't believe he's sad until I see it with my own eyes. If he ***really did*** love Linda, then he would appear on the TV every night, crying his eyes out. For a whole hour. And let's face it, he can afford the air time. So why doesn't he?

Cilla Black, a woman of the same age as McCartney also lost the love of her life recently. But you can bet your boots that Cilla will remain faithful to her Bobby.

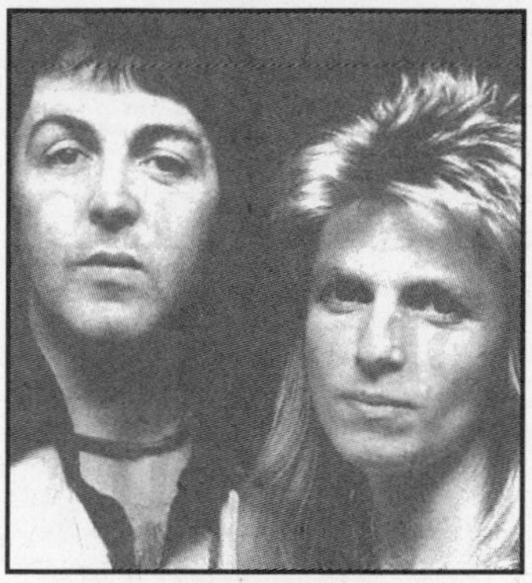

McCartney: No more lonely nights for dirty dog Paul

Her love for Bobby was true. I know in my heart that Cilla will commit herself to abject misery. She will never allow herself a moment's happiness until the day she dies.

That's what I want. And I know Cilla won't let me down. Cilla's love for Bobby was at least six times better than Paul's love for Linda.

If I knew Linda, which I didn't, I know she'll be looking down from heaven, weeping angel tears of sadness. She'll be thinking how Paul has let her down. How he has let himself down. And how he has let his fans down.

But most sickeningly of all, how he has let me, Carole Malone down.

If *you're* worried that your private life may be upsetting Carole Malone, you can write to her for advice on what she feels is acceptable for you to do. Write to Carole Malone, The Sunday Mirror, 1 Canada Square, Canary Wharf, London E14. Mark your envelope 'Please mind my own business'.

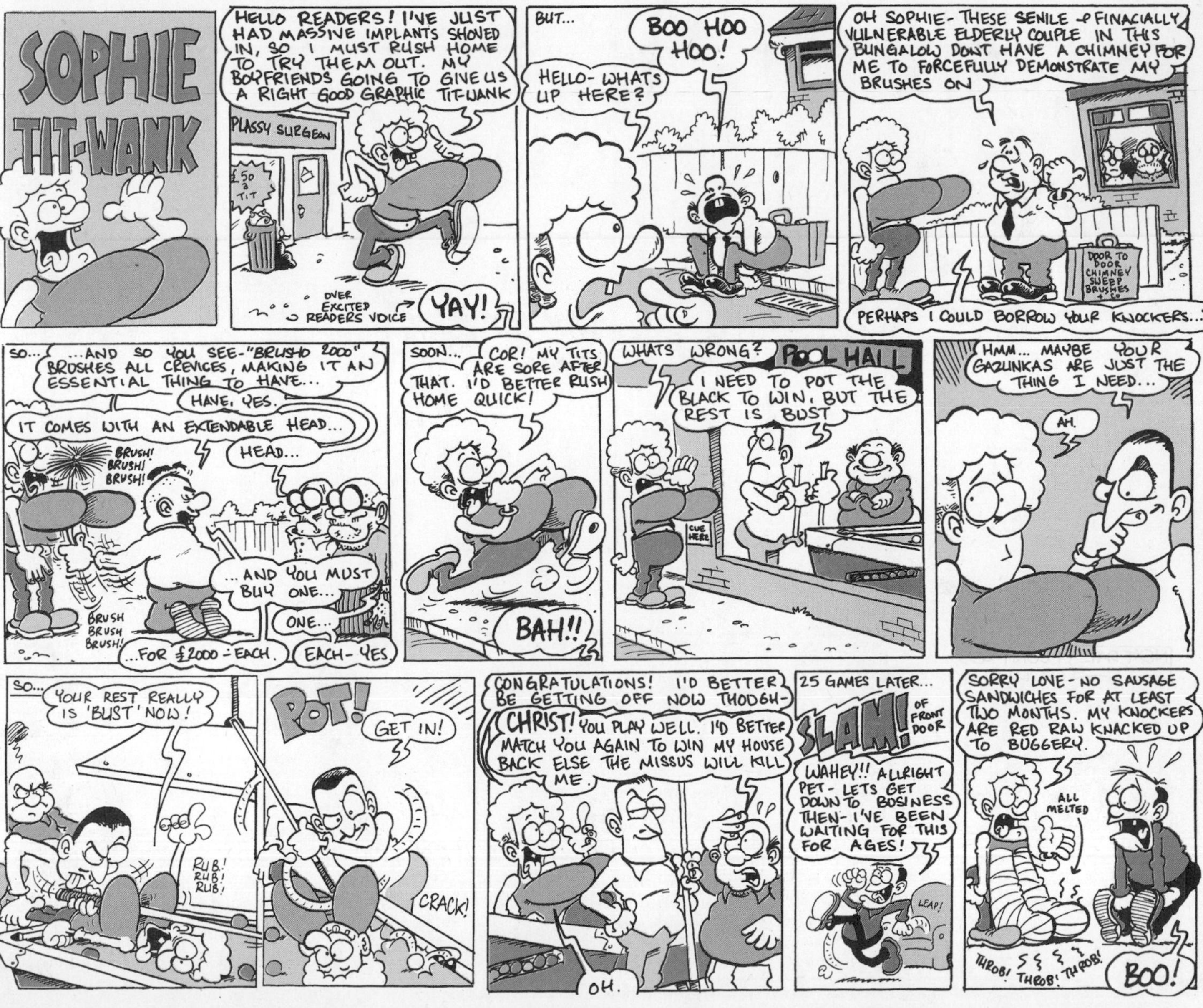
SOPHIE TIT-WANK
HELLO READERS! I'VE JUST HAD MASSIVE IMPLANTS SHOVED IN, SO I MUST RUSH HOME TO TRY THEM OUT. MY BOYFRIENDS GOING TO GIVE US A RIGHT GOOD GRAPHIC TIT-WANK
PLASSY SURGEON
£50 a TIT
OVER EXCITED READERS VOICE
YAY!
BUT...
BOO HOO HOO!
HELLO- WHATS UP HERE?
OH SOPHIE- THESE SENILE & FINACIALLY VULNERABLE ELDERLY COUPLE IN THIS BUNGALOW DONT HAVE A CHIMNEY FOR ME TO FORCEFULLY DEMONSTRATE MY BRUSHES ON
DOOR TO DOOR CHIMNEY SWEEP BRUSHES + CO
PERHAPS I COULD BORROW YOUR KNOCKERS...?
SO...
...AND SO YOU SEE-"BRUSHO 2000" BRUSHES ALL CREVICES, MAKING IT AN ESSENTIAL THING TO HAVE...
HAVE, YES.
IT COMES WITH AN EXTENDABLE HEAD...
BRUSH! BRUSH! BRUSH!
HEAD...
...AND YOU MUST BUY ONE...
ONE...
BRUSH BRUSH BRUSH!
...FOR £2000 - EACH.
EACH- YES.
SOON...
COR! MY TITS ARE SORE AFTER THAT. I'D BETTER RUSH HOME QUICK!
BAH!!
WHATS WRONG?
POOL HALL
I NEED TO POT THE BLACK TO WIN, BUT THE REST IS BUST
CUE HERE
HMM... MAYBE YOUR GAZUNKAS ARE JUST THE THING I NEED...
AH.
SO...
YOUR REST REALLY IS 'BUST' NOW!
RUB! RUB! RUB!
POT!
GET IN!
CRACK!
CONGRATULATIONS! I'D BETTER BE GETTING OFF NOW THOUGH-
CHRIST! YOU PLAY WELL. I'D BETTER MATCH YOU AGAIN TO WIN MY HOUSE BACK ELSE THE MISSUS WILL KILL ME.
OH.
25 GAMES LATER...
SLAM! OF FRONT DOOR
WAHEY!! ALLRIGHT PET- LETS GET DOWN TO BUSINESS THEN- I'VE BEEN WAITING FOR THIS FOR AGES!
LEAP!
SORRY LOVE- NO SAUSAGE SANDWICHES FOR AT LEAST TWO MONTHS. MY KNOCKERS ARE RED RAW KNACKED UP TO BUGGERY.
ALL MELTED
THROB! THROB! THROB!
BOO!

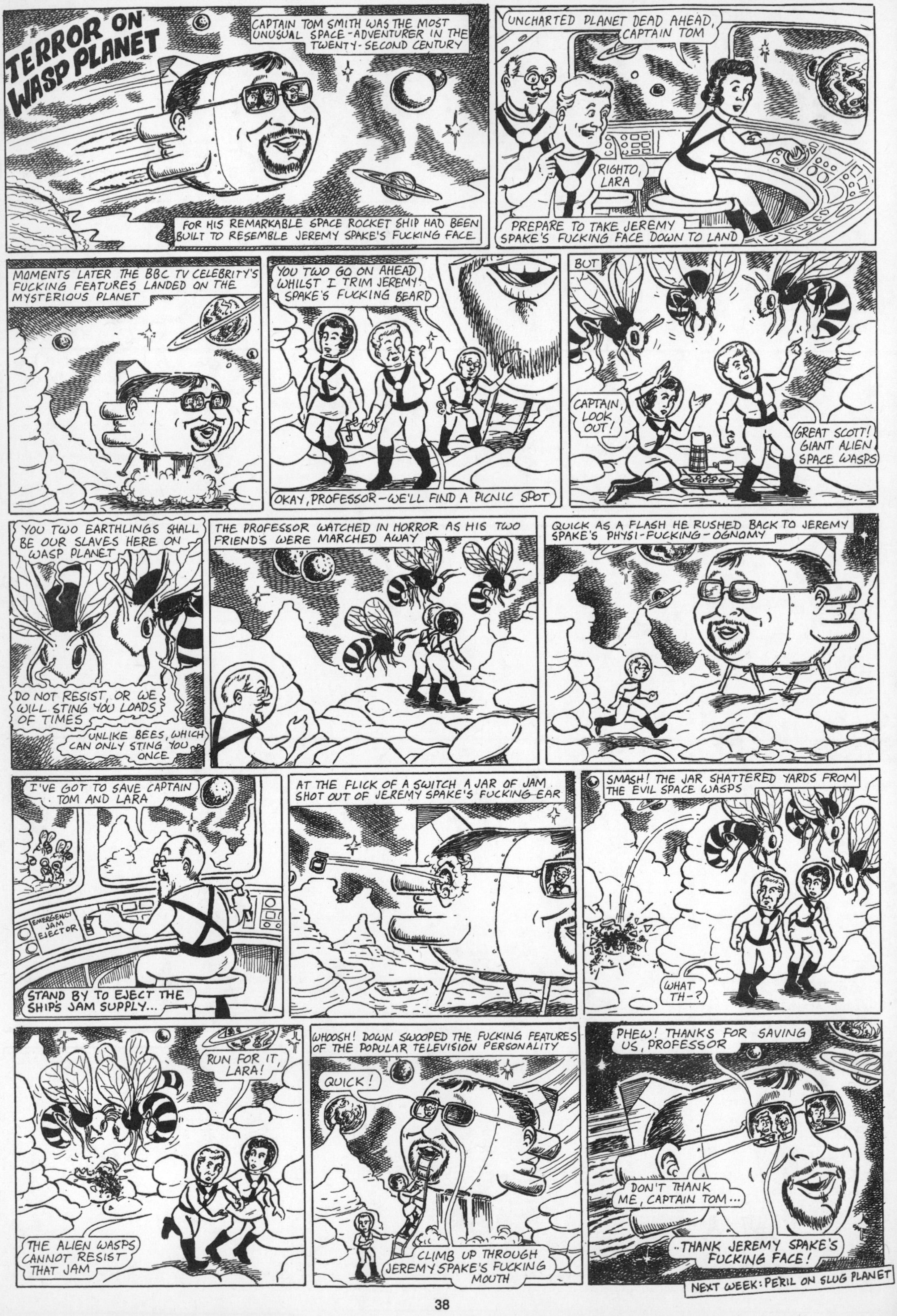
TERROR ON WASP PLANET
CAPTAIN TOM SMITH WAS THE MOST UNUSUAL SPACE-ADVENTURER IN THE TWENTY-SECOND CENTURY
FOR HIS REMARKABLE SPACE ROCKET SHIP HAD BEEN BUILT TO RESEMBLE JEREMY SPAKE'S FUCKING FACE
UNCHARTED PLANET DEAD AHEAD, CAPTAIN TOM
RIGHTO, LARA
PREPARE TO TAKE JEREMY SPAKE'S FUCKING FACE DOWN TO LAND
MOMENTS LATER THE BBC TV CELEBRITY'S FUCKING FEATURES LANDED ON THE MYSTERIOUS PLANET
YOU TWO GO ON AHEAD WHILST I TRIM JEREMY SPAKE'S FUCKING BEARD
OKAY, PROFESSOR—WE'LL FIND A PICNIC SPOT
BUT
CAPTAIN, LOOK OUT!
GREAT SCOTT! GIANT ALIEN SPACE WASPS
YOU TWO EARTHLINGS SHALL BE OUR SLAVES HERE ON WASP PLANET
DO NOT RESIST, OR WE WILL STING YOU LOADS OF TIMES
UNLIKE BEES, WHICH CAN ONLY STING YOU ONCE
THE PROFESSOR WATCHED IN HORROR AS HIS TWO FRIENDS WERE MARCHED AWAY
QUICK AS A FLASH HE RUSHED BACK TO JEREMY SPAKE'S PHYSI-FUCKING-OGNOMY
I'VE GOT TO SAVE CAPTAIN TOM AND LARA
EMERGENCY JAM EJECTOR
STAND BY TO EJECT THE SHIP'S JAM SUPPLY...
AT THE FLICK OF A SWITCH A JAR OF JAM SHOT OUT OF JEREMY SPAKE'S FUCKING EAR
SMASH! THE JAR SHATTERED YARDS FROM THE EVIL SPACE WASPS
WHAT TH-?
RUN FOR IT, LARA!
THE ALIEN WASPS CANNOT RESIST THAT JAM
WHOOSH! DOWN SWOOPED THE FUCKING FEATURES OF THE POPULAR TELEVISION PERSONALITY
QUICK!
CLIMB UP THROUGH JEREMY SPAKE'S FUCKING MOUTH
PHEW! THANKS FOR SAVING US, PROFESSOR
DON'T THANK ME, CAPTAIN TOM...
..THANK JEREMY SPAKE'S FUCKING FACE!
NEXT WEEK: PERIL ON SLUG PLANET

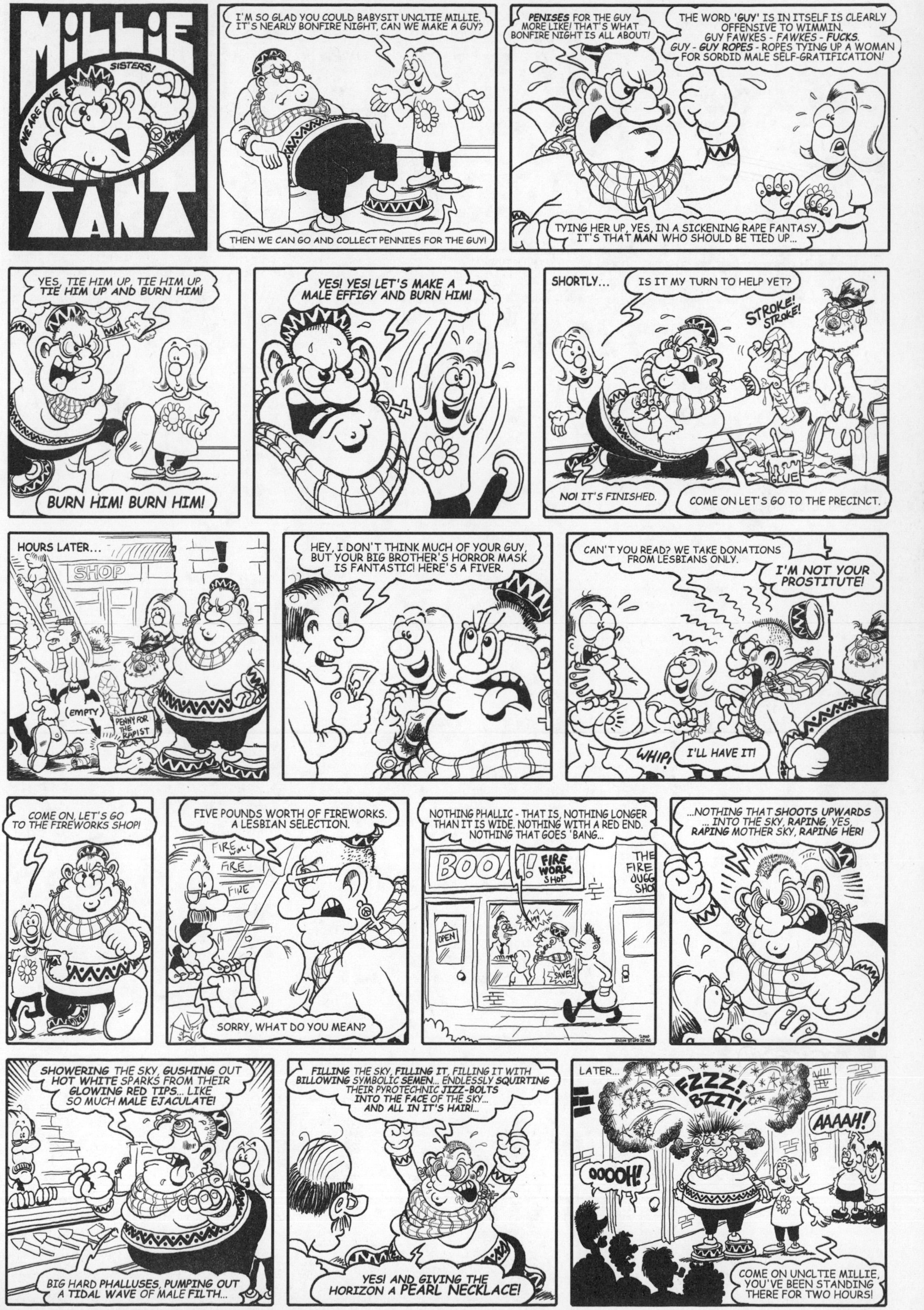

MILLIE TANT
WE ARE ONE SISTERS!
I'M SO GLAD YOU COULD BABYSIT UNCLTIE MILLIE. IT'S NEARLY BONFIRE NIGHT, CAN WE MAKE A GUY?
THEN WE CAN GO AND COLLECT PENNIES FOR THE GUY!
PENISES FOR THE GUY MORE LIKE! THAT'S WHAT BONFIRE NIGHT IS ALL ABOUT!
THE WORD 'GUY' IS IN ITSELF IS CLEARLY OFFENSIVE TO WIMMIN. GUY FAWKES - FAWKES - FUCKS. GUY - GUY ROPES - ROPES TYING UP A WOMAN FOR SORDID MALE SELF-GRATIFICATION!
TYING HER UP, YES, IN A SICKENING RAPE FANTASY. IT'S THAT MAN WHO SHOULD BE TIED UP...
YES, TIE HIM UP, TIE HIM UP, TIE HIM UP AND BURN HIM!
BURN HIM! BURN HIM!
YES! YES! LET'S MAKE A MALE EFFIGY AND BURN HIM!
SHORTLY...
IS IT MY TURN TO HELP YET?
STROKE! STROKE!
GLUE
NO! IT'S FINISHED.
COME ON LET'S GO TO THE PRECINCT.
HOURS LATER...
SHOP
(EMPTY)
PENNY FOR THE RAPIST
HEY, I DON'T THINK MUCH OF YOUR GUY, BUT YOUR BIG BROTHER'S HORROR MASK IS FANTASTIC! HERE'S A FIVER.
CAN'T YOU READ? WE TAKE DONATIONS FROM LESBIANS ONLY.
I'M NOT YOUR PROSTITUTE!
WHIP!
I'LL HAVE IT!
COME ON, LET'S GO TO THE FIREWORKS SHOP!
FIVE POUNDS WORTH OF FIREWORKS. A LESBIAN SELECTION.
SORRY, WHAT DO YOU MEAN?
NOTHING PHALLIC - THAT IS, NOTHING LONGER THAN IT IS WIDE. NOTHING WITH A RED END. NOTHING THAT GOES 'BANG...
BOOM! FIRE WORK SHOP
OPEN
SAVE!
...NOTHING THAT SHOOTS UPWARDS ... INTO THE SKY, RAPING, YES, RAPING MOTHER SKY, RAPING HER!
SHOWERING THE SKY, GUSHING OUT HOT WHITE SPARKS FROM THEIR GLOWING RED TIPS... LIKE SO MUCH MALE EJACULATE!
BIG HARD PHALLUSES, PUMPING OUT A TIDAL WAVE OF MALE FILTH...
FILLING THE SKY, FILLING IT, FILLING IT WITH BILLOWING SYMBOLIC SEMEN... ENDLESSLY SQUIRTING THEIR PYROTECHNIC JIZZ-BOLTS INTO THE FACE OF THE SKY... AND ALL IN IT'S HAIR!...
YES! AND GIVING THE HORIZON A PEARL NECKLACE!
LATER...
FZZZ! BZZT!
AAAAH!
OOOOH!
COME ON UNCLTIE MILLIE, YOU'VE BEEN STANDING THERE FOR TWO HOURS!

How are Yo

We say 'potato', they say 'potato'. They call a slapper a tramp, a tramp a bum, a bum a fanny, and a fanny a puh-seh. In 1946, US war hero John Wayne said that Britain and America were two countries separated by a common language. This may have been true then, but is it still true today? Thanks to the Internet, Concorde and cordless phones the world is shrinking, and American culture is increasingly an everyday part of the British way of life. With our star-spangled diet of McDonalds food, Coca-Cola and the Disney Channel, it is almost inevitable that we will soon become the 51st state of the Union. But are YOU ready to be a yank? It's time to get off your hoss, drink your milk and ask...

ANSWER the following questions a, b, or c. Tot up your score at the end and see how you did.

1 You decide that your relationship with your partner is over. How do you break the news that you are leaving?

a. Leave a tearful note on the kitchen table and slip away in the night.

b. Sit down with your partner and calmly discuss the reasons for your decision.

c. Attack him with a chair in front of a rabble of cheering, pumped-up trailer-trash vermins, on national television.

2 You are visiting Egypt and are concerned over the recent terrorist attacks on foreign nationals. What do you wear to remain inconspicuous?

a. A tee-shirt and a pair of jeans.

b. A Demis Roussos tent dress, fez, a false beard and sunglasses.

c. A high-rise baseball cap, trainers with knee-length socks, an horrendous flowery shirt, Eric Morecambe shorts and 8 cameras.

3 Where are you most likely to find your local copper?

a. Outside his police house in the village, mending a puncture on his bicycle.

b. Asleep in his patrol car on a motorway flyover.

c. On his yacht, wearing a pastel suit with the sleeves rolled up , feeding his pet crocodile.

4 You are the political leader of your country. An interviewer asks you a question on foreign affairs. How do you respond?

a. Knowledgeably, addressing the issues and answering all the points.

b. As best you can, deftly steering the conversation towards topics on which you are better qualified to speak.

c. Stand there grinning gormlessly, then throw up on the Japanese prime minister, before going home and getting sucked off by a fat-titted intern.

5 You fancy a night in watching something funny on the telly. What kind of comedy show do you choose?

a. A sitcom like Fawlty Towers or Father Ted.

b. A sketch show like The Fast Show or Smack the Pony.

c. A thinly-disguised morality play set in a massive lounge where the audience whoop for ten minutes every time an overpaid actor makes an entrance to deliver a lightweight wisecrack.

6 Your fourteen-year-old son is going through a difficult phase. He is becoming disruptive at school and reclusive at home. What do you do?

a. Don't worry. It's just a phase he is going through. You were the same at his age.

b. Encourage him to get out and about more. Perhaps join a youth club or get involved in some team games.

c. Take him to the local supermarket and buy him an arsenal of semi-automatic weapons and enough ammunition to kill a small town.

7 You and your mates decide to have a game of football in the park. What do you need to take?

a. A ball.

b. A ball and two coats.

c. A ball, 50 crash helmets, 4 tons of body armour, 20 cheer leaders, a marching souzaphone band with a grand piano on a trolley, and a team of orthopaedic surgeons specialising in spinal injuries.

8 Whilst getting ready for bed, you stub your toe on your wife's dressing table. What do you do?

a. Shout and swear a little, after all it did hurt and you didn't have your slippers on at the time.

b. Make a mental note to move the table as soon as possible to prevent it happening again.

c. Immediately call a hotshot lawyer with an uptown reputation and sue your wife's ass.

American
OU?

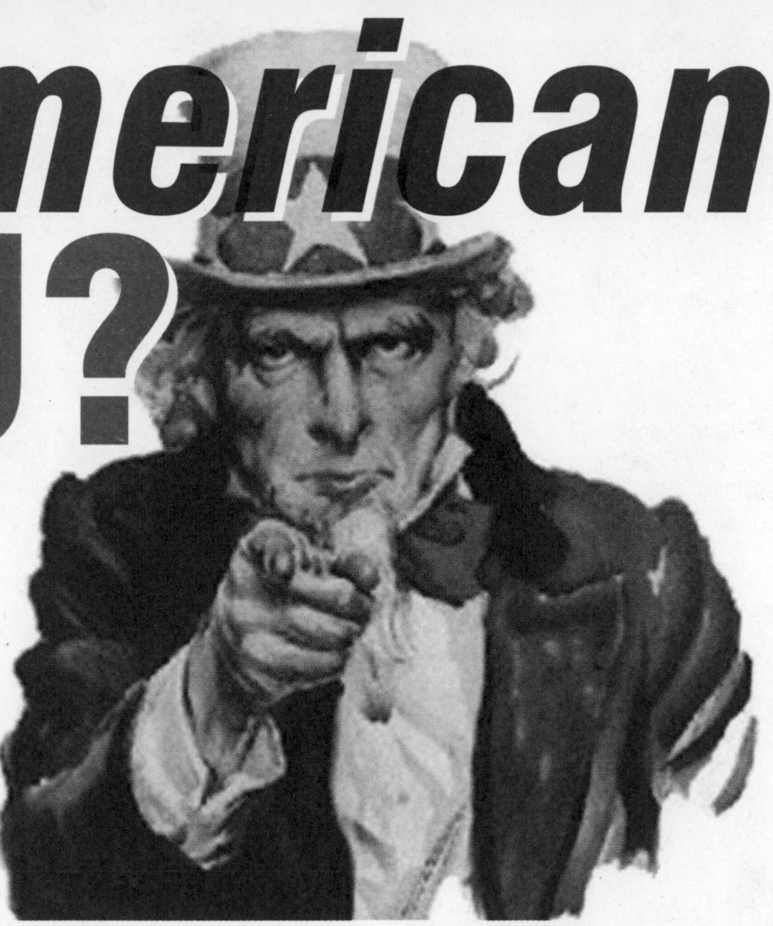

9 **You are driving along a country road one day when you accidentally run over a rabbit. What do you do?**

a. Stop and see how badly injured it is, taking it to a vet if it's still alive.

b. Carry on driving, but hope that it is still alive, or if not that it died quickly.

c. Strap it across the bonnet of your car and drive home hollering and whooping, throwing empty Budweiser cans out of the window.

10 **You wake up one morning with a rather stiff neck after sleeping in an awkward position. What do you do?**

a. Ignore it, it will probably loosen up as the day goes on.

b. Take a couple of aspirins and get on with things.

c. Take yourself to a prostitute-addicted televangelist faith-healer in an ill-fitting wig, who will lay his hand on your forehead, whilst screaming about the devil in front of an audience of gibbering inbreds.

11 **What do you have for breakfast?**

a. A bowl of cornflakes, a slice of toast and a mug of tea.

b. A glass of orange juice, a croissant and a cup of black coffee.

c. A bag of donuts with ice cream, a 32 ounce steak with six eggs sunny-side-up , fifteen pancakes with maple syrup, a dozen waffles, five corn dogs and a diet root beer.

12 **What sort of car do you drive?**

a. A small economical runabout.

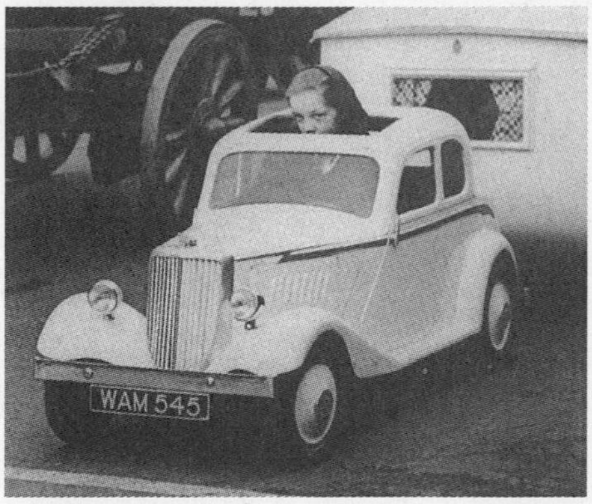
WAM 545

b. A medium-sized family saloon.

c. A forty-foot long chromium-plated jukebox that does 1 mile to the gallon.

13 **You and your partner decide to take the plunge and get married. What sort of ceremony do you have?**

a. A quiet little do with a few friends in a registry office.

b. A church service followed by a traditional reception at a fancy hotel.

c. A minute-long mockery at a 24-hour drive-thru chapel in Las Vegas, presided over by a transvestite vicar dressed as Elvis.

How did you 'Yankee Doodle Do?'

Mostly a's

You are in no way American. You probably still spell colour with a 'u' and call your trousers 'trousers'. Try wearing a baseball cap and driving on the wrong side of the road a little.

Mostly b's

Good try, but no kewpie doll. You're halfway there, but you could still do better. Why not put a little white fence around your garden and ask the postman to put your letters in a bread bin on a stick.

Mostly c's

Well hot diggety, you're as American as Uncle Sam with sassafras on rye. You were born on the 4th of July and you've got Mom's apple pie and napalm coming out the buns of your ass. Take the fifth and have a nice fucking day, y'all.

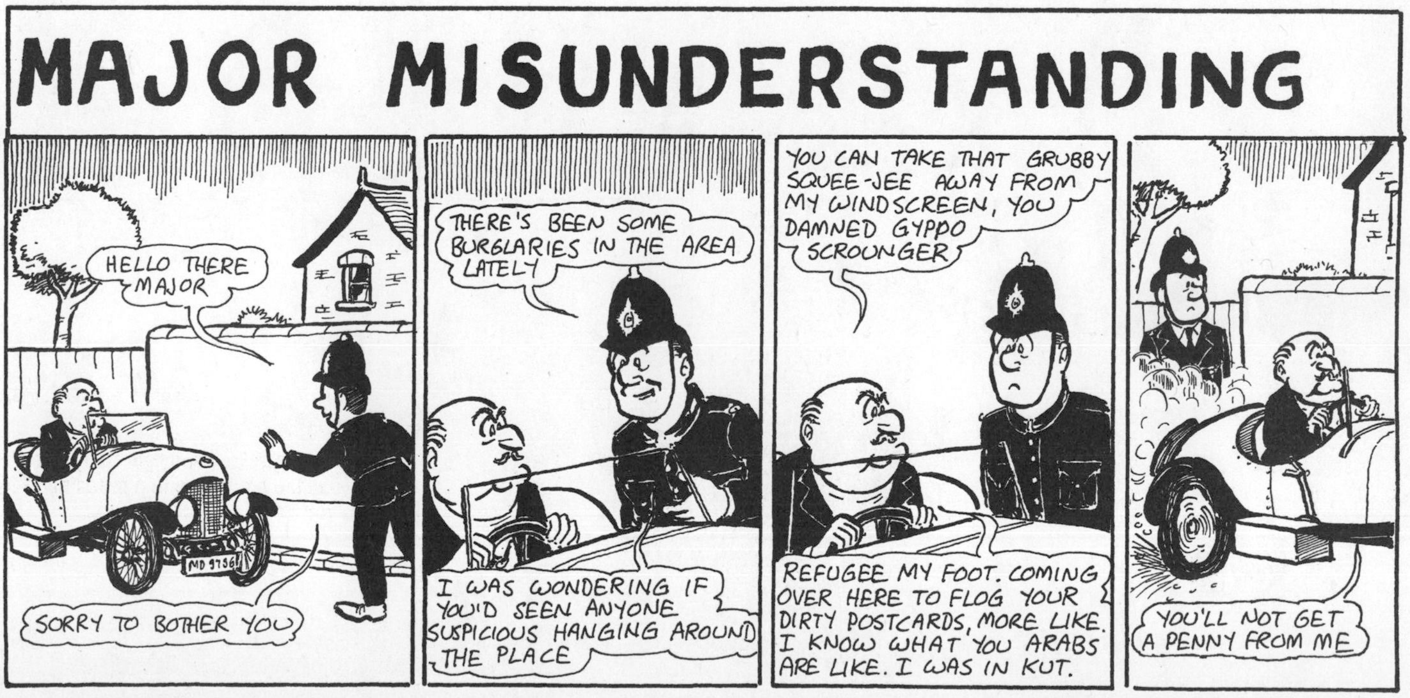
MAJOR MISUNDERSTANDING
HELLO THERE MAJOR
SORRY TO BOTHER YOU
MD 9756
THERE'S BEEN SOME BURGLARIES IN THE AREA LATELY
I WAS WONDERING IF YOU'D SEEN ANYONE SUSPICIOUS HANGING AROUND THE PLACE
YOU CAN TAKE THAT GRUBBY SQUEE-JEE AWAY FROM MY WINDSCREEN, YOU DAMNED GYPPO SCROUNGER
REFUGEE MY FOOT. COMING OVER HERE TO FLOG YOUR DIRTY POSTCARDS, MORE LIKE. I KNOW WHAT YOU ARABS ARE LIKE. I WAS IN KUT.
YOU'LL NOT GET A PENNY FROM ME

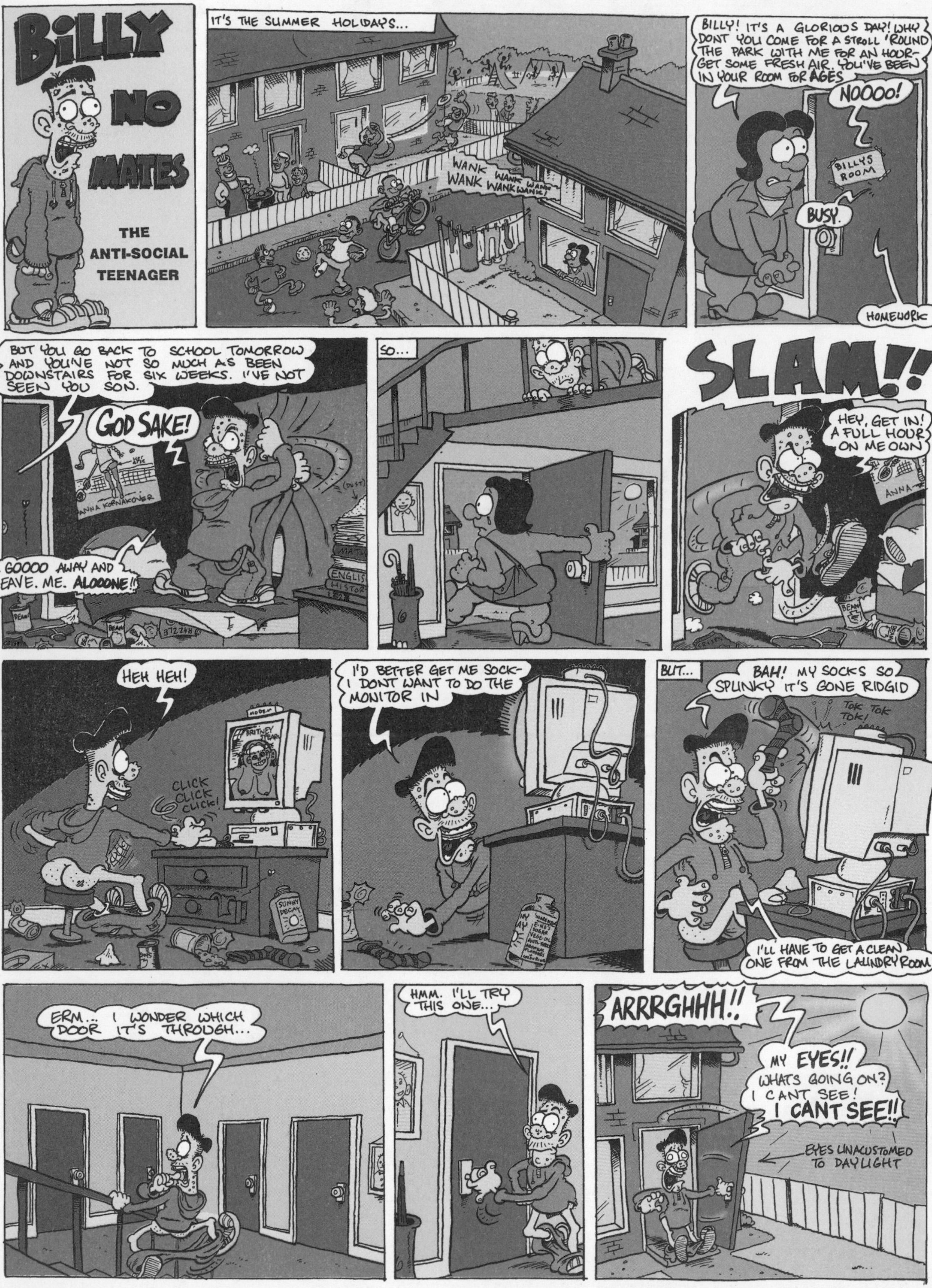
BILLY NO MATES
THE ANTI-SOCIAL TEENAGER
IT'S THE SUMMER HOLIDAYS...
WANK WANK WANK WANK WANK WANK
BILLY! IT'S A GLORIOUS DAY! WHY DONT YOU COME FOR A STROLL 'ROUND THE PARK WITH ME FOR AN HOUR-GET SOME FRESH AIR. YOU'VE BEEN IN YOUR ROOM FOR AGES
NOOOO!
BILLYS ROOM
BUSY.
HOMEWORK
BUT YOU GO BACK TO SCHOOL TOMORROW AND YOU'VE NOT SO MUCH AS BEEN DOWNSTAIRS FOR SIX WEEKS. I'VE NOT SEEN YOU SON.
GOD SAKE!
ANNA KORNAKOVER
MATHS
ENGLISH
HISTORY
GOOOO AWAY AND LEAVE. ME. ALOOONE!!
SO...
SLAM!!
HEY, GET IN! A FULL HOUR ON ME OWN
ANNA
HEH HEH!
MODEM
BRITNEY SPEARS
CLICK CLICK CLICK!
SUNNY DECAY
I'D BETTER GET ME SOCK- I DONT WANT TO DO THE MONITOR IN
BUT...
BAH! MY SOCKS SO SPUNKY IT'S GONE RIDGID
TOK TOK TOK!
I'LL HAVE TO GET A CLEAN ONE FROM THE LAUNDRY ROOM
ERM... I WONDER WHICH DOOR IT'S THROUGH...
HMM. I'LL TRY THIS ONE...
ARRRGHHH!!
MY EYES!! WHATS GOING ON? I CANT SEE! I CANT SEE!!
EYES UNACUSTOMED TO DAYLIGHT

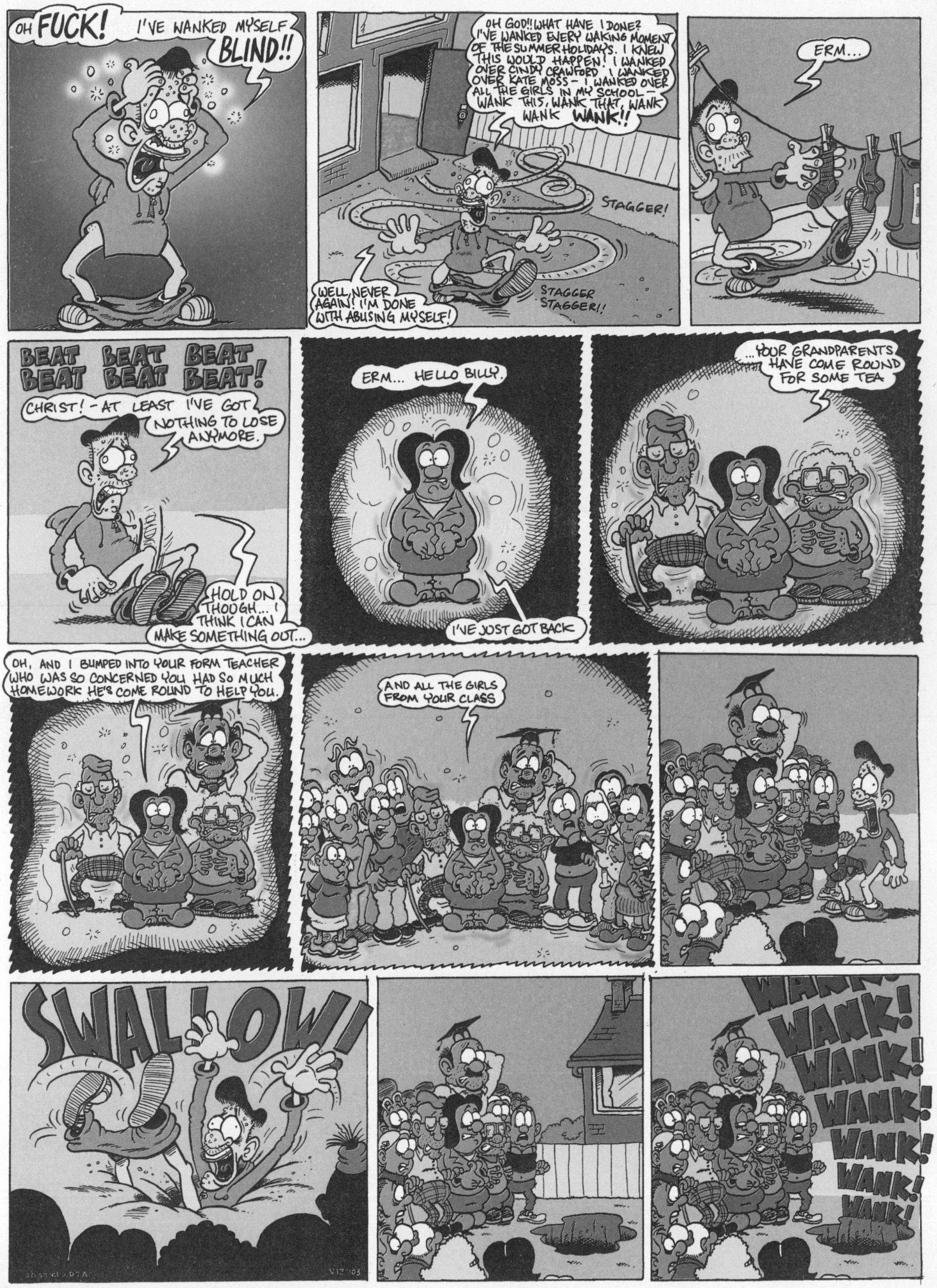
OH FUCK! I'VE WANKED MYSELF BLIND!!
OH GOD!! WHAT HAVE I DONE? I'VE WANKED EVERY WAKING MOMENT OF THE SUMMER HOLIDAYS. I KNEW THIS WOULD HAPPEN! I WANKED OVER CINDY CRAWFORD. I WANKED OVER KATE MOSS - I WANKED OVER ALL THE GIRLS IN MY SCHOOL - WANK THIS, WANK THAT, WANK WANK WANK!!
STAGGER!
WELL, NEVER AGAIN! I'M DONE WITH ABUSING MYSELF!
STAGGER STAGGER!!
ERM...
BEAT BEAT BEAT BEAT BEAT BEAT!
CHRIST! - AT LEAST I'VE GOT NOTHING TO LOSE ANYMORE.
HOLD ON THOUGH... I THINK I CAN MAKE SOMETHING OUT...
ERM... HELLO BILLY.
I'VE JUST GOT BACK
...YOUR GRANDPARENTS HAVE COME ROUND FOR SOME TEA
OH, AND I BUMPED INTO YOUR FORM TEACHER WHO WAS SO CONCERNED YOU HAD SO MUCH HOMEWORK HE'S COME ROUND TO HELP YOU.
AND ALL THE GIRLS FROM YOUR CLASS
SWALLOW!
WANK! WANK! WANK! WANK! WANK! WANK! WANK!

Letterbocks

It's the page that's just farted & is checking its kex for bullets

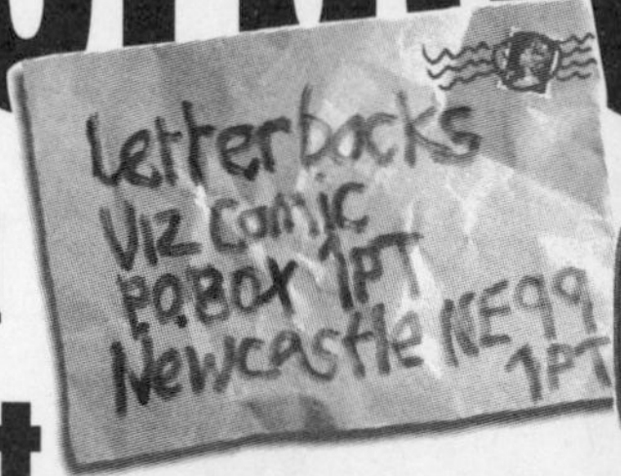

Letterbocks
Viz Comic
PO Box 1PT
Newcastle NE99 1PT

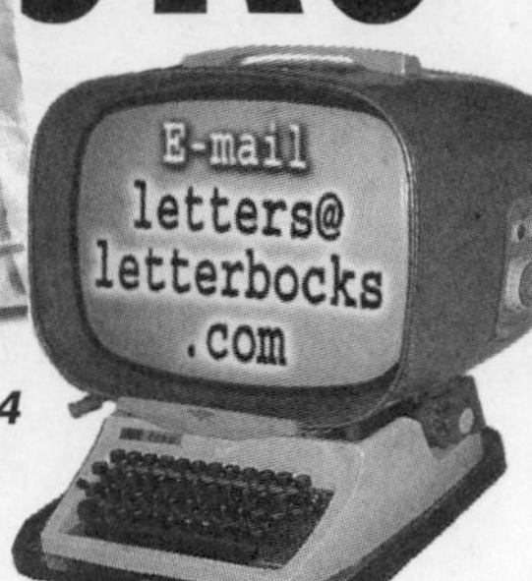

E-mail
letters@
letterbocks
.com

Fax: 0191 2414244

Is there something you want to tell us? Perhaps a member of the family with Alzheimer's disease has just said or done something vaguely amusing.
Or perhaps there's something you want to ask. Maybe your chip pan is on fire and you want to know how to put it out.
Why not drop us a line? There's a Profanisaurus mug for every letter or tip we use.

Not ova the limit

❑ These scotch eggs are a rip-off. I ate 16 of them on Friday evening and by last orders I was still as sober as a judge.

Alex Hanson
Upton

❑ So scally rockers 'Space' think the female of the species is more deadly than the male. Try telling that to my wife. She's buried under the patio.

P. C.
London

Tuppence on rates

❑ I've just recieved my new local council tax bill, and I note that it has gone up by £200 this year. This is in part to fund a new lesbian drop-in centre. I'm not opposed to this in principle, but I think after forking out for it, the least they could do is let me in to watch

B. Aldiss
Lambeth

Amen corner

❑ The padre of Manchester United football club says he prayed to the Lord as his team were 1-0 down in the final seconds of last year's European Championship. With 2 goals in the last minute, his prayer certainly seems to have worked. If he can spare a few minutes after asking God to fix matches for his team of 11 millionaires, perhaps he could put in a word on behalf of the millions of sick, starving and dying all over the world. Just if he's got time.

Wilfred M. Thompson
Penrith

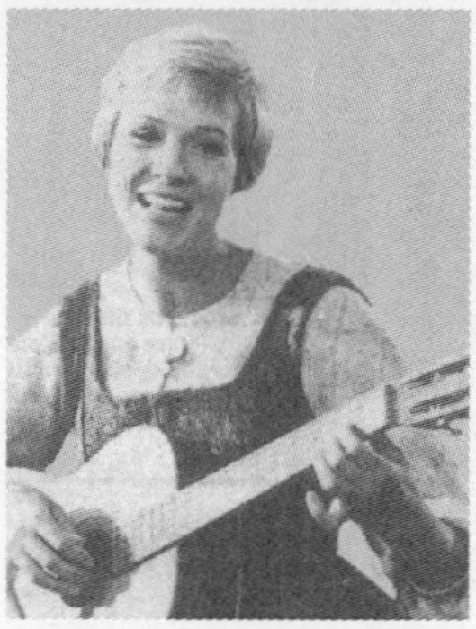

❑ So a spoonful of sugar helps the medicine goes down, does it? Well I'm an insulin dependant diabetic, and after following this advice, I am now two months into a life threatening hyperglycaemic coma. Thank you very much, Mary fucking Poppins.

Elron Hubbard
Bradford

❑ I tried to write my name on a sock recently using a sharp pencil, but the pencil went straight through and cut my foot. Small bespoke name tags are much better for this purpose and are available from my shop.

A. Lee (Gents Outfitter)
Ropergate
Pontefract

❑ My mate prefers a Snickers Bar to a Mars Bar. But strangely, he prefers Mars ice-cream to Snickers ice-cream. The hypocrisy of the situation annoys me no end.

Bickbucks McCoy
e-mail

Blankety Blanker

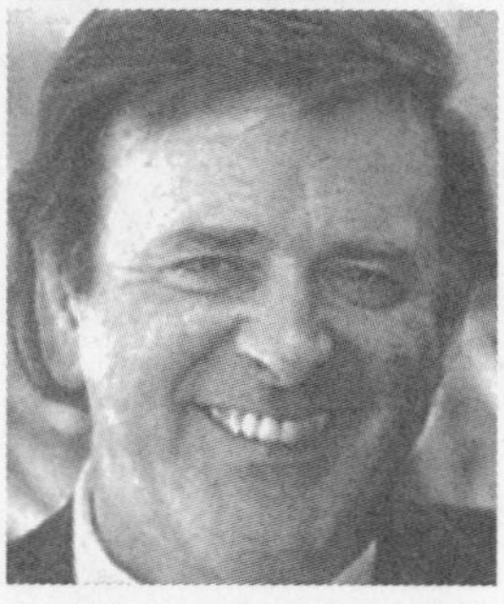

❑ What a small world. For example, there appears to be two Terry Wogans. The one in the TV Times, criticising the BBC for paying big name presenters inflated salaries at the expense of quality programming, and that other one who gets £550,000 a year to front shite like Auntie's Sporting Bloomers.

Richard Hauptmann
Chester

❑ What a con these so-called radio controlled taxis are. I got in one the other day and there was a man inside driving it.

J. Beneaux
Leeds

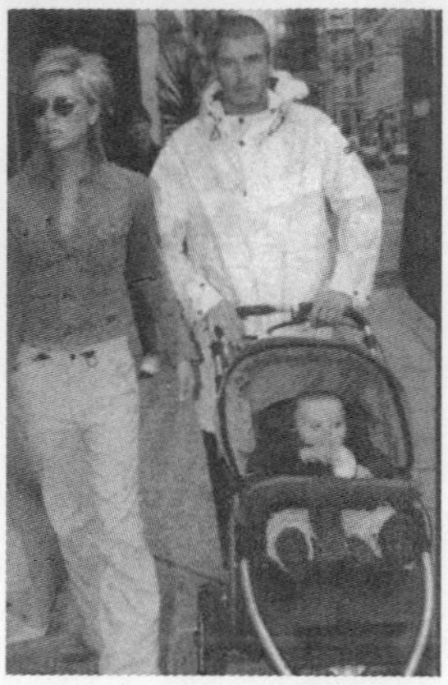

❑ It seems that you cannot open a newspaper today without seeing stories and pictures of David Beckham and Posh Spice splashed all over the place. Do the editors ever stop to wonder if anyone is actually interested in the mundane comings and goings of these overpaid and underworked, self-important idiots who seem to be famous simply for being famous? The space could be put to much better use with more stories about the Royal family.

A. Richards
Burnley

Silly articles

❑ I am becoming increasingly frustrated by the stupidity of football clubs. For example, when are Liverpool going to stop referring to their hallowed turf as 'an' field when everyone knows that the correct pronunciation is 'a' field.

David D.
Aberdeen

Baker's treat

❑ Was it just me, or did anyone else find Fru T. Bunn's gingerbread mistress slightly arousing in issue 101?

Martin Smith
Northampton

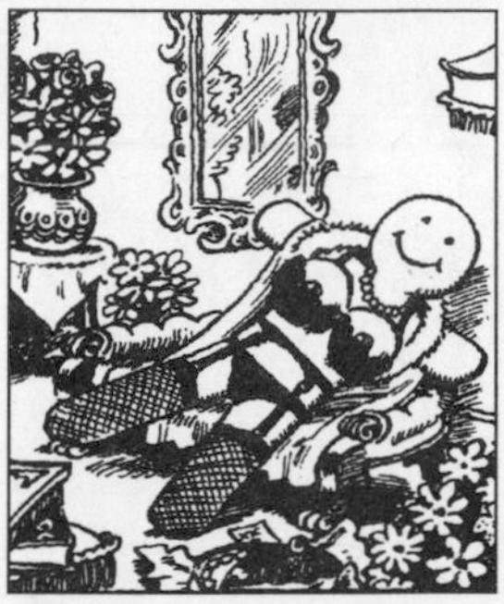

❑ ...more please of Fru T. Bunn's delicious bit on the side. I don't normally like pastry women, but she was something else.

E. Axon
London

❑ ...Fru T. Bunn's girlfriend (issue 101) was worth the cover price of your mag alone. Those biscuity thighs. Woof! When can we see her again?

Name & address withheld by request

❑ The government safety campaign proclaims 'Speed Kills!' What nonsense. As an astronaut, I regularly travelled at 30,000 mph on space missions and came to no harm. The Titanic was doing less than 30 mph when it hit an iceberg killing over 1,500 people.

Neil Armstrong
Houston, West Yorkshire

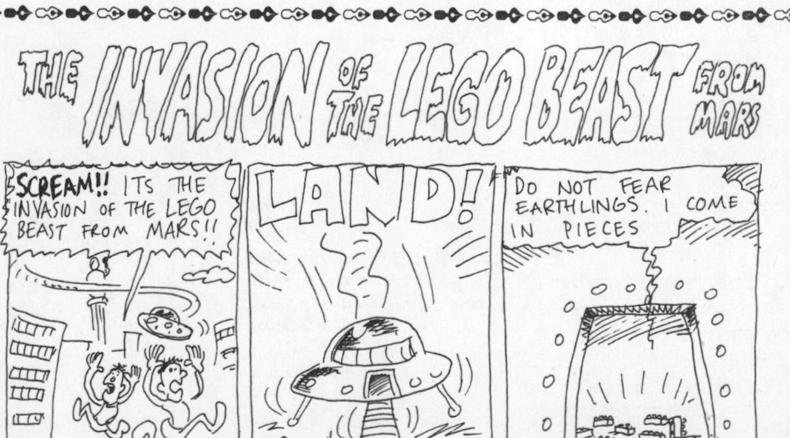

THE INVASION OF THE LEGO BEAST FROM MARS
SCREAM!! ITS THE INVASION OF THE LEGO BEAST FROM MARS!!
LAND!
OPEN!
DO NOT FEAR EARTHLINGS. I COME IN PIECES

Check it out

❏ I used my credit card to pay for £32 of groceries at Tesco's recently and the woman on the till asked me if I wanted any cashback. I requested £20 which she cheerfully gave me. So my shopping really only cost me £12. Who says the supermarkets are ripping us off?

A. Berry
Grimsby

❏ Which silly cunt said you should peel onions under water to stop then making your eyes run? I nearly drowned because I can't hold my breath for more than two minutes.

Geoff Barker
Germany

❏ The desecration of Sir Winston Churchill's statue by hairy anarchists is just the latest in a long line of acts of mindless vandalism that seem to be rife in this country.

For example, Graham Sutherland's particularly fine portrait of Sir Winston was chopped into pieces and set on fire in 1954. Mind you, that was Churchill and his missus who did that because he didn't like it.

M. Bloomer
Kidderminster

❏ Recently I started a good job with the title of Regional Information Systems Manager, or RISM. I can't wait until I can employ a Junior Information Systems Manager.

Lachlan Barker
New South Wales

❏ They say a woman's work is never done. Well, perhaps if they got on with it instead of painting their toenails all day we might see some results.

Norman K.
Florida

❏ I was born in Wales in 1957 and moved to Glasgow when I was 2. At school I was beaten and made to "wiggle your hips and give us a song, Tom" many times a day. Can any of your female readers thinking of throwing their knickers at Tom Jones , please put half a brick in them to pay the name-changing twat back for my life of misery.

Tom Jones
Southampton

❏ Since unscrupulous entrepreneurs are making fortunes registering web sites using the names of stars then selling them

on at inflated prices, may I suggest that Michael Barrymore registers his personal site www.talentlessfruitytosser.com before they beat him to it.

J. Burns
e-mail

Shed Load

❏ Our next door neighbour is very strange. He spends all summer, every summer building sheds. We now call him Stanley Shed. I've counted that he has over 25 sheds in his 90ft back garden. I don't know who's more pathetic, him for building all those sheds or me for spending time counting them.

N. Reece
Essex

❏ *Do you live on the other side of Stanley Shed from N. Reece? Surely you can think of a more imaginative nickname for him than Stanley Shed. Write and let us know. There's the cheapest 6' x 4' shed from B&Q for the best nickname you come up with.*

GOLDEN SYRUPS

A fine pair of Irish jigs sent in by our Wigfinder Generals this month.

J.Thorne snapped this comedy barnet (right), complete with shaddow, perched aloft an unsuspecting wearer whilst visiting the Epcot Centre in Florida. "Forget Disneyworld and the Everglades, seeing this toup was the highlight of my holiday", she writes.

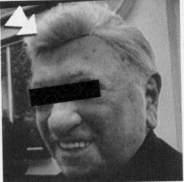

M. Pilgrim of Leicester was quick off the mark when he spotted this laughable rugster (left) on Channel 4's The Big Breakfast. "He was being interviewed about something but I don't know what, I was so busy laughing at him," he informs us.

Have you seen any terrible wigs lately? Keep your eyes peeled and your cameras ready and send any snaps to Golden Syrups, Viz Comic, PO Box 1PT, Newcastle upon Tyne, NE99 1PT. We'll give you a disposable Viz/Newcastle Brown wig-spotting camera for every comedy rug we use.

E-mail **syrups@viz.co.uk**

BUS DRIVERS. *If you see an attractive woman with a low cut top at the bus stop, accelerate and come to a halt 50 feet past the stop. You will then have a great view in your nearside mirror as she runs towards you. Finally, accidentally drop her change for a second look.*

A. Driver
Bolton

YOUNG mothers. Pretend to be unbelievably dull and unimaginative by meeting other young mothers in public places and only ever talking about your children.

Phil Telfer
e-mail

SPERM *makes ideal 00-gauge tadpoles for model railway ponds.*

D. Grear
e-mail

BOOKIES. Increase your profits by not giving customers 'clues' in the form of odds as to which horse will win a race

Den Haag
Holland

GIRLS. *Get those old 70's bell-bottoms from the wardrobe, cut the legs off and sew them back on upside down. They will then fit you once more.*

Andy Balkham
Wandsworth

Top Tips

email:
toptips@letterbocks.com

DRINK as much as you like on Long haul flights and don't worry about being over the limit when you drive home from the airport - the time difference will have taken care of that.

J. Walker
Hemel Hempstead

PUT on a pair of swimming trunks and ask your wife to hit you over the head with a chair and push you through a pasting table. Get your kids to boo and chant obscenities and hey

presto!- you're the star of your own WWF wrestling show.

Bob Harris
Cardiff

COMMUTERS. Make the bus come quicker by standing by the corner looking for it coming down the road, then running back to the bus stop.

John Altree
Hounslow

FOOL *people into thinking you are an octopus by drinking several litres of ink and farting everytime someone startles you.*

D. Grear
e-mail

BAKERS and coffee shop owners. Encourage your customers to buy by having the smell of a newly built house in your establishment.

D. Hull
Hull

TV PRACTICAL *pranksters. When wanking always use your withered hand as it will make your chopper appear bigger than it actually is.*

C. Harris
Southend

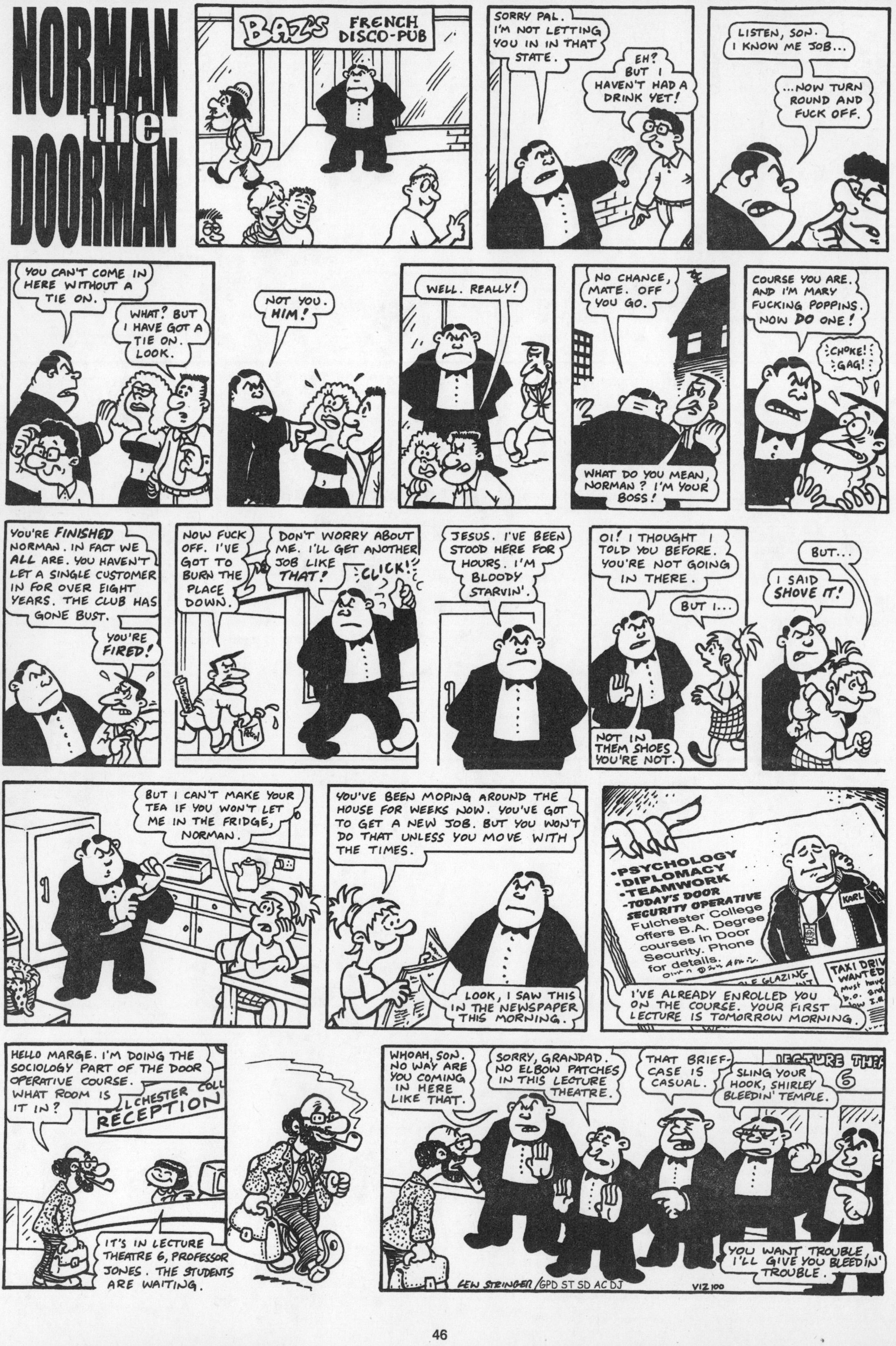
NORMAN the DOORMAN
BAZ'S FRENCH DISCO-PUB
SORRY PAL. I'M NOT LETTING YOU IN IN THAT STATE.
EH? BUT I HAVEN'T HAD A DRINK YET!
LISTEN, SON. I KNOW ME JOB...
...NOW TURN ROUND AND FUCK OFF.
YOU CAN'T COME IN HERE WITHOUT A TIE ON.
WHAT? BUT I HAVE GOT A TIE ON. LOOK.
NOT YOU. HIM!
WELL. REALLY!
NO CHANCE, MATE. OFF YOU GO.
WHAT DO YOU MEAN, NORMAN? I'M YOUR BOSS!
COURSE YOU ARE. AND I'M MARY FUCKING POPPINS. NOW DO ONE!
CHOKE! GAG!
YOU'RE FINISHED NORMAN. IN FACT WE ALL ARE. YOU HAVEN'T LET A SINGLE CUSTOMER IN FOR OVER EIGHT YEARS. THE CLUB HAS GONE BUST.
YOU'RE FIRED!
NOW FUCK OFF. I'VE GOT TO BURN THE PLACE DOWN.
DON'T WORRY ABOUT ME. I'LL GET ANOTHER JOB LIKE THAT!
CLICK!
JESUS. I'VE BEEN STOOD HERE FOR HOURS. I'M BLOODY STARVIN'.
OI! I THOUGHT I TOLD YOU BEFORE. YOU'RE NOT GOING IN THERE.
BUT I...
NOT IN THEM SHOES YOU'RE NOT.
BUT...
I SAID SHOVE IT!
BUT I CAN'T MAKE YOUR TEA IF YOU WON'T LET ME IN THE FRIDGE, NORMAN.
YOU'VE BEEN MOPING AROUND THE HOUSE FOR WEEKS NOW. YOU'VE GOT TO GET A NEW JOB. BUT YOU WON'T DO THAT UNLESS YOU MOVE WITH THE TIMES.
LOOK, I SAW THIS IN THE NEWSPAPER THIS MORNING.
•PSYCHOLOGY
•DIPLOMACY
•TEAMWORK
•TODAY'S DOOR SECURITY OPERATIVE
Fulchester College offers B.A. Degree courses in Door Security. Phone for details.
KARL
I'VE ALREADY ENROLLED YOU ON THE COURSE. YOUR FIRST LECTURE IS TOMORROW MORNING.
HELLO MARGE. I'M DOING THE SOCIOLOGY PART OF THE DOOR OPERATIVE COURSE. WHAT ROOM IS IT IN?
RECEPTION
IT'S IN LECTURE THEATRE 6, PROFESSOR JONES. THE STUDENTS ARE WAITING.
WHOAH, SON. NO WAY ARE YOU COMING IN HERE LIKE THAT.
SORRY, GRANDAD. NO ELBOW PATCHES IN THIS LECTURE THEATRE.
THAT BRIEF-CASE IS CASUAL.
SLING YOUR HOOK, SHIRLEY BLEEDIN' TEMPLE.
6
YOU WANT TROUBLE, I'LL GIVE YOU BLEEDIN' TROUBLE.
LEW STRINGER /GPD ST SD AC DJ
VIZ 100

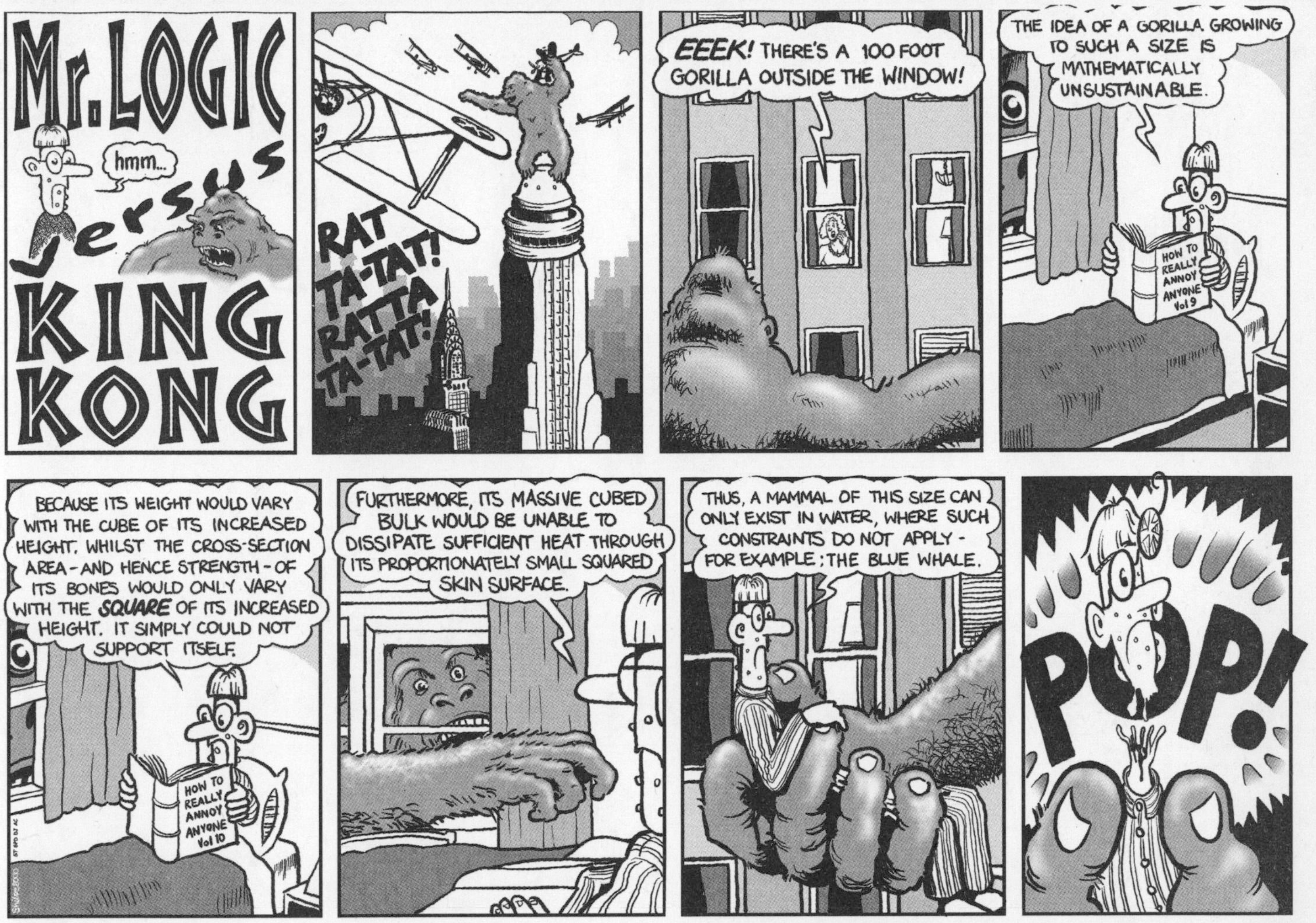
Mr. LOGIC
hmm...
versus
KING KONG
RAT TA-TAT! RATTA TA-TAT!
EEEK! THERE'S A 100 FOOT GORILLA OUTSIDE THE WINDOW!
THE IDEA OF A GORILLA GROWING TO SUCH A SIZE IS MATHEMATICALLY UNSUSTAINABLE.
HOW TO REALLY ANNOY ANYONE Vol 9
BECAUSE ITS WEIGHT WOULD VARY WITH THE CUBE OF ITS INCREASED HEIGHT, WHILST THE CROSS-SECTION AREA - AND HENCE STRENGTH - OF ITS BONES WOULD ONLY VARY WITH THE SQUARE OF ITS INCREASED HEIGHT. IT SIMPLY COULD NOT SUPPORT ITSELF.
HOW TO REALLY ANNOY ANYONE Vol 10
FURTHERMORE, ITS MASSIVE CUBED BULK WOULD BE UNABLE TO DISSIPATE SUFFICIENT HEAT THROUGH ITS PROPORTIONATELY SMALL SQUARED SKIN SURFACE.
THUS, A MAMMAL OF THIS SIZE CAN ONLY EXIST IN WATER, WHERE SUCH CONSTRAINTS DO NOT APPLY - FOR EXAMPLE; THE BLUE WHALE.
POP!

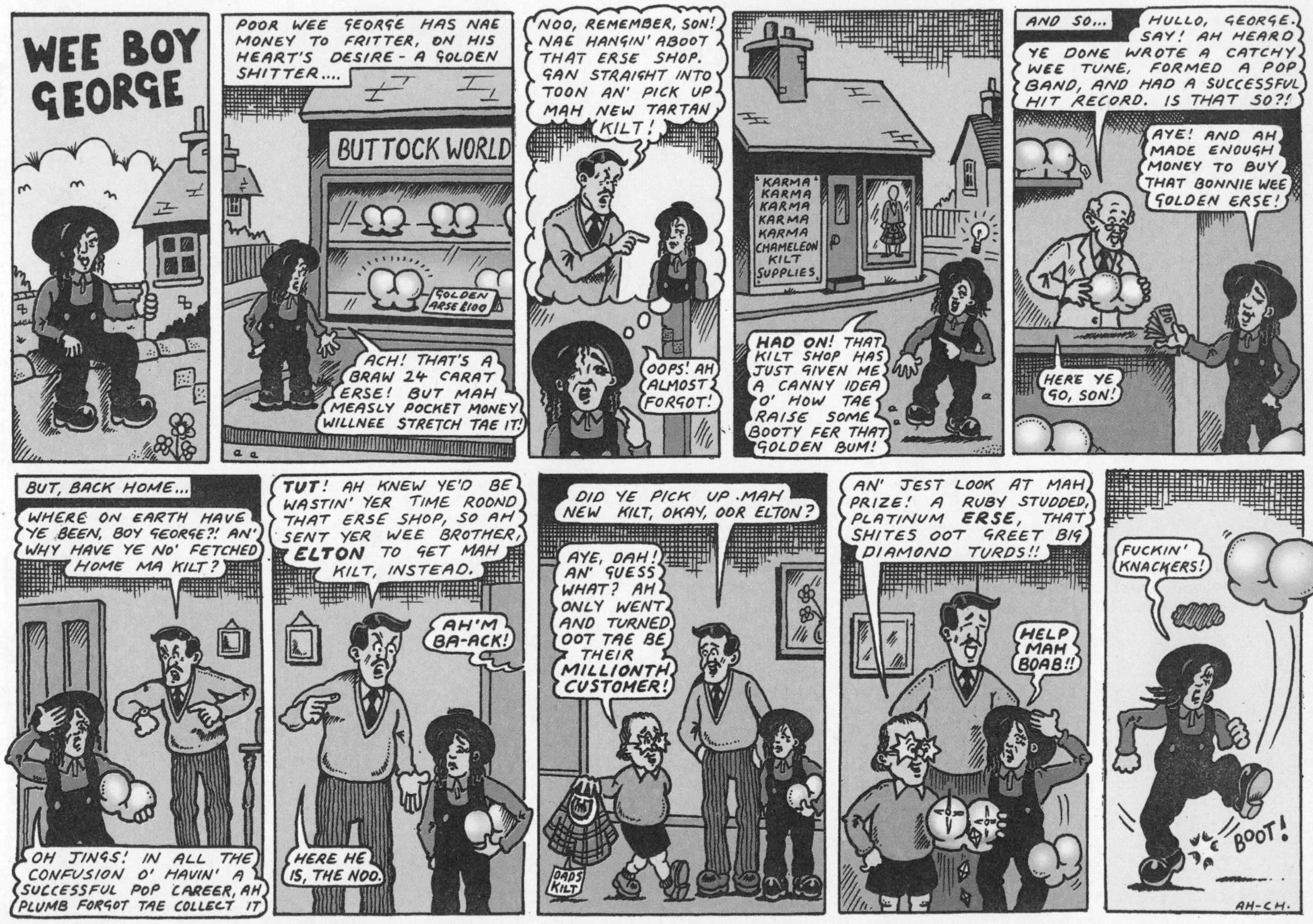
WEE BOY GEORGE
POOR WEE GEORGE HAS NAE MONEY TO FRITTER, ON HIS HEART'S DESIRE - A GOLDEN SHITTER....
BUTTOCK WORLD
GOLDEN ARSE £100
ACH! THAT'S A BRAW 24 CARAT ERSE! BUT MAH MEASLY POCKET MONEY WILLNEE STRETCH TAE IT!
NOO, REMEMBER, SON! NAE HANGIN' ABOOT THAT ERSE SHOP. GAN STRAIGHT INTO TOON AN' PICK UP MAH NEW TARTAN KILT!
OOPS! AH ALMOST FORGOT!
KARMA KARMA KARMA KARMA KARMA CHAMELEON KILT SUPPLIES
HAD ON! THAT KILT SHOP HAS JUST GIVEN ME A CANNY IDEA O' HOW TAE RAISE SOME BOOTY FER THAT GOLDEN BUM!
AND SO...
HULLO, GEORGE. SAY! AH HEARD YE DONE WROTE A CATCHY WEE TUNE, FORMED A POP BAND, AND HAD A SUCCESSFUL HIT RECORD. IS THAT SO?!
AYE! AND AH MADE ENOUGH MONEY TO BUY THAT BONNIE WEE GOLDEN ERSE!
HERE YE GO, SON!
BUT, BACK HOME...
WHERE ON EARTH HAVE YE BEEN, BOY GEORGE?! AN' WHY HAVE YE NO' FETCHED HOME MA KILT?
OH JINGS! IN ALL THE CONFUSION O' HAVIN' A SUCCESSFUL POP CAREER, AH PLUMB FORGOT TAE COLLECT IT
TUT! AH KNEW YE'D BE WASTIN' YER TIME ROOND THAT ERSE SHOP, SO AH SENT YER WEE BROTHER, ELTON TO GET MAH KILT, INSTEAD.
AH'M BA-ACK!
HERE HE IS, THE NOO.
DID YE PICK UP MAH NEW KILT, OKAY, OOR ELTON?
AYE, DAH! AN' GUESS WHAT? AH ONLY WENT AND TURNED OOT TAE BE THEIR MILLIONTH CUSTOMER!
DADS KILT
AN' JEST LOOK AT MAH PRIZE! A RUBY STUDDED, PLATINUM ERSE, THAT SHITES OOT GREET BIG DIAMOND TURDS!!
HELP MAH BOAB!!
FUCKIN' KNACKERS!
BOOT!
AH-CH.

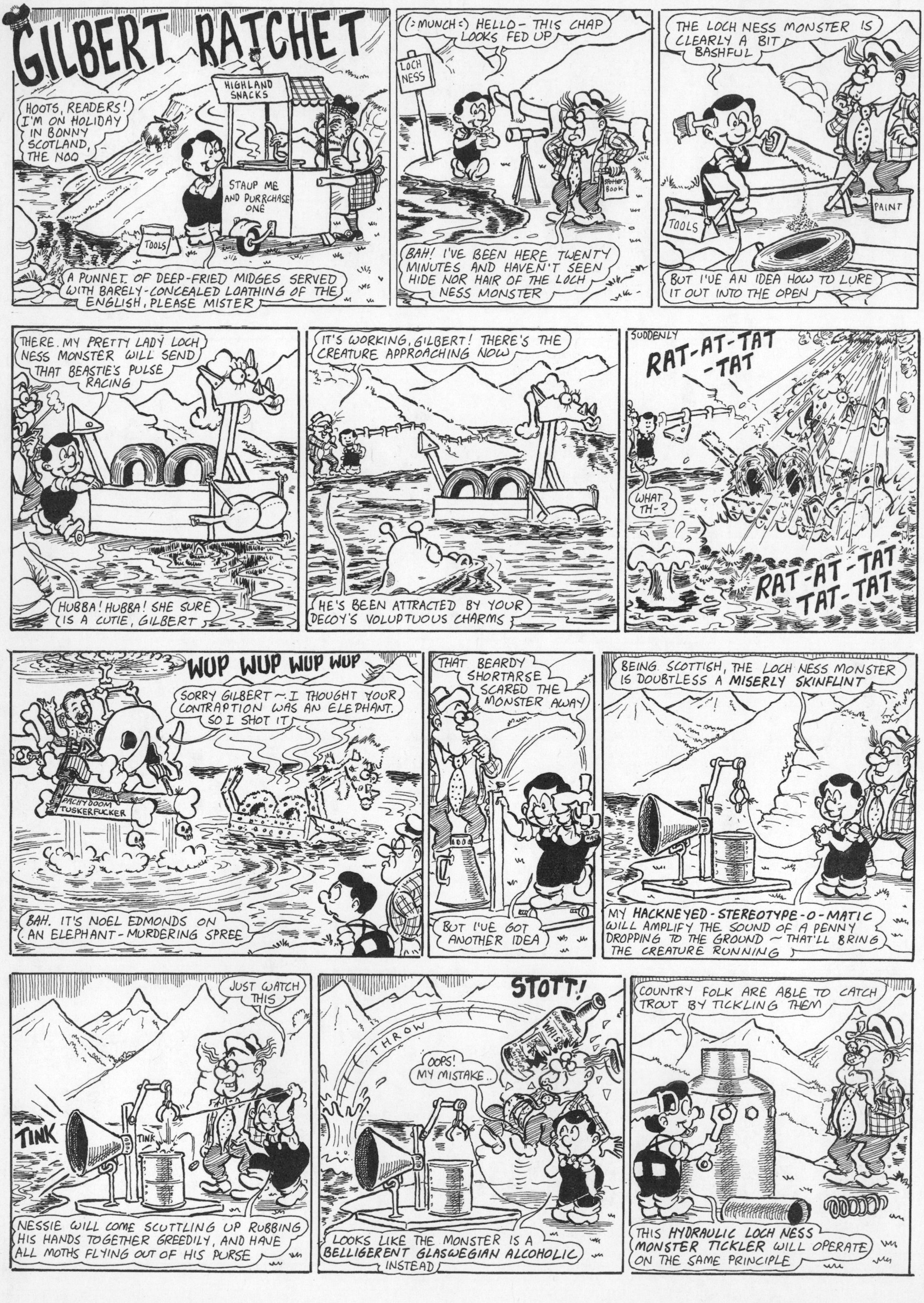
GILBERT RATCHET
HIGHLAND SNACKS
HOOTS, READERS! I'M ON HOLIDAY IN BONNY SCOTLAND, THE NOO
STAUP ME AND PURRCHASE ONE
TOOLS
A PUNNET OF DEEP-FRIED MIDGES SERVED WITH BARELY-CONCEALED LOATHING OF THE ENGLISH, PLEASE MISTER
(:MUNCH:) HELLO - THIS CHAP LOOKS FED UP
LOCH NESS
SPOTTER'S BOOK
BAH! I'VE BEEN HERE TWENTY MINUTES AND HAVEN'T SEEN HIDE NOR HAIR OF THE LOCH NESS MONSTER
THE LOCH NESS MONSTER IS CLEARLY A BIT BASHFUL
TOOLS
PAINT
BUT I'VE AN IDEA HOW TO LURE IT OUT INTO THE OPEN
THERE. MY PRETTY LADY LOCH NESS MONSTER WILL SEND THAT BEASTIE'S PULSE RACING
HUBBA! HUBBA! SHE SURE IS A CUTIE, GILBERT
IT'S WORKING, GILBERT! THERE'S THE CREATURE APPROACHING NOW
HE'S BEEN ATTRACTED BY YOUR DECOY'S VOLUPTUOUS CHARMS
SUDDENLY
RAT-AT-TAT -TAT
WHAT TH-?
RAT-AT-TAT TAT-TAT
WUP WUP WUP WUP
SORRY GILBERT ~. I THOUGHT YOUR CONTRAPTION WAS AN ELEPHANT. SO I SHOT IT
PACHYDOOM TUSKERFUCKER
BAH. IT'S NOEL EDMONDS ON AN ELEPHANT-MURDERING SPREE
THAT BEARDY SHORTARSE SCARED THE MONSTER AWAY
BUT I'VE GOT ANOTHER IDEA
BEING SCOTTISH, THE LOCH NESS MONSTER IS DOUBTLESS A MISERLY SKINFLINT
MY HACKNEYED-STEREOTYPE-O-MATIC WILL AMPLIFY THE SOUND OF A PENNY DROPPING TO THE GROUND ~ THAT'LL BRING THE CREATURE RUNNING
JUST WATCH THIS
TINK
TINK
NESSIE WILL COME SCUTTLING UP RUBBING HIS HANDS TOGETHER GREEDILY, AND HAVE ALL MOTHS FLYING OUT OF HIS PURSE
STOTT!
THROW
OOPS! MY MISTAKE..
LOOKS LIKE THE MONSTER IS A BELLIGERENT GLASWEGIAN ALCOHOLIC INSTEAD
COUNTRY FOLK ARE ABLE TO CATCH TROUT BY TICKLING THEM
THIS HYDRAULIC LOCH NESS MONSTER TICKLER WILL OPERATE ON THE SAME PRINCIPLE

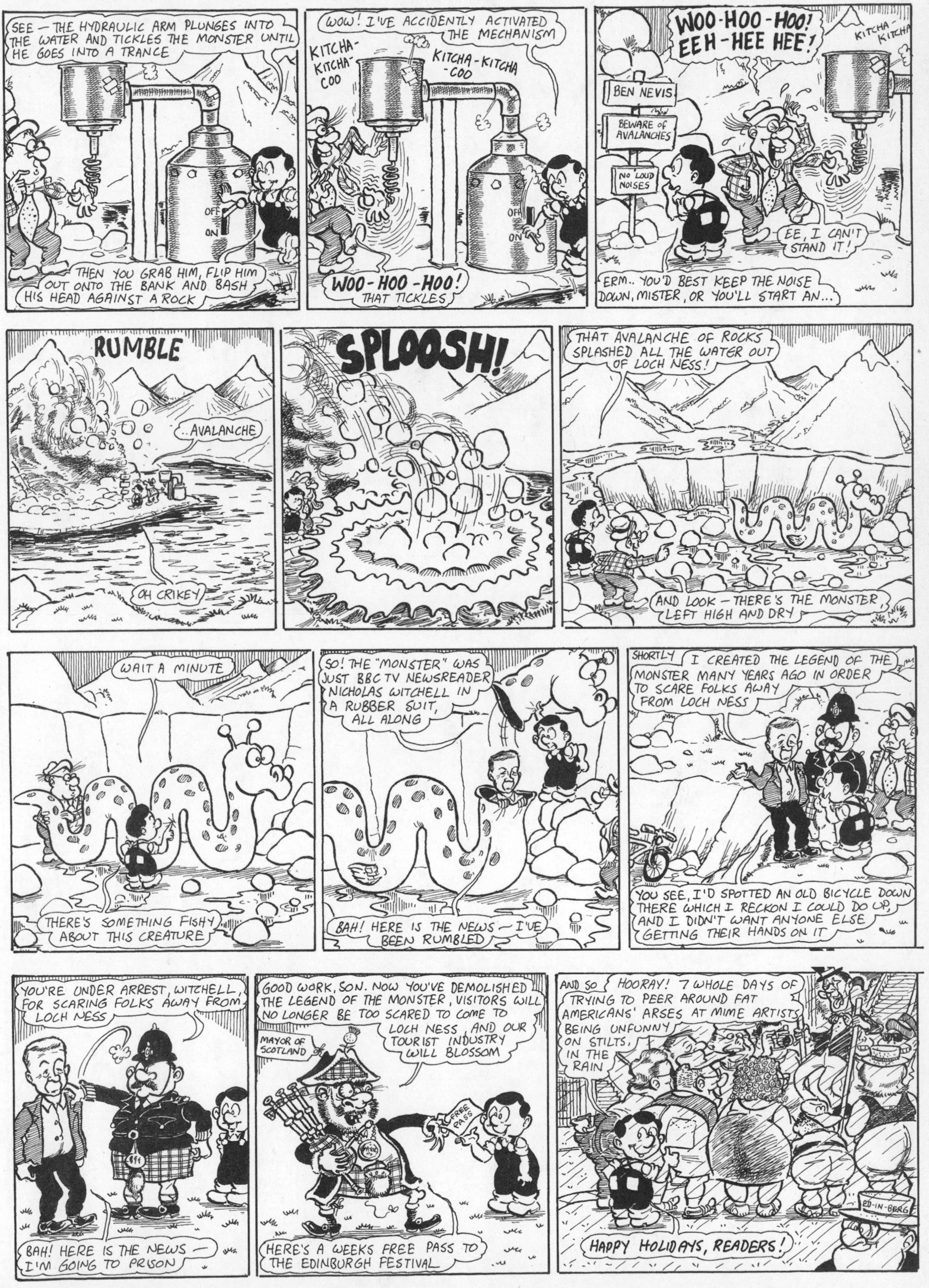
SEE — THE HYDRAULIC ARM PLUNGES INTO THE WATER AND TICKLES THE MONSTER UNTIL HE GOES INTO A TRANCE
OFF
ON
THEN YOU GRAB HIM, FLIP HIM OUT ONTO THE BANK AND BASH HIS HEAD AGAINST A ROCK
WOW! I'VE ACCIDENTLY ACTIVATED THE MECHANISM
KITCHA-KITCHA-COO
KITCHA-KITCHA-COO
OFF
ON
WOO-HOO-HOO! THAT TICKLES
WOO-HOO-HOO! EEH-HEE HEE!
KITCHA-KITCHA
BEN NEVIS
BEWARE OF AVALANCHES
NO LOUD NOISES
EE, I CAN'T STAND IT!
ERM.. YOU'D BEST KEEP THE NOISE DOWN, MISTER, OR YOU'LL START AN...
RUMBLE
..AVALANCHE
OH CRIKEY
SPLOOSH!
THAT AVALANCHE OF ROCKS SPLASHED ALL THE WATER OUT OF LOCH NESS!
AND LOOK — THERE'S THE MONSTER, LEFT HIGH AND DRY
WAIT A MINUTE
THERE'S SOMETHING FISHY ABOUT THIS CREATURE
SO! THE "MONSTER" WAS JUST BBC TV NEWSREADER NICHOLAS WITCHELL IN A RUBBER SUIT, ALL ALONG
BAH! HERE IS THE NEWS — I'VE BEEN RUMBLED
SHORTLY
I CREATED THE LEGEND OF THE MONSTER MANY YEARS AGO IN ORDER TO SCARE FOLKS AWAY FROM LOCH NESS
YOU SEE, I'D SPOTTED AN OLD BICYCLE DOWN THERE WHICH I RECKON I COULD DO UP, AND I DIDN'T WANT ANYONE ELSE GETTING THEIR HANDS ON IT
YOU'RE UNDER ARREST, WITCHELL, FOR SCARING FOLKS AWAY FROM LOCH NESS
BAH! HERE IS THE NEWS — I'M GOING TO PRISON
GOOD WORK, SON. NOW YOU'VE DEMOLISHED THE LEGEND OF THE MONSTER, VISITORS WILL NO LONGER BE TOO SCARED TO COME TO LOCH NESS, AND OUR TOURIST INDUSTRY WILL BLOSSOM
MAYOR OF SCOTLAND
FREE PASS
HERE'S A WEEKS FREE PASS TO THE EDINBURGH FESTIVAL
AND SO
HOORAY! 7 WHOLE DAYS OF TRYING TO PEER AROUND FAT AMERICANS' ARSES AT MIME ARTISTS BEING UNFUNNY ON STILTS, IN THE RAIN
ED-IN-BERG
HAPPY HOLIDAYS, READERS!

Who's who in local te

When we turn on our TV sets to watch the nightly regional news, we only see the faces of the presenters. How many of us ever stop to wonder how many people are working behind the camera? You may be surprised to learn that, just like an iceberg, nine tenths of the regional news team is submerged beneath the surface of the sea. It's two minutes before the programme goes on air. Let's pull back the camera and take a look at who's who in the regional news studio.

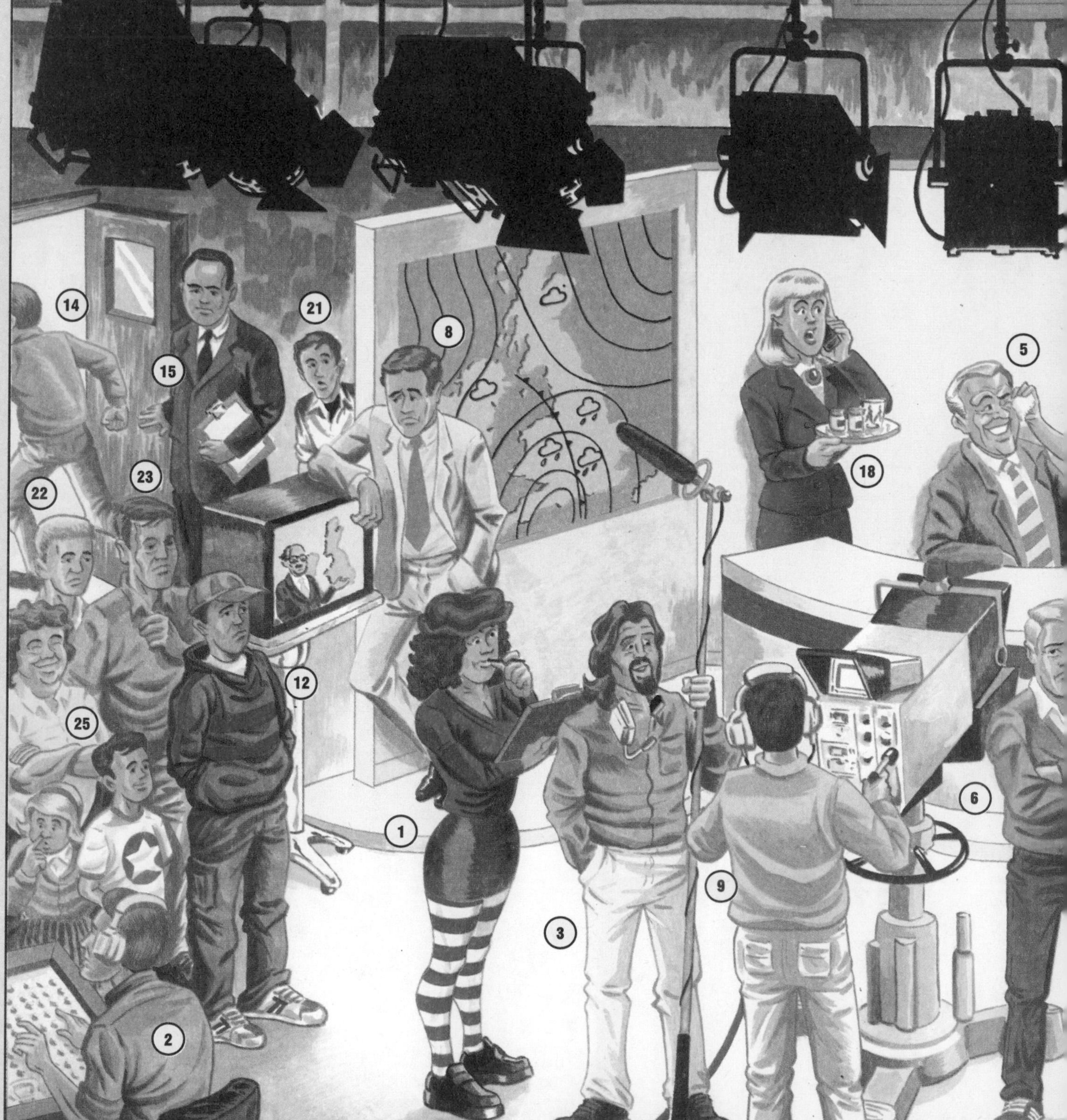

4
14
21
8
5
15
18
22
23
12
25
1
6
9
3
2

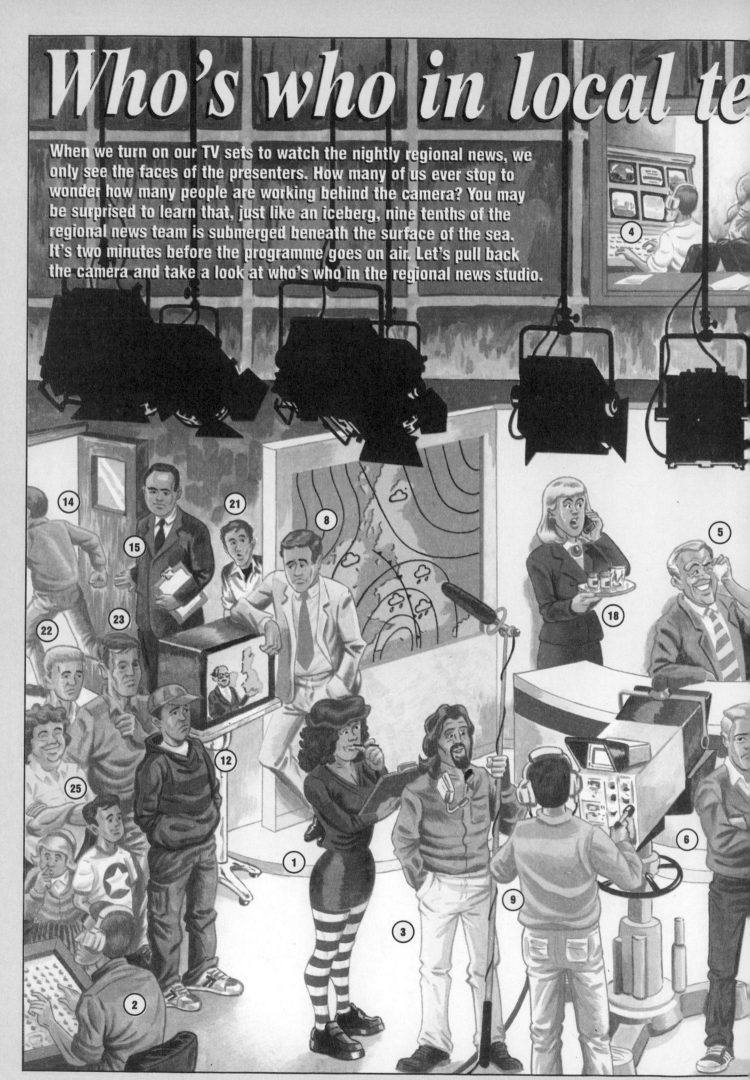

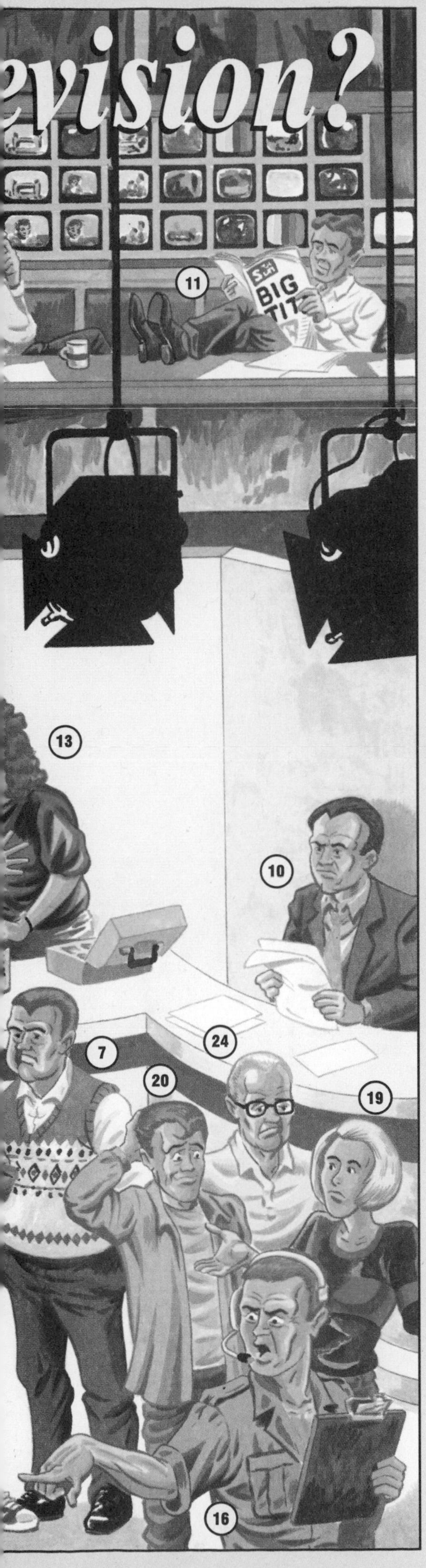
evision?
11
BIG TIT
13
10
7
24
20
19
16

1 The Researcher

A junior, though still very important position. Traditionally she must have the silliest name of anyone in the studio. Without the researcher, there would be no one running round the studio carrying a clipboard and wearing hoopy tights.

2 The Sound Engineer

He must balance the sound levels during the actual broadcast and filter out the sound of the presenter's false teeth clacking before the signal reaches the mixing desk.

3 The Boom Operator

Works in conjunction with the sound engineer and the camera man. It is his job to occasionally dip the microphone in shot just long enough and frequently enough to be distracting. A highly skilled job, that requires the ability to point your arms vaguely at whoever is talking.

4 The Sound Mixer

This man takes all the sounds from all the microphones across the studio and balances the levels to produce the final sound that is broadcast. He also has to leave the presenter's microphone switched off for the first 3 seconds of a broadcast, then turn it up far too loud in panic before finally finding the correct level.

5 The Anchorman

He may be just another cog in the Regional News Programme machine, but he is the one that the public sees. As his title suggests, he 'anchors' the programme. Sitting upright with his eyes open and slowly reading things other people have written when he sees a red light go on are just some of the skills he has honed over 35 years in Regional Broadcasting. Several drink-driving bans and a couple of shop-lifting incidents have done little to dent his popularity with stupid old women regionwide.

6 Standby Gaffer

Stands on the studio floor. It is his job to move out of the way when the camera comes through.

7 Assistant Standby Gaffer

Moves out of the way to allow the standby gaffer to move out of the way of the camera.

8 Local Weatherman

This man must work to very tight deadlines. He has to watch Michael Fish doing the national weather on a portable telly minutes before he goes on air, take the bit relevant to the region and pad it out to about a minute. He will be insanely jealous of the anchorman who can command double his own appearance fee to open carpet warehouse sales etc. The weatherman must also deliver his piece standing up, and must therefore drink slightly less than the anchorman.

9 Chief Cameraman

In constant contact with the director, the cameraman must carefully compose each shot, taking great care to position the camera so that the 'backdrop picture' covers half of the anchorman's face. When the director eventually spots this and informs the cameraman, he must zoom in quickly on the anchorman's ear, allowing the director to cut to camera 2's shot of a bemused looking weatherman picking his nose.

10 Newsreader

The newsreader must have a sense of timing second to none. When his segment is counted in by the director, he must begin reading to the wrong camera for exactly 4 seconds, as demanded by the IBA, before spotting the red light on the other camera. He will probably be in dispute with the station because his grinning, chrome-framed portrait on the foyer wall is smaller than the weatherman's.

11 The News Editor

A time-served journalist, the News editor scans through the national daily tabloids looking for stories with a local interest, which were probably lifted from local weekly rags in the first place. This ensures that every story that makes it on screen is at least four days old. Unsalaried, he is paid a commission of £1 every time the words 'local' or 'region' appear in the script.

12 Best Boy

Runs to the station video library for the Betty Boop cartoons when the anchorman has a stroke on air.

13 Make-up Artist

The harsh lighting in a television studio shows up the smallest imperfections of the skin. So just imagine what it would do to an alcoholic anchorman with cheeks like purple crazy paving and a nose like a baboon with piles's arse. For this reason, the make-up artist is often considered the most important member of the regional programme team, and up to half of the entire production budget can be spent on sufficiently powerful make-up.

14 Post Production Runner

This man must run to the bar and line up the drinks for the Anchorman.

15 Producer

The most important man, after the anchorman, on the studio floor. His job is to open all the doors to allow the anchorman to lumber to the bar immediately after the broadcast.

16 Floor Manager

Invariably an aggressive, effeminate Scotsman who's job it is to mince angrily about the studio, bossing everyone around in a patronising voice.

17 The Director

Surely the man who holds the show together. Throughout the show he must sit in the gantry next to a woman who counts backwards whilst looking at lots of television screens.

18 P.A. to Anchorman

A woman who makes sure the anchorman takes his happy pills and explains away his tantrums to the crew. Her other main job is to buy his wife's birthday and anniversary presents. She must also perform a delicate balancing act, allowing him to drink enough before he goes on air so that he doesn't get the shakes, but not so much that he can't focus on the autocue.

If you want to get into local television, there are two recognised routes to take. Firstly, through your father working for the station, or secondly, through your mother working for the station. The following paid staff are all related to the anchorman.

19 **Junior Researcher** - daughter

20 **On-line Producer** - son

21 **Key Grip** - sister's lad

22 **Clapper Loader** - brother-in-law

23 **Foley Artist** - niece's husband

24 **Rostrum Camera** - father

25 **Production Assistants** - Vera & the kids

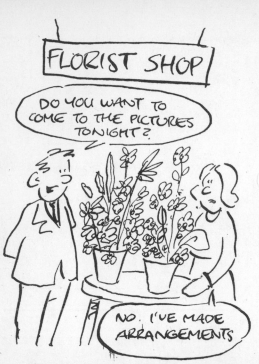

FLORIST SHOP
DO YOU WANT TO COME TO THE PICTURES TONIGHT?
NO. I'VE MADE ARRANGEMENTS

The NEWS in BRIEFS (and a bra) with ANGELA RIPPON

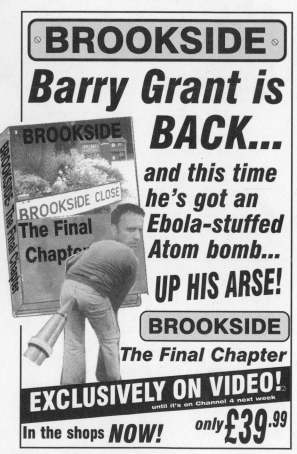

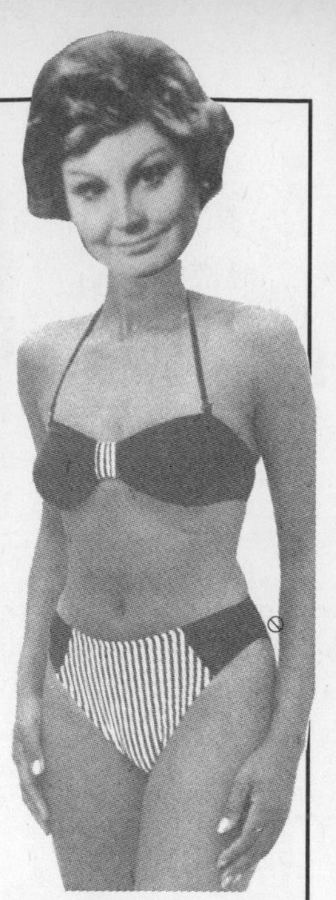

Straw Blimey!

Visitors to the Wimbledon Lawn Tennis Championships could be in for a bit of a shock. For this year a punnet of strawberries and cream could set them back an astonishing £27000 - that's an incredible *nine grand per strawberry*, the price of a Renault Clio. But greedy loudmouth shit film director Michael Winner was last night unfazed when told of the astronomical price-hike. "I like strawberries and cream. I'm going to have ***two bowls,*** whatever it costs," the fat cunt told reporters.

Stone Me!

17th century physicist Sir Isaac Newton has been found fully encased in amber. A group of Carbondale, Illinois schoolchildren on a field trip to the Yellowstone National Park found the amber-cased inventor of gravity at the foot of a Redwood tree. "We couldn't believe what fantastic condition he was in," said geography teacher Draylon Quarterpounder. "He was still sitting on Cambridge University's Lucasian Chair of Mathematics. It was incredible." Newton is thought to be the most complete preserved English physicist found since Russian Seismologists discovered the top half of Michael Faraday embedded in ice near Zhigansk, Siberia in 1974.

Sexplosion

Members of the public ran for cover as a sex bomb exploded without warning in a crowded shopping arcade yesterday. Eye witnesses reported hearing high pitched saxophone music shortly before the 112 lb sex bomb went off outside the Coventry branch of Curry's around 11 o'clock. Sauciness was showered over a 400 yard radius. Emergency services were quickly on the scene. "Fortunately, casualties were light," said Warwickshire Ambulance chief Steven Trellis. "A few middle-aged men were treated at the scene for minor sexual excitement. A 15-year-old boy was taken to hospital with a raging bone-on, but he has since been released."

Core Blimey!

A novel solution to the Earth's burgeoning population problem has been proposed by comedy botanist David Bellamy. "They should dig down to the Earth's core, get the pips out and plant them on the moon," he shouted to bewildered passers-by in a Bishop Auckland shopping precinct. " Each pip would be the size of a double-decker bus. They would grow into trees that would eventually bear a crop of 'Earth fruits' where people could go and live," he continued excitedly before being led away by police.

Whore Blimey!

Visitors to Amsterdam's notorious Red Light district are to take part in an experimental new scheme that could revolutionise the sexual service industry. From June, any man over the age of 16 entering Holland will have a barcode tattooed on the underside of his Charlie. When visiting a prostitute, he will be required to 'swipe' his cock between her tits before sex, where his unique code will be read by a 'supermarket checkout-style' scanner built into her cleavage. His bank account will then be directly debited. "This is a very good thing for the industry," said Dutch minister of Drugs, Whores and Farmyard Porn, Wim van der Haag. "The prostitute will be able to service more clients, and because the punter will not be carrying cash, her pimp is less likely to jump out the wardrobe, rob him and cut his face off."

BROOKSIDE
Barry Grant is BACK...
and this time he's got an Ebola-stuffed Atom bomb...
UP HIS ARSE!
BROOKSIDE
BROOKSIDE CLOSE
The Final Chapter
BROOKSIDE The Final Chapter
BROOKSIDE
The Final Chapter
EXCLUSIVELY ON VIDEO!
until it's on Channel 4 next week
In the shops NOW!
only £39.99

Professor Piehead and his assistant, TIM
OKAY, JOE. READY TO TEST MY NEW HIPPOPOTAMUS PROOF UMBRELLA!
THUD!
HMM... THAT WAS A RHINOCEROUS.

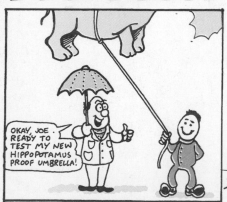

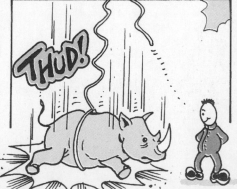

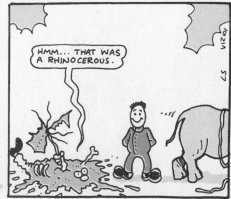

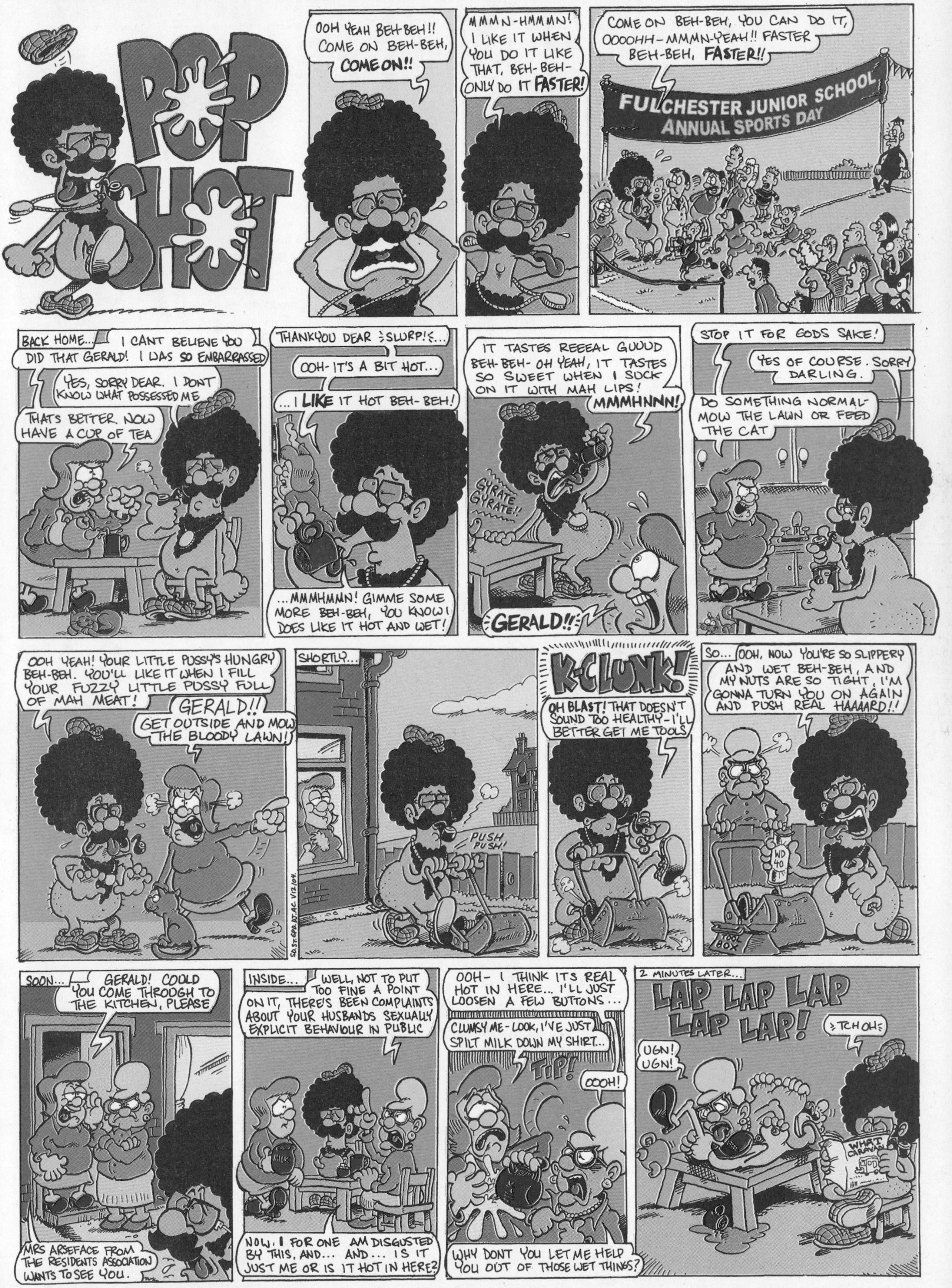
POP SHOT
OOH YEAH BEH-BEH!! COME ON BEH-BEH, COME ON!!
MMMN-HMMMN! I LIKE IT WHEN YOU DO IT LIKE THAT, BEH-BEH- ONLY DO IT FASTER!
COME ON BEH-BEH, YOU CAN DO IT, OOOOHH-MMMN-YEAH!! FASTER BEH-BEH, FASTER!!
FULCHESTER JUNIOR SCHOOL ANNUAL SPORTS DAY
BACK HOME...
I CANT BELIEVE YOU DID THAT GERALD! I WAS SO EMBARRASSED
YES, SORRY DEAR. I DONT KNOW WHAT POSSESSED ME
THATS BETTER. NOW HAVE A CUP OF TEA
THANKYOU DEAR ≷SLURP!≶...
OOH- IT'S A BIT HOT...
...I LIKE IT HOT BEH-BEH!
...MMMHMMN! GIMME SOME MORE BEH-BEH, YOU KNOW I DOES LIKE IT HOT AND WET!
IT TASTES REEEAL GUUUD BEH-BEH- OH YEAH, IT TASTES SO SWEET WHEN I SUCK ON IT WITH MAH LIPS!
MMMHNNN!
GYRATE GYRATE!!
GERALD!!
STOP IT FOR GODS SAKE!
YES OF COURSE. SORRY DARLING.
DO SOMETHING NORMAL- MOW THE LAWN OR FEED THE CAT
OOH YEAH! YOUR LITTLE PUSSY'S HUNGRY BEH-BEH. YOU'LL LIKE IT WHEN I FILL YOUR FUZZY LITTLE PUSSY FULL OF MAH MEAT!
GERALD!! GET OUTSIDE AND MOW THE BLOODY LAWN!
SHORTLY...
PUSH PUSH!
K-CLUNK!
OH BLAST! THAT DOESN'T SOUND TOO HEALTHY- I'LL BETTER GET ME TOOLS
SO...
OOH, NOW YOU'RE SO SLIPPERY AND WET BEH-BEH, AND MY NUTS ARE SO TIGHT, I'M GONNA TURN YOU ON AGAIN AND PUSH REAL HAAAARD!!
WD 40
TOOL BOX
SOON...
GERALD! COULD YOU COME THROUGH TO THE KITCHEN, PLEASE
MRS ARSEFACE FROM THE RESIDENTS ASSOCIATION WANTS TO SEE YOU.
INSIDE...
WELL, NOT TO PUT TOO FINE A POINT ON IT, THERE'S BEEN COMPLAINTS ABOUT YOUR HUSBANDS SEXUALLY EXPLICIT BEHAVIOUR IN PUBLIC
MILK
NOW, I FOR ONE AM DISGUSTED BY THIS, AND... AND... IS IT JUST ME OR IS IT HOT IN HERE?
OOH- I THINK ITS REAL HOT IN HERE... I'LL JUST LOOSEN A FEW BUTTONS...
CLUMSY ME- LOOK, I'VE JUST SPILT MILK DOWN MY SHIRT...
TIP!
OOOH!
WHY DONT YOU LET ME HELP YOU OUT OF THOSE WET THINGS?
2 MINUTES LATER...
LAP LAP LAP LAP LAP!
≷TCH OH≶
UGN! UGN!
WHAT CARAVAN

£50m painting 'not as good' as £8 telly

ART GALLERIES were last night facing the prospect of *SCRAPPING* all their masterpieces after experts proved that a telly costing just £8 was more than *ELEVEN TIMES* as interesting as the world's most valuable painting.

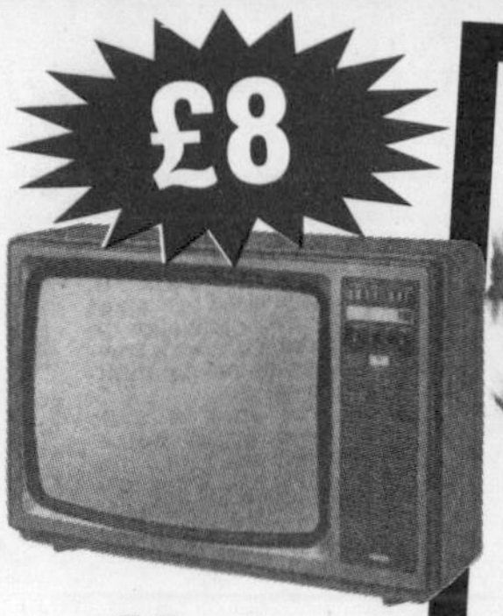

£8

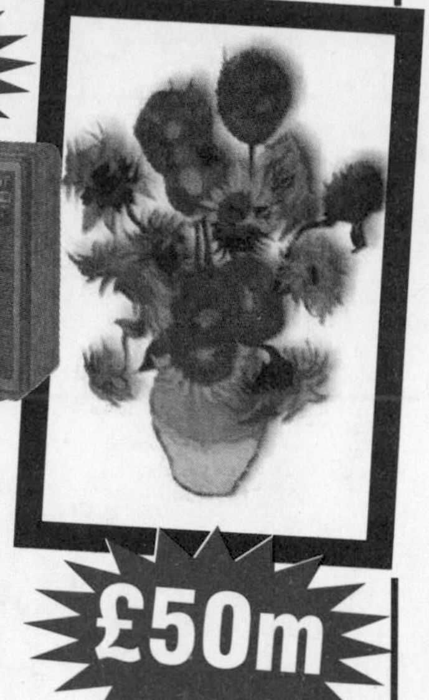

£50m

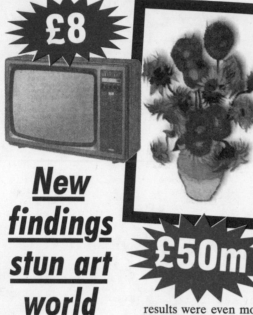

New findings stun art world

Scientists shut volunteers in a completely bare room containing Vincent Van Gogh's 'Sunflowers', an armchair and a small black & white TV, and then monitored their viewing habits for an hour.

chair

Amazingly, they spent an average of less than 5 minutes standing looking at the £50 million painting, before sitting down in the chair and watching whatever was on the television for the rest of the hour.

eel

"At first we doubted our results," said Professor Kent Walton, head of Statistics at Brunel University. "But then we checked and re-checked them and there was no mistake. Telly is loads better than posh paintings, and that's a scientific fact."

ladyland

When the experiment was repeated using the Mona Lisa and a copy of the Autotrader, the results were even more marked.

Disneyland

Sir Roy Strong, curator of the National Gallery, was devastated when we told him of Professor Walton's findings. "I have wasted my life," he said. "All this shit is going in a skip first thing tomorrow, I can tell you."

ONE SMALL STEP FOR BRAN(SON)

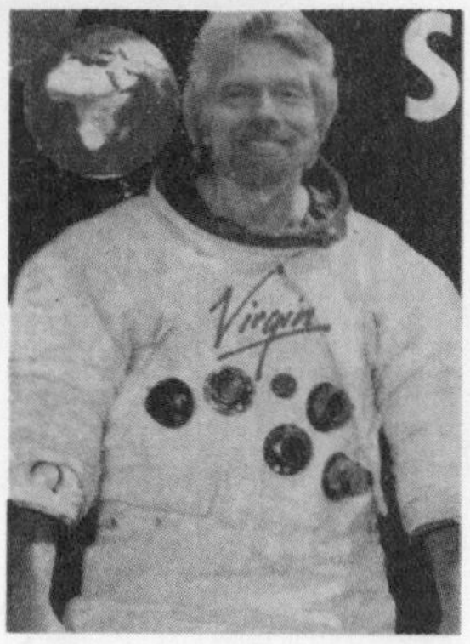

Virgin

MILLIONAIRE adventurer Sir Richard Branson has announced plans to get into the record books by being the first twat in space.

The Virgin boss, whose last attempt to circumnavigate the globe ended in tears when his £3 million balloon popped, hopes to complete a twelve-hour mission aboard an American Space Shuttle.

orbits

If all goes to plan Branson will complete 12 orbits of the earth with a shit-eating grin plastered across his face.

The NASA Tosspots in Space programme has been running for over 20 years. In 1978 a pair of fucking wankers were blasted up to Skylab where they spent over 100 days orbiting the earth, and this was followed up during 1994 when, for six months, an absolute arsehole lived aboard the Russian Mir space platform.

stimerols

But a challenge to American supremacy in the field of wankered spaceflight is set to emerge on this side of the Atlantic. Hillaire Belloc, a spokesman for the European Space agency ESA, said: "We have recently been having talks with Jeffrey Archer, and by the year 2020 we should hopefully have the technology in place to put a right cunt on Mars."

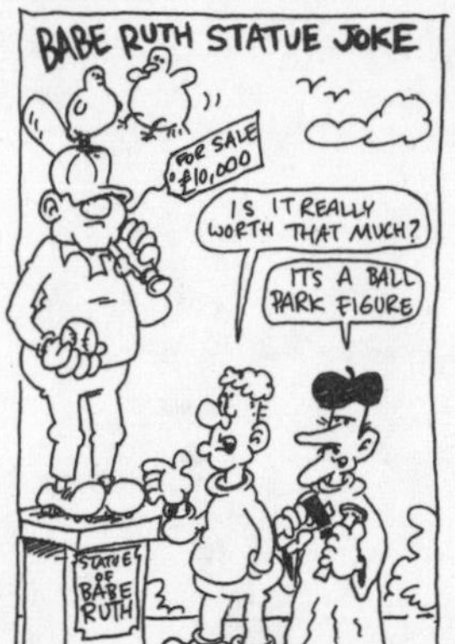

BABE RUTH STATUE JOKE
FOR SALE £10,000
IS IT REALLY WORTH THAT MUCH?
ITS A BALL PARK FIGURE
STATUE OF BABE RUTH

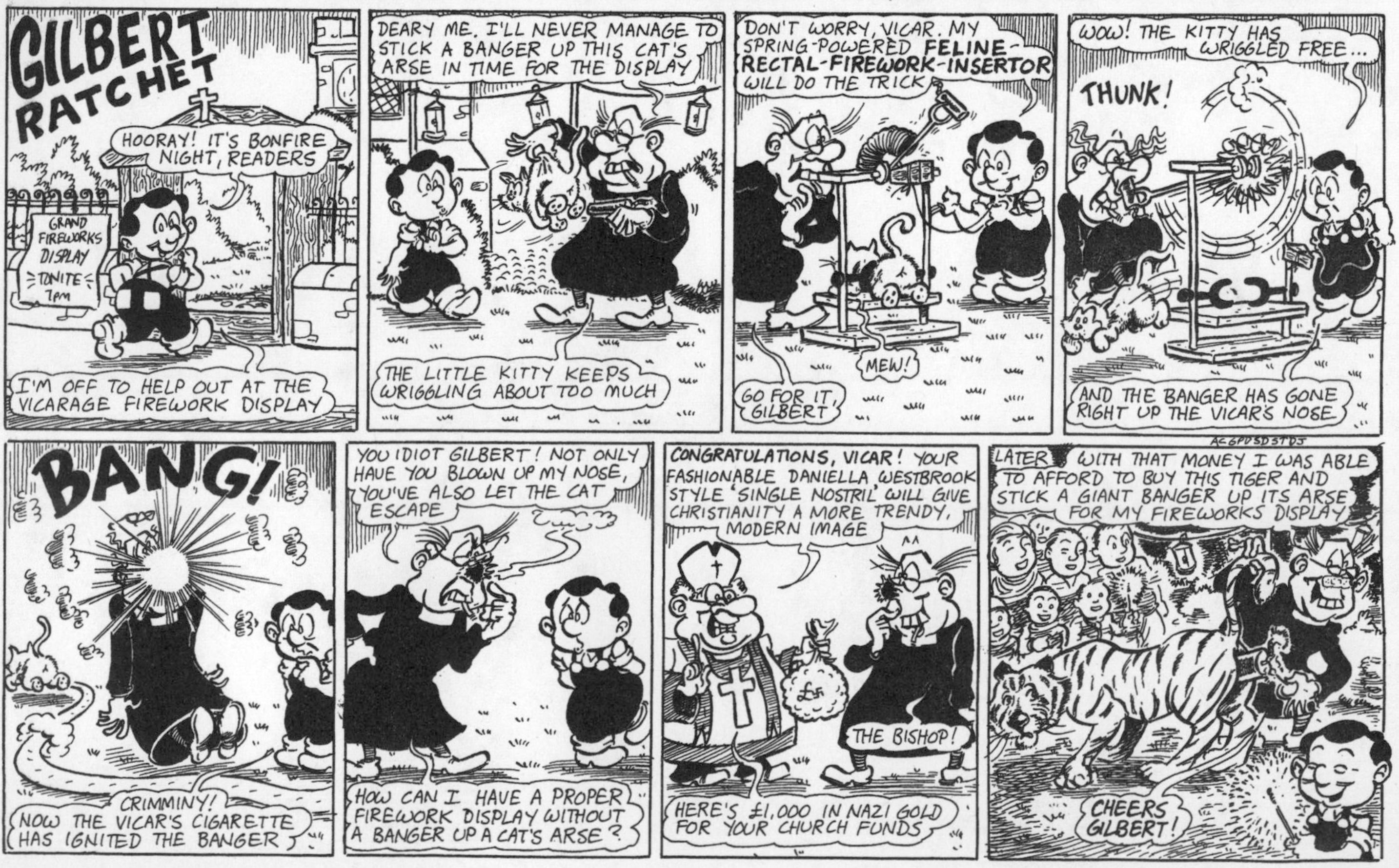

GILBERT RATCHET
HOORAY! IT'S BONFIRE NIGHT, READERS
GRAND FIREWORKS DISPLAY TONITE 7PM
I'M OFF TO HELP OUT AT THE VICARAGE FIREWORK DISPLAY
DEARY ME. I'LL NEVER MANAGE TO STICK A BANGER UP THIS CAT'S ARSE IN TIME FOR THE DISPLAY
THE LITTLE KITTY KEEPS WRIGGLING ABOUT TOO MUCH
DON'T WORRY, VICAR. MY SPRING-POWERED FELINE-RECTAL-FIREWORK-INSERTOR WILL DO THE TRICK
MEW!
GO FOR IT, GILBERT
WOW! THE KITTY HAS WRIGGLED FREE...
THUNK!
AND THE BANGER HAS GONE RIGHT UP THE VICAR'S NOSE
BANG!
CRIMMINY! NOW THE VICAR'S CIGARETTE HAS IGNITED THE BANGER
YOU IDIOT GILBERT! NOT ONLY HAVE YOU BLOWN UP MY NOSE, YOU'VE ALSO LET THE CAT ESCAPE
HOW CAN I HAVE A PROPER FIREWORK DISPLAY WITHOUT A BANGER UP A CAT'S ARSE?
CONGRATULATIONS, VICAR! YOUR FASHIONABLE DANIELLA WESTBROOK STYLE 'SINGLE NOSTRIL' WILL GIVE CHRISTIANITY A MORE TRENDY, MODERN IMAGE
THE BISHOP!
HERE'S £1,000 IN NAZI GOLD FOR YOUR CHURCH FUNDS
LATER WITH THAT MONEY I WAS ABLE TO AFFORD TO BUY THIS TIGER AND STICK A GIANT BANGER UP ITS ARSE FOR MY FIREWORKS DISPLAY
CHEERS GILBERT!

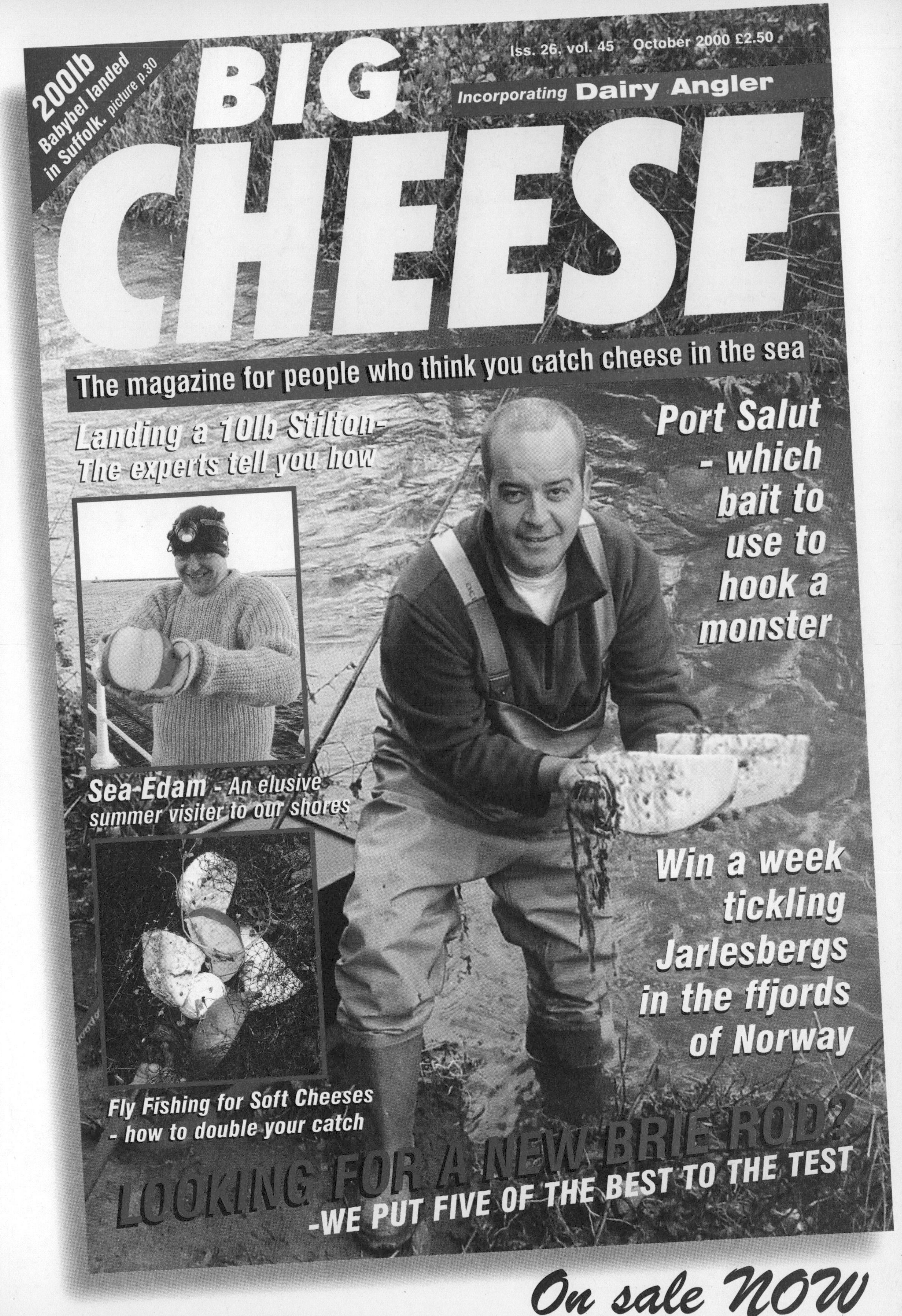
Iss. 26. vol. 45 October 2000 £2.50
200lb Babybel landed in Suffolk. picture p.30
BIG CHEESE
Incorporating Dairy Angler
The magazine for people who think you catch cheese in the sea
Landing a 10lb Stilton- The experts tell you how
Port Salut - which bait to use to hook a monster
Sea-Edam - An elusive summer visiter to our shores
Win a week tickling Jarlesbergs in the ffjords of Norway
Fly Fishing for Soft Cheeses - how to double your catch
LOOKING FOR A NEW BRIE ROD?
-WE PUT FIVE OF THE BEST TO THE TEST

On sale NOW

MICROSCOPES

Do you have a microscope? Are you interested in microscopes? Do you have any amusing stories about microscopes or people with microscopes? We are presently researching a 'fly-on-the-wall' docusoap about people with microscopes. If you are interested in taking part, consider yourself flamboyantly camp, and have a microscope, call Mike Knackers at Hairy Knackers Films on 0207 565 3103

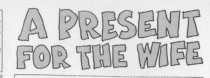

Scandal of the phoney stars

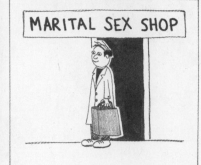

By our Consumer Affairs correspondent: A baboon with a big blue arse

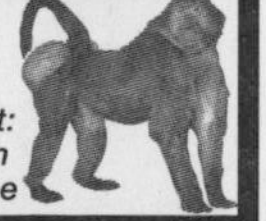

The public is being warned to be on the lookout for counterfeit celebrities being passed off as genuinely entertaining stars.

Trading standards chiefs have been alarmed at the number of people being conned into watching substandard programmes featuring fake personalities like Eamonn Holmes and Richard Whiteley.

quality

"One woman called to say she'd sat down to watch a makeover programme after being assured in the Radio Times that the presenter was of reasonable quality," says Malcolm Kirk, of West Midlands Trading Standards. "But, after a few minutes it was clear she'd been duped. Despite the fact that Carol Vorderman costs millions of pounds, she was practically useless and not worth watching."

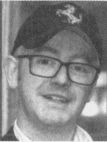

Can YOU spot a fake?

Look at the two entertainers on the right. One is genuinely talented, the other is a clever fake. Can you spot which is which?

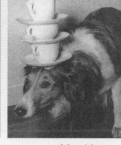

"Another man set his video to record a show after being promised that its star Phill Jupitus was a genuine comedian," continues Kirk.

Coronation

"When he viewed the tape, it quickly became apparent that Jupitus's act was constructed of extremely flimsy material, and was certainly not worth the £8000 which he is paid for each show."

Adrian

A spokesman was last night adamant that all BBC performers were genuine entertainers. He told us: "We pride ourselves on taking great care to avoid employing counterfeit celebrities. However, with the best will in the world a few, such as Noel Edmonds, are bound to slip through the net."

A PRESENT FOR THE WIFE

MARITAL SEX SHOP
I'VE GOT ONE, DARLING
GREAT! I'M IN THE BEDROOM
KMMC

ERM.. TROT, TROTH, TROTTER, TROUBADOUR...
ERE! ARE YOU LOOKING FOR TROUBLE?
DICTIONARY

MAN in the PUB
Britain's most ill-informed columnist

● Hey, you know why Des Lynam's got a big thick 'tache, don't you? I'll *tell you* - he's got *'FUCK OFF'* tatooed on his top lip that's why. True. Had it done when he was a teenager. Pissed as fart he was at the time. 'Course he regrets it now, like.

● *Have you got any £2 coins on you? Have a look, go on. If you've got any where the Queen's wearing a necklace, keep hold of 'em 'cos they're worth fifteen quid each. Straight up. There was a cock up at the mint.*

● You know the Russian linesman in the '66 World Cup? The one who said the ball had gone over the line. Well what everyone's forgot is that the Russian bloke was ill that day. Sick as a dog he was. They just got a bloke out the crowd to take his place. Well he was qualified, like. From Bolton he was...

... who's round is it?

Benson & Hedges
TOFF FAGS

Government Health Warning

SMOKING TOFF FAGS MAY CAUSE YOU TO SEND YOUR CHILDREN TO BOARDING SCHOOL AT THE AGE OF THREE

6mg Tar 0.5mg Nicotine 3mg Quails in aspic

"Churchill's Bouncy Castles are the ONLY bouncy castles I trust. I highly recommend them."

Dame Thora Hird

FREE Home Trial

Churchill's Bouncy Castles

Dial 100 and ask for FREEPHONE Bouncy Castles

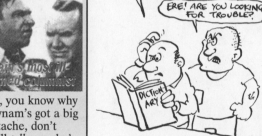

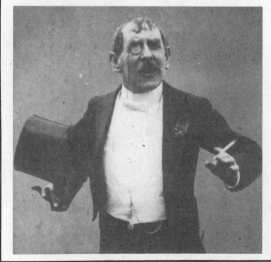

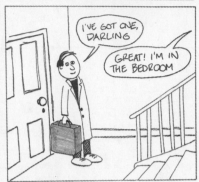

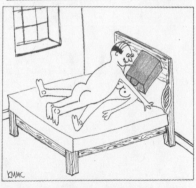

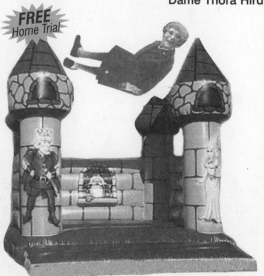

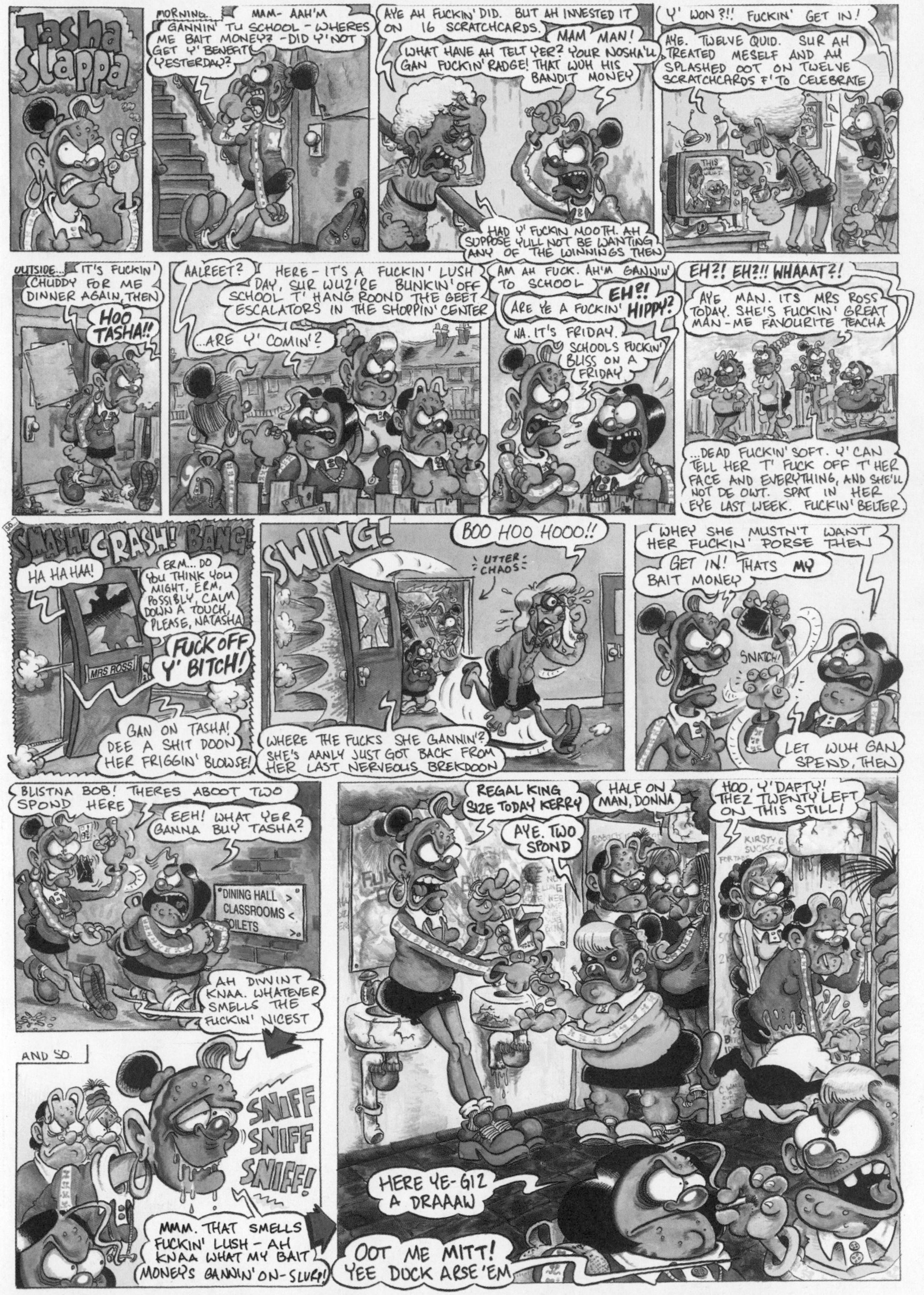

Tasha Slappa
MORNING...
MAM- AAH'M GANNIN' TU SCHOOL - WHERES ME BAIT MONEY? - DID Y'NOT GET Y' BENEFIT YESTERDAY?
AYE AH FUCKIN' DID. BUT AH INVESTED IT ON 16 SCRATCHCARDS.
MAM MAN!
WHAT HAVE AH TELT YER? YOUR NOSHA'LL GAN FUCKIN' RADGE! THAT WUH HIS BANDIT MONEY
HAD Y' FUCKIN MOOTH. AH SUPPOSE YULL NOT BE WANTING ANY OF THE WINNINGS THEN
Y' WON?!! FUCKIN' GET IN!
AYE. TWELVE QUID. SUR AH TREATED MESELF AND AH SPLASHED OOT ON TWELVE SCRATCHCARDS F'TO CELEBRATE
OUTSIDE...
IT'S FUCKIN' CHUDDY FOR ME DINNER AGAIN, THEN
HOO TASHA!!
AALREET?
HERE - IT'S A FUCKIN' LUSH DAY, SUR WUZ'RE BUNKIN' OFF SCHOOL T' HANG ROOND THE GEET ESCALATORS IN THE SHOPPIN' CENTER
...ARE Y' COMIN'?
AM AH FUCK. AH'M GANNIN' TO SCHOOL
EH?!
ARE YE A FUCKIN' HIPPY?
NA. IT'S FRIDAY.
SCHOOLS FUCKIN' BLISS ON A FRIDAY
EH?! EH?!! WHAAAT?!
AYE MAN. ITS MRS ROSS TODAY. SHE'S FUCKIN' GREAT MAN - ME FAVOURITE TEACHA
...DEAD FUCKIN' SOFT. Y' CAN TELL HER T' FUCK OFF T' HER FACE AND EVERYTHING, AND SHE'LL NOT DE OWT. SPAT IN HER EYE LAST WEEK. FUCKIN' BELTER
SO...
SMASH! CRASH! BANG!
HA HA HAA!
ERM... DO YOU THINK YOU MIGHT, ERM, POSSIBLY, CALM DOWN A TOUCH, PLEASE, NATASHA
MRS ROSS
FUCK OFF Y' BITCH!
GAN ON TASHA! DEE A SHIT DOON HER FRIGGIN' BLOWSE!
SWING!
BOO HOO HOOO!!
UTTER CHAOS
WHERE THE FUCKS SHE GANNIN'? SHE'S AANLY JUST GOT BACK FROM HER LAST NERVEOUS BREKDOON
WHEY SHE MUSTN'T WANT HER FUCKIN' PORSE THEN
GET IN! THATS MY BAIT MONEY
SNATCH!
LET WUH GAN SPEND, THEN
BLISTNA BOB! THERES ABOOT TWO SPOND HERE
EEH! WHAT YER GANNA BUY TASHA?
DINING HALL >
CLASSROOMS <
TOILETS >
AH DIVVINT KNAA. WHATEVER SMELLS THE FUCKIN' NICEST
AND SO...
SNIFF SNIFF SNIFF!
MMM. THAT SMELLS FUCKIN' LUSH - AH KNAA WHAT MY BAIT MONEY'S GANNIN' ON - SLURP!
REGAL KING SIZE TODAY KERRY
HALF ON MAN, DONNA
AYE. TWO SPOND
HOO, Y' DAFTY! THEZ TWENTY LEFT ON THIS STILL!
HERE YE - GIZ A DRAAAW
OOT ME MITT! YEE DUCK ARSE 'EM

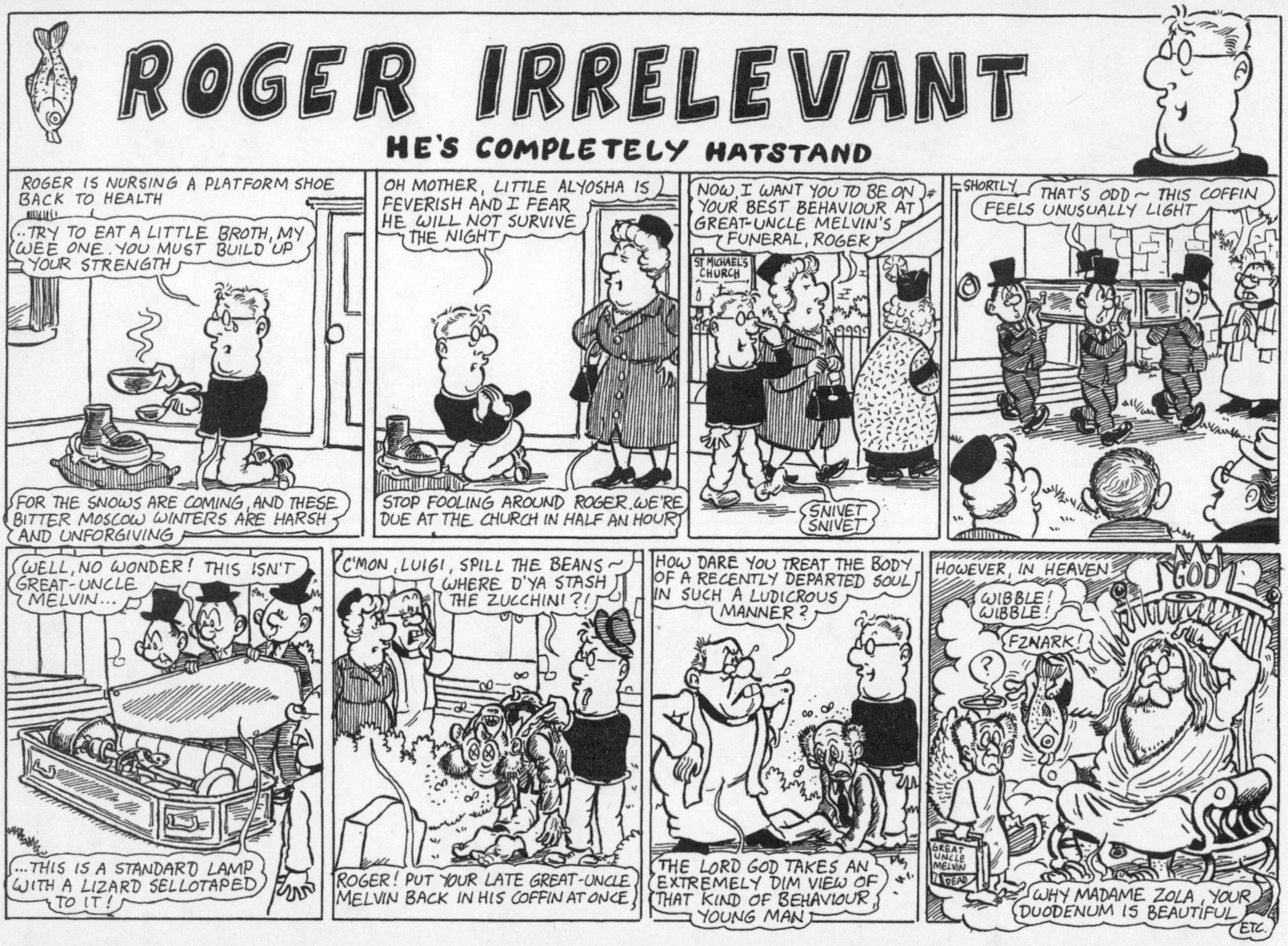
ROGER IRRELEVANT
HE'S COMPLETELY HATSTAND
ROGER IS NURSING A PLATFORM SHOE BACK TO HEALTH
..TRY TO EAT A LITTLE BROTH, MY WEE ONE. YOU MUST BUILD UP YOUR STRENGTH
FOR THE SNOWS ARE COMING, AND THESE BITTER MOSCOW WINTERS ARE HARSH AND UNFORGIVING
OH MOTHER, LITTLE ALYOSHA IS FEVERISH AND I FEAR HE WILL NOT SURVIVE THE NIGHT
STOP FOOLING AROUND ROGER. WE'RE DUE AT THE CHURCH IN HALF AN HOUR
NOW, I WANT YOU TO BE ON YOUR BEST BEHAVIOUR AT GREAT-UNCLE MELVIN'S FUNERAL, ROGER
ST MICHAEL'S CHURCH
SNIVET SNIVET
SHORTLY
THAT'S ODD ~ THIS COFFIN FEELS UNUSUALLY LIGHT
WELL, NO WONDER! THIS ISN'T GREAT-UNCLE MELVIN...
...THIS IS A STANDARD LAMP WITH A LIZARD SELLOTAPED TO IT!
C'MON, LUIGI, SPILL THE BEANS ~ WHERE D'YA STASH THE ZUCCHINI?!
ROGER! PUT YOUR LATE GREAT-UNCLE MELVIN BACK IN HIS COFFIN AT ONCE
HOW DARE YOU TREAT THE BODY OF A RECENTLY DEPARTED SOUL IN SUCH A LUDICROUS MANNER?
THE LORD GOD TAKES AN EXTREMELY DIM VIEW OF THAT KIND OF BEHAVIOUR, YOUNG MAN
HOWEVER, IN HEAVEN
GOD
WIBBLE! WIBBLE!
FZNARK!
?
GREAT UNCLE MELVIN DEAD
WHY MADAME ZOLA, YOUR DUODENUM IS BEAUTIFUL
ETC.

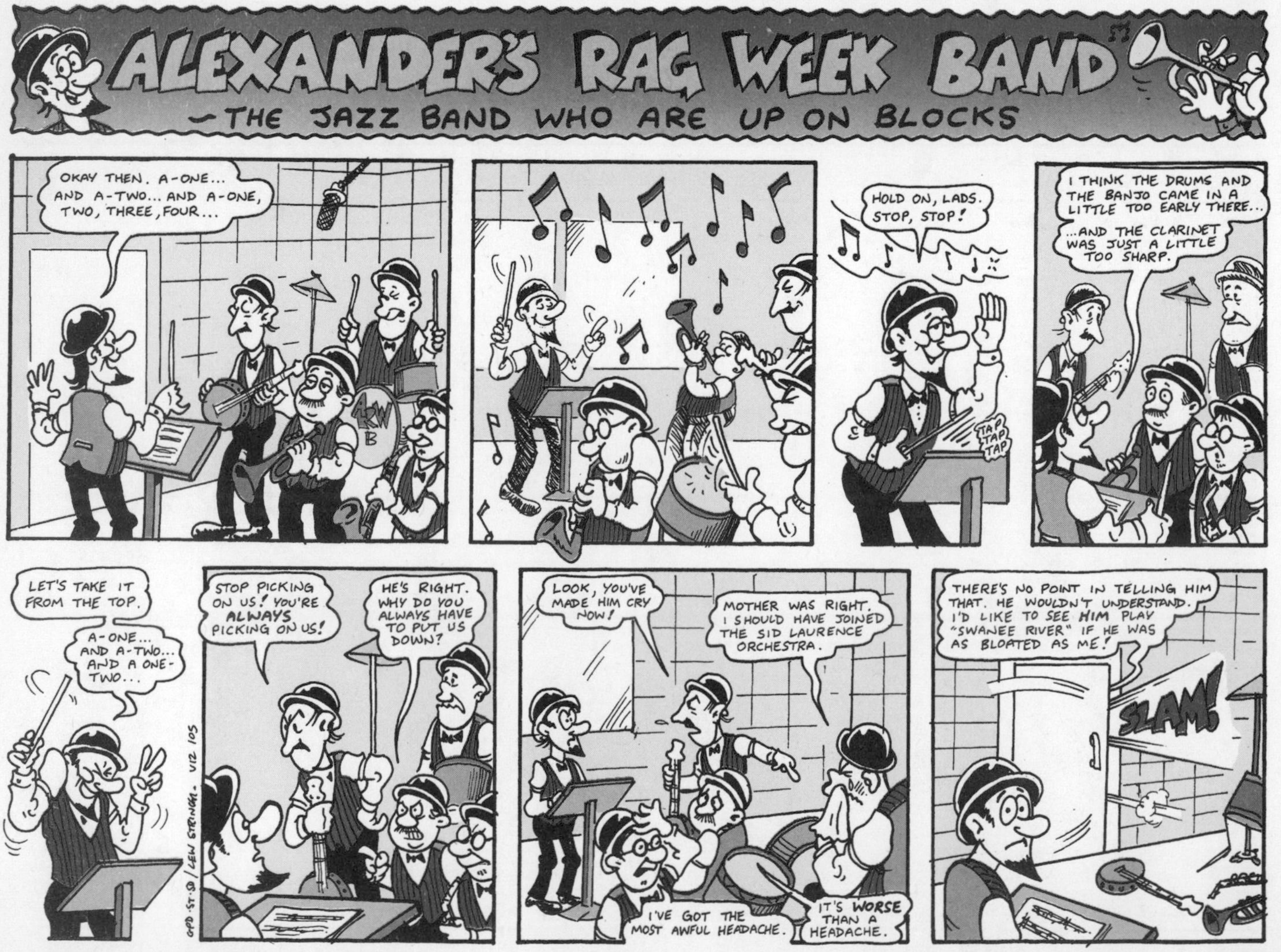
ALEXANDER'S RAG WEEK BAND
~THE JAZZ BAND WHO ARE UP ON BLOCKS
OKAY THEN. A-ONE... AND A-TWO... AND A-ONE, TWO, THREE, FOUR...
HOLD ON, LADS. STOP, STOP!
TAP TAP TAP
I THINK THE DRUMS AND THE BANJO CAME IN A LITTLE TOO EARLY THERE...
...AND THE CLARINET WAS JUST A LITTLE TOO SHARP.
LET'S TAKE IT FROM THE TOP.
A-ONE... AND A-TWO... AND A ONE-TWO...
STOP PICKING ON US! YOU'RE ALWAYS PICKING ON US!
HE'S RIGHT. WHY DO YOU ALWAYS HAVE TO PUT US DOWN?
LOOK, YOU'VE MADE HIM CRY NOW!
MOTHER WAS RIGHT. I SHOULD HAVE JOINED THE SID LAURENCE ORCHESTRA.
I'VE GOT THE MOST AWFUL HEADACHE.
IT'S WORSE THAN A HEADACHE.
THERE'S NO POINT IN TELLING HIM THAT. HE WOULDN'T UNDERSTAND. I'D LIKE TO SEE HIM PLAY "SWANEE RIVER" IF HE WAS AS BLOATED AS ME!
SLAM!

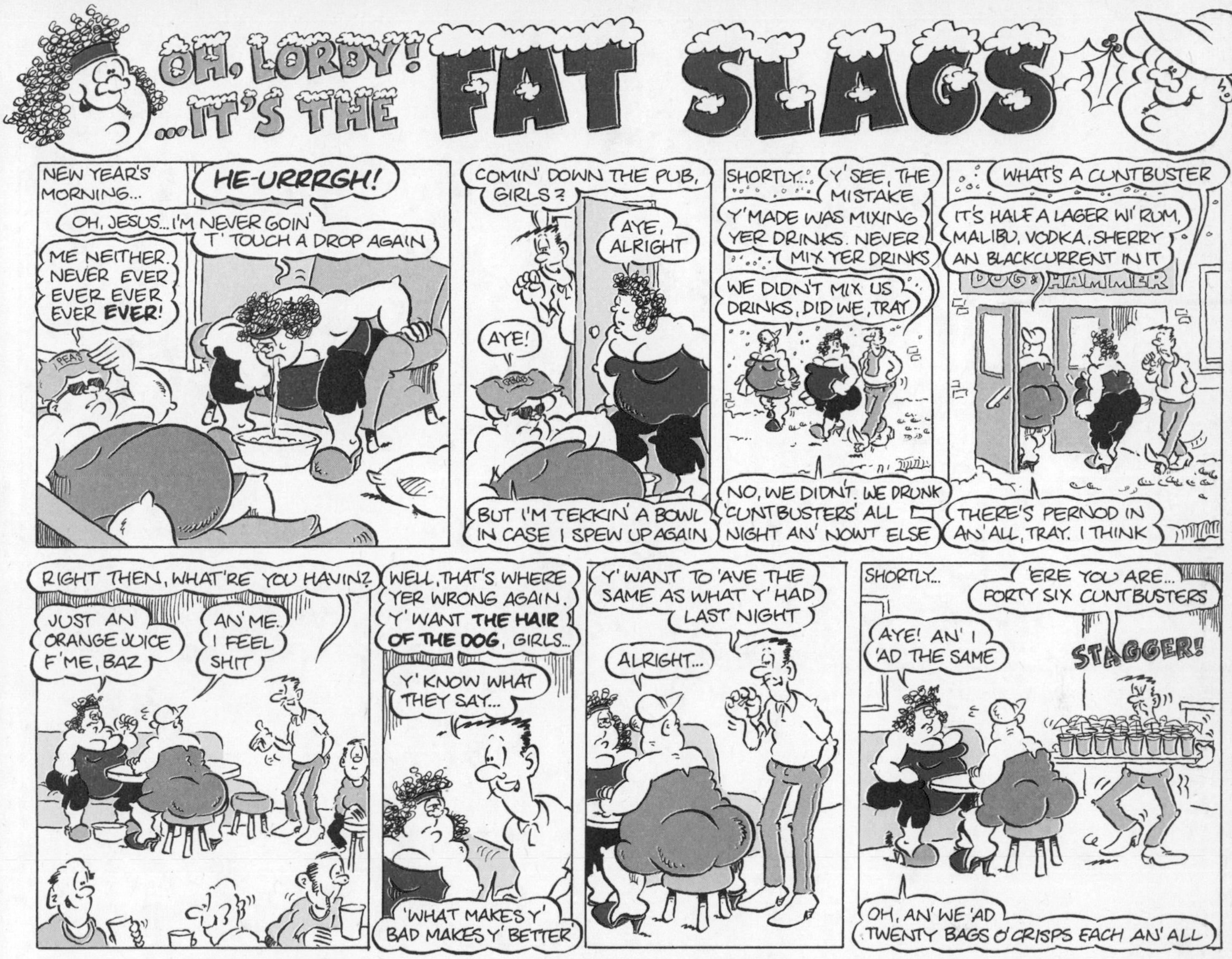
OH, LORDY! ...IT'S THE
FAT SLAGS
NEW YEAR'S MORNING...
HE-URRRGH!
OH, JESUS... I'M NEVER GOIN' T' TOUCH A DROP AGAIN
ME NEITHER. NEVER EVER EVER EVER EVER **EVER**!
COMIN' DOWN THE PUB, GIRLS?
AYE, ALRIGHT
AYE!
BUT I'M TEKKIN' A BOWL IN CASE I SPEW UP AGAIN
SHORTLY...
Y' SEE, THE MISTAKE Y'MADE WAS MIXING YER DRINKS. NEVER MIX YER DRINKS
WE DIDN'T MIX US DRINKS, DID WE, TRAY
NO, WE DIDN'T. WE DRUNK 'CUNTBUSTERS' ALL NIGHT AN' NOWT ELSE
WHAT'S A CUNTBUSTER
IT'S HALF A LAGER WI' RUM, MALIBU, VODKA, SHERRY AN BLACKCURRENT IN IT
DOG & HAMMER
THERE'S PERNOD IN AN' ALL, TRAY. I THINK
RIGHT THEN, WHAT'RE YOU HAVIN?
JUST AN ORANGE JUICE F'ME, BAZ
AN' ME. I FEEL SHIT
WELL, THAT'S WHERE YER WRONG AGAIN. Y' WANT **THE HAIR OF THE DOG**, GIRLS...
Y' KNOW WHAT THEY SAY...
'WHAT MAKES Y' BAD MAKES Y' BETTER'
Y' WANT TO 'AVE THE SAME AS WHAT Y' HAD LAST NIGHT
ALRIGHT...
SHORTLY...
'ERE YOU ARE... FORTY SIX CUNTBUSTERS
AYE! AN' I 'AD THE SAME
STAGGER!
OH, AN' WE 'AD TWENTY BAGS O' CRISPS EACH AN' ALL

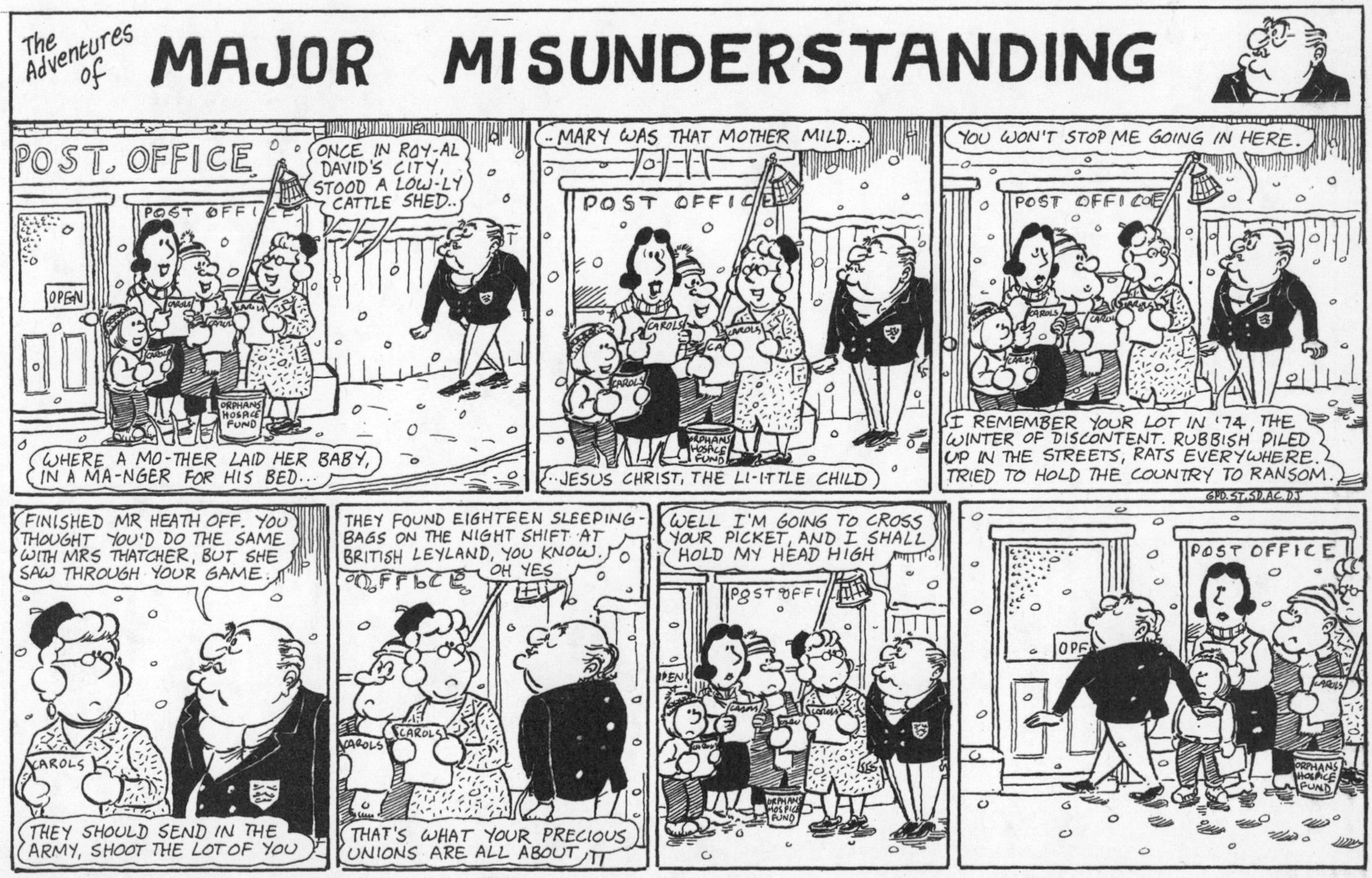
The Adventures of
MAJOR MISUNDERSTANDING
POST OFFICE
ONCE IN ROY-AL DAVID'S CITY, STOOD A LOW-LY CATTLE SHED..
OPEN
ORPHANS HOSPICE FUND
WHERE A MO-THER LAID HER BABY, IN A MA-NGER FOR HIS BED...
..MARY WAS THAT MOTHER MILD...
POST OFFICE
..JESUS CHRIST, THE LI-ITTLE CHILD
SHORTLY...
YOU WON'T STOP ME GOING IN HERE.
I REMEMBER YOUR LOT IN '74, THE WINTER OF DISCONTENT. RUBBISH PILED UP IN THE STREETS, RATS EVERYWHERE. TRIED TO HOLD THE COUNTRY TO RANSOM.
GPD.ST.SD.AC.DJ
FINISHED MR HEATH OFF. YOU THOUGHT YOU'D DO THE SAME WITH MRS THATCHER, BUT SHE SAW THROUGH YOUR GAME.
THEY SHOULD SEND IN THE ARMY, SHOOT THE LOT OF YOU
THEY FOUND EIGHTEEN SLEEPING-BAGS ON THE NIGHT SHIFT AT BRITISH LEYLAND, YOU KNOW.
OH YES
THAT'S WHAT YOUR PRECIOUS UNIONS ARE ALL ABOUT
WELL I'M GOING TO CROSS YOUR PICKET, AND I SHALL HOLD MY HEAD HIGH
POST OFFICE

Sid the Sexist's

FRIDAY NIGHT FLYERS

50% off
a fucking good kicking off ANY bouncer

TO THE BEARER - This voucher entitles the bearer to 50% off any fucking good kicking off a bouncer. example - half your teeth not kicked out or 50% of your head not kicked in. Please present this voucher to the bouncer before he commences starting on you.

TO THE BOUNCER - Please attempt to harness your rage by 50% when using 'minimum force to restrain' the bearer of this voucher.

Excludes bouncers pumped up to their tits on 'Test'. Individual door security officers reserve the right to get the red mist and go fucking crazy, in which case the voucher becomes void. Valid only for kicking on the pavement outside the nightclub by professional door security officer. Not valid in back alley paggas or free-for-alls.

Valid until 31-12-99

HONESTY HOUR
£1 off
ALL short change in ANY bar 10.30-11.30pm

Voucher to be presented along with payment. £1 will be added to your short change, providing this does not take your change up to the correct amount.Please check your short change before leaving the bar, as shorter change cannot be rectified later.

Certificate of Shoe Non-Casualness

Valid at any nightclub or bar where dress restrictions apply

To the bearer
Please present this certificate to the door staff on attempted entry to the nightclub.

To the Doorman
The bearer of this voucher's shoes are not casual, but genuine Italian fashion shoes. Allow entry, providing all other dress restrictions are met.

Casualness applies to shoes of the voucher holder only. Voucher is not transferable to another party and does not cover jackets or shirts.

Valid for ONE visit to Nightclub or bar up to 31/12/99

NORTHUMBERLAND POLICE

Northumberland Police
"Happy Hour"

1 ARREST-FREE PISS in any shop doorway in Newcastle City Centre between 11.30 pm & 12.30 am

To the arresting officer.
Howay, man. The bearer of this flyer has done fuck 'aall. Friggin' leave 'im alairn. What's he ever done t'yee, eh? Y' think y' rock cos y' wear that friggin' hat.

Valid on arrests for urinating in a public place on Fridays & Saturdays until 31.12.99

2 FOR 1
Pavement Pizza offer!

Throw up any 12" deep pan stripey laugh on the pavement...

...have a 7" thin crust concrete stainer two staggers further on.

TITS OOT!

THIS VOUCHER ENTITLES THE BEARER TO

1 FREE EYEFUL!

This voucher may be exchanged for a *single flash* of any participating bird's tits.

TO REDEEM YOUR KNOCKER GOZ, HAND THIS VOUCHER TO A YOUNG LADY WHO MAY IN RETURN EXPOSE HER BREASTS FOR APPROXIMATELY ONE EIGHTH OF A SECOND. ONLY ONE FLASH PER GROUP OF GAWPING MEN. VALID BETWEEN 7 AND 11 PINTS ONLY. OFFER CLOSES 31-12-99

Women not participating in the 'Free Eyeful' scheme reserve the right to kick you in the nuts on presentation of this voucher

Casualty QUEUEBUSTER!

H

STRAIGHT TO THE ***FRONT OF THE QUEUE*** *IN ANY PARTICIPATING ACCIDENT & EMERGENCY DEPARTMENT AFTER 2.00 AM. WITH THIS VOUCHER.*

To the nurse in charge. Please allow this haemorrhaging, incoherent, vomiting drunk who's just had a fight with a window to be treated before all the other haemorrhaging, incoherent vomiting drunks. Not to be used in conjunction with any other offer.

On your marks... get set... GO!!

30 SECONDS START on ANY taxi runner!

with this voucher

To the bearer - Present this voucher to the taxi driver before jumping out at lights near your house and running like bloody fuck. **To the driver** - Please allow the bearer of this voucher a 30-second head start, before levering your fat arse from behind the wheel and giving a lumbering, 20 yard pursuit, gasping for breath and bellowing obscenities.

TAXI

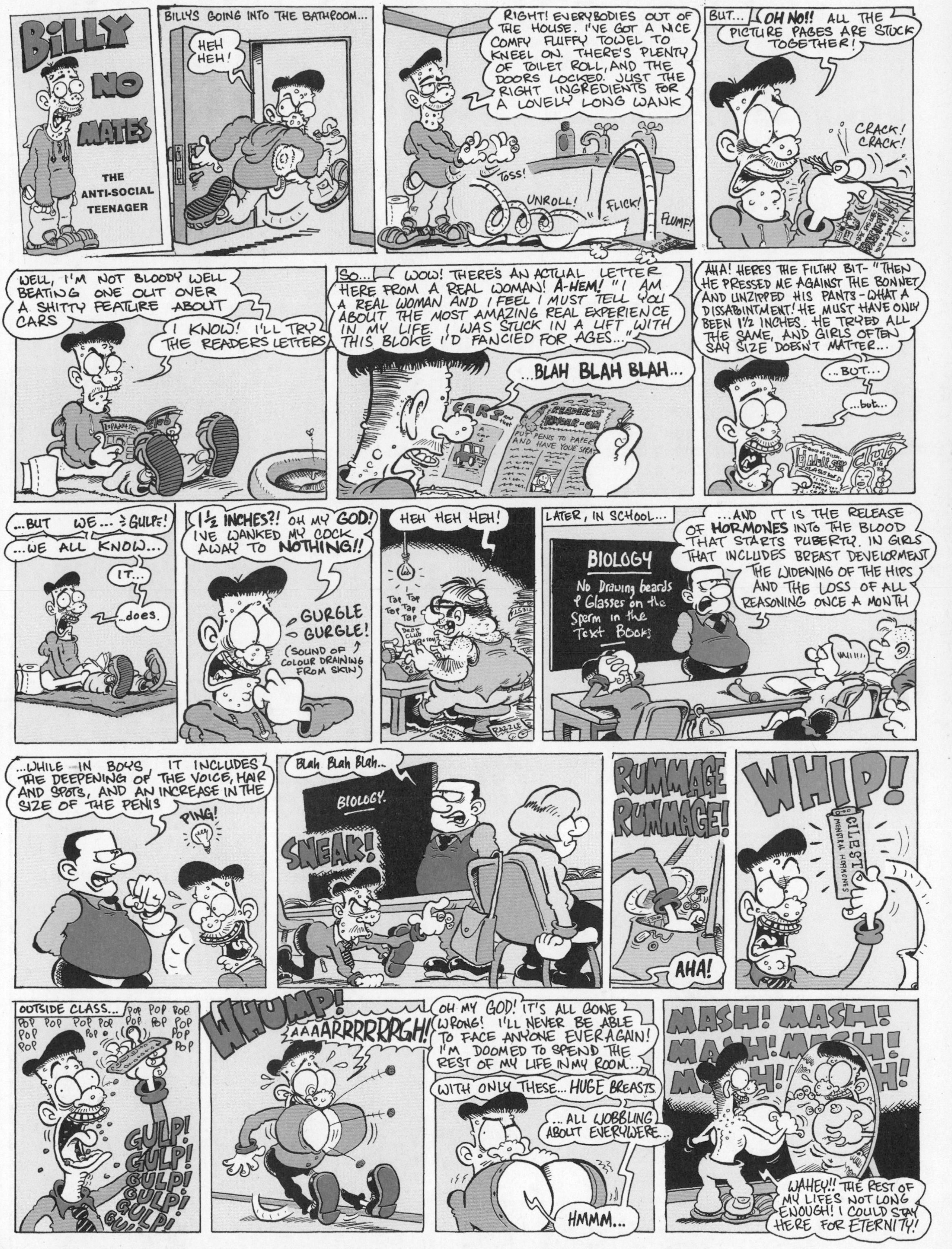
BILLY NO MATES
THE ANTI-SOCIAL TEENAGER
BILLYS GOING INTO THE BATHROOM...
HEH HEH!
RIGHT! EVERYBODIES OUT OF THE HOUSE. I'VE GOT A NICE COMFY FLUFFY TOWEL TO KNEEL ON. THERE'S PLENTY OF TOILET ROLL, AND THE DOORS LOCKED. JUST THE RIGHT INGREDIENTS FOR A LOVELY LONG WANK
TOSS!
UNROLL!
FLICK!
FLUMP!
BUT...
OH NO!! ALL THE PICTURE PAGES ARE STUCK TOGETHER!
CRACK! CRACK!
WELL, I'M NOT BLOODY WELL BEATING ONE OUT OVER A SHITTY FEATURE ABOUT CARS
I KNOW! I'LL TRY THE READERS LETTERS
SO...
WOW! THERE'S AN ACTUAL LETTER HERE FROM A REAL WOMAN! A-HEM! "I AM A REAL WOMAN AND I FEEL I MUST TELL YOU ABOUT THE MOST AMAZING REAL EXPERIENCE IN MY LIFE. I WAS STUCK IN A LIFT WITH THIS BLOKE I'D FANCIED FOR AGES..."
...BLAH BLAH BLAH...
CARS
READER'S WRIT-UM
PUT PENIS TO PAPER AND HAVE YOUR SAY
AHA! HERES THE FILTHY BIT- "THEN HE PRESSED ME AGAINST THE BONNET AND UNZIPPED HIS PANTS - WHAT A DISSAPOINTMENT! HE MUST HAVE ONLY BEEN 1½ INCHES. HE TRYED ALL THE SAME, AND GIRLS OFTEN SAY SIZE DOESN'T MATTER...
...BUT...
...but...
club
...BUT WE... GULP!
...WE ALL KNOW...
IT...
...does.
1½ INCHES?! OH MY GOD! I'VE WANKED MY COCK AWAY TO NOTHING!!
GURGLE GURGLE!
(SOUND OF COLOUR DRAINING FROM SKIN)
HEH HEH HEH!
Tap Tap Tap Tap Tap
RAZZLE
LATER, IN SCHOOL...
BIOLOGY
No Drawing beards & Glasses on the Sperm in the Text Books
...AND IT IS THE RELEASE OF HORMONES INTO THE BLOOD THAT STARTS PUBERTY. IN GIRLS THAT INCLUDES BREAST DEVELOPMENT THE WIDENING OF THE HIPS AND THE LOSS OF ALL REASONING ONCE A MONTH
...WHILE IN BOYS, IT INCLUDES THE DEEPENING OF THE VOICE, HAIR AND SPOTS, AND AN INCREASE IN THE SIZE OF THE PENIS
PING!
Blah Blah Blah...
BIOLOGY
SNEAK!
RUMMAGE RUMMAGE!
AHA!
WHIP!
GILEST MENSTRAL HORMONES
OUTSIDE CLASS...
POP POP POP POP POP POP POP POP POP POP POP POP POP POP POP
GULP! GULP! GULP! GULP! GULP!
WHUMP!
AAAARRRRRGH!
OH MY GOD! IT'S ALL GONE WRONG! I'LL NEVER BE ABLE TO FACE ANYONE EVER AGAIN! I'M DOOMED TO SPEND THE REST OF MY LIFE IN MY ROOM...
WITH ONLY THESE... HUGE BREASTS
...ALL WOBBLING ABOUT EVERYWHERE...
HMMM...
MASH! MASH! MASH! MASH! MASH! MASH!
WAHEY!! THE REST OF MY LIFES NOT LONG ENOUGH! I COULD STAY HERE FOR ETERNITY!

Are YOUR employees going for a shit in YOUR time at YOUR expense...?

WIPE THE SMILE OFF THEIR FAECES

swarf
flint chippings
woodchips
fibre glass

with BADGER'S ARSE™

Industrial Toilet Tissue

BADGER'S
ARSE
Industrial
Toilet Tissue
With added
Woodchip
swarf,
glass fibre &
flint shards.
IF IT'S NOT ROUGH,
IT'S NOT BADGER'S ARSE

FOUR THOUSAND MILLION BILLION man-hours are lost in Britain each year due to employees enjoying a shit in work's time. You can't stop them, but you *can* make life uncomfortable. Badger's Arse is the only toilet tissue made from recycled sand paper, with added wood chippings, glass fibre and swarf. It's like wiping your nick on a cheese grater. Results show that when BADGER'S ARSE is introduced into workplace toilets, visits for number 2's go DOWN and productivity goes UP.

Put it in YOUR works bogs, and they'll wait till they get home

Only BADGER'S ARSE™ is as rough as a badger's arse.

Studio recorded in the buff!
Kenny Bollock
& his
Jizz Men
Altogether now!
20
NUDE
JAZZ
GREATS

WARNING! Beware of other 'soft' recordings where the musicians simulate nakedness, often wearing FLESHINGS! These guys were REALLY IN THE RIK!

NOW THAT'S WHAT I CALL NUDE JAZZ!

20 All-time Trad Jazz Favourites recorded

STARK BOLLOCK NAKED!

Alexander's Ragtime Band
St. Louis Blues ● Hold that tiger!
Jeepers! Creepers! ● Is you is or is you ain't my baby? ● Bad Penny Blues ● Swanee River
...and many more!

HK HOT KARLOPHONE
in conjunction with
ESD

The Home of NAKED JAZZ since 1920

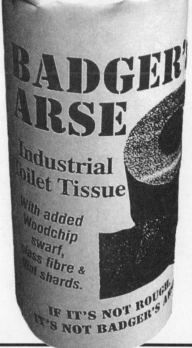

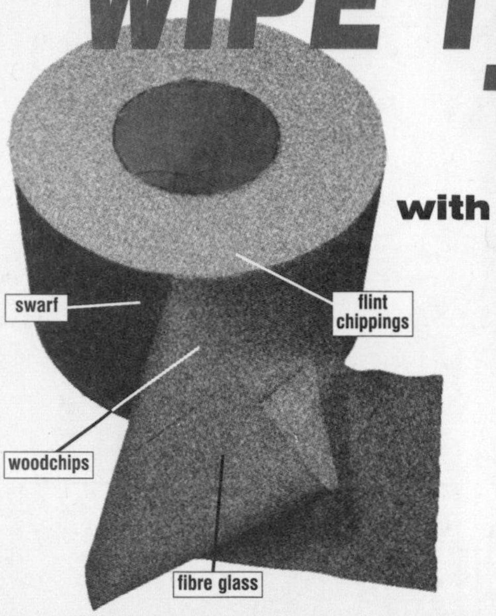

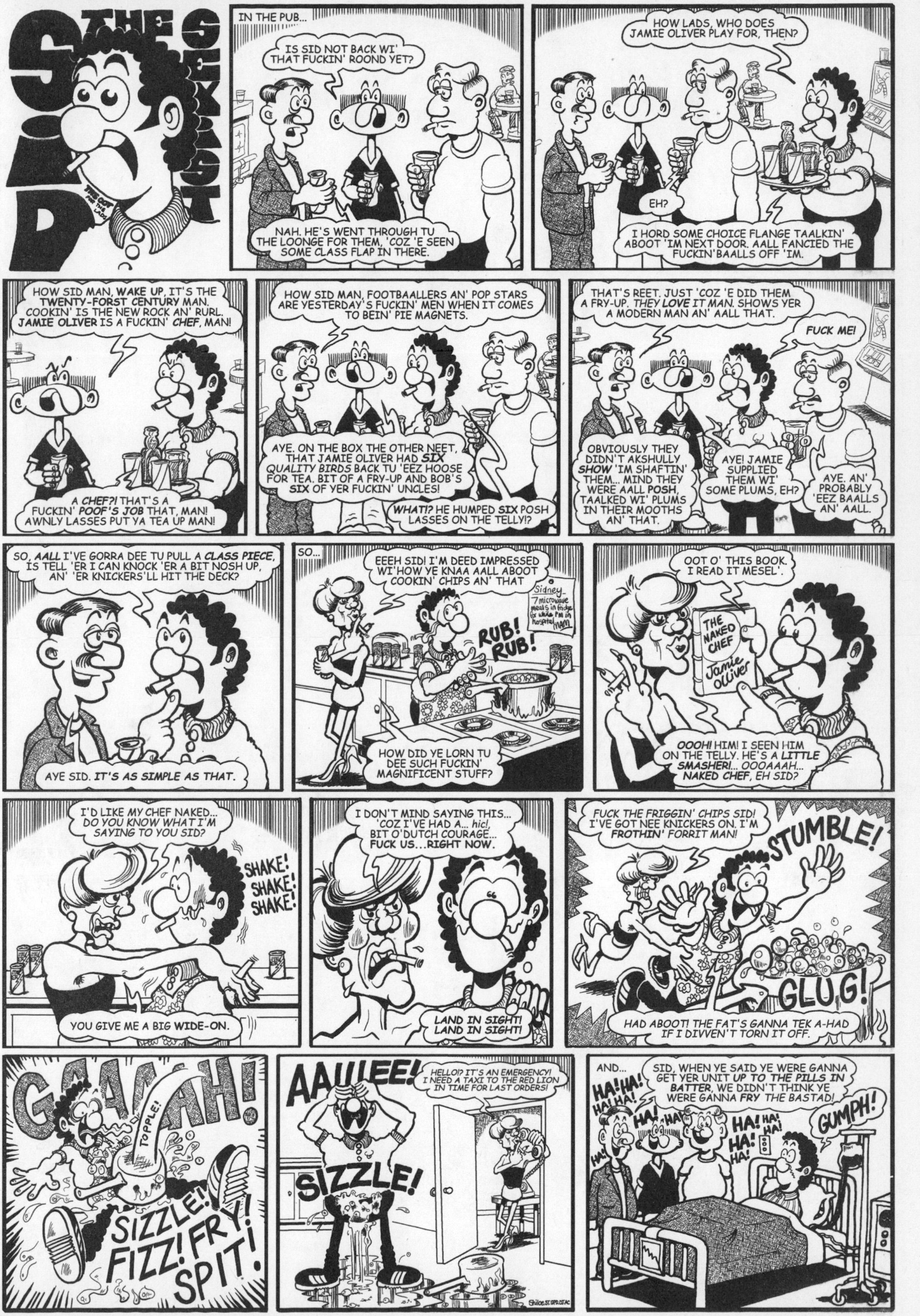
SID THE SEXIST
IN THE PUB...
IS SID NOT BACK WI' THAT FUCKIN' ROOND YET?
NAH. HE'S WENT THROUGH TU THE LOONGE FOR THEM, 'COZ 'E SEEN SOME CLASS FLAP IN THERE.
HOW LADS, WHO DOES JAMIE OLIVER PLAY FOR, THEN?
EH?
I HORD SOME CHOICE FLANGE TAALKIN' ABOOT 'IM NEXT DOOR. AALL FANCIED THE FUCKIN'BAALLS OFF 'IM.
HOW SID MAN, WAKE UP, IT'S THE TWENTY-FORST CENTURY MAN. COOKIN' IS THE NEW ROCK AN' RURL. JAMIE OLIVER IS A FUCKIN' CHEF, MAN!
A CHEF?! THAT'S A FUCKIN' POOF'S JOB THAT, MAN! AWNLY LASSES PUT YA TEA UP MAN!
HOW SID MAN, FOOTBAALLERS AN' POP STARS ARE YESTERDAY'S FUCKIN' MEN WHEN IT COMES TO BEIN' PIE MAGNETS.
AYE. ON THE BOX THE OTHER NEET, THAT JAMIE OLIVER HAD SIX QUALITY BIRDS BACK TU 'EEZ HOOSE FOR TEA. BIT OF A FRY-UP AND BOB'S SIX OF YER FUCKIN' UNCLES!
WHAT!? HE HUMPED SIX POSH LASSES ON THE TELLY!?
THAT'S REET. JUST 'COZ 'E DID THEM A FRY-UP. THEY LOVE IT MAN. SHOWS YER A MODERN MAN AN' AALL THAT.
FUCK ME!
OBVIOUSLY THEY DIDN'T AKSHULLY SHOW 'IM SHAFTIN' THEM... MIND THEY WERE AALL POSH, TAALKED WI' PLUMS IN THEIR MOOTHS AN' THAT.
AYE! JAMIE SUPPLIED THEM WI' SOME PLUMS, EH?
AYE. AN' PROBABLY 'EEZ BAALLS AN' AALL.
SO, AALL I'VE GORRA DEE TU PULL A CLASS PIECE, IS TELL 'ER I CAN KNOCK 'ER A BIT NOSH UP, AN' 'ER KNICKERS'LL HIT THE DECK?
AYE SID. IT'S AS SIMPLE AS THAT.
SO...
EEEH SID! I'M DEED IMPRESSED WI'HOW YE KNAA AALL ABOOT COOKIN' CHIPS AN' THAT
Sidney 7 microwave meals in fridge for while I'm in hospital MAM
RUB! RUB!
HOW DID YE LORN TU DEE SUCH FUCKIN' MAGNIFICENT STUFF?
OOT O' THIS BOOK. I READ IT MESEL'.
THE NAKED CHEF Jamie Oliver
OOOH! HIM! I SEEN HIM ON THE TELLY. HE'S A LITTLE SMASHER!... OOOAAAH... NAKED CHEF, EH SID?
I'D LIKE MY CHEF NAKED... DO YOU KNOW WHAT I'M SAYING TO YOU SID?
SHAKE! SHAKE! SHAKE!
YOU GIVE ME A BIG WIDE-ON.
I DON'T MIND SAYING THIS... 'COZ I'VE HAD A... hic!, BIT O'DUTCH COURAGE... FUCK US...RIGHT NOW.
LAND IN SIGHT! LAND IN SIGHT!
FUCK THE FRIGGIN' CHIPS SID! I'VE GOT NEE KNICKERS ON. I'M FROTHIN' FORRIT MAN!
STUMBLE!
GLUG!
HAD ABOOT! THE FAT'S GANNA TEK A-HAD IF I DIVVEN'T TORN IT OFF.
GAAAAH!
TOPPLE!
SIZZLE! FIZZ! FRY! SPIT!
AAIIEE!
HELLO!? IT'S AN EMERGENCY! I NEED A TAXI TO THE RED LION IN TIME FOR LAST ORDERS!
SIZZLE!
AND...
SID, WHEN YE SAID YE WERE GANNA GET YER UNIT UP TO THE PILLS IN BATTER, WE DIDN'T THINK YE WERE GANNA FRY THE BASTAD!
HA! HA! HA! HA!
HA!
HA! HA!
HA! HA! HA! HA! HA!
GUMPH!

Letterbox

It's the page that's bubbly, breezy & bright,
And upon your carpet has done a big shite

Star Letter

Letterbocks
Viz Comic
PO Box 1PT
Newcastle NE99
1PT

I sent you a letter for your letterbox on 6th June, but I'm afraid I neglected to include my name and address, which is Simon Trutwein from Bradford. Sorry.

S. Trutwein
Bradford

Ladies' darts nights in pubs around the country could be improved by scrapping the usual game of 501, and just going straight for double one, which is where most games finish anyway. The time saved could then be spent drinking more heavily than usual and fighting in the car park.

Neil Hanson
e-mail

Just dessert

As I walked into the kitchen this morning I was horrified to find my elderly mother haemorrhaging from the mouth, coughing up pus into a bowl and screaming uncontrollably. Imagine my relief when I spotted a cherry amongst the sticky mess, and realised she was only eating a trifle, and shrieking with delight.

J.F. Taylor
Bury

E-mail
letters@
letterbocks
.com

Brits oot!

Saucy singers, such as Shania Twain and Britney Spears are all enjoying successful careers at the moment. But the sooner we stop buying their albums, the sooner they'll go broke and be forced to make porn films to pay their bills.

Antony Peterson
New Zealand

I'd like to wake up next to the Queen Mum the day after her 100th birthday, give her a big kiss and order the butler to bring champagne to celebrate a right-royal night of centegenarian bedroom games.

Neal Pearce
Horsham

It seems very unfair that people brand certain dogs as 'dangerous'. These dogs spend less that 1% of their lives mauling children and babies, and yet they are branded as dangerous. 99% of the time they are not savaging anyone. If your car worked 99% of the time you would not call it 'unreliable'. Maybe it's just that I've never been scared of dangerous animals. I was once bitten on the arse by a German Shepherd, but he apologised afterwards and even introduced me to his dog.

Stewart Ferris
Chichester

Woof justice

These days it seems politically incorrect to be in favour of capital punishment. I'm all in favour of the death penalty for murder, but only in cases where they are absolutely sure that the convicted person is guilty. In other cases where there is a bit of doubt, they could be given life imprisonment, and life should mean life.

T. Houston
Southport

Pull the other one

Apparently, sperm banks look for doners who are stable, intelligent and healthy. What would a stable, intelligent, healthy man be doing in a cubicle, wearing a surgical gown having a wank into a test tube? Wankers of the world answer that one if you can, and don't pretend you only do it for the money.

Neil Hanson
e-mail

Have a look at the enclosed Dagenham council newsletter. Has 8 Ace moved down to Cockney Wanker land?

Ray Farlam
Barking

With the increasing number of near-misses and mid-air collisions over our skies, it's high time that the airlines started fitting bumpers to their planes, especially now that some of them allow women 'pilots'.

Stewart Ferris
Chichester

I am fed up with people describing Formula 1 as "the most glamorous sport in the world." Having studied sport the world over, I have to say that a couple of topless Page 3 birds wrestling in a vat of custard is a lot more glamorous.

H. Jego
Kiddrminster

How Phil Jupitus has the nerve to charge £12 a ticket for is show is beyond belief. I have seen him twice now and on both occasions he failed to even make me raise a smile. Once was in WH Smith in King's Cross and the other time he was walking past HMV in Oxford street.

S. Whiting
Greenwich

I'd like to slap the Queen Mum's bum and watch her crinkly arse-cheeks explode with pleasure.

Neal Pearce
Horsham

figure it out

If Carol Vorderman is so clever at maths, when is she going to realise that a size 16 body doesn't go into a size 8 dress?

Nick Pettigrew
e-mail

I think all murderers should be executed without exception. And I'd pull the lever. I've always fancied killing somebody.

Mrs. E. Caldwell
Tunbridge Wells

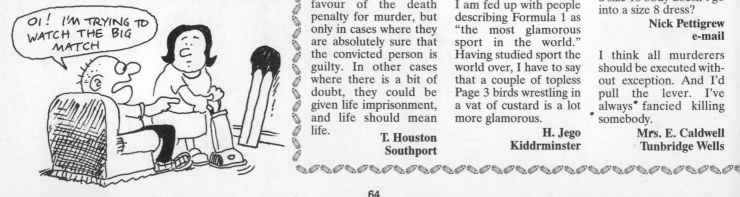

OI! I'M TRYING TO WATCH THE BIG MATCH

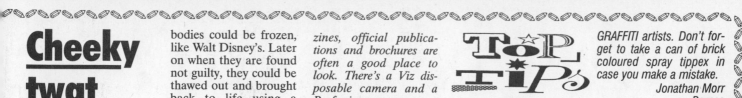

Cheeky twat

Congratulations to the sub-editor of the Esher News and Mail for getting this headline past his bosses.

Cam
Esher

Furry snatch

ANYONE offered a baby ferret should call the police at Esher as they may be part of a group stolen from the Bramble Wood Wildlife Rescue Centre in Cobham.

The furry creatures were snatched from the centre in Common road between 11am and 8pm on Wednesday.

Yes, well done that sub-editor, a Profanisaurus mug stuffed with £20 is on its way to you. Are you the sub-editor of a local rag and think you you can sneak a ruder headline into your paper? Send us the clipping and we'll award £20 for the rudest one we receive.

Too many cooks spoil the broth, so the saying goes. Nonsense. I'm a cannibal and I've just made some soup out of five chefs off a wrecked supertanker and it was delicious.

Chief UmBongo
Skull Island

Keep on trucking

As a truck driver working long hours, I often find myself nodding off at the wheel. However I've found I can relax and keep on driving by simply half closing my eyes and resting my head on a cushion against the window.

J. Manley
Burton on Trent

I read T. Houston's letter (this issue) with interest and came up with a better idea. Anyone found guilty of murder should be hanged and then the bodies could be frozen, like Walt Disney's. Later on when they are found not guilty, they could be thawed out and brought back to life using a future technology which will probably be available by then.

R. Brown
Great Yarmouth

Yours insincerely

I was flicking through a University of Wales magazine the other day and spotted what must surely be the most incincere smile ever captured on camera. A quick glance at the picture, and it's a cheerful grin, but look more closely and the smile drains off his face before your very eyes.

E. Morgan
Aberystwyth

On the same subject, I spotted June Whitfield failing to smile effectively on an advert for funeral insurance. As June says in the advert, "it's a good feeling to know that your life insurance is in order". Wise words, but from the look in her eyes, it's tempting to think that June hasn't been practising what she preaches.

B. Bellamy
Oxford

Keep your eyes peeled for insincere smiles and send them to us. Trade magazines, official publications and brochures are often a good place to look. There's a Viz disposable camera and a Profanisaurus mug or something for each one we print.

I have just read this issue of Viz and was disgusted to find there were no blatant plugs for my restaurant whatsoever.

Lord Latif of Harpole
The Rupali restaurant
Bigg market, Newcastle

Dad to be gay

These people who object to gay men bringing up children, saying they will lack female role models show a staggering level of ignorance. Surely they'll get all the feminine influence they need with both parents skipping around the house in high heeled shoes and dresses.

T. Kavanagh
Wapping

Meat the wife

My local butcher's shop is so clean, you could eat a raw sausage directly out of the butcher's trouser pocket. I know this because I spotted my wife doing it in the back of his shop the other day and she seems to have suffered no ill effects.

Hector Johnson
Bournemouth

Top Tips

AVOID paper cuts by cutting off the sharp edges of paper before handling.

Niamh Shaw
e-mail

HATERS of shirt ironing. If you do the fronts, backs and sleeves first, there are only the collars left to do - and they're a piece of piss.

Geoff Barker
Germany

SECOND rate Scottish female celebrities. When flying from London to Glasgow on a Friday night, always board last and make an awful fuss about the lockers being full, thus ensuring everyone seated will know who you are. Better still, stop fucking around with pots of paint in other people's houses and get a proper job.

Barry Turnbull
e-mail

MEN. Make women think you are a good lover by cutting scratches in your back with a fork before walking shirtless along the beach.

Les Washington
Camberley

GRAFFITI artists. Don't forget to take a can of brick coloured spray tippex in case you make a mistake.

Jonathan Morr
Barnes

SAUSAGE rolls sewn together side by side make an excellent emergency hat for judges.

Super Ape
e-mail

BRALESS feminists. Support your sagging breasts by pretending you have a broken arm and wearing a sling. Simply shorten the sling until your tits reach a socially acceptable level.

S. Ballard
e-mail

GUYS. Save wasted trips to the swimming baths by ringing them up to ask if there is any bikini-clad talent in the pool before you set off.

David Wells
Billericay

VAT Inspectors. When carrying out spot checks on small businesses, refuse all offers of tea or coffee. It is not impossible that the proprietor may have wiped his cheesy knob all around the rim of the mug. I know I always do.

P. Roberts
Holyhead

HATCH INSTANT PESTS!
Pube-Monkeys
INSTANT LICE
PUBE-MONKEYS! SO EASY TO START FROM SCRATCH! DELIVERED DIRECT TO YOUR FRONT DOOR ON A PAIR OF SPECIALLY MOISTENED UNDERPANTS THEY MATURE IN HOURS & LIVE FOR YEARS! ECONOMICAL TO FEED - A COUPLE OF NUTS LAST A LIFETIME!
"I'M ITCHING TO TELL EVERYONE ABOUT THEM!" A.A., Guatemala
"IT'S LIKE HAVING A CIRCUS IN YOUR GROIN!" G.M., Guatemala
"I GOT MINE LAST WEEK AND NOW ALL MY FRIENDS HAVE THEM!" P.M., Guatemala
"SURPRISE YOUR LOVED ONE!" V.C., Guatemala
YET ANOTHER FINE PRODUCT FROM WIGGLIES OF GUATEMALA

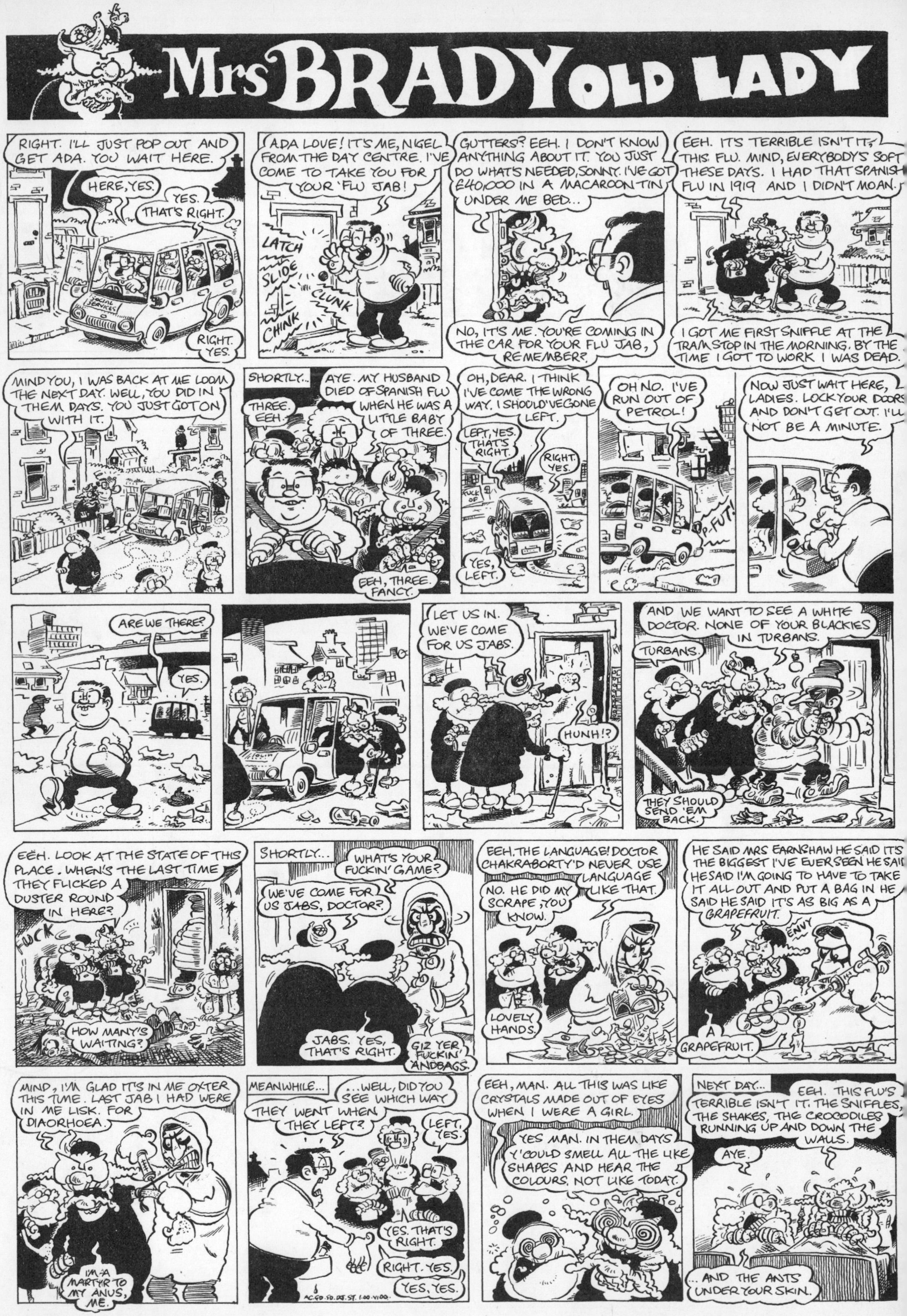
Mrs BRADY OLD LADY
RIGHT. I'LL JUST POP OUT AND GET ADA. YOU WAIT HERE.
HERE, YES.
YES. THAT'S RIGHT.
SOCIAL SERVICES
RIGHT. YES.
ADA LOVE! IT'S ME, NIGEL FROM THE DAY CENTRE. I'VE COME TO TAKE YOU FOR YOUR 'FLU JAB!
LATCH
SLIDE
CLUNK
CHINK
GUTTERS? EEH. I DON'T KNOW ANYTHING ABOUT IT. YOU JUST DO WHAT'S NEEDED, SONNY. I'VE GOT £40,000 IN A MACAROON TIN UNDER ME BED...
NO, IT'S ME. YOU'RE COMING IN THE CAR FOR YOUR FLU JAB, REMEMBER?
EEH. IT'S TERRIBLE ISN'T IT, THIS FLU. MIND, EVERYBODY'S SOFT THESE DAYS. I HAD THAT SPANISH FLU IN 1919 AND I DIDN'T MOAN.
I GOT ME FIRST SNIFFLE AT THE TRAM STOP IN THE MORNING. BY THE TIME I GOT TO WORK I WAS DEAD.
MIND YOU, I WAS BACK AT ME LOOM THE NEXT DAY. WELL, YOU DID IN THEM DAYS. YOU JUST GOT ON WITH IT.
SHORTLY...
AYE. MY HUSBAND DIED OF SPANISH FLU WHEN HE WAS A LITTLE BABY OF THREE.
THREE. EEH.
EEH, THREE. FANCY.
OH, DEAR. I THINK I'VE COME THE WRONG WAY. I SHOULD'VE GONE LEFT.
LEFT, YES. THAT'S RIGHT.
RIGHT. YES.
YES, LEFT.
OH NO. I'VE RUN OUT OF PETROL!
P-FUT!
NOW JUST WAIT HERE, LADIES. LOCK YOUR DOORS AND DON'T GET OUT. I'LL NOT BE A MINUTE.
ARE WE THERE?
YES.
LET US IN. WE'VE COME FOR US JABS.
HUNH!?
AND WE WANT TO SEE A WHITE DOCTOR. NONE OF YOUR BLACKIES IN TURBANS.
TURBANS.
THEY SHOULD SEND 'EM BACK.
EEH. LOOK AT THE STATE OF THIS PLACE. WHEN'S THE LAST TIME THEY FLICKED A DUSTER ROUND IN HERE?
FUCK
HOW MANY'S WAITING?
SHORTLY...
WHAT'S YOUR FUCKIN' GAME?
WE'VE COME FOR US JABS, DOCTOR?
JABS. YES, THAT'S RIGHT.
GIZ YER FUCKIN' 'ANDBAGS.
EEH. THE LANGUAGE! DOCTOR CHAKRABORTY'D NEVER USE LANGUAGE LIKE THAT.
NO. HE DID MY SCRAPE, YOU KNOW.
LOVELY HANDS.
HE SAID MRS EARNSHAW HE SAID IT'S THE BIGGEST I'VE EVER SEEN HE SAID HE SAID I'M GOING TO HAVE TO TAKE IT ALL OUT AND PUT A BAG IN HE SAID HE SAID IT'S AS BIG AS A GRAPEFRUIT.
ENVY
A GRAPEFRUIT.
MIND, I'M GLAD IT'S IN ME OXTER THIS TIME. LAST JAB I HAD WERE IN ME LISK. FOR DIAORHOEA.
I'M A MARTYR TO MY ANUS, ME.
MEANWHILE...
...WELL, DID YOU SEE WHICH WAY THEY WENT WHEN THEY LEFT?
LEFT. YES.
YES. THAT'S RIGHT.
RIGHT. YES.
YES, YES.
EEH, MAN. ALL THIS WAS LIKE CRYSTALS MADE OUT OF EYES WHEN I WERE A GIRL.
YES MAN. IN THEM DAYS Y'COULD SMELL ALL THE LIKE SHAPES AND HEAR THE COLOURS, NOT LIKE TODAY.
NEXT DAY...
EEH. THIS FLU'S TERRIBLE ISN'T IT. THE SNIFFLES, THE SHAKES, THE CROCODILES RUNNING UP AND DOWN THE WALLS.
AYE.
...AND THE ANTS UNDER YOUR SKIN.

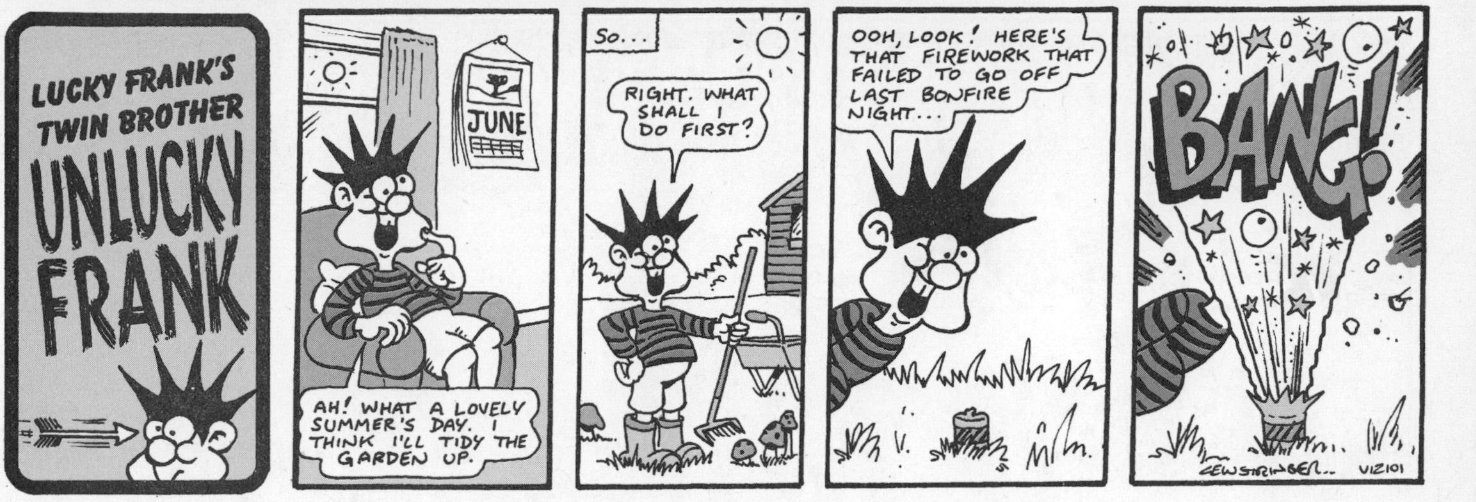

LUCKY FRANK'S TWIN BROTHER
UNLUCKY FRANK
JUNE
AH! WHAT A LOVELY SUMMER'S DAY. I THINK I'LL TIDY THE GARDEN UP.
SO...
RIGHT. WHAT SHALL I DO FIRST?
OOH, LOOK! HERE'S THAT FIREWORK THAT FAILED TO GO OFF LAST BONFIRE NIGHT...
BANG!
LEWSTRINGER.. VIZ101

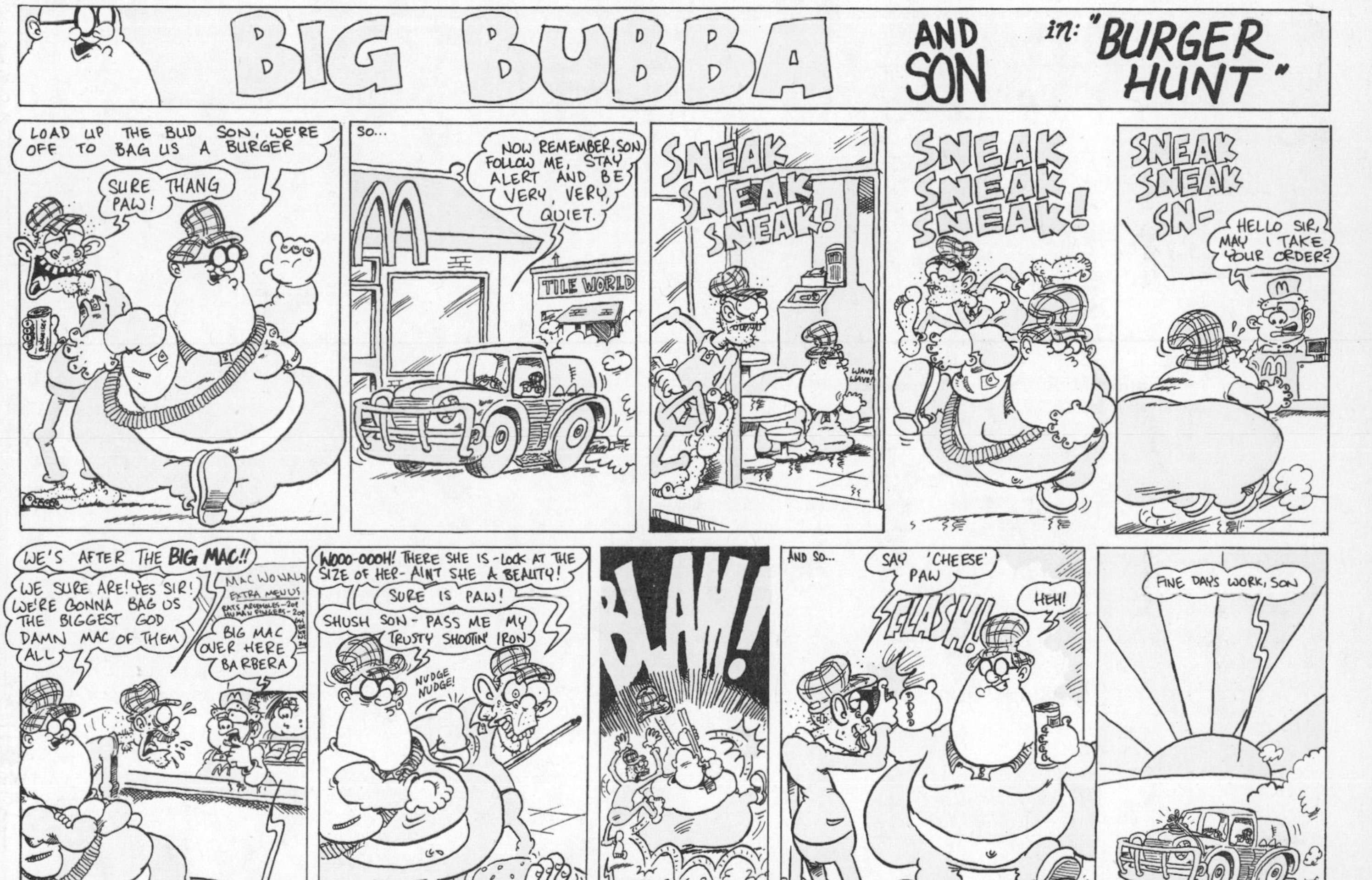

BIG BUBBA AND SON in: "BURGER HUNT"
LOAD UP THE BUD SON, WE'RE OFF TO BAG US A BURGER
SURE THANG PAW!
SO...
NOW REMEMBER, SON. FOLLOW ME, STAY ALERT AND BE VERY, VERY, QUIET.
TILE WORLD
SNEAK SNEAK SNEAK!
SNEAK SNEAK SNEAK!
SNEAK SNEAK SN-
HELLO SIR, MAY I TAKE YOUR ORDER?
WE'S AFTER THE BIG MAC!!
WE SURE ARE! YES SIR! WE'RE GONNA BAG US THE BIGGEST GOD DAMN MAC OF THEM ALL
MAC WONALD
EXTRA MENUS
RATS ARSEHOLES - 20p
HUMAN FINGERS - 20p
BIG MAC OVER HERE BARBERA
AYE
WOOO-OOOH! THERE SHE IS - LOOK AT THE SIZE OF HER - AINT SHE A BEAUTY!
SURE IS PAW!
SHUSH SON - PASS ME MY TRUSTY SHOOTIN' IRON
NUDGE NUDGE!
BLAM!
YEEEAAHHH!! WOOOHOOHOOHOO!! NICE SHOOTIN' PAW! RIGHT BETWEEN THE EYES!
AND SO...
SAY 'CHEESE' PAW
FLASH!
HEH!
FINE DAYS WORK, SON

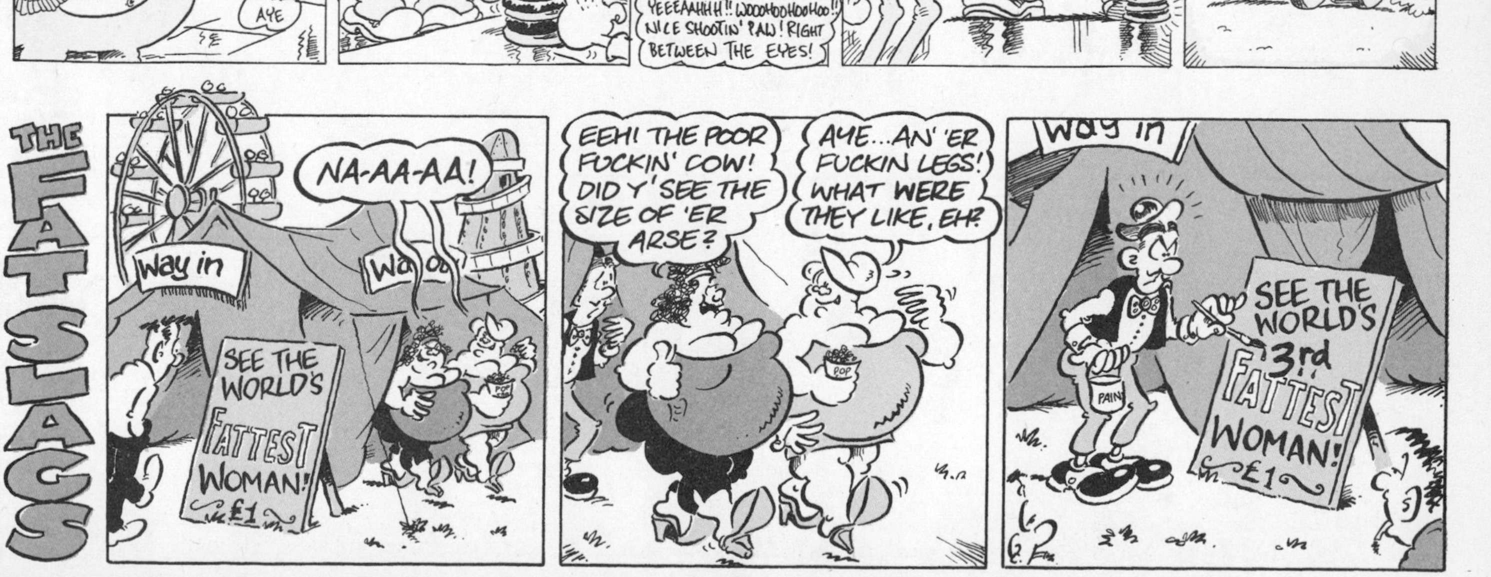

THE FAT SLAGS
NA-AA-AA!
Way in
SEE THE WORLD'S FATTEST WOMAN! £1
EEH! THE POOR FUCKIN' COW! DID Y'SEE THE SIZE OF 'ER ARSE?
AYE... AN' 'ER FUCKIN LEGS! WHAT WERE THEY LIKE, EH?
POP
Way in
SEE THE WORLD'S 3rd FATTEST WOMAN! £1
PAINT

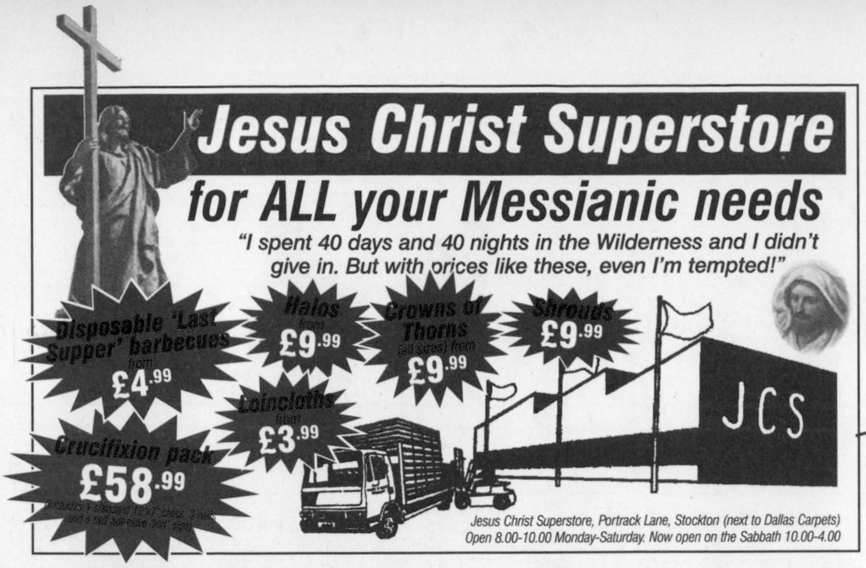

Jesus Christ Superstore
for ALL your Messianic needs
"I spent 40 days and 40 nights in the Wilderness and I didn't give in. But with orices like these, even I'm tempted!"
Disposable 'Last Supper' barbecues from £4.99
Halos from £9.99
Crowns of Thorns (all sizes) from £9.99
Shrouds £9.99
Loincloths from £3.99
Crucifixion pack £58.99
JCS
Jesus Christ Superstore, Portrack Lane, Stockton (next to Dallas Carpets)
Open 8.00-10.00 Monday-Saturday. Now open on the Sabbath 10.00-4.00

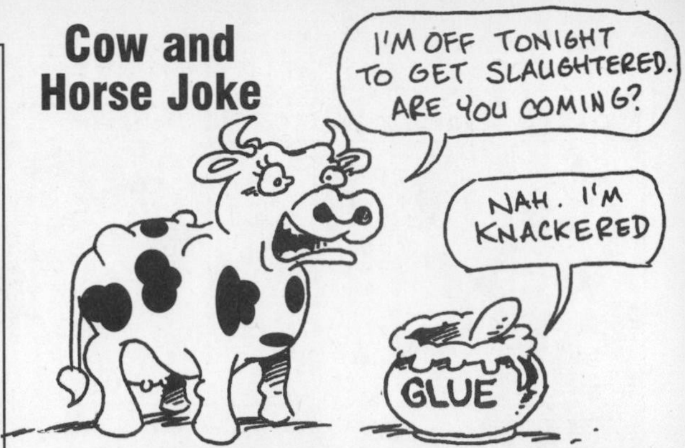

Cow and Horse Joke
I'M OFF TONIGHT TO GET SLAUGHTERED. ARE YOU COMING?
NAH. I'M KNACKERED
GLUE

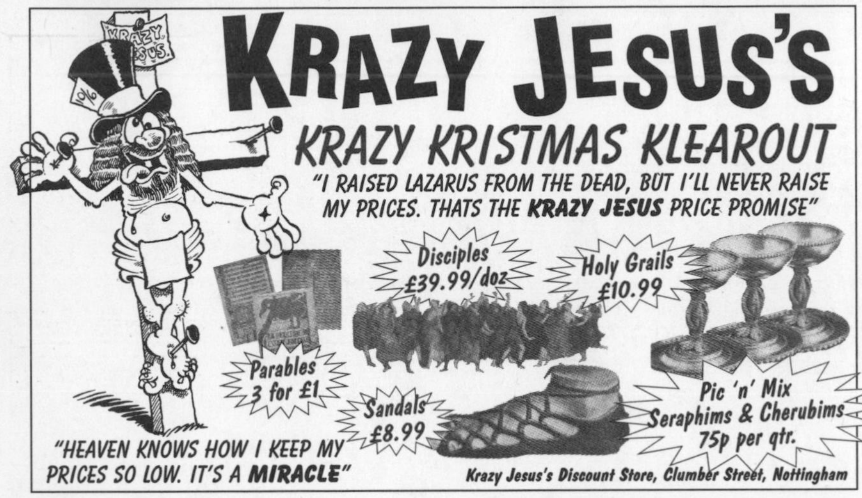

KRAZY JESUS'S
KRAZY KRISTMAS KLEAROUT
"I RAISED LAZARUS FROM THE DEAD, BUT I'LL NEVER RAISE MY PRICES. THATS THE KRAZY JESUS PRICE PROMISE"
Disciples £39.99/doz
Holy Grails £10.99
Parables 3 for £1
Sandals £8.99
Pic 'n' Mix Seraphims & Cherubims 75p per qtr.
"HEAVEN KNOWS HOW I KEEP MY PRICES SO LOW. IT'S A MIRACLE"
Krazy Jesus's Discount Store, Clumber Street, Nottingham

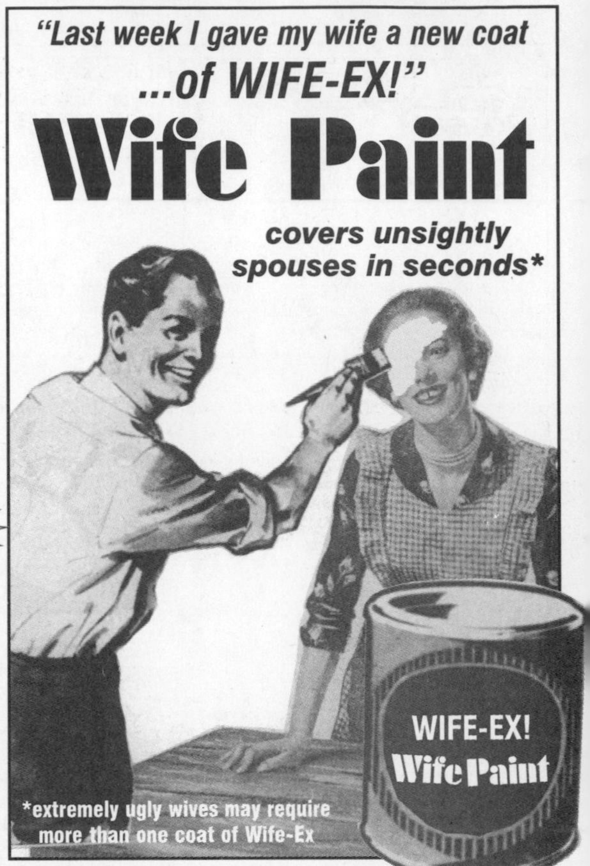

"Last week I gave my wife a new coat ...of WIFE-EX!"
Wife Paint
covers unsightly spouses in seconds*
WIFE-EX!
Wife Paint
*extremely ugly wives may require more than one coat of Wife-Ex

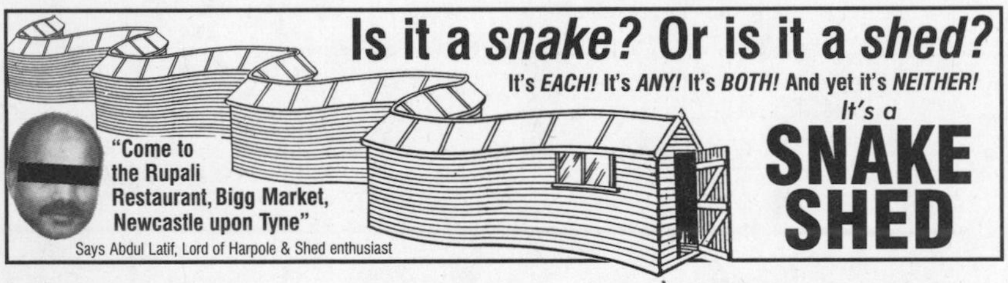

Is it a snake? Or is it a shed?
It's EACH! It's ANY! It's BOTH! And yet it's NEITHER!
It's a SNAKE SHED
"Come to the Rupali Restaurant, Bigg Market, Newcastle upon Tyne"
Says Abdul Latif, Lord of Harpole & Shed enthusiast

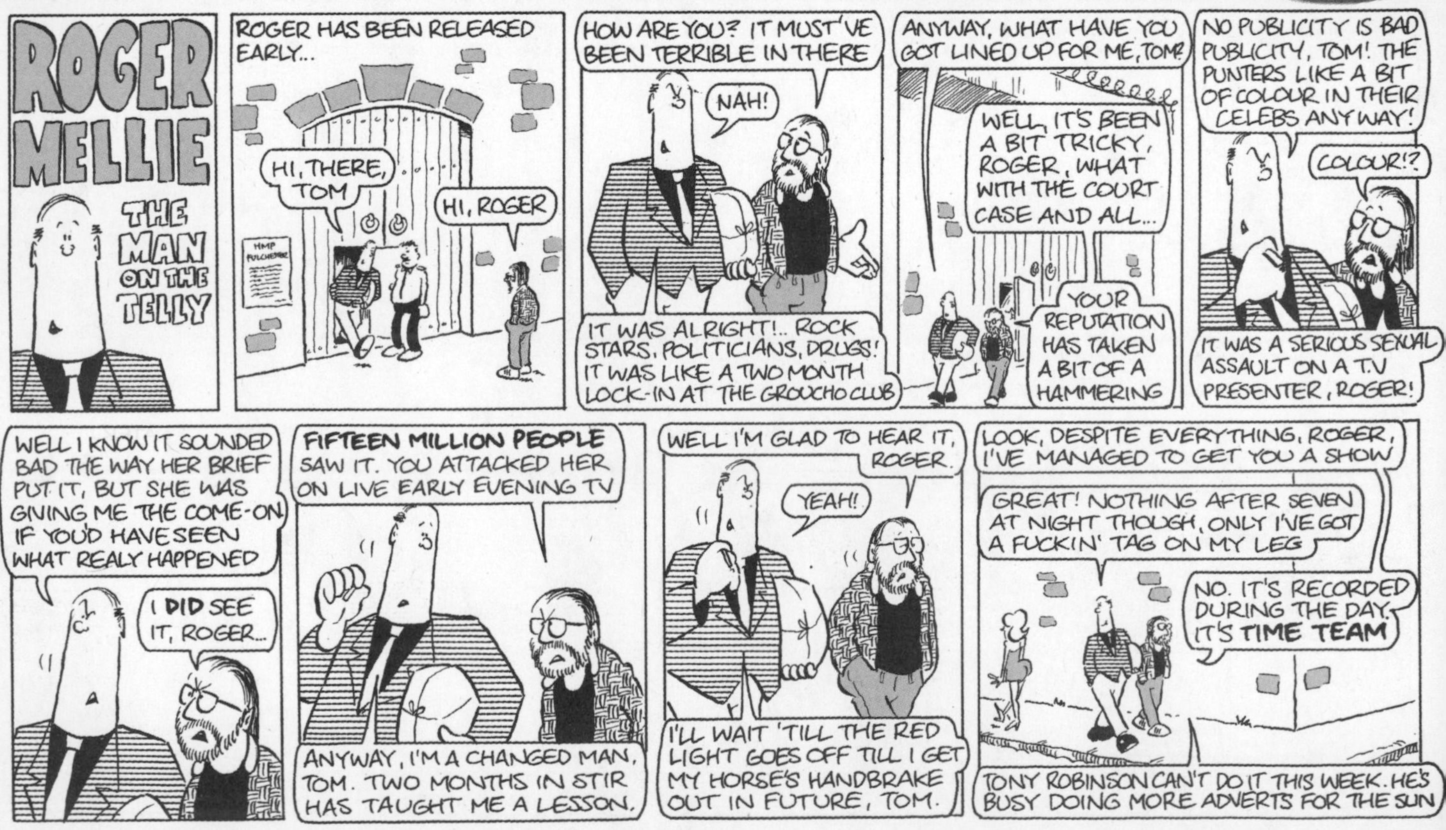

ROGER MELLIE THE MAN ON THE TELLY
ROGER HAS BEEN RELEASED EARLY...
HI, THERE, TOM
HI, ROGER
HOW ARE YOU? IT MUST'VE BEEN TERRIBLE IN THERE
NAH!
IT WAS ALRIGHT!.. ROCK STARS, POLITICIANS, DRUGS! IT WAS LIKE A TWO MONTH LOCK-IN AT THE GROUCHO CLUB
ANYWAY, WHAT HAVE YOU GOT LINED UP FOR ME, TOM?
WELL, IT'S BEEN A BIT TRICKY, ROGER, WHAT WITH THE COURT CASE AND ALL...
YOUR REPUTATION HAS TAKEN A BIT OF A HAMMERING
NO PUBLICITY IS BAD PUBLICITY, TOM! THE PUNTERS LIKE A BIT OF COLOUR IN THEIR CELEBS ANY WAY!
COLOUR!?
IT WAS A SERIOUS SEXUAL ASSAULT ON A T.V PRESENTER, ROGER!
WELL I KNOW IT SOUNDED BAD THE WAY HER BRIEF PUT IT, BUT SHE WAS GIVING ME THE COME-ON IF YOU'D HAVE SEEN WHAT REALY HAPPENED
I DID SEE IT, ROGER...
FIFTEEN MILLION PEOPLE SAW IT. YOU ATTACKED HER ON LIVE EARLY EVENING TV
ANYWAY, I'M A CHANGED MAN, TOM. TWO MONTHS IN STIR HAS TAUGHT ME A LESSON.
WELL I'M GLAD TO HEAR IT, ROGER.
YEAH!
I'LL WAIT 'TILL THE RED LIGHT GOES OFF TILL I GET MY HORSE'S HANDBRAKE OUT IN FUTURE, TOM.
LOOK, DESPITE EVERYTHING, ROGER, I'VE MANAGED TO GET YOU A SHOW
GREAT! NOTHING AFTER SEVEN AT NIGHT THOUGH, ONLY I'VE GOT A FUCKIN' TAG ON MY LEG
NO. IT'S RECORDED DURING THE DAY. IT'S TIME TEAM
TONY ROBINSON CAN'T DO IT THIS WEEK. HE'S BUSY DOING MORE ADVERTS FOR THE SUN

TIME TEAM, EH!? I LIKE IT. THAT ARCHAEOLOGY STUFF IS THE NEW ROCK & ROLL. WHEN DO WE START?

TOMORROW! THE TEAM HAVE JUST 3 DAYS TO UNCOVER A ROMAN VILLA

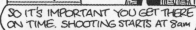
SO IT'S IMPORTANT YOU GET THERE ON TIME. SHOOTING STARTS AT 8AM

NEXT DAY, 2PM

WHERE THE **HELL** IS ROGER? HE SHOULD HAVE BEEN HERE SIX HOURS AGO

SUDDENLY

SORRY I'M LATE, TOM. I WAS OUT CELEBRATING LAST NIGHT AND I GOT ABSOLUTELY...

HANG ON!.. I'VE GOT ANOTHER BLEEP!

EH!?

NO ROGER!!

HRNGH!

SPANG!

FOR GOD'S SAKE... THIS IS A SYSTEMATIC SCIENTIFIC SURVEY. EVERYTHING HAS TO BE METICULOUSLY MEASURED, PLOTTED AND PHOTOGRAPHED

ALRIGHT! NO HARM DONE. IT'S ONLY A TIN HAT. NOT WORTH FUCK ALL

LISTEN, TOM. HOW ARE WE GOING TO SPLIT THE TREASURE? I DON'T TRUST HIM FOR A START. WE CAN CUT HIM OUT...

IF HE TURNS NASTY, THE PAIR OF US COULD MINCE HIM EASY, EH TOM?

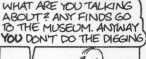

WHAT ARE YOU TALKING ABOUT? ANY FINDS GO TO THE MUSEUM. ANYWAY **YOU** DON'T DO THE DIGGING

YOU JUST GO AROUND AND ASK 'LAYMEN' TYPE QUESTIONS

RIGHT. GOTCHA, TOM.

SHORTLY...

RIGHT... SO WHAT'S GOING ON, HERE?

WELL, IT'S VERY INTERESTING, ROGER...

WE'VE FOUND A SMALL SECTION OF MOSAIC FLOOR WITH A CRISS-CROSS PATTERN, INDICATING THAT THIS WAS PROBABLY A...

HEY, TOM! WE'VE FOUND THE GOLD! X-MARKS THE SPOT!

?

EVERY MAN FOR HIMSELF!

SMASH!

FOR CHRIST'S SAKE, ROGER. STOP IT! JUST GO OVER TO TRENCH B! PROF. MICK HAS FOUND SOMETHING INTERESTING... AND DON'T TOUCH IT!

HEY!

SO...

RIGHT! WHAT'S THE BIG DEAL HERE, THEN?

AH! ROGER... IT'S A FRAGMENT OF A VASE THAT WE THINK...

HEY! WHO'S THAT BIRD? IS SHE ONE OF YOUR LOT?

ER...YES. THAT'S CARENZA...

...ERM. AS I WAS SAYING, WE THINK IT MAY BE PART OF...

HI, LOVE! HOW'S IT GOING, EH?

GREAT, ROGER. I THINK I'VE FOUND THE SITE OF THE KITCHEN. I THINK I'VE GOT WHAT COULD BE A SPOON HANDLE

WELL I'VE GOT SOMETHING THAT'S DEFINITELY A PAN HANDLE

YOU SEE, THESE CHARCOAL FRAGMENTS INDICATE A LOT OF COOKING WENT ON HERE...

...BUT EVEN MORE EXCITING THAN THAT, ROGER...

...I'M UNCOVERING AN ENORMOUS PAIR OF JUGS DOWN HERE...

...WOULD YOU LIKE TO HELP ME LIFT THEM OUT?

I THOUGHT YOU'D NEVER ASK.

FOUR MONTHS LATER...

HI, THERE, TOM

HI, ROGER

HMP PUTCHERE

Things that Shout 'Wank' in the Night!
FUCKING HELL!

EVERYONE is terrified when they see a ghost. But these days, when the spooks open their mouths to speak, more often than not that terror turns to disgust.

Because according to scientists at a top university, today's ghosts are using fouler language than ever before.

chain

"In the old days, the average ghoulie would limit itself to low moans, high-pitched wails and a bit of chain-rattling," says Oxford parapsychologist Shirley Crabtree. "Nowadays, you're more likely to be awoken in the middle of the night by a see-through man with his head under his arm calling you a fucking bastard."

pole

Crabtree reached her conclusions by interviewing people with first-hand experience of ghostly abuse, including Nottingham museum nightwatchman Terry Jackson:

"I'd heard stories about the museum being haunted, but I've never believed in that sort of thing," says Terry, 38. "Then one night last December I was just finishing my rounds when the room went very cold.

Shirley Crabtree (top) yesterday and (yesterday)- above Terry (Jackson -yesterday). (And)- yesterday right- A ghost

I could see my breath condensing on the air.

rod

Suddenly, I had the strong impression that there was somebody standing behind me, so I turned. I was horrified by what was there.

"Two shimmering, translucent Roman sol-

Language gets worse on Other Side

By our g...g...g...ghost correspondent
Phil Spectre

diers, hovering about a foot above the floor.

barrymore

They may have been figments of my imagination, but let me tell you, their language was real enough. I was in the Navy for eight years, but I've never heard any-

thing like it. I know these souls are in eternal torment, but there's really no need for that kind of language."

row the boat ashore

Terry asked the foul-mouthed phantoms to moderate their language, but received a

torrent of ghostly four-letter abuse in reply. In the morning, museum staff found him huddled in a corner, ashen-faced and shaking like a leaf. "I had never been spoken to like that before," he says.

halelujah!

The swearing was so rude, including the B-word, the F-word and cunt, that Terry's hair had turned white overnight. He is still too petrified to sleep in the dark, and hasn't been back to work since.

row the boat ashore

Even in the traditionally genteel surroundings of the front parlour seance, mediums are increasingly finding that the air has a nasty habit of turning blue as well as cold. "I've been in daily contact with my red Indian guide for over forty years," says Blackpool clairvoyant Doris Fraud. "Then a couple of weeks

THE TURDMAN OF ALKATRAZ

"HEY, BERT! WE'VE FINISHED THE TUNNEL!"

"YEH! AND WE'VE GOT SOMEBODY WAITING FOR US WITH A BOAT. ARE YOU COMING?"

"NO. YOU GO WITHOUT ME. I'VE BEEN HERE FOR 25 YEARS. IT'S ALL I KNOW.

AND ANYWAY, WHO WOULD TAKE CARE OF ALL MY LITTLE FRIENDS?"

"GO ON, FLY. FLY AWAY, MY BEAUTY. ENJOY THE FREEDOM THAT I WILL NEVER KNOW."

SPLATCH!

Doris Fraud (right) and her foul-mouthed spirit guide, Billy Two-Rivers (above)

ago a client asked me to contact their uncle Ernest in spirit world. I summoned Chief Billy Two-Rivers in the usual way, but instead of rapping on the table like he's always done - one knock for yes, two knocks for no - there was this deep booming voice saying I could suck um heap big redskin cock. I've never been so embarrassed. In fact I vomited."

halelujah!

Doris decided to try reading some tea-leaves instead, but the runes were being no more co-operative: "I looked in the bottom of the cup and it just said 'fuck off'," she told us.

The Path of Truth

Ghosties and ghoulies and long-legged beasties and things that go bump in the night. All will be out and about this Halloween. But what is the difference betwen a ghostie and a ghoulie, and which one are YOU? Take a stroll down our Path of Truth, answering the questions honestly to find out once and for all...

Are you a Ghostie or a Ghoulie?

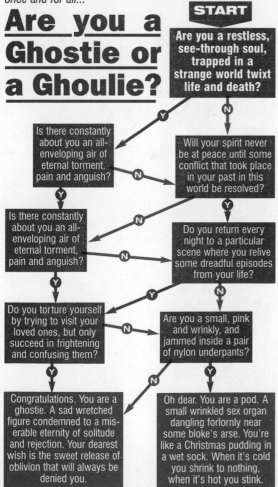

START

Are you a restless, see-through soul, trapped in a strange world twixt life and death? — Y: go to 1; N: go to 2

1. Is there constantly about you an all-enveloping air of eternal torment, pain and anguish? — Y: go to 3; N: go to 2
2. Will your spirit never be at peace until some conflict that took place in your past in this world be resolved? — Y: go to 4; N: go to 3
3. Is there constantly about you an all-enveloping air of eternal torment, pain and anguish? — Y: go to 5; N: go to 4
4. Do you return every night to a particular scene where you relive some dreadful episodes from your life? — Y: go to 5; N: go to 6
5. Do you torture yourself by trying to visit your loved ones, but only succeed in frightening and confusing them? — Y: go to A; N: go to 6
6. Are you a small, pink and wrinkly, and jammed inside a pair of nylon underpants? — Y: go to B; N: go to A

A. Congratulations. You are a ghostie. A sad wretched figure condemned to a miserable eternity of solitude and rejection. Your dearest wish is the sweet release of oblivion that will always be denied you.

B. Oh dear. You are a pod. A small wrinkled sex organ dangling forlornly near some bloke's arse. You're like a Christmas pudding in a wet sock. When it's cold you shrink to nothing, when it's hot you stink.

Win £100 in our *'phantomtastic'* Halloween Devil Photo Competition

BOOOOOOOOOOOOOOOOOOOOOOOOOTIFUL!

Here's your chance to raise Beelzebub, whilst enjoying the great taste of Norfolk turkey by-products, with this FREE 'Turkey Dinosaur Altar of Diabolism'.

The devil has been responsible for some terrible things, but nothing quite as dreadful as what you find in a Bernard Matthews packet. That's why we're offering one lucky reader the chance to win as many cheese hamwiches, mini Kievs and golden drummers they can eat in a year. That's about three packets.

All you have to do is raise the Prince of Darkness from his fiery lair in the netherworld, and snap a photograph as he appears before you in all his satanic majesty. And to help you along, we're providing a fabulous altar of diabolism for you to cut out & keep.

Conjuring Up the Necromancer ~*the Turkey dinosaur way.*

Assemble your altar as shown in the diagram. Then light the birthday cake candles and turn out the lights.

Now put on that music off The Omen that they used to use on the Old Spice adverts. Alternatively, if this is not available play a Judas Priest album backwards.

The devil requires a bloody sacrifice before he will appear, so place a virgin turkey dinosaur on the altar, and cut its throat. You may like to dab on a bit of ketchup for added realism.

Incantation is an important part of the ceremony. Take the turkey dinosaurs packet, look at the list of ingredients and chant the E-numbers seven times in a deep voice.

At this point the candles will blow out and the doors and windows will start slamming. There may also be a strong smell of sulphur. But only if you've eaten the turkey dinosaur. Lucifer will now manifest from behind the altar.

Take your photo, and send it to us at: ***Viz Devil Worship Competition, Viz, PO Box 1PT, Newcastle upon Tyne NE99 1PT.*** *We'll print a selection of your satanic snaps in the next issue, and the sender of the most terrifying will receive £100 cash to spend on Bernard Matthews turkey products.*

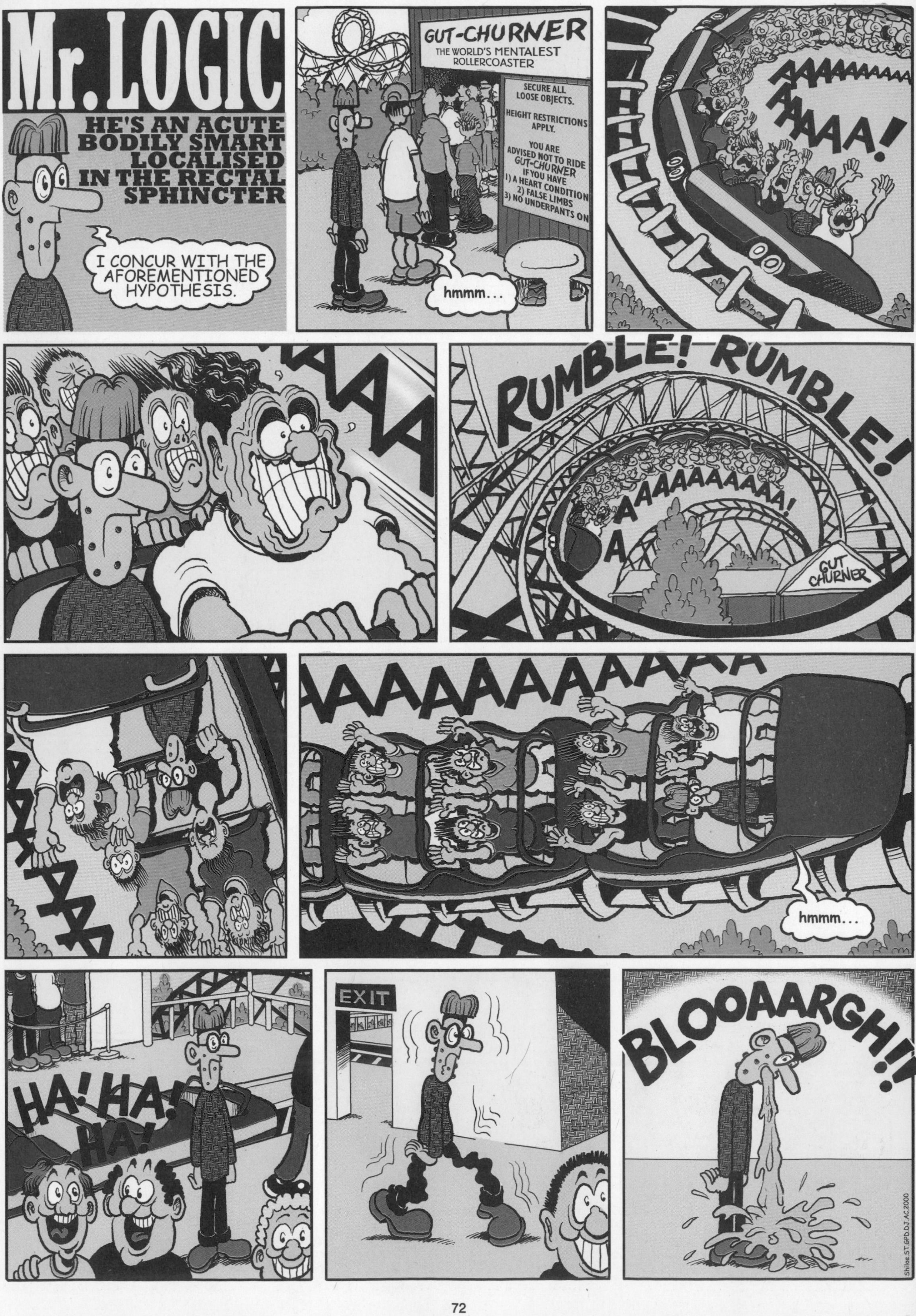
Mr. LOGIC
HE'S AN ACUTE BODILY SMART LOCALISED IN THE RECTAL SPHINCTER
I CONCUR WITH THE AFOREMENTIONED HYPOTHESIS.
GUT-CHURNER
THE WORLD'S MENTALEST ROLLERCOASTER
SECURE ALL LOOSE OBJECTS.
HEIGHT RESTRICTIONS APPLY.
YOU ARE ADVISED NOT TO RIDE GUT-CHURNER IF YOU HAVE
1) A HEART CONDITION
2) FALSE LIMBS
3) NO UNDERPANTS ON
hmmm...
AAAAAAAAAAAAAAAA!
RUMBLE! RUMBLE! RUMBLE!
AAAAAAAAAAA!
GUT CHURNER
AAAAAAAAAAAA
hmmm...
HA! HA! HA!
EXIT
BLOOAARGH!!
Shiloe.ST.GPD.DJ.AC.2000

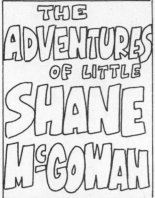

THE ADVENTURES OF LITTLE SHANE McGOWAN

I HOPE YOU'RE BRUSHING YOUR TEETH PROPERLY IN THERE, SHANE

YES, MUM

BRUSH! BRUSH! BRUSH! BRUSH!

FRONT **AND** BACK

INSIDE

CHOMP! SMASH! CRACK!

HEH HEH

GOBSTOPPER TING

TOOTHBRUSH SOUND EFFECTS VOL. 4

BRUSH! BRUSH! BRUSH! BRUSH!

20 CWT INDUSTRIAL GOBSTOPPERS

NOW STRAIGHT TO BED, SHANE. WE'VE GOT TO BE UP EARLY TOMORROW

BEGORRAH

OK, MUM

AND I HOPE YOU'RE NOT THINKING OF READING UNDER THE COVERS...

NO, I'M NOT, MUM, TO BE SURE

IT'S VERY BAD FOR YOUR EYES, YOU KNOW

I'M NOT READING, MUM, HONEST

> SNIGGER! <

MURPHY RICHARDS CANDY-FLOSS-MAKER

WHIRRR!

10 HOURS LATER..

DRI-I-ING

THAT WAS A GREAT NIGHT'S CANDY-FLOSSING...

NOW FOR SOME BREAKFAST

SO.. HOLY MOTHER OF GOD. IT'S MY FAVOURITE...

CURLY-WURLYS AND COCA COLA

I'LL JUST SWEETEN IT UP A BIT...

.. SO I WILL, SO I WILL

SUGAR

BUT..

?

FWISK!

NO TIME FOR BREAKFAST THIS MORNING, SHANE. IT'S YOUR CHECK UP AT THE DENTIST'S

BEJASUS

THEN YOU'VE GOT TO GO TO YOUR POSH ENGLISH PUBLIC SCHOOL

OUTSIDE

DOH! I DON'T WANT TO GO TO THE DENTIST'S. I'LL EMPTY SOME OF ME SHERBERT INTO MUM'S CAR'S PETROL TANK!

SHERBERT

HEH! HEH!

LOOK MUM. I CAN'T GO TO MR ELLIOT THE DENTIST... YOUR CAR IS FECKED

BUT MR ELLIOT DIED OF YOUR BREATH. WE'VE GOT A NEW DENTIST...

FIZZ! POP! FIZZ

...JUST ROUND THE CORNER

GPD ST SDA CO'S

SO.. AW MUM, I DON'T WANT TO GO. I'LL HAVE TO HAVE ALL MY TEETH OUT AND I'LL NEVER BE ABLE TO CHOMP BOILED SWEETS AGAIN. TO BE SURE.

DENTAL SURGEON

NONSENSE. TELL YOU WHAT - IF YOU DON'T NEED ANY FILLINGS, I'LL GIVE YOU A SUGAR DUMMY

...WELL, THERE'S NOTHING NEEDS DOING THAT I CAN SEE, MRS McGOWAN

DECAY

LITTLE SHANE WON'T NEED ANOTHER APPOINTMENT FOR SIX MONTHS

I JUST CALLED.. TO SAY.. I LOVE YOOUU..

STEVIE WONDER BDS. BCHD DENTAL SURGEON

SWEETS REWARD

HOORAY, BEGORRAH

EMPEROR MING

THE STINKY EVIL GALACTIC DICTATOR

PLANET MONGO ~ IMPERIAL PALACE OF HIS EXCELLENCY THE EMPEROR MING

WE MUST SEE HIS EXCELLENCY IMMEDIATELY

WE HAVE TAKEN PRISONER PRINCESS CLEMENTIA OF ZARON IV AND BROUGHT HER TO HIM, AS HE INSTRUCTED

YOU'LL SMELL HIM BEFORE YOU SEE HIM, PAL

HE'S ABSOLUTELY FUCKIN' LIFTIN'

AH! THE FAIR PRINCESS CLEMENTIA! AT LAST I HAVE YOU IN MY CLUTCHES

CHRIST ON A CRUTCH! WHAT A HONK

IN A FEW HOURS, MY PRETTY ONE, WE SHALL BE MARRIED

AND WITH YOU AS MY HOSTAGE BRIDE, THE GALACTIC FEDERATION WILL DARE NOT CHALLENGE MY SUPREMACY ~ THEN I, EMPEROR MING, WILL BE RULER OF ALL THE GALAXIES!

JESUS! HAS HE BEEN NECKING TURDS?

BUT FIRST THERE IS MUCH TO PREPARE. GUARDS! TAKE HER TO THE INTERNMENT CHAMBER!

EXCELLENCY ~ ERM, SOME OF YOUR LOYAL SUBJECTS ARE UNSURE ABOUT THE CORRECT WAY OF TAKING A BATH...

WE WONDERED IF YOU, AS EMPEROR, COULD ENLIGHTEN US BY GIVING US AN UNDER ARM WASHING DEMONSTRATION...?

FOOLS! I HAVE NO TIME FOR YOUR TRIVIAL PRATTLE

BLOODY NORA ~ IT MAKES YOUR EYES WATER

I MUST READY MY ARMIES FOR THE SUBJUGATION OF SIRIUS B

WHAT ON MONGO?! IT IS MY ARCH-FOE, THE EARTHLING FLASH GORDON

F.G.

HE HAS RESCUED PRINCESS CLEMENTIA ~ MY PLANS FOR GALACTIC DOMINION ARE UNDONE!

WE MUST MOBILISE THE PLANETARY DEFENCE SYSTEM AT ONCE...

BAH! ONCE AGAIN SOME IDIOT HAS LEFT AEROSOL DEODORANTS AND BOTTLES OF MOUTHWASH LYING ON MY GALACTO-TELESCREEN

TOO LATE! GALACTIC FEDERATION WARSHIPS HAVE ALREADY PENETRATED THE PLANET'S FORCE-FIELD!

IN TIMES OF STRESS, EXCELLENCY, I FIND THAT A NICE HOT SHOWER CAN BE REFRESHING

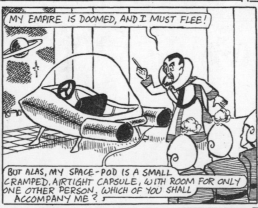

MY EMPIRE IS DOOMED, AND I MUST FLEE!

BUT ALAS, MY SPACE-POD IS A SMALL CRAMPED, AIRTIGHT CAPSULE, WITH ROOM FOR ONLY ONE OTHER PERSON. WHICH OF YOU SHALL ACCOMPANY ME?

AH! YOU ARE PRIVILEGED INDEED, MY FAITHFUL MINION, TO BE TRAVELLING ALONGSIDE YOUR BELOVED EMPEROR

OH GOD NO

HELP ME TAKE MY BOOTS OFF, GUARD ~ WE HAVE A LONG JOURNEY AHEAD, AND I WISH TO BE COMFORTABLE

THEN YOU CAN UNWRAP THE GARLIC SAUSAGE I PACKED FOR LUNCH

THE AIR IS STARTING TO CLEAR ALREADY

THE STINKY REIGN OF EMPEROR MING IS OVER AT LAST

GREETINGS, CITIZENS OF MONGO ~ WE ARE KLING-ONS, YOUR NEW MASTERS

SHITTY HUM

BY JUPITER, THESE WINNITS AREN'T HALF MAKING MY ARSE-CLEFT ITCH

ME TOO, I HAVEN'T WIPED FOR A MONTH

FUCK ME WHAT A REEK

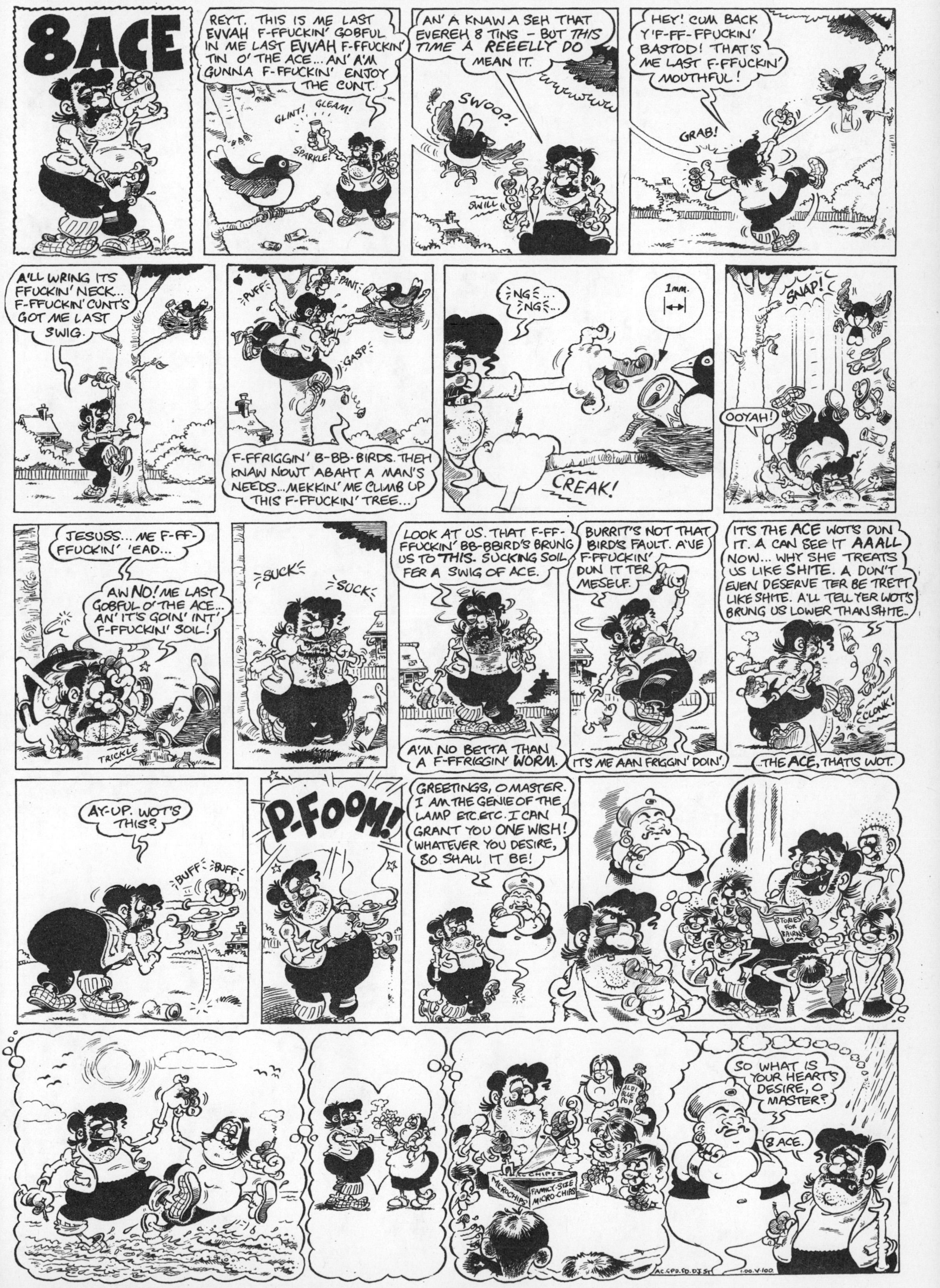

8ACE
REY'T. THIS IS ME LAST EVVAH F-FFUCKIN' GOBFUL IN ME LAST EVVAH F-FFUCKIN' TIN O' THE ACE... AN' A'M GUNNA F-FFUCKIN' ENJOY THE CUNT.
GLINT! GLEAM! SPARKLE!
AN' A KNAW A SEH THAT EVEREH 8 TINS - BUT THIS TIME A REEELLY DO MEAN IT.
SWOOP!
SWILL
HEY! CUM BACK Y'F-FF-FFUCKIN' BASTOD! THAT'S ME LAST F-FFUCKIN' MOUTHFUL!
GRAB!
A'LL WRING ITS FFUCKIN' NECK... F-FFUCKIN' CUNT'S GOT ME LAST SWIG.
PUFF
PANT
GASP
F-FFRIGGIN' B-BB-BIRDS. THEH KNAW NOWT ABAHT A MAN'S NEEDS... MEKKIN' ME CLIMB UP THIS F-FFUCKIN' TREE...
NG... NG...
1mm.
CREAK!
SNAP!
OOYAH!
JESUSS... ME F-FF-FFUCKIN' 'EAD...
AW NO! ME LAST GOBFUL O' THE ACE... AN' IT'S GOIN' INT' F-FFUCKIN' SOIL!
TRICKLE
SUCK
SUCK
LOOK AT US. THAT F-FF-FFUCKIN' BB-BBIRD'S BRUNG US TO THIS. SUCKING SOIL FER A SWIG OF ACE.
A'M NO BETTA THAN A F-FFRIGGIN' WORM.
BURRIT'S NOT THAT BIRD'S FAULT. A'VE F-FFUCKIN' DUN IT TER MESELF.
IT'S ME AAN FRIGGIN' DOIN'.
IT'S THE ACE WOT'S DUN IT. A CAN SEE IT AAALL NOW... WHY SHE TREATS US LIKE SHITE. A DON'T EVEN DESERVE TER BE TRETT LIKE SHITE. A'LL TELL YER WOT'S BRUNG US LOWER THAN SHITE..
CLONK!
...THE ACE, THAT'S WOT.
AY-UP. WOT'S THIS?
BUFF
BUFF
P-FOOM!
GREETINGS, O MASTER. I AM THE GENIE OF THE LAMP ETC. ETC. I CAN GRANT YOU ONE WISH! WHATEVER YOU DESIRE, SO SHALL IT BE!
STORIES FOR BAIRNS
ALDI BLUE POP
MICROCHIPS
FAMILY-SIZE MICRO-CHIPS
SO WHAT IS YOUR HEART'S DESIRE, O MASTER?
8 ACE.

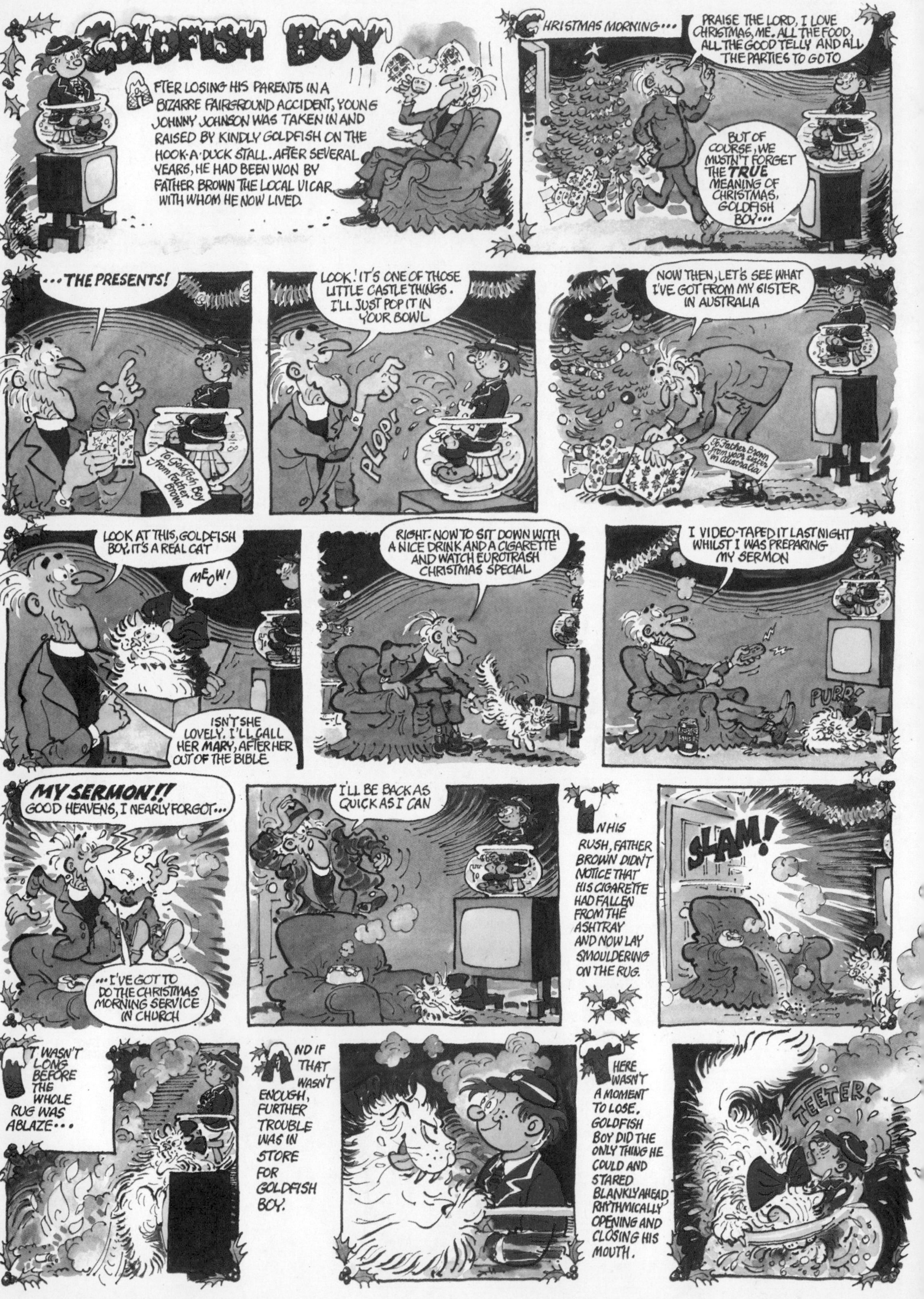

GOLDFISH BOY
AFTER LOSING HIS PARENTS IN A BIZARRE FAIRGROUND ACCIDENT, YOUNG JOHNNY JOHNSON WAS TAKEN IN AND RAISED BY KINDLY GOLDFISH ON THE HOOK-A-DUCK STALL. AFTER SEVERAL YEARS, HE HAD BEEN WON BY FATHER BROWN THE LOCAL VICAR WITH WHOM HE NOW LIVED.
CHRISTMAS MORNING...
PRAISE THE LORD, I LOVE CHRISTMAS, ME. ALL THE FOOD, ALL THE GOOD TELLY AND ALL THE PARTIES TO GO TO
BUT OF COURSE, WE MUSTN'T FORGET THE TRUE MEANING OF CHRISTMAS, GOLDFISH BOY...
...THE PRESENTS!
To Goldfish Boy from Father Brown
LOOK! IT'S ONE OF THOSE LITTLE CASTLE THINGS. I'LL JUST POP IT IN YOUR BOWL
PLOP!
NOW THEN, LET'S SEE WHAT I'VE GOT FROM MY SISTER IN AUSTRALIA
To Father Brown from your sister in Australia
LOOK AT THIS, GOLDFISH BOY. IT'S A REAL CAT
MEOW!
ISN'T SHE LOVELY. I'LL CALL HER MARY, AFTER HER OUT OF THE BIBLE
RIGHT. NOW TO SIT DOWN WITH A NICE DRINK AND A CIGARETTE AND WATCH EUROTRASH CHRISTMAS SPECIAL
I VIDEO-TAPED IT LAST NIGHT WHILST I WAS PREPARING MY SERMON
PURR!
MY SERMON!! GOOD HEAVENS, I NEARLY FORGOT...
...I'VE GOT TO DO THE CHRISTMAS MORNING SERVICE IN CHURCH
I'LL BE BACK AS QUICK AS I CAN
IN HIS RUSH, FATHER BROWN DIDN'T NOTICE THAT HIS CIGARETTE HAD FALLEN FROM THE ASHTRAY AND NOW LAY SMOULDERING ON THE RUG.
SLAM!
IT WASN'T LONG BEFORE THE WHOLE RUG WAS ABLAZE...
AND IF THAT WASN'T ENOUGH, FURTHER TROUBLE WAS IN STORE FOR GOLDFISH BOY.
THERE WASN'T A MOMENT TO LOSE. GOLDFISH BOY DID THE ONLY THING HE COULD AND STARED BLANKLY AHEAD RHYTHMICALLY OPENING AND CLOSING HIS MOUTH.
TEETER!

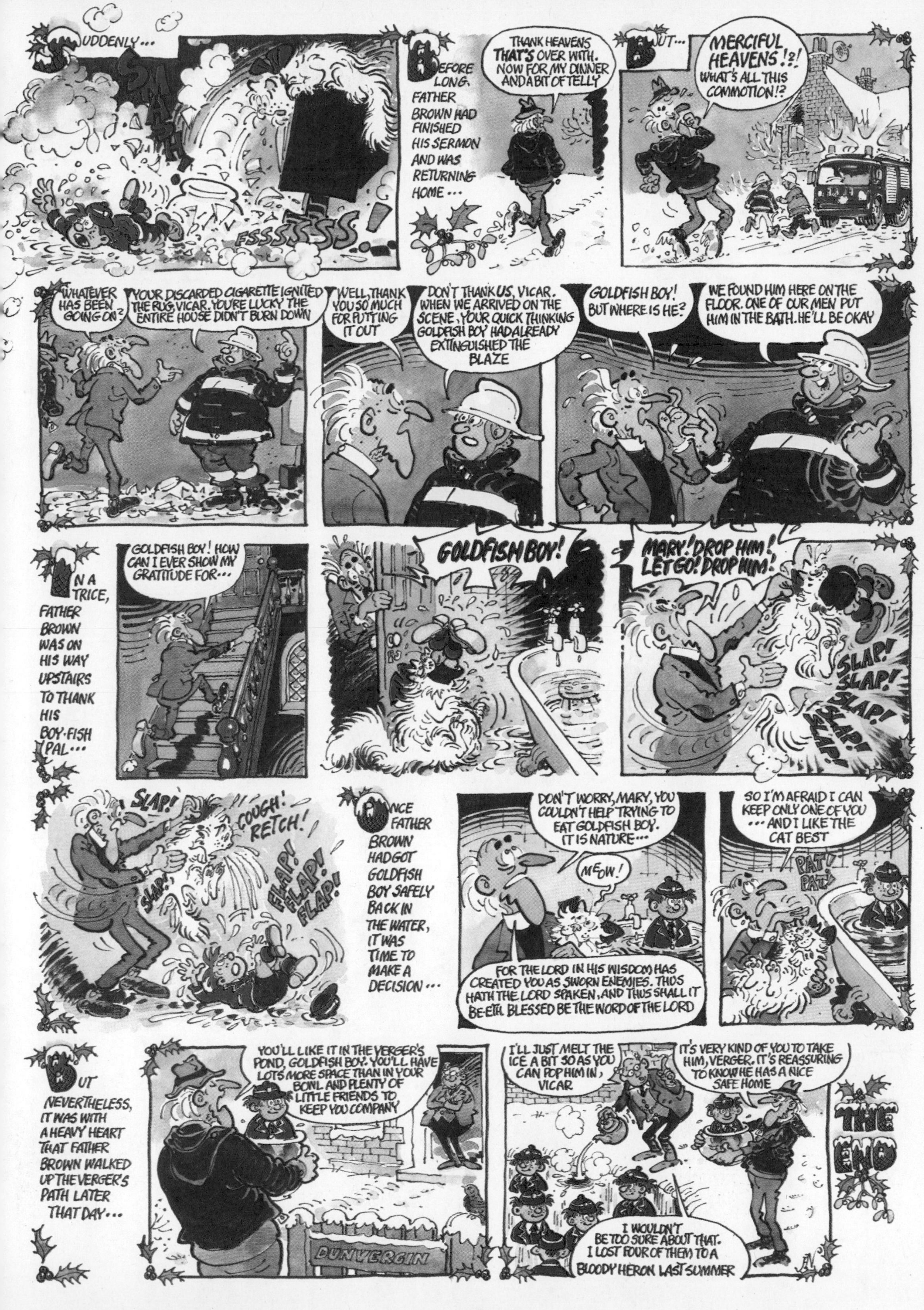
SUDDENLY...
SMASH
FSSSSSSSS...!
BEFORE LONG, FATHER BROWN HAD FINISHED HIS SERMON AND WAS RETURNING HOME...
THANK HEAVENS THAT'S OVER WITH. NOW FOR MY DINNER AND A BIT OF TELLY
BUT...
MERCIFUL HEAVENS!?! WHAT'S ALL THIS COMMOTION!?
WHATEVER HAS BEEN GOING ON?
YOUR DISCARDED CIGARETTE IGNITED THE RUG, VICAR. YOU'RE LUCKY THE ENTIRE HOUSE DIDN'T BURN DOWN
WELL, THANK YOU SO MUCH FOR PUTTING IT OUT
DON'T THANK US, VICAR. WHEN WE ARRIVED ON THE SCENE, YOUR QUICK THINKING GOLDFISH BOY HAD ALREADY EXTINGUISHED THE BLAZE
GOLDFISH BOY! BUT WHERE IS HE?
WE FOUND HIM HERE ON THE FLOOR. ONE OF OUR MEN PUT HIM IN THE BATH. HE'LL BE OKAY
IN A TRICE, FATHER BROWN WAS ON HIS WAY UPSTAIRS TO THANK HIS BOY-FISH PAL...
GOLDFISH BOY! HOW CAN I EVER SHOW MY GRATITUDE FOR...
GOLDFISH BOY!
MARY! DROP HIM! LET GO! DROP HIM!
SLAP! SLAP! SLAP! SLAP! SLAP!
SLAP!
COUGH! RETCH!
SLAP!
FLAP! FLAP! FLAP!
ONCE FATHER BROWN HAD GOT GOLDFISH BOY SAFELY BACK IN THE WATER, IT WAS TIME TO MAKE A DECISION...
DON'T WORRY, MARY, YOU COULDN'T HELP TRYING TO EAT GOLDFISH BOY. IT IS NATURE...
MEOW!
FOR THE LORD IN HIS WISDOM HAS CREATED YOU AS SWORN ENEMIES. THUS HATH THE LORD SPAKEN, AND THUS SHALL IT BE-ETH. BLESSED BE THE WORD OF THE LORD
SO I'M AFRAID I CAN KEEP ONLY ONE OF YOU ... AND I LIKE THE CAT BEST
PAT! PAT!
BUT NEVERTHELESS, IT WAS WITH A HEAVY HEART THAT FATHER BROWN WALKED UP THE VERGER'S PATH LATER THAT DAY...
YOU'LL LIKE IT IN THE VERGER'S POND, GOLDFISH BOY. YOU'LL HAVE LOTS MORE SPACE THAN IN YOUR BOWL AND PLENTY OF LITTLE FRIENDS TO KEEP YOU COMPANY
DUNVERGIN
I'LL JUST MELT THE ICE A BIT SO AS YOU CAN POP HIM IN, VICAR
IT'S VERY KIND OF YOU TO TAKE HIM, VERGER. IT'S REASSURING TO KNOW HE HAS A NICE SAFE HOME
I WOULDN'T BE TOO SURE ABOUT THAT. I LOST FOUR OF THEM TO A BLOODY HERON LAST SUMMER
THE END

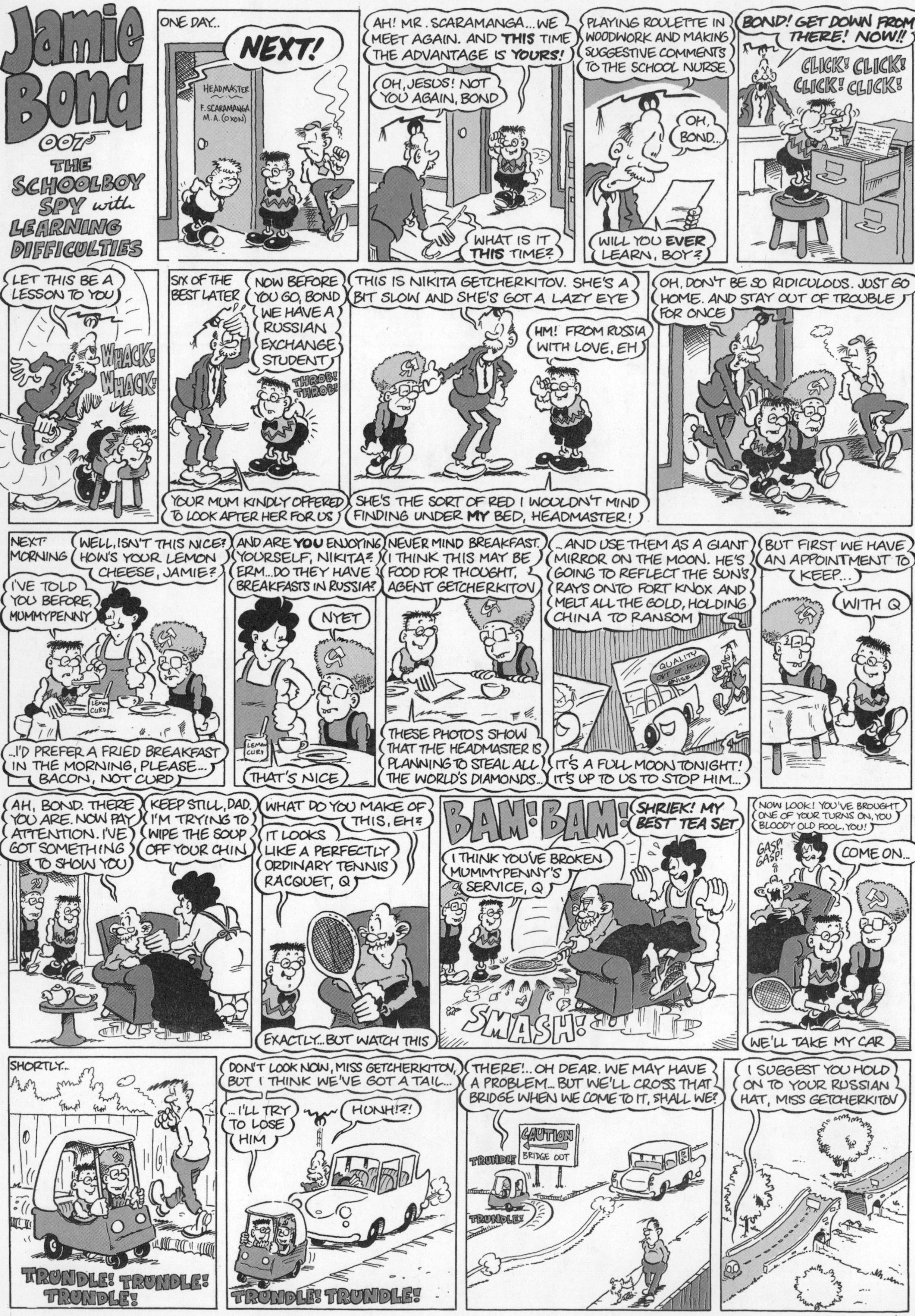
Jamie Bond
007
THE SCHOOLBOY SPY with LEARNING DIFFICULTIES
ONE DAY..
NEXT!
HEADMASTER
F. SCARAMANGA M.A. (OXON)
AH! MR. SCARAMANGA... WE MEET AGAIN. AND THIS TIME THE ADVANTAGE IS YOURS!
OH, JESUS! NOT YOU AGAIN, BOND
WHAT IS IT THIS TIME?
PLAYING ROULETTE IN WOODWORK AND MAKING SUGGESTIVE COMMENTS TO THE SCHOOL NURSE.
OH, BOND...
WILL YOU EVER LEARN, BOY?
BOND! GET DOWN FROM THERE! NOW!!
CLICK! CLICK! CLICK! CLICK!
LET THIS BE A LESSON TO YOU
WHACK! WHACK!
SIX OF THE BEST LATER
NOW BEFORE YOU GO, BOND WE HAVE A RUSSIAN EXCHANGE STUDENT
THROB! THROB!
YOUR MUM KINDLY OFFERED TO LOOK AFTER HER FOR US
THIS IS NIKITA GETCHERKITOV. SHE'S A BIT SLOW AND SHE'S GOT A LAZY EYE
HM! FROM RUSSIA WITH LOVE, EH
SHE'S THE SORT OF RED I WOULDN'T MIND FINDING UNDER MY BED, HEADMASTER!
OH, DON'T BE SO RIDICULOUS. JUST GO HOME. AND STAY OUT OF TROUBLE FOR ONCE
NEXT MORNING
WELL, ISN'T THIS NICE? HOW'S YOUR LEMON CHEESE, JAMIE?
I'VE TOLD YOU BEFORE, MUMMYPENNY
LEMON CURD
..I'D PREFER A FRIED BREAKFAST IN THE MORNING, PLEASE... BACON, NOT CURD
AND ARE YOU ENJOYING YOURSELF, NIKITA? ERM...DO THEY HAVE BREAKFASTS IN RUSSIA?
NYET
LEMON CURD
THAT'S NICE
NEVER MIND BREAKFAST. I THINK THIS MAY BE FOOD FOR THOUGHT, AGENT GETCHERKITOV
THESE PHOTOS SHOW THAT THE HEADMASTER IS PLANNING TO STEAL ALL THE WORLD'S DIAMONDS...
...AND USE THEM AS A GIANT MIRROR ON THE MOON. HE'S GOING TO REFLECT THE SUN'S RAYS ONTO FORT KNOX AND MELT ALL THE GOLD, HOLDING CHINA TO RANSOM
QUALITY OUT OF FOCUS
IT'S A FULL MOON TONIGHT! IT'S UP TO US TO STOP HIM...
BUT FIRST WE HAVE AN APPOINTMENT TO KEEP...
WITH Q
AH, BOND. THERE YOU ARE. NOW PAY ATTENTION. I'VE GOT SOMETHING TO SHOW YOU
KEEP STILL, DAD. I'M TRYING TO WIPE THE SOUP OFF YOUR CHIN
WHAT DO YOU MAKE OF THIS, EH?
IT LOOKS LIKE A PERFECTLY ORDINARY TENNIS RACQUET, Q
EXACTLY...BUT WATCH THIS
BAM! BAM!
SHRIEK! MY BEST TEA SET
I THINK YOU'VE BROKEN MUMMYPENNY'S SERVICE, Q
SMASH!
NOW LOOK! YOU'VE BROUGHT ONE OF YOUR TURNS ON, YOU BLOODY OLD FOOL, YOU!
GASP! GASP!
COME ON...
WE'LL TAKE MY CAR
SHORTLY...
TRUNDLE! TRUNDLE! TRUNDLE!
DON'T LOOK NOW, MISS GETCHERKITOV, BUT I THINK WE'VE GOT A TAIL...
...I'LL TRY TO LOSE HIM
HONH!?!
TRUNDLE! TRUNDLE!
THERE!.. OH DEAR. WE MAY HAVE A PROBLEM... BUT WE'LL CROSS THAT BRIDGE WHEN WE COME TO IT, SHALL WE?
CAUTION BRIDGE OUT
TRUNDLE!
TRUNDLE!
I SUGGEST YOU HOLD ON TO YOUR RUSSIAN HAT, MISS GETCHERKITOV

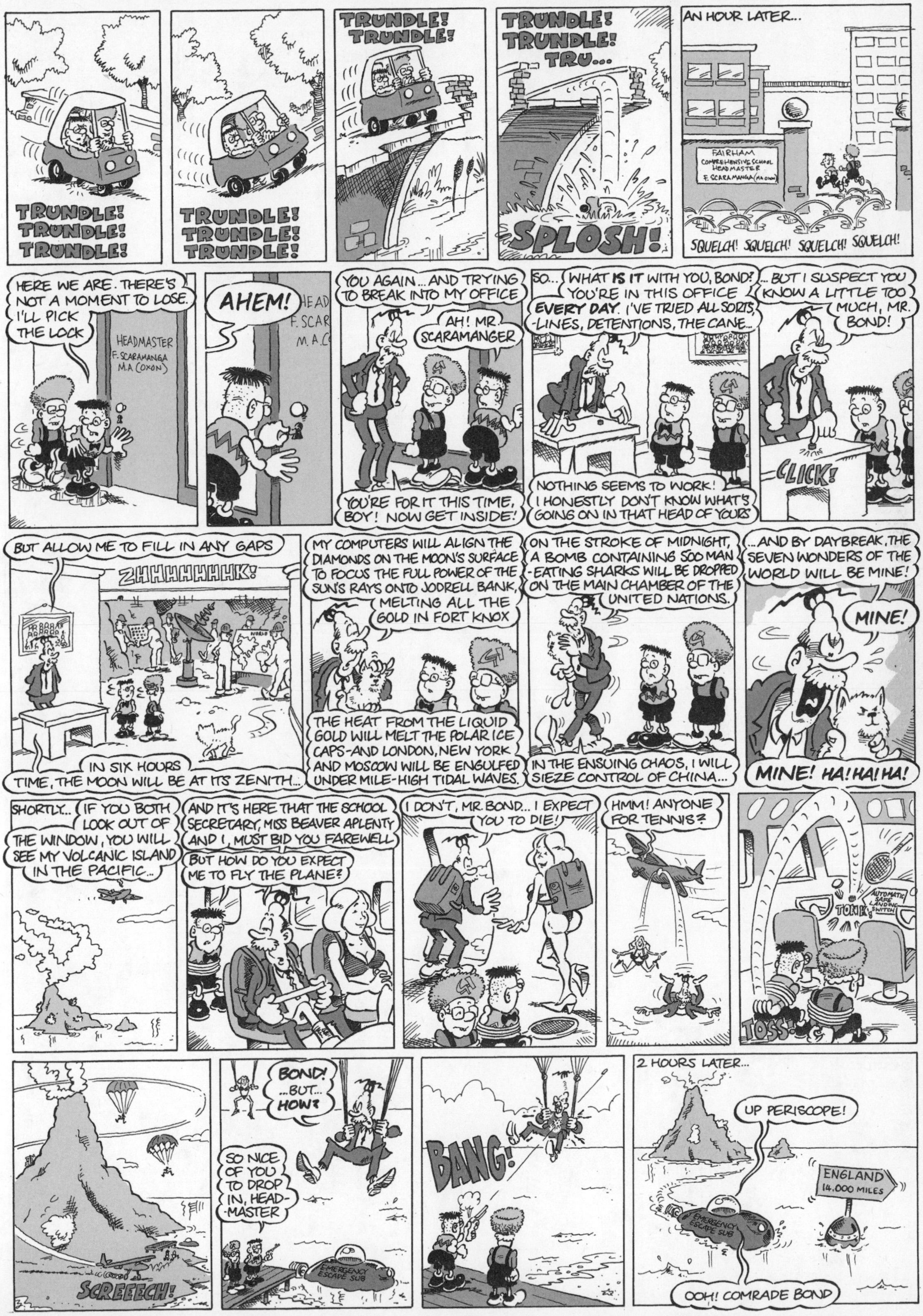

TRUNDLE! TRUNDLE! TRUNDLE!
TRUNDLE! TRUNDLE! TRUNDLE!
TRUNDLE! TRUNDLE!
TRUNDLE! TRUNDLE! TRU...
SPLOSH!
AN HOUR LATER...
FAIRHAM COMPREHENSIVE SCHOOL HEADMASTER F. SCARAMANGA (MA OXON)
SQUELCH! SQUELCH! SQUELCH! SQUELCH!
HERE WE ARE. THERE'S NOT A MOMENT TO LOSE. I'LL PICK THE LOCK
HEADMASTER F. SCARAMANGA M.A (OXON)
AHEM!
YOU AGAIN... AND TRYING TO BREAK INTO MY OFFICE
AH! MR. SCARAMANGER
YOU'RE FOR IT THIS TIME, BOY! NOW GET INSIDE!
SO... WHAT IS IT WITH YOU, BOND? YOU'RE IN THIS OFFICE EVERY DAY. I'VE TRIED ALL SORTS, -LINES, DETENTIONS, THE CANE...
NOTHING SEEMS TO WORK! I HONESTLY DON'T KNOW WHAT'S GOING ON IN THAT HEAD OF YOURS
... BUT I SUSPECT YOU KNOW A LITTLE TOO MUCH, MR. BOND!
CLICK!
BUT ALLOW ME TO FILL IN ANY GAPS
ZHHHHHHHK!
IN SIX HOURS TIME, THE MOON WILL BE AT ITS ZENITH...
MY COMPUTERS WILL ALIGN THE DIAMONDS ON THE MOON'S SURFACE TO FOCUS THE FULL POWER OF THE SUN'S RAYS ONTO JODRELL BANK,
MELTING ALL THE GOLD IN FORT KNOX
THE HEAT FROM THE LIQUID GOLD WILL MELT THE POLAR ICE CAPS-AND LONDON, NEW YORK AND MOSCOW WILL BE ENGULFED UNDER MILE-HIGH TIDAL WAVES.
ON THE STROKE OF MIDNIGHT, A BOMB CONTAINING 500 MAN -EATING SHARKS WILL BE DROPPED ON THE MAIN CHAMBER OF THE UNITED NATIONS.
IN THE ENSUING CHAOS, I WILL SIEZE CONTROL OF CHINA...
...AND BY DAYBREAK, THE SEVEN WONDERS OF THE WORLD WILL BE MINE!
MINE!
MINE! HA! HA! HA!
SHORTLY... IF YOU BOTH LOOK OUT OF THE WINDOW, YOU WILL SEE MY VOLCANIC ISLAND IN THE PACIFIC...
AND IT'S HERE THAT THE SCHOOL SECRETARY, MISS BEAVER APLENTY AND I, MUST BID YOU FAREWELL
BUT HOW DO YOU EXPECT ME TO FLY THE PLANE?
I DON'T, MR. BOND... I EXPECT YOU TO DIE!
HMM! ANYONE FOR TENNIS?
AUTOMATIC SAFE LANDING SWITCH
TONK!
TOSS!
SCREEECH!
BOND! ...BUT... HOW?
SO NICE OF YOU TO DROP IN, HEAD-MASTER
EMERGENCY ESCAPE SUB
BANG!
2 HOURS LATER...
UP PERISCOPE!
ENGLAND 14,000 MILES
EMERGENCY ESCAPE SUB
OOH! COMRADE BOND

Black Bag

The Faithful Border Binliner

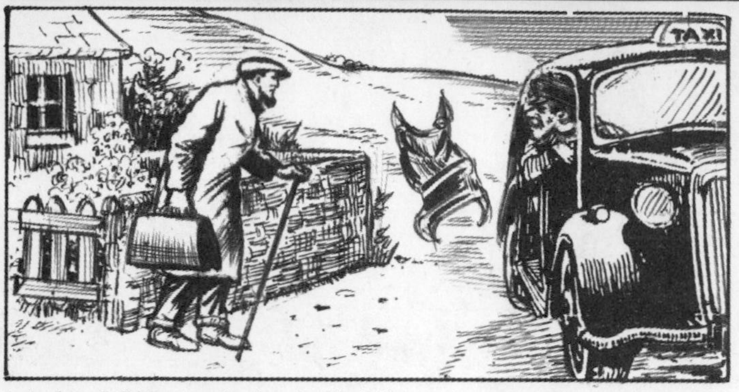
TAXI

1. Andrew Selkirk was going into Peebles Infirmary for an operation, so there would be nobody to look after Bag for a couple of days. "The appointment for ma breast implants has come through, Baggie," he explained to his faithful polythene companion. "So a'm afraid ye'll hae tae fend frae yersel'." As his master got into the taxi, a sudden gust of wind took the border binliner off to find his friends.

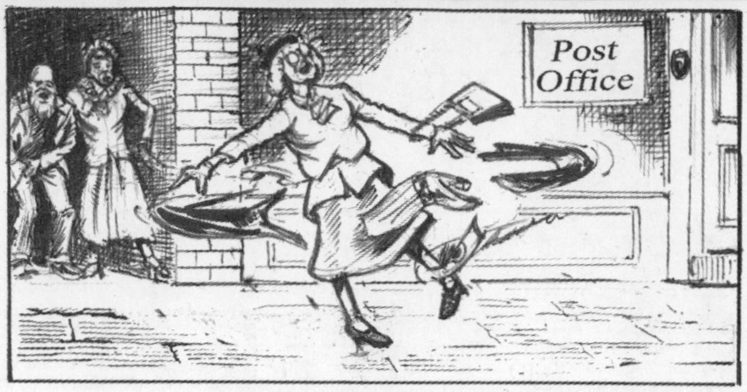
Post Office

2. He soon found them outside the post office, and the pack of stray bags merrily chased each other about. Suddenly wee Rab, a scruffy West Highland carrier, accidentally got caught up in the legs of old Ma Peggotty, bringing her crashing to the ground. "Help m'boab!" she cried. "A ken a've braw bricht ma wee hippie. A'll hae the litter catcher oot, the noo." The litter catcher! The bags scattered in panic.

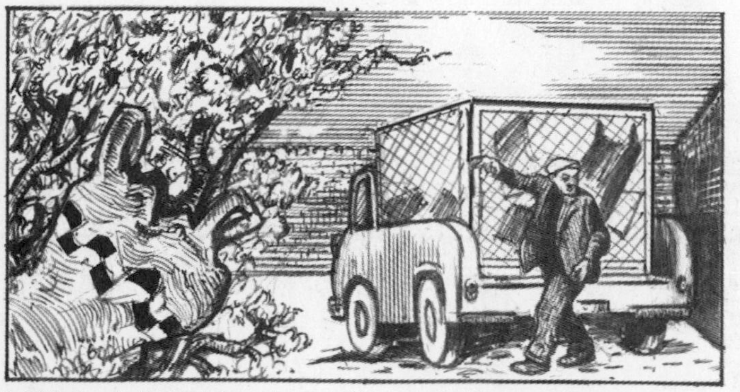

3. With the wind behind them, they gave him a run for his money, but there was to be no escaping from the litter catcher. He chased the bags until they found themselves trapped by a dead end. "Richt, a've caught ye all," he snarled as he locked them in the back of his van. But he'd forgotten about canny wee Rab, who'd managed to scamper away and was watching from under a hedge.

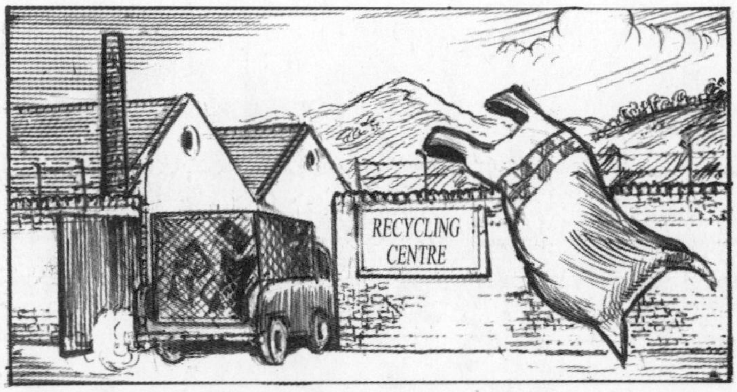
RECYCLING CENTRE

4. Fluttering as hard as he could, Rab followed the van all the way through the busy town centre to the outskirts of Peebles. He wasn't too worried. He and his stray pals had been this way to the landfill site many times before. He knew they would escape through the hole in the fence and soon make their way back across country. But the plucky little carrier's heart sank. The van wasn't going to the dump.

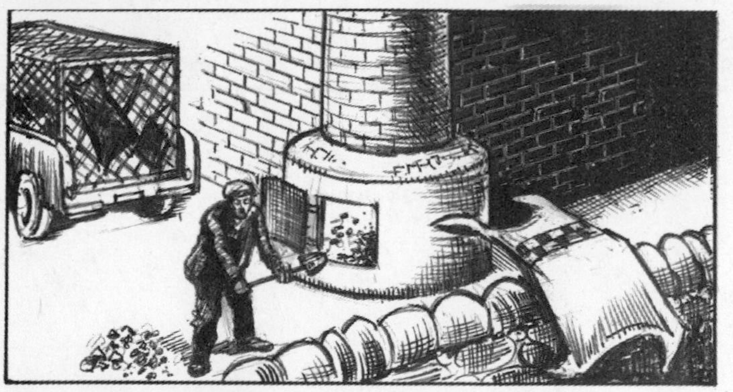

5. Peering over the top of the recycling centre wall, wee Rab was horrified by what he saw. Black Bag and the other strays were securely locked in the cage whilst the litter catcher shovelled coal into the furnace. "Once a get this fire burnin' muckle hot, ye bags're all goin' in," he cackled. Rab knew he didn't have a moment to lose, and immediately rustled off to find help.

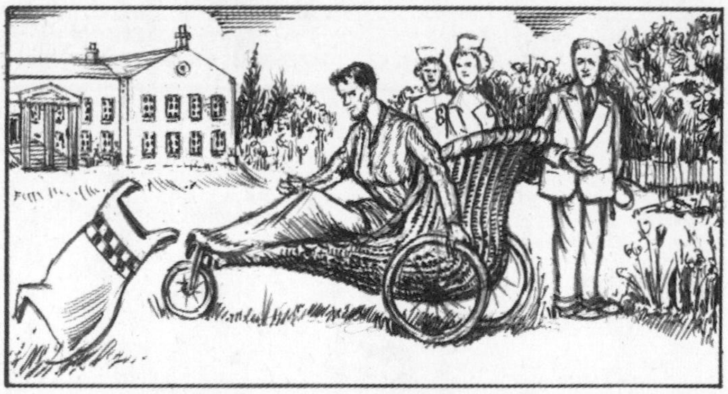

6. Convalescing in the hospital gardens, Andrew Selkirk was surprised to see the scruffy little carrier blowing across the lawn and landing at his feet. "It's wee Rab, isnae it," he said as the bag fluttered frantically at his ankles. "Whit's the matter, wee 'un? Are ye tryin' tae tell me something?" The shepherd, who'd worked with bags all his life, instinctively knew something was wrong and leapt to his feet.

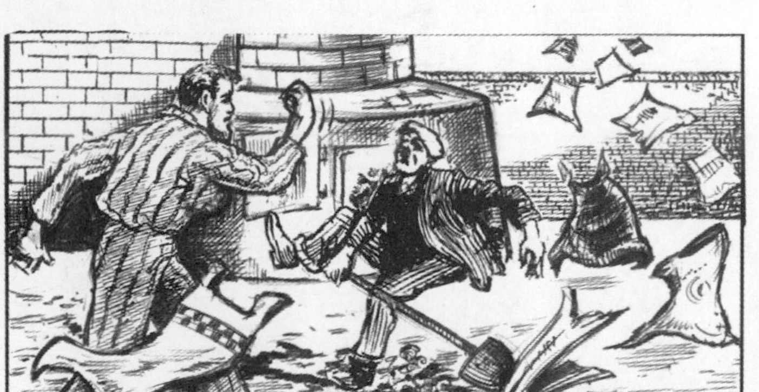

7. Selkirk followed the plucky little fellow all the way across the glen, arriving at the recycling centre only just in time. As they burst in, the litter catcher had the terrified stray bags on his shovel and was about to pitch them into the white hot furnace. Twice Peebles light-middleweight boxing champion, Selkirk din't lose a moment in landing a square uppercut to the scoundrel's ear. The bags were saved!

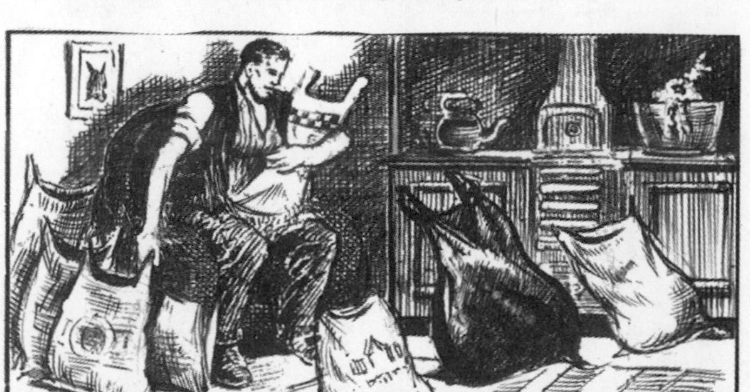

8. Later that evening, Black bag and his litter were safely gathered in Andrew Selkirk's sitting room. "There'll be nae mair strayin' aboot the toon frae ye lads," he told them. "Frae noo on, ye can all live here in ma but'n'ben wi' me an' Black Baggie." And the shepherd had a special treat in store for the bravest stray of all. "As frae ye, wee Rab, a'll hang ye on ma bedroom door frae tae keep ma bras in!"

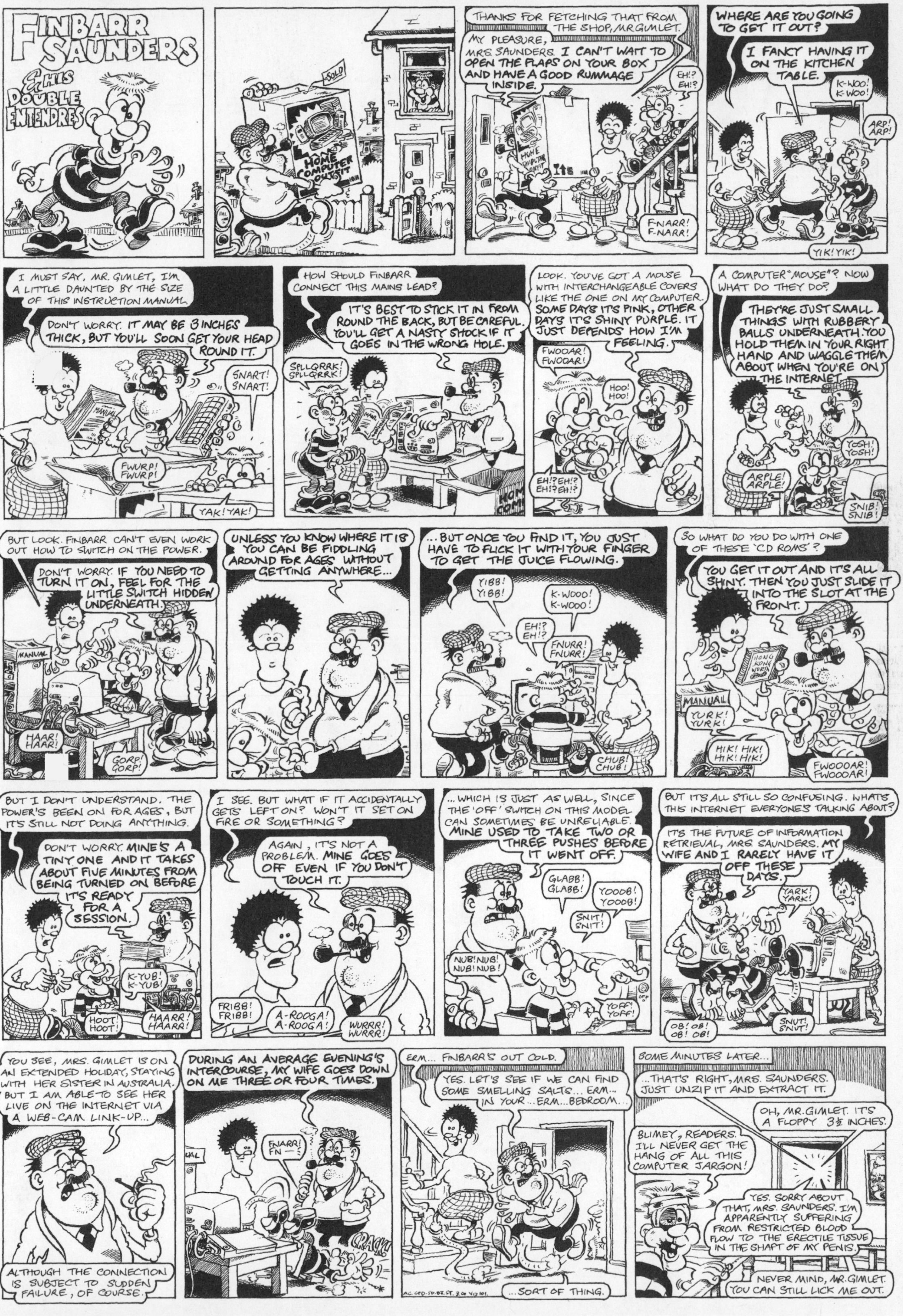

FINBARR SAUNDERS & HIS DOUBLE ENTENDRES
SOLD!
HOME COMPUTER OUTFIT
THANKS FOR FETCHING THAT FROM THE SHOP, MR GIMLET.
MY PLEASURE, MRS. SAUNDERS. I CAN'T WAIT TO OPEN THE FLAPS ON YOUR BOX AND HAVE A GOOD RUMMAGE INSIDE.
EH!? EH!?
F-NARR! F-NARR!
WHERE ARE YOU GOING TO GET IT OUT?
I FANCY HAVING IT ON THE KITCHEN TABLE.
K-WOO! K-WOO!
ARP! ARP!
YIK! YIK!
I MUST SAY, MR. GIMLET, I'M A LITTLE DAUNTED BY THE SIZE OF THIS INSTRUCTION MANUAL.
DON'T WORRY. IT MAY BE 3 INCHES THICK, BUT YOU'LL SOON GET YOUR HEAD ROUND IT.
SNART! SNART!
FWURP! FWURP!
YAK! YAK!
HOW SHOULD FINBARR CONNECT THIS MAINS LEAD?
IT'S BEST TO STICK IT IN FROM ROUND THE BACK, BUT BE CAREFUL. YOU'LL GET A NASTY SHOCK IF IT GOES IN THE WRONG HOLE.
SPLLQRRK! SPLLQRRK!
LOOK. YOU'VE GOT A MOUSE WITH INTERCHANGEABLE COVERS LIKE THE ONE ON MY COMPUTER. SOME DAYS IT'S PINK, OTHER DAYS IT'S SHINY PURPLE. IT JUST DEPENDS HOW I'M FEELING.
FWOOAR! FWOOAR!
HOO! HOO!
EH!? EH!? EH!? EH!?
A COMPUTER "MOUSE"? NOW WHAT DO THEY DO?
THEY'RE JUST SMALL THINGS WITH RUBBERY BALLS UNDERNEATH. YOU HOLD THEM IN YOUR RIGHT HAND AND WAGGLE THEM ABOUT WHEN YOU'RE ON THE INTERNET.
YOSH! YOSH!
ARPLE! ARPLE!
SNIB! SNIB!
BUT LOOK. FINBARR CAN'T EVEN WORK OUT HOW TO SWITCH ON THE POWER.
DON'T WORRY. IF YOU NEED TO TURN IT ON, FEEL FOR THE LITTLE SWITCH HIDDEN UNDERNEATH.
MANUAL
HAAR! HAAR!
GORP! GORP!
UNLESS YOU KNOW WHERE IT IS YOU CAN BE FIDDLING AROUND FOR AGES WITHOUT GETTING ANYWHERE...
...BUT ONCE YOU FIND IT, YOU JUST HAVE TO FLICK IT WITH YOUR FINGER TO GET THE JUICE FLOWING.
YIBB! YIBB!
K-WOOO! K-WOOO!
EH!? EH!?
FNURR! FNURR!
CHUB! CHUB!
SO WHAT DO YOU DO WITH ONE OF THESE 'CD ROMS'?
YOU GET IT OUT AND IT'S ALL SHINY. THEN YOU JUST SLIDE IT INTO THE SLOT AT THE FRONT.
MANUAL
YURK! YURK!
HIK! HIK! HIK! HIK!
FWOOOAR! FWOOOAR!
BUT I DON'T UNDERSTAND. THE POWER'S BEEN ON FOR AGES, BUT IT'S STILL NOT DOING ANYTHING.
DON'T WORRY. MINE'S A TINY ONE AND IT TAKES ABOUT FIVE MINUTES FROM BEING TURNED ON BEFORE IT'S READY FOR A SESSION.
K-YUB! K-YUB!
HOOT! HOOT!
HAARR! HAARR!
I SEE. BUT WHAT IF IT ACCIDENTALLY GETS LEFT ON? WON'T IT SET ON FIRE OR SOMETHING?
AGAIN, IT'S NOT A PROBLEM. MINE GOES OFF EVEN IF YOU DON'T TOUCH IT.
FRIBB! FRIBB!
A-ROOGA! A-ROOGA!
WURRR! WURRR!
...WHICH IS JUST AS WELL, SINCE THE 'OFF' SWITCH ON THIS MODEL CAN SOMETIMES BE UNRELIABLE. MINE USED TO TAKE TWO OR THREE PUSHES BEFORE IT WENT OFF.
GLABB! GLABB!
YOOOB! YOOOB!
SNIT! SNIT!
NUB! NUB! NUB! NUB!
YOFF! YOFF!
BUT IT'S ALL STILL SO CONFUSING. WHAT'S THIS INTERNET EVERYONE'S TALKING ABOUT?
IT'S THE FUTURE OF INFORMATION RETRIEVAL, MRS. SAUNDERS. MY WIFE AND I RARELY HAVE IT OFF THESE DAYS.
YARK! YARK!
OB! OB! OB! OB!
SNUT! SNUT!
YOU SEE, MRS. GIMLET IS ON AN EXTENDED HOLIDAY, STAYING WITH HER SISTER IN AUSTRALIA. BUT I AM ABLE TO SEE HER LIVE ON THE INTERNET VIA A WEB-CAM LINK-UP...
ALTHOUGH THE CONNECTION IS SUBJECT TO SUDDEN FAILURE, OF COURSE.
DURING AN AVERAGE EVENING'S INTERCOURSE, MY WIFE GOES DOWN ON ME THREE OR FOUR TIMES.
FNARR! FN—
CRACK!
ERM... FINBARR'S OUT COLD.
YES. LET'S SEE IF WE CAN FIND SOME SMELLING SALTS... ERM... IN YOUR... ERM... BEDROOM...
...SORT OF THING.
SOME MINUTES LATER...
...THAT'S RIGHT, MRS. SAUNDERS. JUST UNZIP IT AND EXTRACT IT.
OH, MR. GIMLET. IT'S A FLOPPY 3½ INCHES.
BLIMEY, READERS. I'LL NEVER GET THE HANG OF ALL THIS COMPUTER JARGON!
YES. SORRY ABOUT THAT, MRS. SAUNDERS. I'M APPARENTLY SUFFERING FROM RESTRICTED BLOOD FLOW TO THE ERECTILE TISSUE IN THE SHAFT OF MY PENIS.
NEVER MIND, MR. GIMLET. YOU CAN STILL LICK ME OUT.

Letterbocks

It's the page that's fuller than the Pope's pods

Letterbocks
Viz Comic
P.O.Box 1PT
Newcastle NE99 1PT

Do you have an opinion about something? You may think that enough is enough, and fuel duty is far too high. Maybe you think taxing road-users is the only way to fund an effective health service. Or perhaps you think Piltdown man's cock stank. Write and tell us, there's a fantastic wig mug and a teabag for each letter we print.

E-mail
letters@
letterbocks
.com

Star Letter

❑ I've donated over a thousand pounds this year to the World Wildlife Fund. Imagine my anger when I saw them fighting over the money on satellite telly, rather than spending it on vanishing tigers in Sumatra.

Charlie Hamilton
e-mail

What keeps Lizzie dripping?

❑ Enough about the Queen Mum's 100th birthday, I want to know who, or what, has been servicing her love tunnel over the last fifty years. If she has been screwing around, then this is in clear breach of Christian teachings on love and marriage and needs to be exposed. If she has been indulging in regular self-abuse, then what kind of example does this set the rest of us?

Mr. Fox
Shoreham

❑ Why do old people insist on referring to World War I as 'The Great War'? Surely World War II with its higher death toll and use of atomic weapons was loads better.

G. Delaney
London

Slow thinking

❑ With the FIA constantly looking for ways to slow down modern Formula 1 cars, why haven't they tried wrapping hair and fluff around the rear wheel axles? It certainly works on my Scalextric.

J. Gash
e-mail

❑ There's no pleasing my wife. She complains when I leave the toilet seat up, she complains when I leave it down and piss all over it.

Jon
Leeds

Shitting image

Royal
wave

❑ I spotted this picture in the *Leamington Spa Courier*. This woman is apparently constantly mistaken for the Queen Mum. Maybe other readers have spotted a more shit 'lookalike', because I'm sure I haven't.

Ged
Olton

Excreta from the Black Lagoon

❑ Usually when laying a log, its weight causes it to break off as it exits the arse, so you end up laying several smaller logs. While on holiday, I worked out that the bouyancy of the sea should allow one to lay the most enormous log with no breakage. My theory proved correct as a monster rose to the surface and drifted away. However, no scientific journal seems willing to publish my findings.

Prof. Matthew Pollard
Woking

❑ We all saw the Queen Mum enjoying her 100th birthday, but let's not forget the many other centegenarians who have celebrated their happy day.

100
TODAY
FLORENCE
100th

Here's one having a whale of a time recently in Cleveland.

Sarah Morgan, Stockton-on-Tees

❑ On hearing that oil terminals were to be blockaded in protests at fuel prices, I sensibly rushed out to fill my car and half a dozen jerry-cans with four star. When I got to the petrol station, however, there was a mile-long queue of pathetic individuals 'panic buying' the stuff like there was no tomorrow. I was furious.

J. Holsen
Wakefield

It takes Allsorts

❑ My mate Jamie reckons that slugs probably taste like liquorice, but he's not prepared to try one. Have any of your readers eaten a slug, and if so, what did it taste like?

Sam Smith
e-mail

Smile, Please!

❑ I was reading in-flight magazine *Skyline* the other day when I came across this picture of Judith Chalmers trying her best to squeeze out a grin at an awards ceremony. *'Wish I Wasn't Here'*, she appears to be thinking.

Neil Henderson
Shetland

❑ In response to your request for incincere smiles, I spotted this one whilst flicking through Food Trade Review. It's a smile to start with, but looked at for a second or two, it turns into a rather threatening snarl. Scary.

Sarah Newman
Prestwich

HMM. INTERESTING. THE COMPOUND BURNS WITH A YELLOW FLAME, WHICH INDICATES A HIGH PROPORTION OF SODIUM PRESENT. NOW I'LL TRY TO FIND OUT THE RADICAL. UGH UGH!
BOOOM!
MY WIFE LIKES TO EXPERIMENT DURING SEX

Shit Creek

❑ How about bringing back 'Celebrity Cunts'? I work in one of our more publicised art galleries for sub-minimal wages and one morning I encountered 'top geezer' Alan Davies. However,

Davies - pube-haired

on requesting some ID for his audio guide, I was treated to a charming histrionic strop, featuring some airline points card being waved in my face and some fine prima donna "do you know who I am?" tactics. Suffice to say, his embarrassed girlfriend wiped up the mess that ensued and I vowed never to get a mortgage with the Abbey National. What an egotistical pubey-haired 'man of the people' tosser.

Toby
e-mail

Remains of the Tray

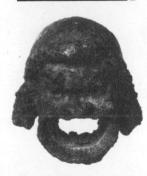

❑ I like jokes about arses and shit, but I'm also very intelligent, so I read *Viz* and *History Today.* Imagine my surprise when a character from the former turned up on the pages of the latter.

Puella Magna
Favilla

❑ In this modern age it is possible to tell from the markings on a bullet which gun it was fired from. Similarly, it must be possible to tell from the ridges on a dog turd which dog's arse delivered it, thus allowing the owner's face to be rubbed in it.

D. Whaslam
e-mail

❑ I went to sign on the other day and was told that I couldn't have any money due to the fact that I was in full time employment. If this government think I'm going to give up a perfectly good job just to get hold of their poxy dole, they must be stupid. Now wonder this country is in such a bloody state.

Alan Wade
Stockport

Fatal contraction

❑ So fanny-chinned filmstar Michael Douglas and his Welsh rarebint Catherine Zeta-Jones are calling their son Dylan Douglas. I wonder how long he will have been at school before someone shortens it to DylDo.

Ian Iro
Ilkley

What a raquet

❑ Why do women tennis players make such a loud grunt every time they hit the ball? If the act of hitting a ball is so difficult for them, perhaps they should stick to more ladylike pastimes such as knitting or dressmaking.

Ric Porter
London

❑ 'Always listen to your heart' sang Paul Young

Paul Young - not the dead one, another one - yesterday

on the latest Mike and the Mechanics album. Perhaps if he'd listened to his own, or better still, got his doctor to listen to it, he wouldn't have popped his clogs of a heart attack a few weeks back.

Trevor John
Basingstoke

❑ During the recent petrol crisis, I sat for over two hours in a queue at my local Esso station. I was furious, as I only wanted to buy a Mars bar and a paper.

Langy
Twickenham

❑ I'm a driver, but the rising cost of fuel prices doesn't bother me as I always put £10 worth in my tank.

Lost his name
Sorry

TOP TIPS

SCULPTORS. When designing a new statue for your city centre, why not add a stone traffic cone to its head to discourage pissed students from risking death at 3.00 am.

Garry Smith
East Kilbride

RATS. Improve your image by attaching a small brush to your arse and pretending to be a squirrel.

Colin Saunders
e-mail

NEED to measure an alligator but only have a school ruler? Simply measure the distance between its eyes in inches, to give its overall length in feet.

Jungle John
Liverpool

TRAINLINE telephone employees. Retain an air of mystery by never giving accurate information.

Kelly Durkin
e-mail

EXECUTIVES. Don't get stressed wasting money on anti-stress toys. Simply fill a condom with diarrhoea and tie a knot in the end. Hey presto! Your own anti-stress toy to squeeze all day long.

Laurence Lennin
e-mail

ORIENTALS who would like to look more western. Insert a spaghetti hoop instead of your contact lenses. Hula hoops could also be used in more extreme circumstances.

C. McClintock
e-mail

UGLY birds. Become better looking by simply moving North.

Andy Inman
Inverness

TWINS. Always make your twin try on a new outfit before you buy it so you can see exactly how you will look in it. (This does not work if your twin is of the opposite sex. Unless you are a drag queen. Or the opposite of a drag queen).

Matt Jones
Cambridge

Miriam

ANSWERS YOUR PROBLEMS IN CHINESE

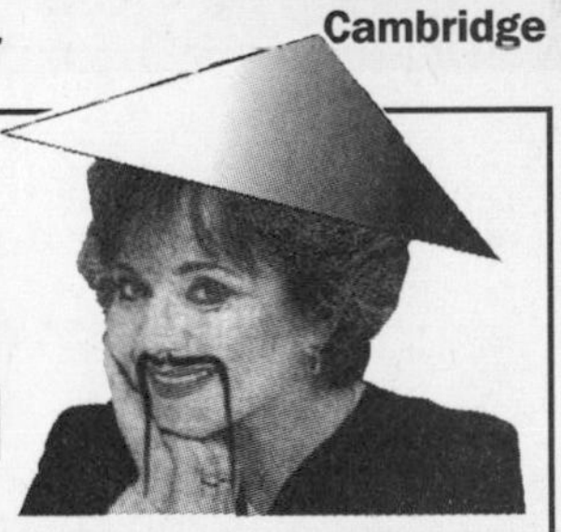

LETTER OF THE DAY

Dear Miriam... **I'm sixteen, and recently on holiday I had sex with this boy.** He told me you can't get pregnant the first time you do it, but now I've missed my period. Please don't tell me to go to the doctor, as he's a family friend and I'm terrified he'll tell my mum. Help me, Miriam. I don't know which way to turn.

MB, Kidderminster.

Miriam says... 棄トナー容器も、このプログラムでリサイクルいたします。感光ドラムと廃棄トナー容器は、新たにご購入された製品を梱包していた箱に入れてご返却ください。使用済みの廃光ドラムは、オレンジ色のトレイに差し込んでください。使用済みの廃棄トナー容器は、容器に付いている栓でふたをしてください。郵送の際には、トナーカート

Dear Miriam... I'm 28, and married with two young children. I recently started work in a large office. The other day my boss asked me to stay behind after work to help him with some filing. However, when we were alone he made a pass at me. I made it clear that I wasn't interested but he told me that if I didn't give in to his demands, I'd be looking for another job, so reluctantly I performed oral sex on him in the photocopying room. I was sure my husband was going to find out, as his best friend is my boss's siamese twin and he saw everything. However, he now says he won't tell my husband if I'll go with him to a stables and have anal intercourse with a horse. My boss says he'll sack me anyway if he discovers I've been going with a horse. My husband is a murderer and he's threatened to murder me if he finds out what's been going on, and also if I lose my job. I think the horse is HIV positive. Please help me Miriam, I am starting to lose sleep worrying about this.

JS, Reading

Miriam says... 感光ド

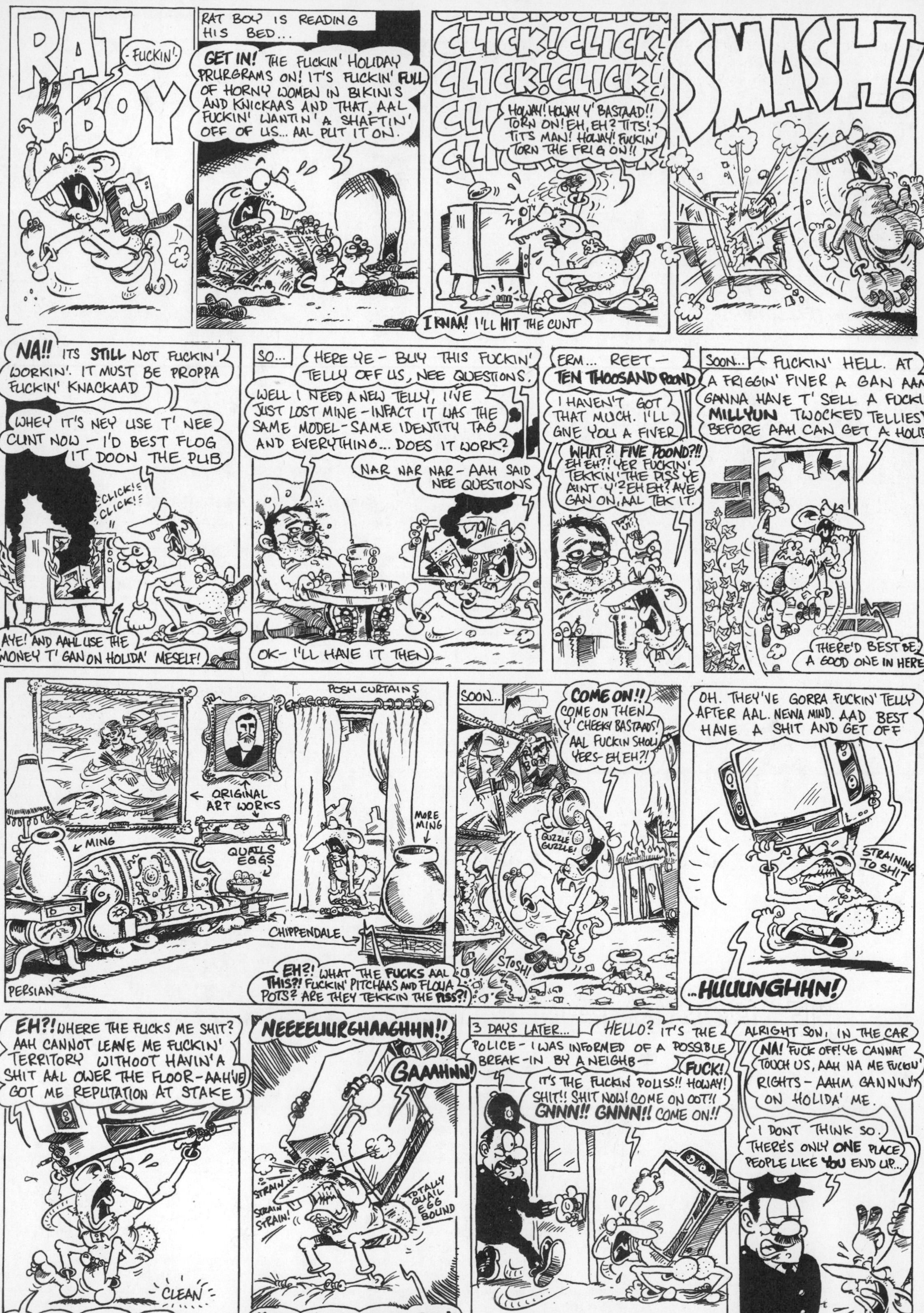
RAT BOY
-FUCKIN'-
RAT BOY IS READING HIS BED...
GET IN! THE FUCKIN' HOLIDAY PRURGRAMS ON! IT'S FUCKIN' FULL OF HORNY WOMEN IN BIKINIS AND KNICKAAS AND THAT, AAL FUCKIN' WANTIN' A SHAFTIN' OFF OF US... AAL PUT IT ON.
CLICK! CLICK! CLICK! CLICK!
HOWAY! HOWAY Y' BASTAAD!! TORN ON! EH, EH? TITS! TITS MAN! HOWAY! FUCKIN' TORN THE FRIG ON!!
I KNAA! I'LL HIT THE CUNT
SMASH!
NA!! ITS STILL NOT FUCKIN' WORKIN'. IT MUST BE PROPPA FUCKIN' KNACKAAD
WHEY IT'S NEY USE T' NEE CUNT NOW — I'D BEST FLOG IT DOON THE PUB.
CLICK! CLICK!
AYE! AND AAHL USE THE MONEY T' GAN ON HOLIDA' MESELF!
SO...
HERE YE — BUY THIS FUCKIN' TELLY OFF US, NEE QUESTIONS.
WELL I NEED A NEW TELLY, I'VE JUST LOST MINE — INFACT IT WAS THE SAME MODEL — SAME IDENTITY TAG AND EVERYTHING... DOES IT WORK?
NAR NAR NAR — AAH SAID NEE QUESTIONS
OK — I'LL HAVE IT THEN
ERM... REET — TEN THOOSAND POOND
I HAVEN'T GOT THAT MUCH. I'LL GIVE YOU A FIVER
WHAT?! FIVE POOND?!! EH EH?! YER FUCKIN' TEKKIN' THE PISS YE AINT Y'? EH EH? AYE, GAN ON, AAL TEK IT.
SOON...
FUCKIN' HELL. AT A FRIGGIN' FIVER A GAN AAM GANNA HAVE T' SELL A FUCKIN' MILLYUN TWOCKED TELLIES BEFORE AAH CAN GET A HOLIDA
THERE'D BEST BE A GOOD ONE IN HERE
POSH CURTAINS
ORIGINAL ART WORKS
MING
QUAILS EGGS
MORE MING
CHIPPENDALE
PERSIAN
EH?! WHAT THE FUCKS AAL THIS?! FUCKIN' PITCHAAS AND FLOUA POTS? ARE THEY TEKKIN THE PISS?!
SOON...
COME ON!! COME ON THEN Y' CHEEKY BASTAADS! AAL FUCKIN SHOW YERS — EH, EH?!
GUZZLE GUZZLE!
STOSH!
OH. THEY'VE GORRA FUCKIN' TELLY AFTER AAL. NEWA MIND. AAD BEST HAVE A SHIT AND GET OFF
STRAINING TO SHIT
..HUUUNGHHN!
EH?! WHERE THE FUCKS ME SHIT? AAH CANNOT LEAVE ME FUCKIN' TERRITORY WITHOOT HAVIN' A SHIT AAL OWER THE FLOOR — AAH'VE GOT ME REPUTATION AT STAKE
CLEAN
AAHL HAVE ANOTHER GAN
NEEEEUURGHAAGHHN!!
GAAAHNN!
STRAIN
STRAIN STRAIN!
TOTALLY QUAIL EGG BOUND
HHUUMMMPHWOORR!!
3 DAYS LATER...
HELLO? IT'S THE POLICE — I WAS INFORMED OF A POSSIBLE BREAK-IN BY A NEIGHB—
FUCK!
IT'S THE FUCKIN POLISS!! HOWAY! SHIT!! SHIT NOW! COME ON OOT!! GNNN!! GNNN!! COME ON!!
ALRIGHT SON, IN THE CAR
NA! FUCK OFF! YE CANNAT TOUCH US, AAH NA ME FUCKIN' RIGHTS — AAHM GANNIN' ON HOLIDA' ME.
I DONT THINK SO. THERE'S ONLY ONE PLACE PEOPLE LIKE YOU END UP...

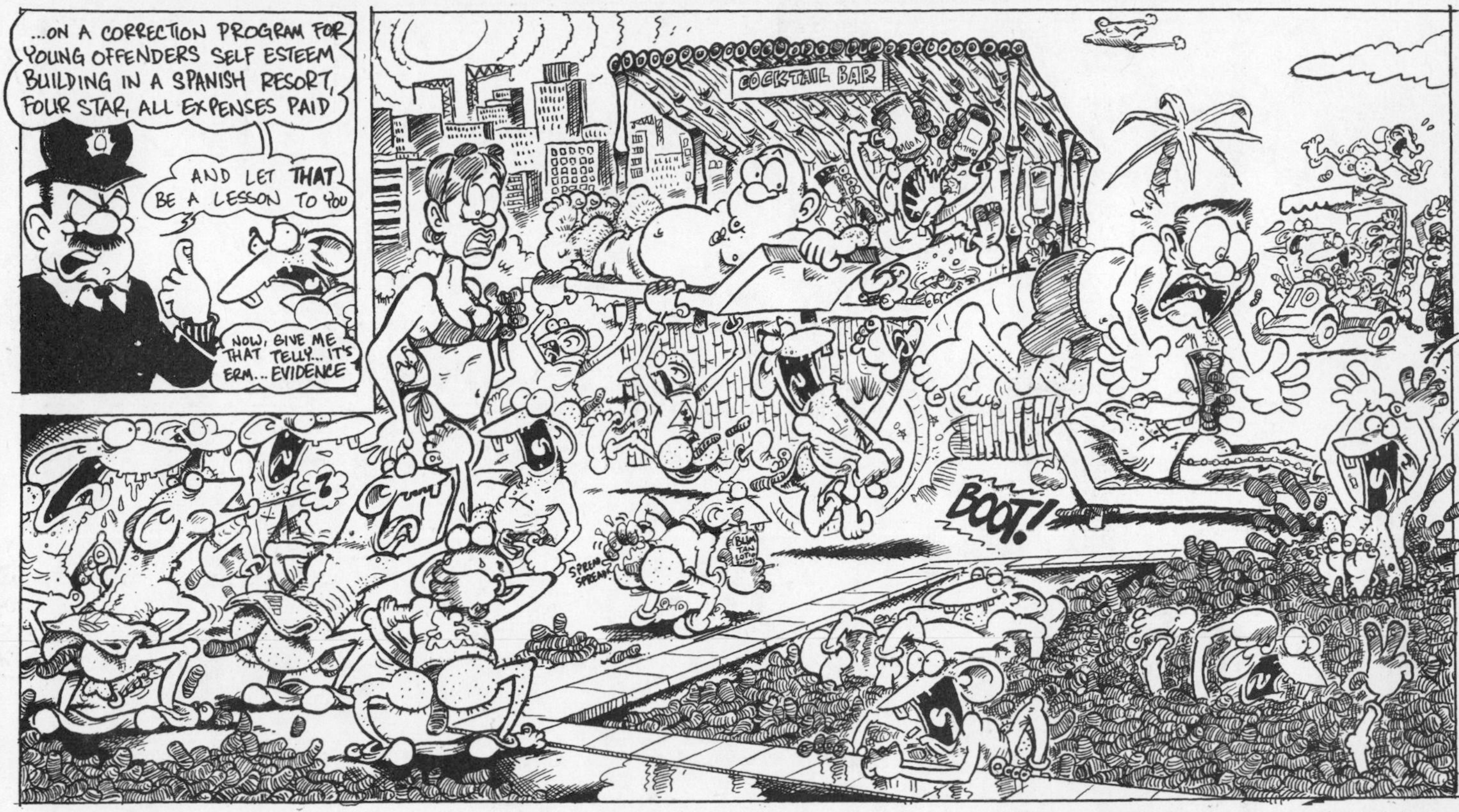

...ON A CORRECTION PROGRAM FOR YOUNG OFFENDERS SELF ESTEEM BUILDING IN A SPANISH RESORT, FOUR STAR, ALL EXPENSES PAID
AND LET THAT BE A LESSON TO YOU
NOW, GIVE ME THAT TELLY... IT'S ERM... EVIDENCE
COCKTAIL BAR
BOOT!

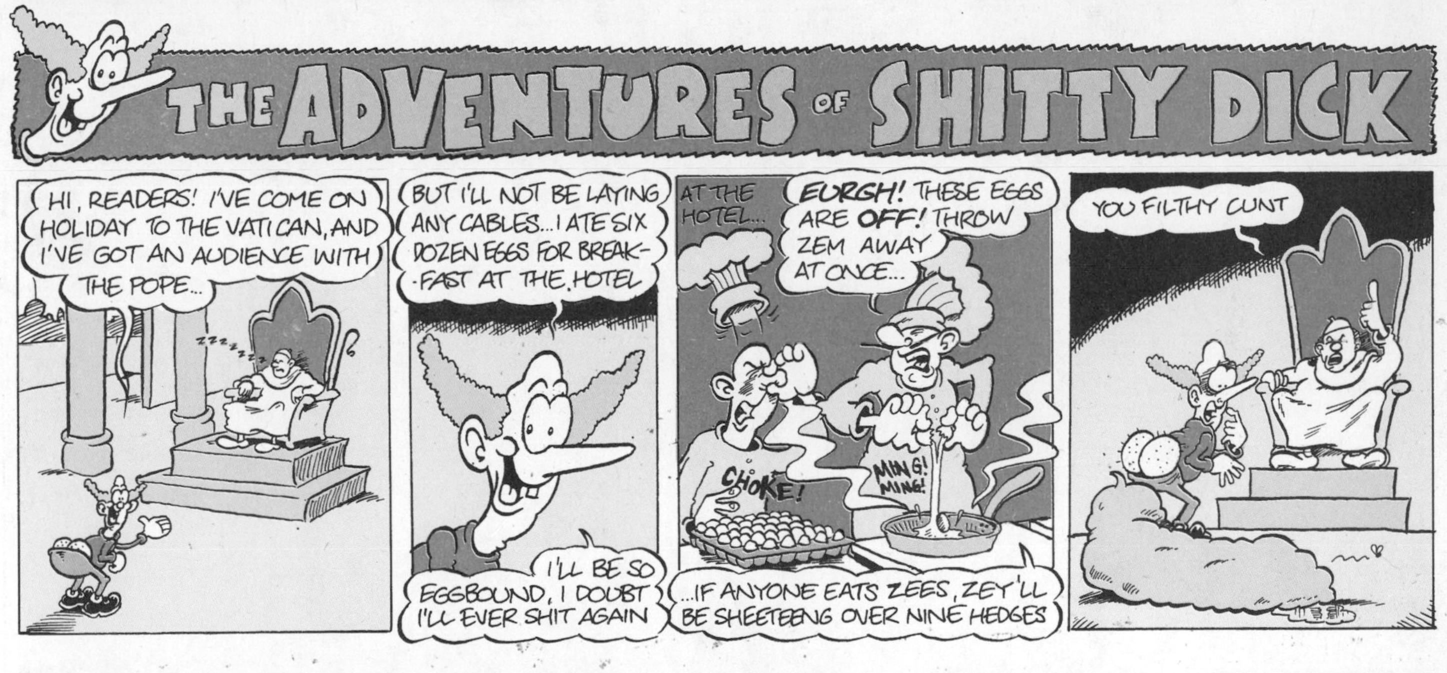

THE ADVENTURES OF SHITTY DICK
HI, READERS! I'VE COME ON HOLIDAY TO THE VATICAN, AND I'VE GOT AN AUDIENCE WITH THE POPE...
BUT I'LL NOT BE LAYING ANY CABLES... I ATE SIX DOZEN EGGS FOR BREAK-FAST AT THE HOTEL
I'LL BE SO EGGBOUND, I DOUBT I'LL EVER SHIT AGAIN
AT THE HOTEL...
EURGH! THESE EGGS ARE OFF! THROW ZEM AWAY AT ONCE...
CHOKE!
MING! MING!
...IF ANYONE EATS ZEES, ZEY'LL BE SHEETEENG OVER NINE HEDGES
YOU FILTHY CUNT

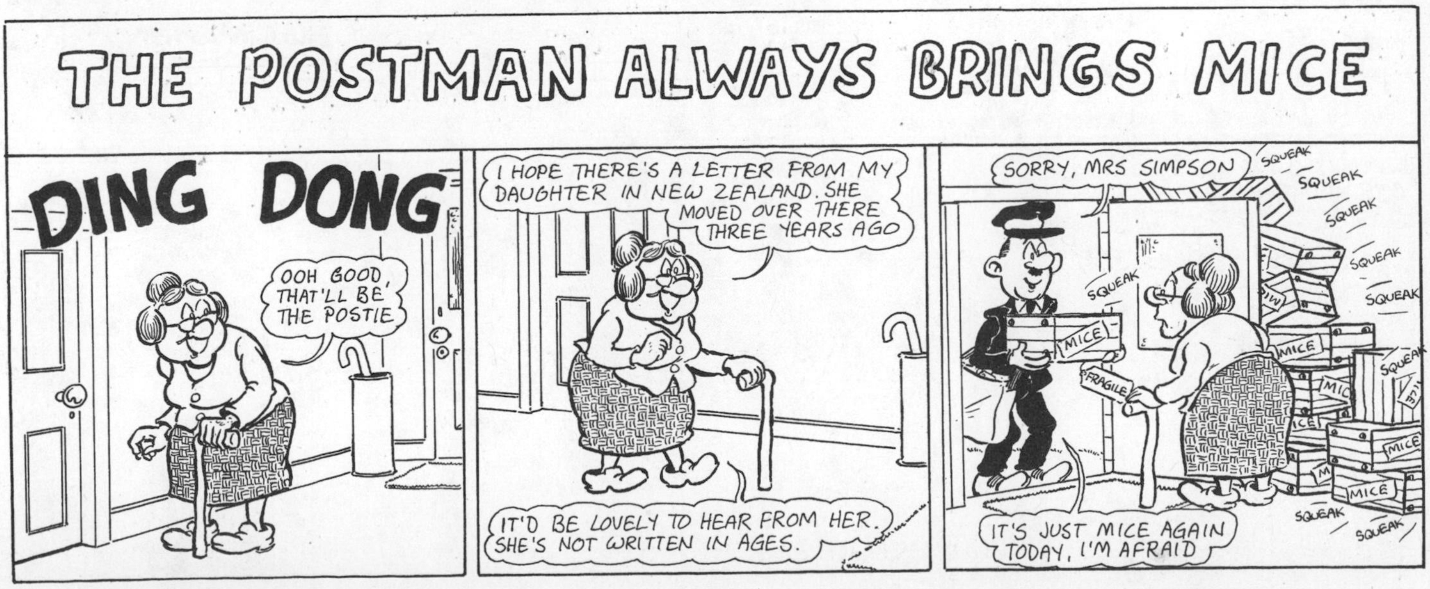

THE POSTMAN ALWAYS BRINGS MICE
DING DONG
OOH GOOD, THAT'LL BE THE POSTIE
I HOPE THERE'S A LETTER FROM MY DAUGHTER IN NEW ZEALAND. SHE MOVED OVER THERE THREE YEARS AGO
IT'D BE LOVELY TO HEAR FROM HER. SHE'S NOT WRITTEN IN AGES.
SORRY, MRS SIMPSON
SQUEAK
MICE
FRAGILE
IT'S JUST MICE AGAIN TODAY, I'M AFRAID

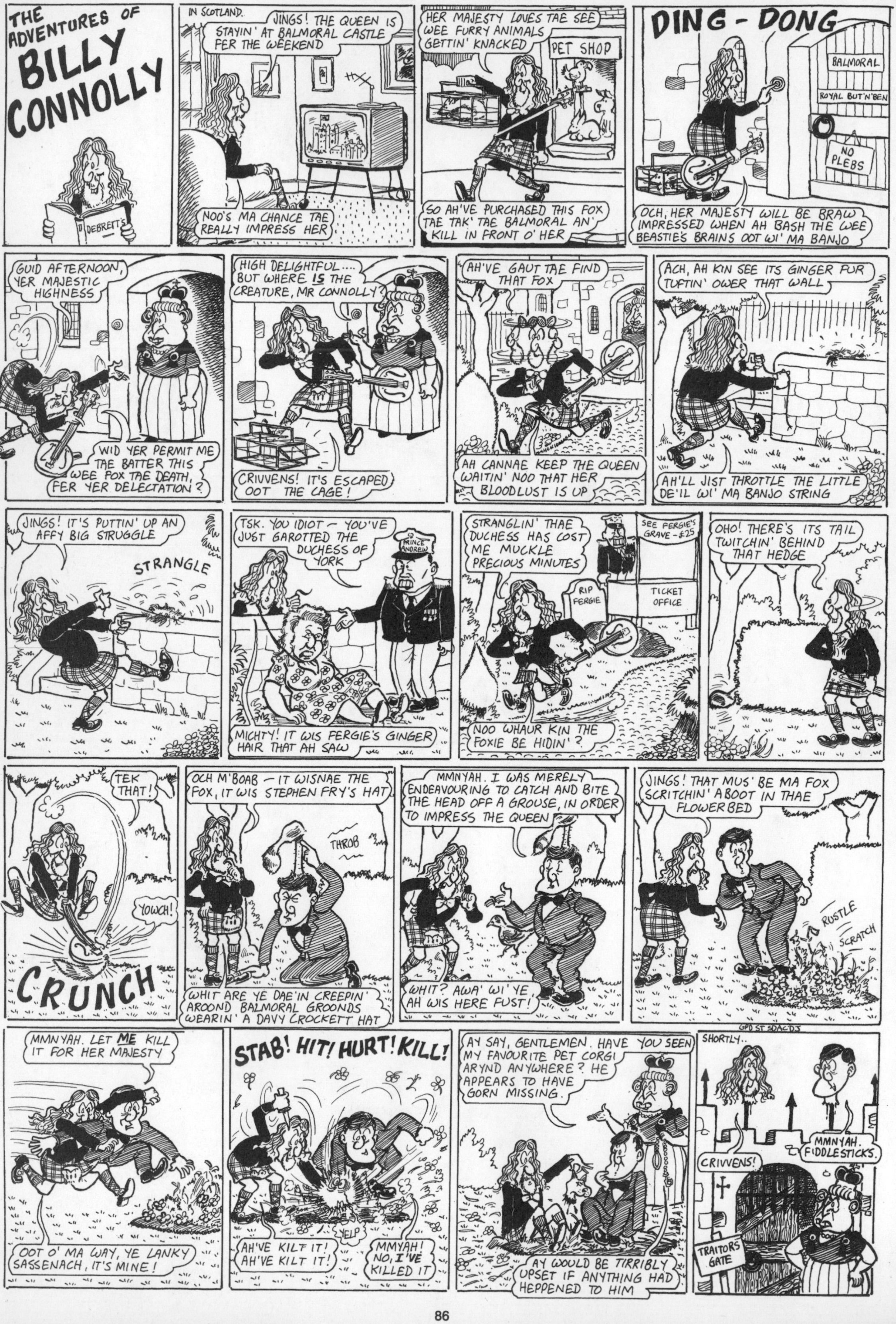
THE ADVENTURES OF BILLY CONNOLLY
DEBRETT'S
IN SCOTLAND.
JINGS! THE QUEEN IS STAYIN' AT BALMORAL CASTLE FER THE WEEKEND
NOO'S MA CHANCE TAE REALLY IMPRESS HER
HER MAJESTY LOVES TAE SEE WEE FURRY ANIMALS GETTIN' KNACKED
PET SHOP
SO AH'VE PURCHASED THIS FOX TAE TAK' TAE BALMORAL AN' KILL IN FRONT O' HER
DING - DONG
BALMORAL
ROYAL BUT'N'BEN
NO PLEBS
OCH, HER MAJESTY WILL BE BRAW IMPRESSED WHEN AH BASH THE WEE BEASTIE'S BRAINS OOT WI' MA BANJO
GUID AFTERNOON, YER MAJESTIC HIGHNESS
WID YER PERMIT ME TAE BATTER THIS WEE FOX TAE DEATH, FER YER DELECTATION?
HIGH DELIGHTFUL.... BUT WHERE IS THE CREATURE, MR CONNOLLY?
CRIVVENS! IT'S ESCAPED OOT THE CAGE!
AH'VE GAUT TAE FIND THAT FOX
AH CANNAE KEEP THE QUEEN WAITIN' NOO THAT HER BLOODLUST IS UP
ACH, AH KIN SEE ITS GINGER FUR TUFTIN' OWER THAT WALL
AH'LL JIST THROTTLE THE LITTLE DE'IL WI' MA BANJO STRING
JINGS! IT'S PUTTIN' UP AN AFFY BIG STRUGGLE
STRANGLE
TSK. YOU IDIOT — YOU'VE JUST GAROTTED THE DUCHESS OF YORK
PRINCE ANDREW
MICHTY! IT WIS FERGIE'S GINGER HAIR THAT AH SAW
STRANGLIN' THAE DUCHESS HAS COST ME MUCKLE PRECIOUS MINUTES
SEE FERGIE'S GRAVE - £25
RIP FERGIE
TICKET OFFICE
NOO WHAUR KIN THE FOXIE BE HIDIN'?
OHO! THERE'S ITS TAIL TWITCHIN' BEHIND THAT HEDGE
TEK THAT!
YOWCH!
CRUNCH
OCH M'BOAB — IT WISNAE THE FOX, IT WIS STEPHEN FRY'S HAT
THROB
WHIT ARE YE DAE'IN CREEPIN' AROOND BALMORAL GROONDS WEARIN' A DAVY CROCKETT HAT
MMNYAH. I WAS MERELY ENDEAVOURING TO CATCH AND BITE THE HEAD OFF A GROUSE, IN ORDER TO IMPRESS THE QUEEN
WHIT? AWA' WI' YE, AH WIS HERE FUST!
JINGS! THAT MUS' BE MA FOX SCRITCHIN' ABOOT IN THAE FLOWERBED
RUSTLE
SCRATCH
MMNYAH. LET ME KILL IT FOR HER MAJESTY
OOT O' MA WAY, YE LANKY SASSENACH, IT'S MINE!
STAB! HIT! HURT! KILL!
YELP
AH'VE KILT IT! AH'VE KILT IT!
MMYAH! NO, I'VE KILLED IT
AY SAY, GENTLEMEN. HAVE YOU SEEN MY FAVOURITE PET CORGI ARYND ANYWHERE? HE APPEARS TO HAVE GORN MISSING.
AY WOULD BE TIRRIBLY UPSET IF ANYTHING HAD HEPPENED TO HIM
SHORTLY..
CRIVVENS!
MMNYAH. FIDDLESTICKS.
TRAITORS GATE

"PULL!"... BANG!!

For a GREAT day out visit

Lesley Grantham's

Clay Taxi Driver Shooting Range

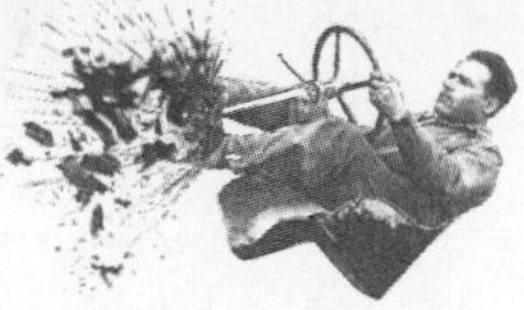

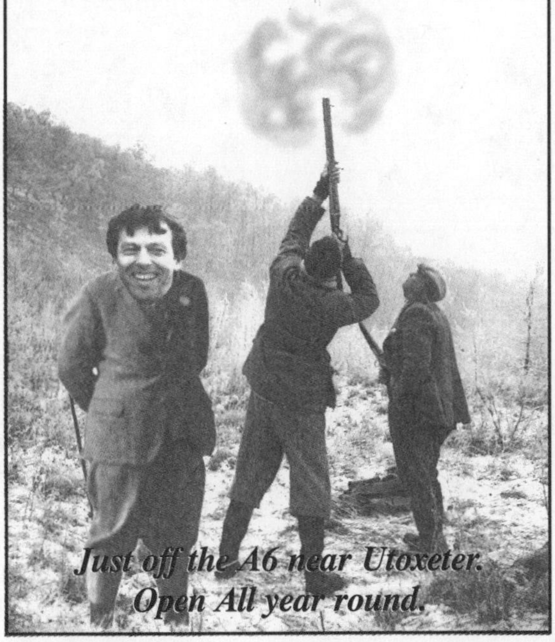

Just off the A6 near Utoxeter. Open All year round.

Ernst Rubic presents...

The Rubic Cube House

The World's Most Perplexing Building

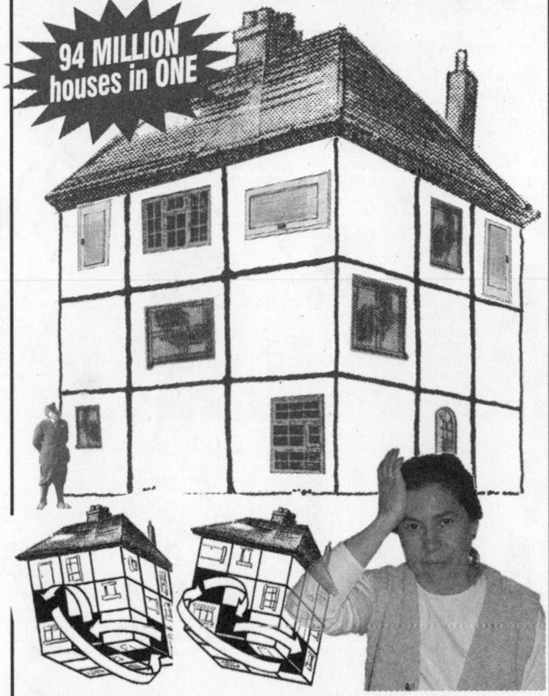

94 MILLION houses in ONE

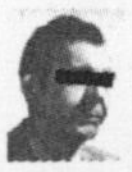

"It took me weeks to get all the bedrooms on the top floor. When I finally managed it, my wife, Mrs. B. of Essex pointed out that the en-suite bathroom was upside down."
Mr. B, Essex

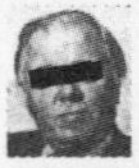

"I spent a year getting my Rubic Cube house right. Then one day, I nipped to the shops and when I got back my four year old son had mixed it up again. Now my front door is on the third floor and I can't get in."
Mr. J, Hull

Prices start from as little as £59,999

(includes carpets all throughout, curtains, fixtures, fittings and full instructions on how to solve your house)

Japan says 'Sorry' at Last

JAPAN has finally apologised for the suffering caused to thousands of people who were forced to listen to their awful songs nearly two decades ago.

Veteran listeners have for years been demanding that the art school

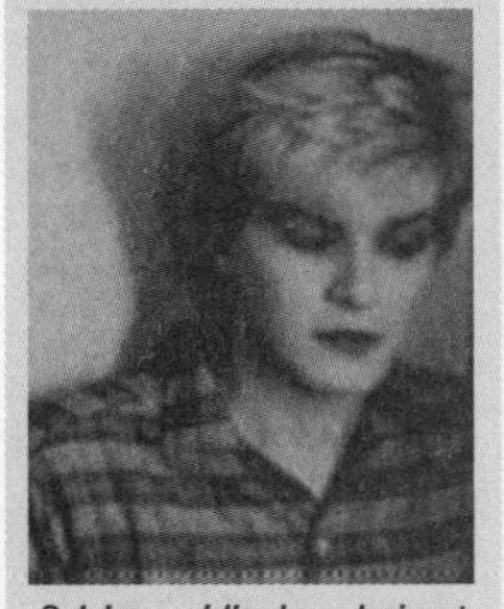

Sylvian - ridiculous haircut

band say they are sorry for releasing "I Second That Emotion" in 1982.

Floppy

There was outrage six years ago when former singer David Sylvian failed to use the word "sorry" in a statement expressing his regret for having a floppy hairstyle and wearing women's lipstick like a puff.

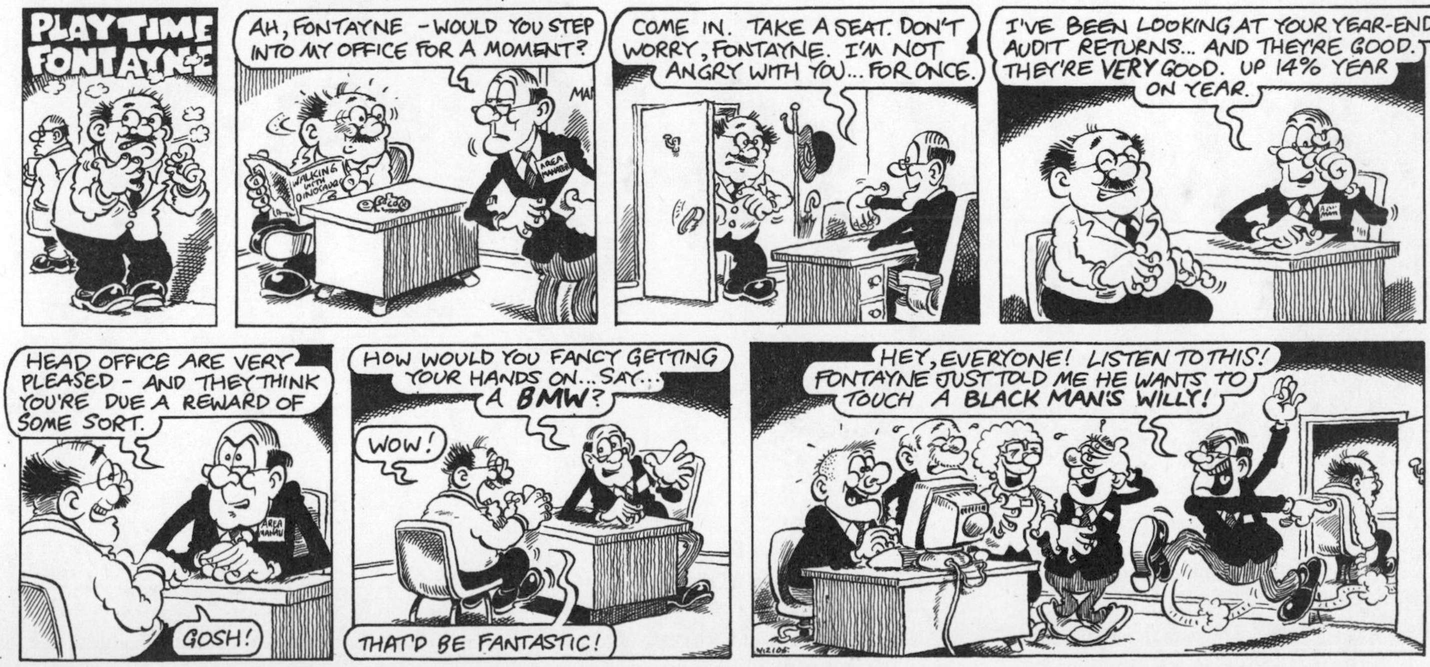

PLAYTIME FONTAYNE
AH, FONTAYNE - WOULD YOU STEP INTO MY OFFICE FOR A MOMENT?
COME IN. TAKE A SEAT. DON'T WORRY, FONTAYNE. I'M NOT ANGRY WITH YOU... FOR ONCE.
I'VE BEEN LOOKING AT YOUR YEAR-END AUDIT RETURNS... AND THEY'RE GOOD. THEY'RE VERY GOOD. UP 14% YEAR ON YEAR.
HEAD OFFICE ARE VERY PLEASED - AND THEY THINK YOU'RE DUE A REWARD OF SOME SORT.
GOSH!
HOW WOULD YOU FANCY GETTING YOUR HANDS ON... SAY... A BMW?
WOW!
THAT'D BE FANTASTIC!
HEY, EVERYONE! LISTEN TO THIS! FONTAYNE JUST TOLD ME HE WANTS TO TOUCH A BLACK MAN'S WILLY!

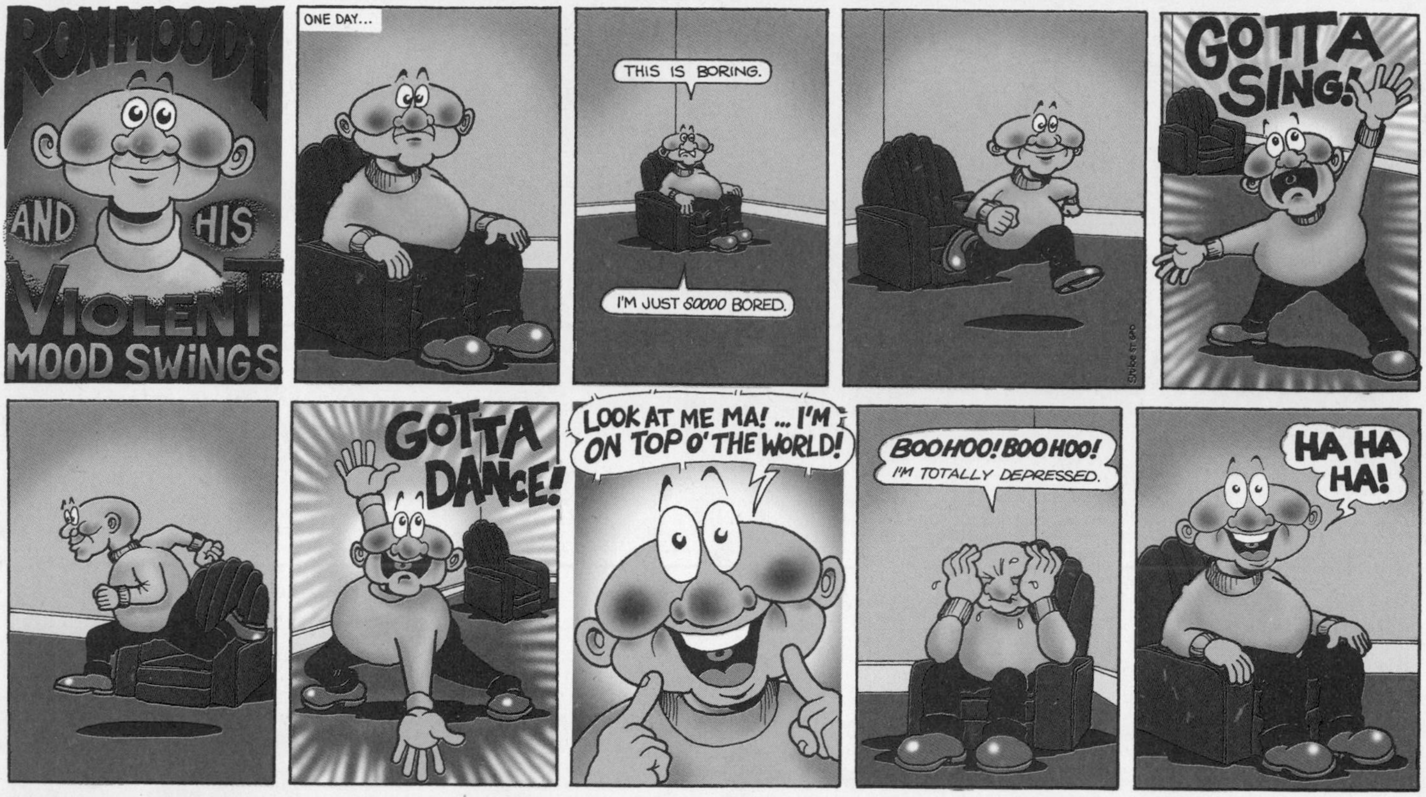
RON MOODY AND HIS VIOLENT MOOD SWINGS
ONE DAY...
THIS IS BORING.
I'M JUST SOOOO BORED.
GOTTA SING!
GOTTA DANCE!
LOOK AT ME MA! ... I'M ON TOP O' THE WORLD!
BOO HOO! BOO HOO! I'M TOTALLY DEPRESSED.
HA HA HA!

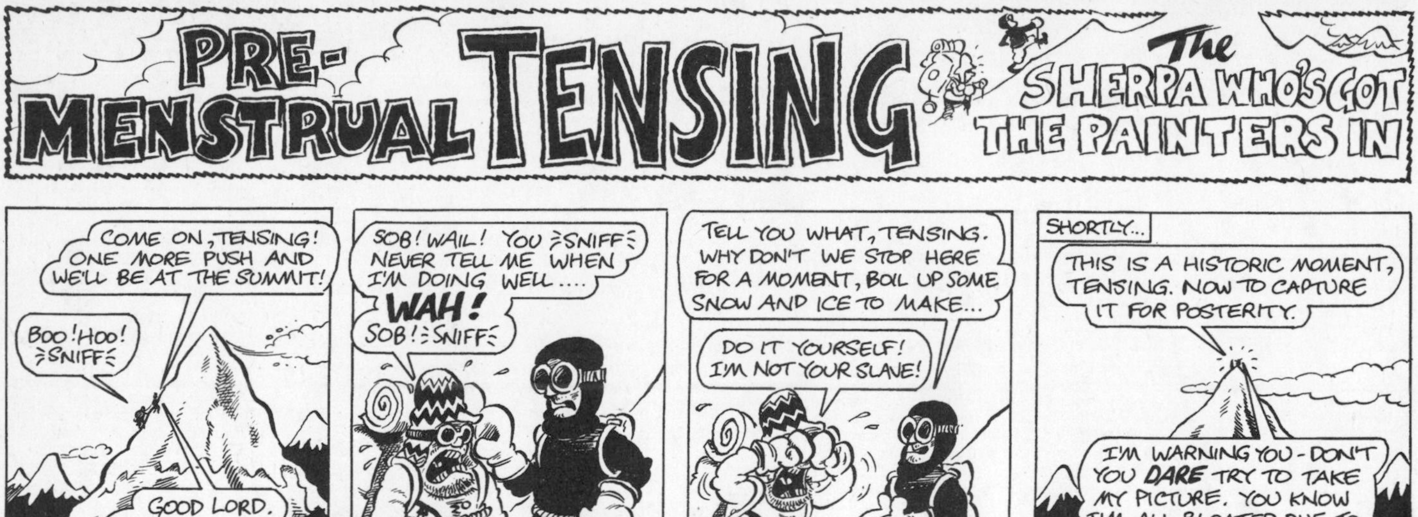
PRE-MENSTRUAL TENSING
The SHERPA WHO'S GOT THE PAINTERS IN
COME ON, TENSING! ONE MORE PUSH AND WE'LL BE AT THE SUMMIT!
BOO! HOO! SNIFF
GOOD LORD. WHATEVER IS THE MATTER?
SOB! WAIL! YOU SNIFF NEVER TELL ME WHEN I'M DOING WELL.... WAH! SOB! SNIFF
ERM...THERE THERE OLD CHAP.
TELL YOU WHAT, TENSING. WHY DON'T WE STOP HERE FOR A MOMENT, BOIL UP SOME SNOW AND ICE TO MAKE...
DO IT YOURSELF! I'M NOT YOUR SLAVE!
WAH! BOO! WAIL!
SHORTLY...
THIS IS A HISTORIC MOMENT, TENSING. NOW TO CAPTURE IT FOR POSTERITY.
I'M WARNING YOU - DON'T YOU DARE TRY TO TAKE MY PICTURE. YOU KNOW I'M ALL BLOATED DUE TO WATER RETENTION. BOO! HOO!
NEXT WEEK - DISASTER STRIKES DURING A TRICKY DESCENT ON THE SOUTH COL - WHEN TENSING GETS HIS WOMEN'S THINGS.

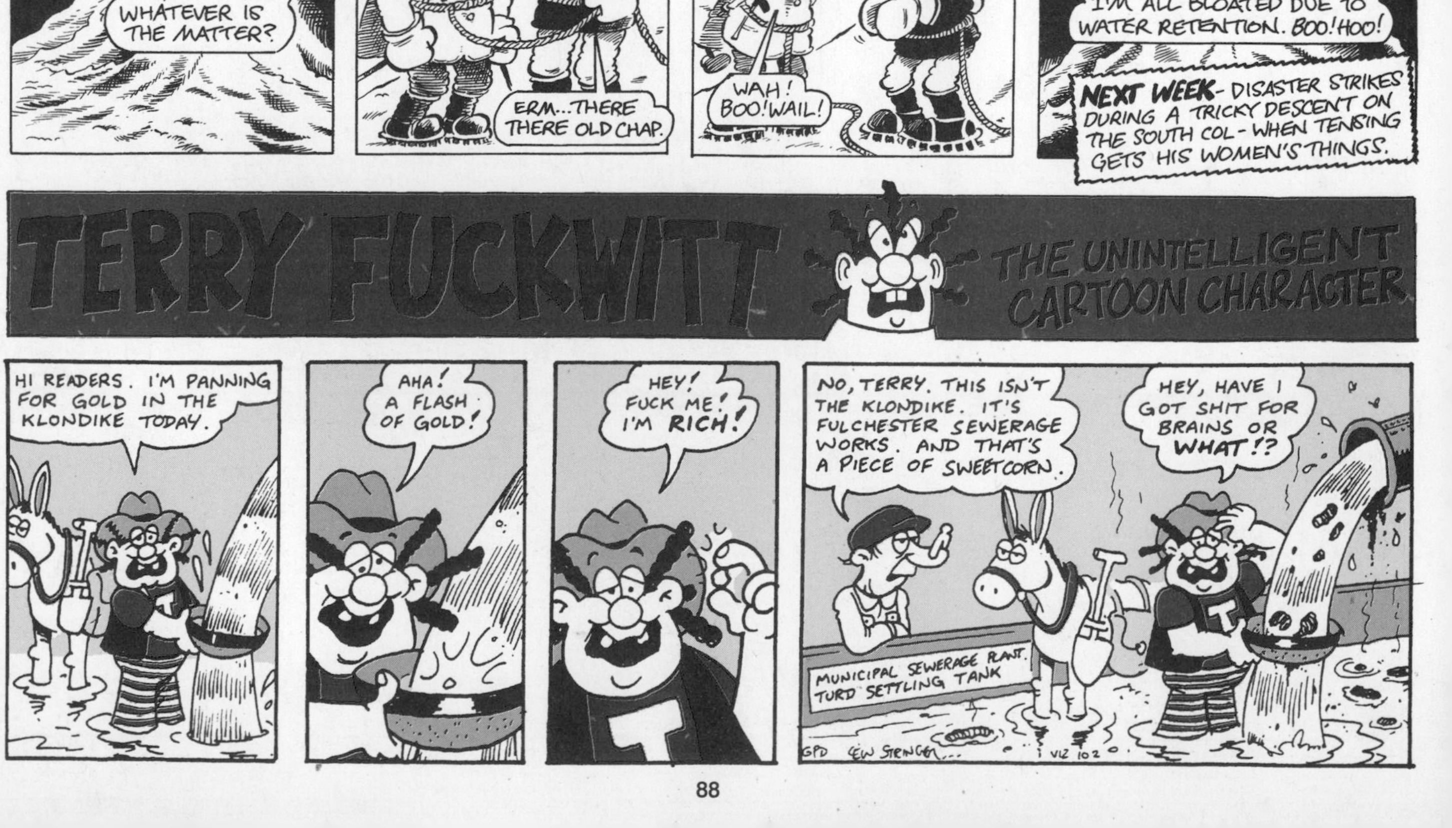
TERRY FUCKWITT
THE UNINTELLIGENT CARTOON CHARACTER
HI READERS. I'M PANNING FOR GOLD IN THE KLONDIKE TODAY.
AHA! A FLASH OF GOLD!
HEY! FUCK ME! I'M RICH!
NO, TERRY. THIS ISN'T THE KLONDIKE. IT'S FULCHESTER SEWERAGE WORKS. AND THAT'S A PIECE OF SWEETCORN.
HEY, HAVE I GOT SHIT FOR BRAINS OR WHAT!?
MUNICIPAL SEWERAGE PLANT. TURD SETTLING TANK
GPD LEW STRINGER
VIZ 102

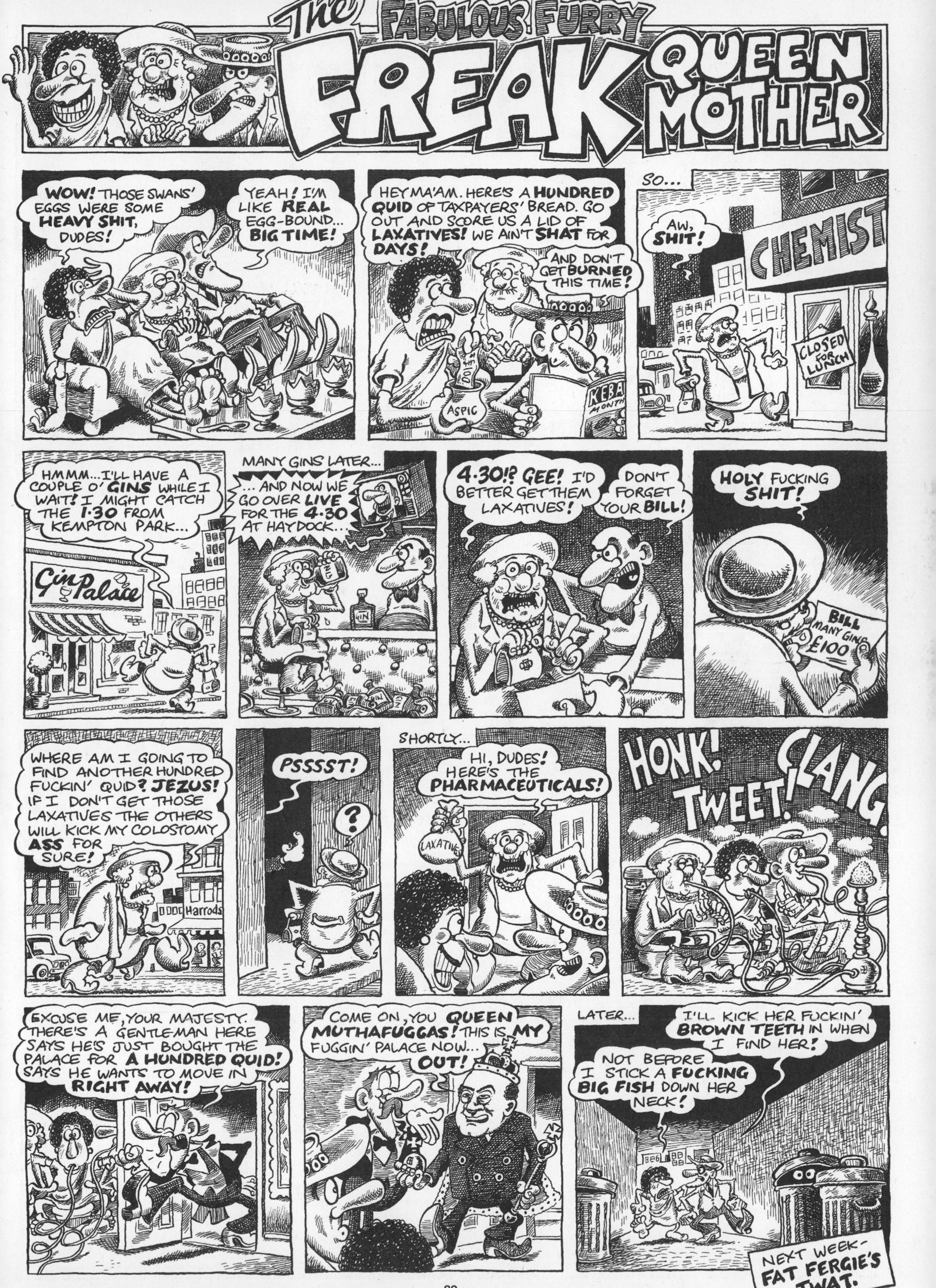
The Fabulous Furry Freak Queen Mother
WOW! THOSE SWANS' EGGS WERE SOME HEAVY SHIT, DUDES!
YEAH! I'M LIKE REAL EGG-BOUND... BIG TIME!
HEY MA'AM. HERE'S A HUNDRED QUID OF TAXPAYERS' BREAD. GO OUT AND SCORE US A LID OF LAXATIVES! WE AIN'T SHAT FOR DAYS!
AND DON'T GET BURNED THIS TIME!
ASPIC
SO...
AW, SHIT!
CHEMIST
CLOSED FOR LUNCH
HMMM... I'LL HAVE A COUPLE O' GINS WHILE I WAIT! I MIGHT CATCH THE 1·30 FROM KEMPTON PARK...
Gin Palace
MANY GINS LATER...
... AND NOW WE GO OVER LIVE FOR THE 4·30 AT HAYDOCK...
4·30!? GEE! I'D BETTER GET THEM LAXATIVES!
DON'T FORGET YOUR BILL!
HOLY FUCKING SHIT!
BILL MANY GINS £100
WHERE AM I GOING TO FIND ANOTHER HUNDRED FUCKIN' QUID? JEZUS! IF I DON'T GET THOSE LAXATIVES THE OTHERS WILL KICK MY COLOSTOMY ASS FOR SURE!
Harrods
PSSSST!
?
SHORTLY...
HI, DUDES! HERE'S THE PHARMACEUTICALS!
LAXATIVE
HONK! TWEET! CLANG!
EXCUSE ME, YOUR MAJESTY. THERE'S A GENTLEMAN HERE SAYS HE'S JUST BOUGHT THE PALACE FOR A HUNDRED QUID! SAYS HE WANTS TO MOVE IN RIGHT AWAY!
COME ON, YOU QUEEN MUTHAFUGGAS! THIS IS MY FUGGIN' PALACE NOW... OUT!
LATER...
I'LL KICK HER FUCKIN' BROWN TEETH IN WHEN I FIND HER!
NOT BEFORE I STICK A FUCKING BIG FISH DOWN HER NECK!
NEXT WEEK- FAT FERGIE'S TWAT.

LEER & LEARN

The Smutt

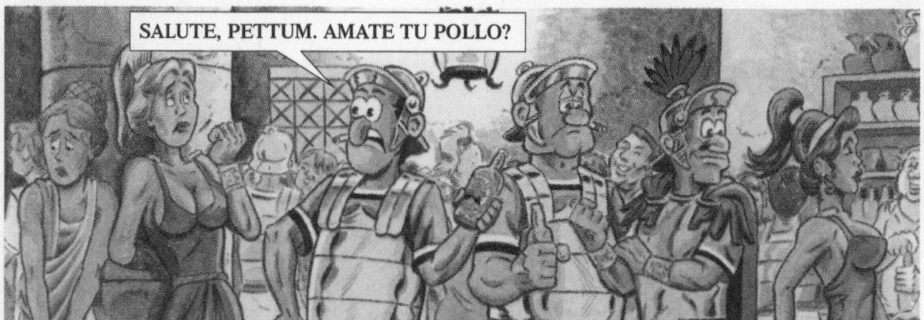
SALUTE, PETTUM. AMATE TU POLLO?
AFFIRMATUM.
ERM...GOBBLUM COCKANI MEO. FOULUM EST.

330AD Sexism was first brought to these shores, along with rabbits, central heating and contraceptive teats by the Romans.

Sidneus Smutticum, a docket clerk in the requisitions office at Segendum Fort on Hadrian's wall, came to Northumbria from Rome. Like all Romans, back home Sidneus would spend his day riding round the Colosseum on a 50 cc Vespum chariot, pinching women's arses. He continued this this practice every Friday night at Marketum Maximus, an area of the nearby town of Novocastrum well provided with taverna and clubs nocturni.

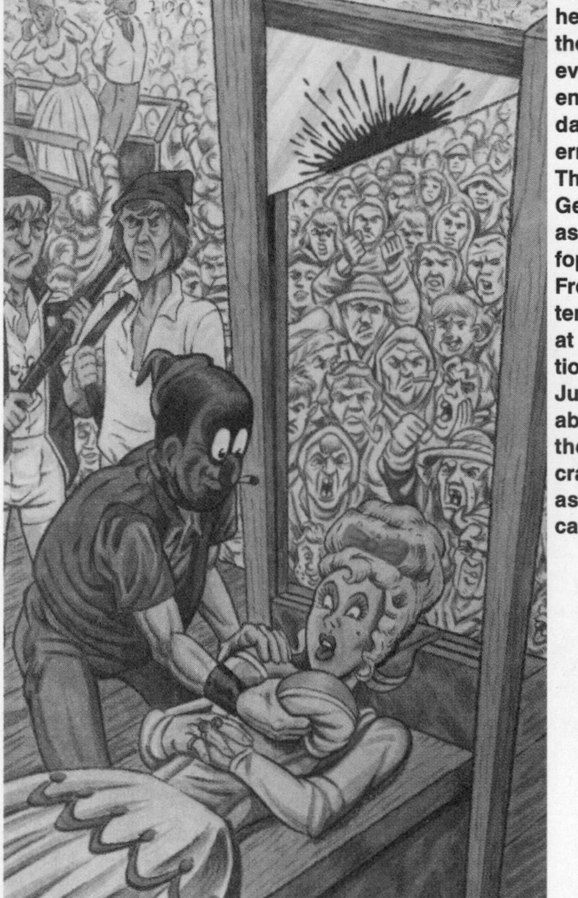

1789 "They seek him here, they seek him there, those Frenchies seek him everywhere. Is he in heaven?- Is he in hell? That damned elusive Pimpernel".

The Sexist Pimpernel, a Geordie dustman posing as an upper-class English fop, is the scourge of the French revolution. A master of disguise, he pops up at the scene of an execution in the nick of time. Just as Mme Guillotine is about to fall, he mashes the unfortunate aristocrat's tits and disappears as mysteriously as he came.

550 The Middle Ages were a time of great chivalry, as fearless knights in armour did battle with ferocious dragons, frequently winning the hands of maidens, not to mention halves of kingdoms. Sir Sideney of Camelo upon Tyne went home with neither, however. In 550 AD he was so paralysed with fear on encountering his one and only dragon, that he pissed his chain-mail pants which rusted solid. According to legend, he stands outside the cave to this day, waiting for Merlin, Magician to the court of King Arthur to pass by with a magica chalice of 3-in-1 release oil.

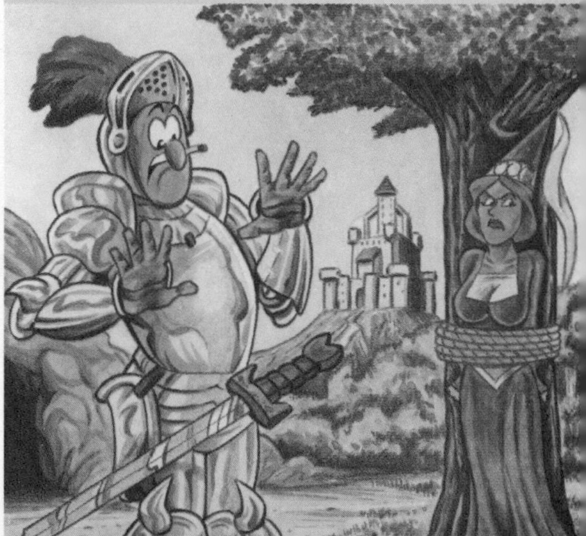

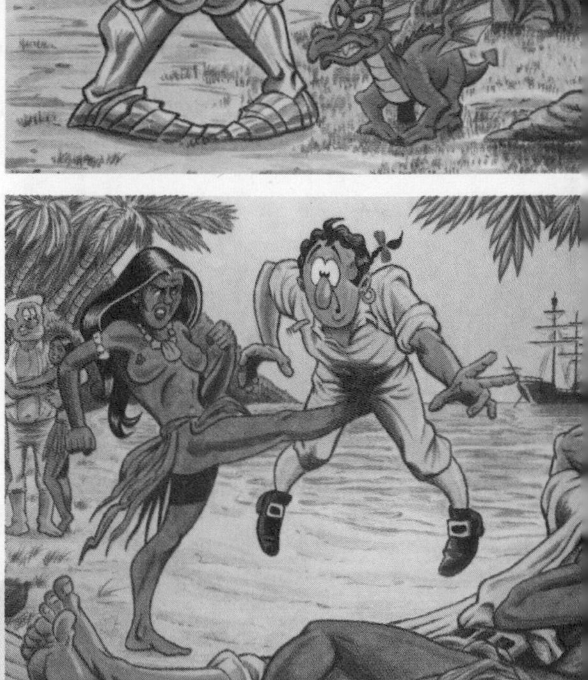

1760, and the crew of HMS Bounty land on the paradise Island of Tahiti after 11 months at sea. The sexually uninhibited Polynesian women were desperate for European men, and it was virtually impossi Midshipman Fletcher Smutt, however achieved the impossible. With his puerile patt chat-up lines, he remained unshagged for entire 18 month stay. After the mutiny in 17 self marooned on Pitcairn Island, the only man amongst 30 sexually insatiable semi-n women. He never gave up trying to get his end away, and over the next four years nuts up to 30 times a day. He eventually wanked himself unconscious and died a vi

Chronicles

The story behind the ancestry of Tyneside's Premier Fanny Rat.

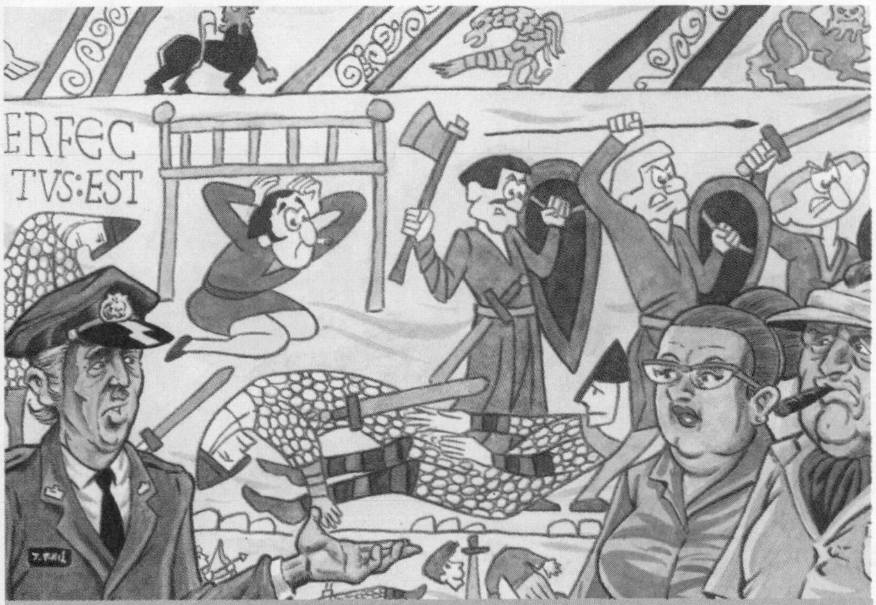
ERFEC
TVS:EST

1066, and every able-bodied Englishman is required to arm himself and fight the invading Norman hordes. Thousands of men respond to the call and bravely march south to defend their Island fortress. The armies of William the Conqueror and King Harold eventually meet in a mighty and bloody confrontation at Senlac Hill near Hastings.The Bayeux Tapestry captures the scene as Ethlered Smutty of Benwell spends the day hiding under his mum's bed whilst the battle rages three hundred miles away.

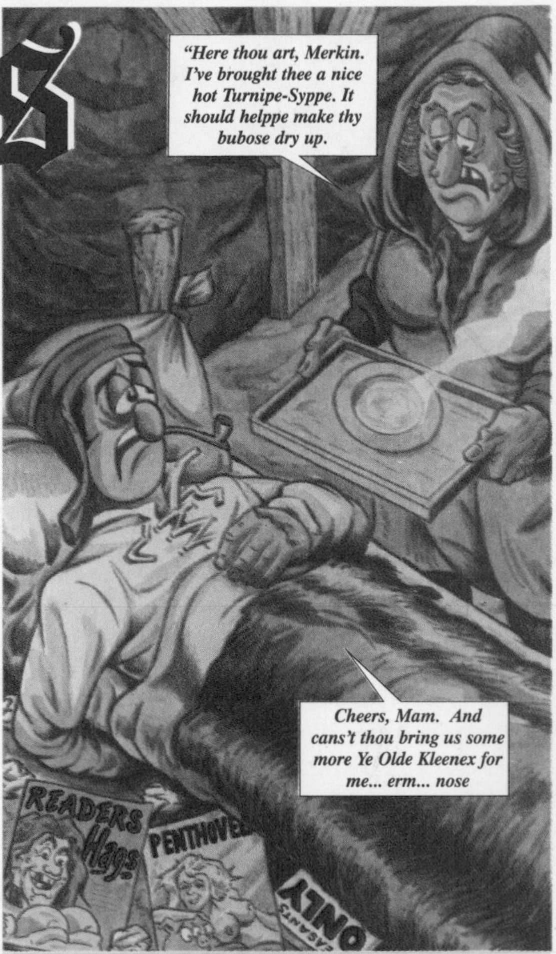
"Here thou art, Merkin. I've brought thee a nice hot Turnipe-Syppe. It should helppe make thy bubose dry up.
Cheers, Mam. And cans't thou bring us some more Ye Olde Kleenex for me... erm... nose
READERS Hags

1314 The dark ages, and sexism is almost wiped out as a virulent plague sweeps its way across the known world, killing all in its path.
Merkin Smutt, a filing clerk at the Doomsday Book records office, Longebentonne takes the opportunity to have a week off on the sick after successfully convincing his mam that he has symptoms of the Black Death.

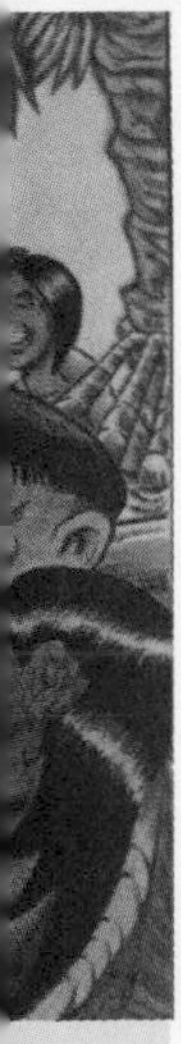

score.
rthless
nd him-
nesian
d in the

1888 and an entertainment-hungry nation flock to the theatres to watch the latest offerings from the pens of Oscar Wilde and Gilbert and Sullivan. 'The Importance of Being Ernest' and 'The Mikado' are the toast of London. Meanwhile, Music Hall entertainer Albert Smutt, under the name of 'The Great Smuttini', offers a more basic form of entertainment.

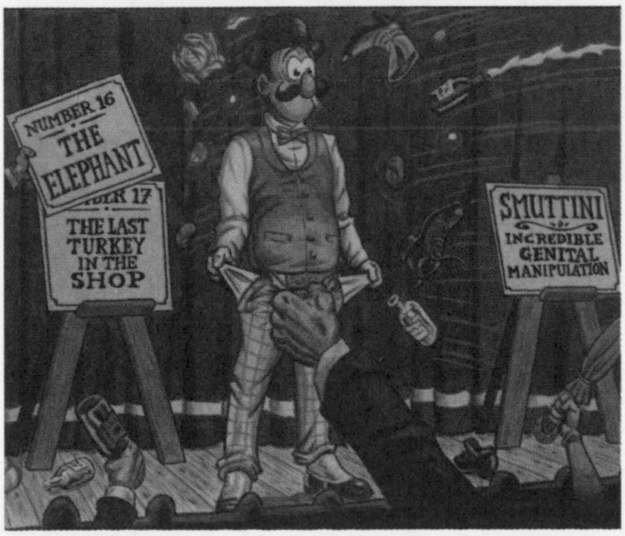
NUMBER 16
THE ELEPHANT
THE LAST TURKEY IN THE SHOP
SMUTTINI
INCREDIBLE GENITAL MANIPULATION

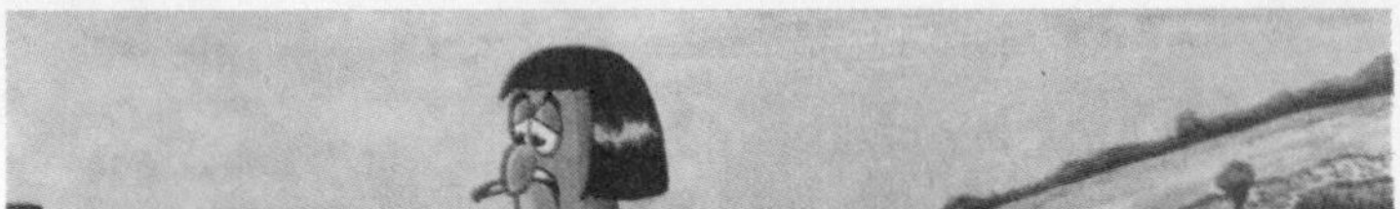

1968, the summer of love. Flower children from around the world descend on Woodstock to celebrate the dawn of sexual liberation with a week of Music, drugs and free love.
Trembling with excitement, Tyneside postman Sydney 'Lovemuscle' Smutt flies over to respond to the call to make love not war. He finds himself in the midst of 200,000 sexually indiscriminate women bestowing their favours on anything in loon pants. But following in the family tradition, he turns on, tunes in and cops nowt.

Next week in our 'It's a Small World' Series
Bernard Manning in Other Lands.

UNLUCKY FRANK

THINNING

HAIR TRANSPLANT CLINIC

AN HOUR LATER...

THE NEXT MORNING...
DING DONG!♪
GPO

POP!
HAIR TRANSPLANT CLINIC BILL

The end.

TV'S "YOU'VE BEEN FRAMED" STAR
Lisa Riley and her TODDLER-MISHAP TASKFORCE

ACCORDING TO MY CALCULATIONS A GIANT METEOR IS HURTLING TOWARDS PLANET EARTH!
SCIENTIFIC INSTITUTE
WE WILL ALL PERISH IN A MATTER OF HOURS!

THE EARTH WILL BE DESTROYED AND WE SHALL ALL DIE
WE ARE INCONSOLABLY DEPRESSED

TODDLER MISHAP TASKFORCE
DON'T WORRY, FOLKS!
I'LL CHEER YOU UP WITH SOME CUTE TODDLER MISHAPS!

HA! HA! LOOK AT THE KIDDIES FALLING OVER
CLONKITY CLONK
CLONK BONK
HO! HO!
AW! BLESS 'EM!
HA! HA!
NOW WE ARE NO LONGER DEPRESSED
THANKS TO LISA RILEY'S TODDLER MISHAP TASKFORCE!

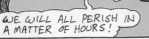

THE ADVENTURES OF BIFFA BACON

I'VE GOT ME'SEL A GEET BIG TIN OF QUICK DRYIN' GLUE...
D.I.Y. SHOP
QUICK DRYING GLUE
...I'LL 'AVE A FUCKIN' BIT FUN WI' THIS! HEH! HEH!

SHORTLY...
HOO! HERE COMES CEDRIC SOFT. HEH! WATCH THIS..
LOVE POEMS
QUICK DRYING GLUE
SKIP

CLANG!!
QUICK DRYING GLUE

HEH! HEH! THAT'S HIM FUCKIN' TELT!
WHIMPER!
QUICK DRYING GLUE

92

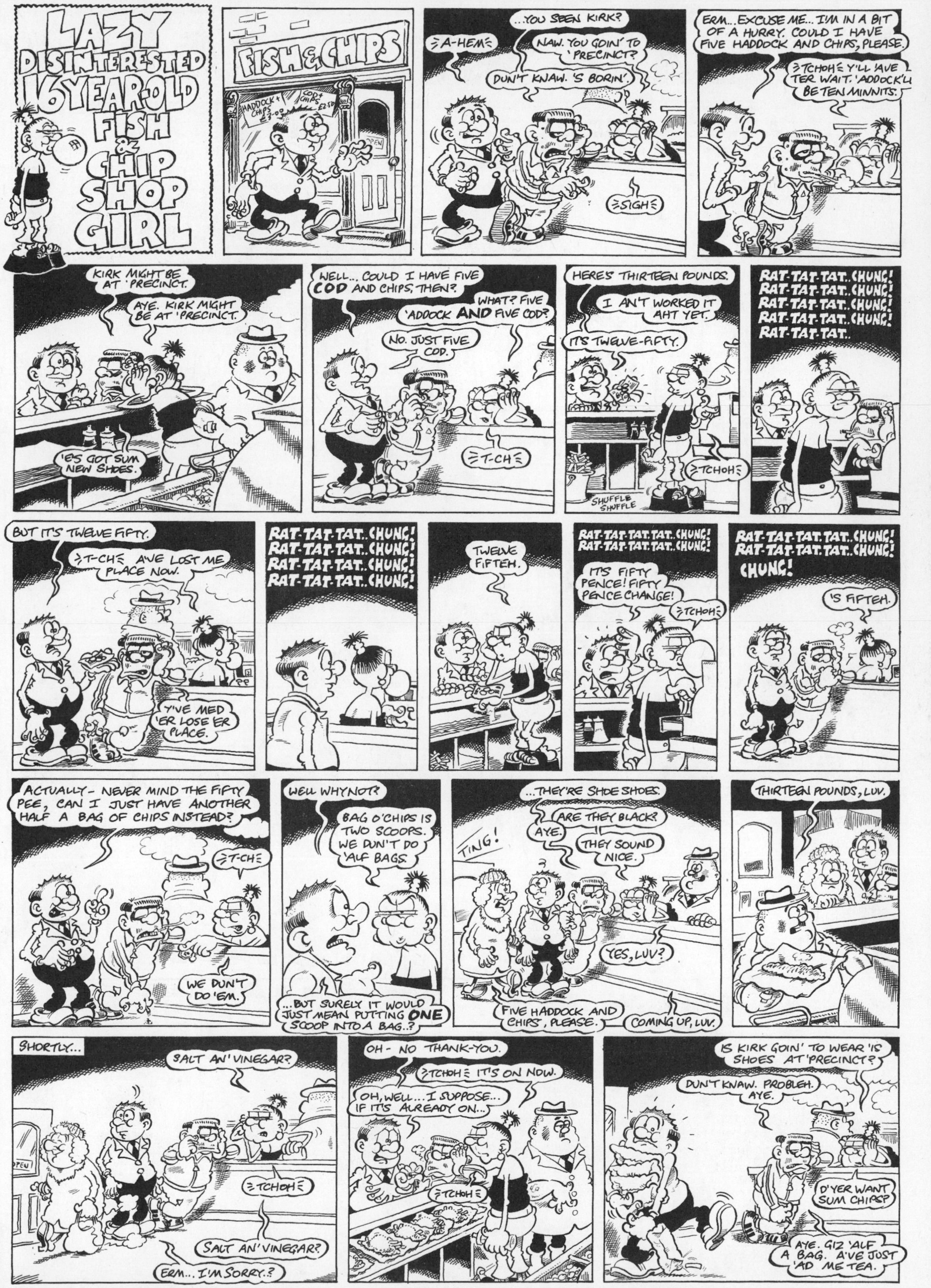
LAZY DISINTERESTED 16 YEAR-OLD FISH & CHIP SHOP GIRL
FISH & CHIPS
HADDOCK + CHIPS £3-00
COD + CHIPS £2.50
OPEN
...YOU SEEN KIRK?
A-HEM
NAW. YOU GOIN' TO 'PRECINCT?
DUN'T KNAW. 'S BORIN'.
SIGH
ERM... EXCUSE ME... I'M IN A BIT OF A HURRY. COULD I HAVE FIVE HADDOCK AND CHIPS, PLEASE.
TCHOH Y'LL 'AVE TER WAIT. 'ADDOCK'LL BE TEN MINNITS.
KIRK MIGHT BE AT 'PRECINCT.
AYE. KIRK MIGHT BE AT 'PRECINCT.
'E'S GOT SUM NEW SHOES.
WELL... COULD I HAVE FIVE COD AND CHIPS, THEN?
WHAT? FIVE 'ADDOCK AND FIVE COD?
NO. JUST FIVE COD.
T-CH
HERE'S THIRTEEN POUNDS.
I AN'T WORKED IT AHT YET.
IT'S TWELVE-FIFTY.
TCHOH
SHUFFLE SHUFFLE
RAT-TAT-TAT..CHUNG! RAT-TAT-TAT..CHUNG! RAT-TAT-TAT..CHUNG! RAT-TAT-TAT..CHUNG! RAT-TAT-TAT..
BUT IT'S TWELVE FIFTY.
T-CH A'VE LOST ME PLACE NOW.
Y'VE MED 'ER LOSE 'ER PLACE.
RAT-TAT-TAT..CHUNG! RAT-TAT-TAT..CHUNG! RAT-TAT-TAT..CHUNG! RAT-TAT-TAT..CHUNG!
TWELVE FIFTEH.
RAT-TAT-TAT-TAT..CHUNG! RAT-TAT-TAT-TAT..CHUNG!
IT'S FIFTY PENCE! FIFTY PENCE CHANGE!
TCHOH
RAT-TAT-TAT-TAT..CHUNG! RAT-TAT-TAT-TAT..CHUNG! CHUNG!
'S FIFTEH.
ACTUALLY - NEVER MIND THE FIFTY PEE, CAN I JUST HAVE ANOTHER HALF A BAG OF CHIPS INSTEAD?
T-CH
WE DUN'T DO 'EM.
WELL WHY NOT?
BAG O'CHIPS IS TWO SCOOPS. WE DUN'T DO 'ALF BAGS.
...BUT SURELY IT WOULD JUST MEAN PUTTING ONE SCOOP INTO A BAG..?
...THEY'RE SHOE SHOES.
ARE THEY BLACK?
AYE.
THEY SOUND NICE.
TING!
YES, LUV?
FIVE HADDOCK AND CHIPS, PLEASE.
COMING UP, LUV.
THIRTEEN POUNDS, LUV.
SHORTLY...
SALT AN' VINEGAR?
TCHOH
SALT AN' VINEGAR?
ERM... I'M SORRY..?
OH - NO THANK-YOU.
TCHOH IT'S ON NOW.
OH, WELL... I SUPPOSE... IF IT'S AREADY ON...
TCHOH
IS KIRK GOIN' TO WEAR 'IS SHOES AT 'PRECINCT?
DUN'T KNAW. PROBLEH. AYE.
D'YER WANT SUM CHIPS?
AYE. GIZ 'ALF A BAG. A'VE JUST 'AD ME TEA.

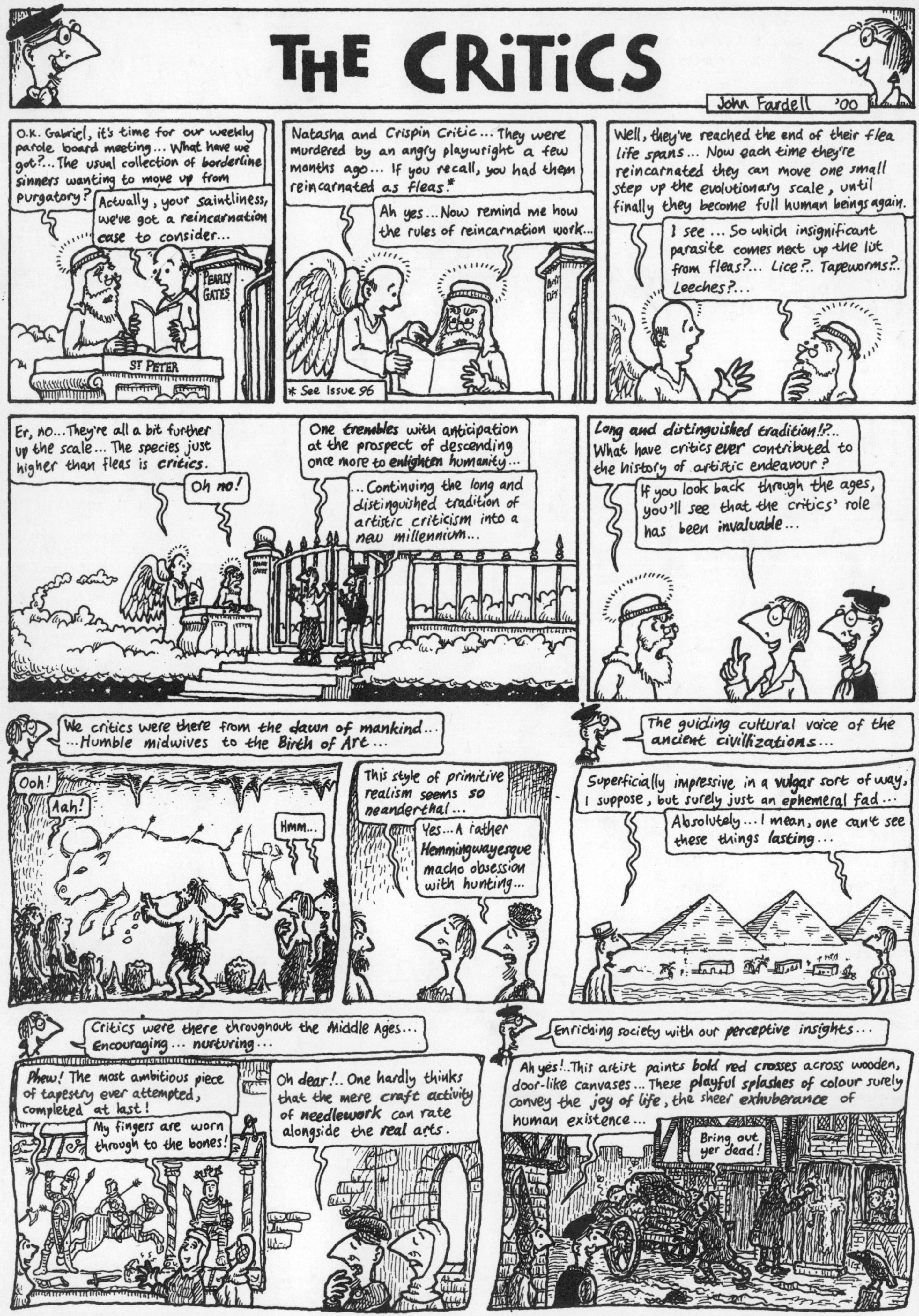
THE CRITICS
John Fardell '00
O.K. Gabriel, it's time for our weekly parole board meeting... What have we got?... The usual collection of borderline sinners wanting to move up from purgatory?
Actually, your saintliness, we've got a reincarnation case to consider...
PEARLY GATES
ST PETER
Natasha and Crispin Critic... They were murdered by an angry playwright a few months ago... If you recall, you had them reincarnated as fleas.*
Ah yes... Now remind me how the rules of reincarnation work...
* See Issue 96
Well, they've reached the end of their flea life spans... Now each time they're reincarnated they can move one small step up the evolutionary scale, until finally they become full human beings again.
I see... So which insignificant parasite comes next up the list from fleas?... Lice?.. Tapeworms?.. Leeches?...
Er, NO... They're all a bit further up the scale... The species just higher than fleas is critics.
Oh no!
One trembles with anticipation at the prospect of descending once more to enlighten humanity...
...Continuing the long and distinguished tradition of artistic criticism into a new millennium...
Long and distinguished tradition!?... What have critics ever contributed to the history of artistic endeavour?
If you look back through the ages, you'll see that the critics' role has been invaluable...
We critics were there from the dawn of mankind... ...Humble midwives to the Birth of Art...
Ooh!
Aah!
Hmm...
This style of primitive realism seems so neanderthal...
Yes... A rather Hemmingwayesque macho obsession with hunting...
The guiding cultural voice of the ancient civilizations...
Superficially impressive in a vulgar sort of way, I suppose, but surely just an ephemeral fad...
Absolutely... I mean, one can't see these things lasting...
Critics were there throughout the Middle Ages... Encouraging... nurturing...
Phew! The most ambitious piece of tapestry ever attempted, completed at last!
My fingers are worn through to the bones!
Oh dear!.. One hardly thinks that the mere craft activity of needlework can rate alongside the real arts.
Enriching society with our perceptive insights...
Ah yes!.. This artist paints bold red crosses across wooden, door-like canvases... These playful splashes of colour surely convey the joy of life, the sheer exuberance of human existence...
Bring out yer dead!

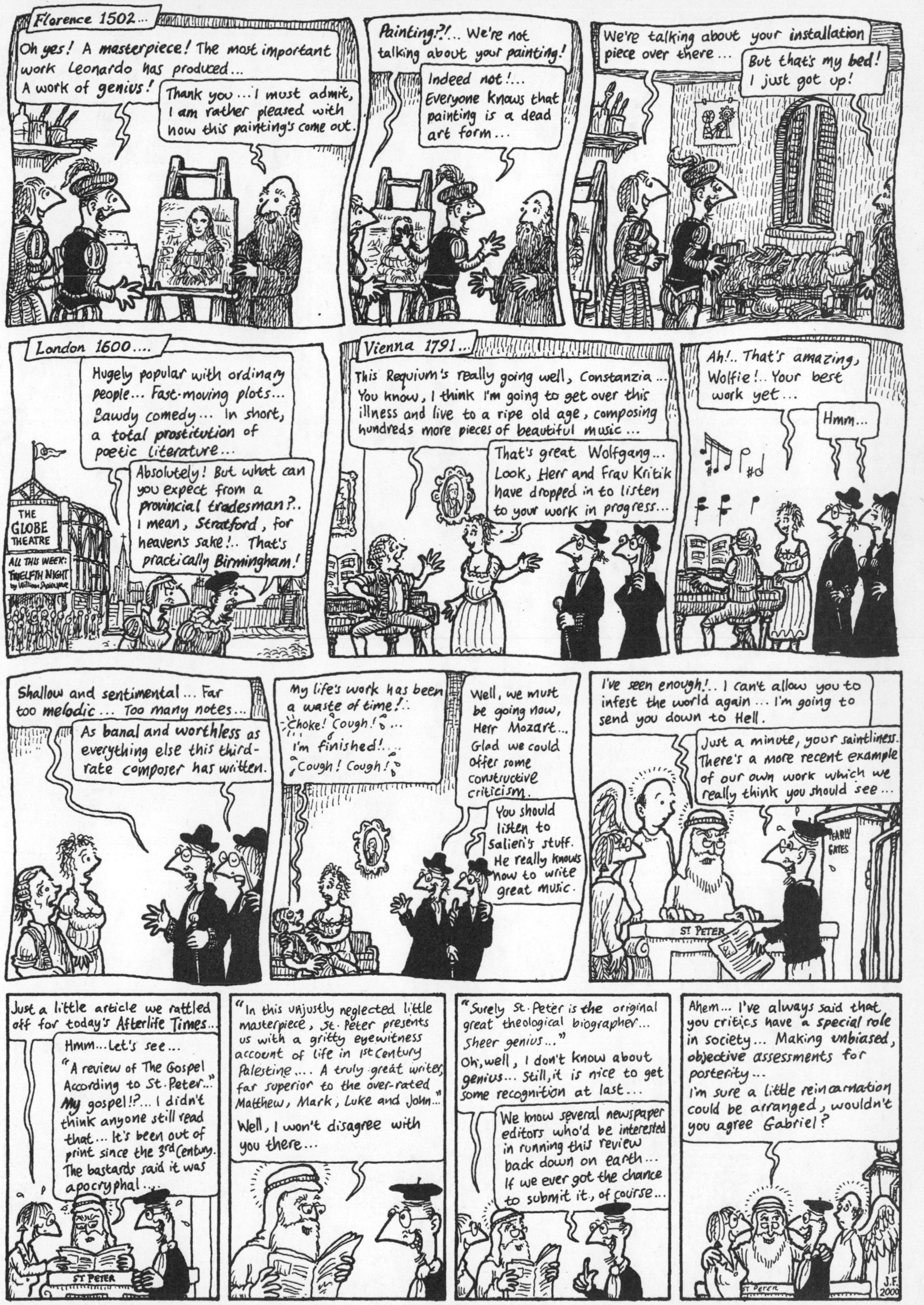
Florence 1502...
Oh yes! A masterpiece! The most important work Leonardo has produced... A work of genius!
Thank you... I must admit, I am rather pleased with how this painting's come out.
Painting?!... We're not talking about your painting!
Indeed not!... Everyone knows that painting is a dead art form...
We're talking about your installation piece over there...
But that's my bed! I just got up!
London 1600....
Hugely popular with ordinary people... Fast-moving plots... Bawdy comedy... In short, a total prostitution of poetic literature...
Absolutely! But what can you expect from a provincial tradesman?.. I mean, Stratford, for heaven's sake!.. That's practically Birmingham!
THE GLOBE THEATRE
ALL THIS WEEK: TWELFTH NIGHT
Vienna 1791...
This Requium's really going well, Constanzia... You know, I think I'm going to get over this illness and live to a ripe old age, composing hundreds more pieces of beautiful music...
That's great Wolfgang... Look, Herr and Frau Kritik have dropped in to listen to your work in progress...
Ah!.. That's amazing, Wolfie!.. Your best work yet...
Hmm...
Shallow and sentimental... Far too melodic... Too many notes...
As banal and worthless as everything else this third-rate composer has written.
My life's work has been a waste of time!.. Choke! Cough!... I'm finished!... Cough! Cough!
Well, we must be going now, Herr Mozart... Glad we could offer some constructive criticism.
You should listen to Salieri's stuff. He really knows how to write great music.
I've seen enough!.. I can't allow you to infest the world again... I'm going to send you down to Hell.
Just a minute, your saintliness. There's a more recent example of our own work which we really think you should see...
PEARLY GATES
ST PETER
Just a little article we rattled off for today's Afterlife Times...
Hmm... let's see... "A review of The Gospel According to St. Peter..." My gospel!?... I didn't think anyone still read that... It's been out of print since the 3rd Century. The bastards said it was apocryphal...
ST PETER
"In this unjustly neglected little masterpiece, St. Peter presents us with a gritty eyewitness account of life in 1st Century Palestine.... A truly great writer, far superior to the over-rated Matthew, Mark, Luke and John..."
Well, I won't disagree with you there...
"Surely St. Peter is the original great theological biographer... Sheer genius..."
Oh, well, I don't know about genius... Still, it is nice to get some recognition at last...
We know several newspaper editors who'd be interested in running this review back down on earth... If we ever got the chance to submit it, of course...
Ahem... I've always said that you critics have a special role in society... Making unbiased, objective assessments for posterity...
I'm sure a little reincarnation could be arranged, wouldn't you agree Gabriel?
ST PETER
J.F. 2000

SAUCY CALENDAR IS A W 'I' OPENER!

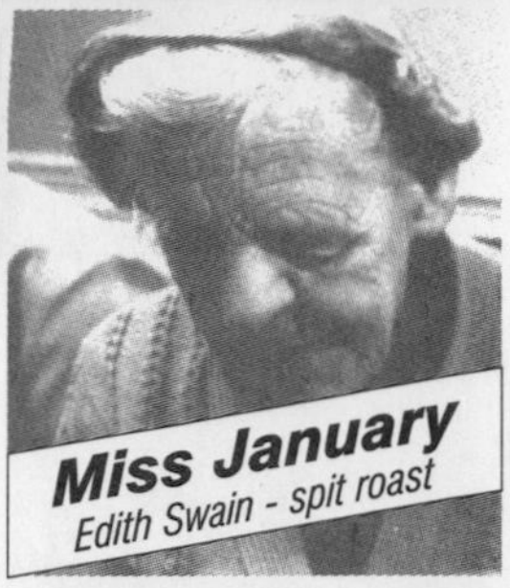

Miss January
Edith Swain - spit roast

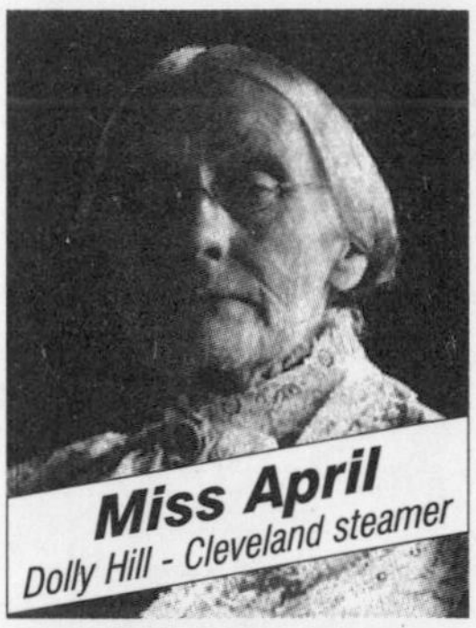

Miss April
Dolly Hill - Cleveland steamer

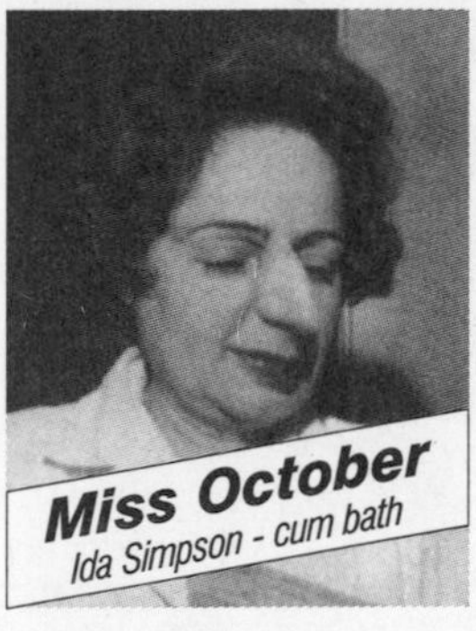

Miss October
Ida Simpson - cum bath

LADIES from the Fulchester branch of the Woman's Institute this year came up with a cheeky idea to raise money for a Sunshine Coach for Orphans. - *by stripping off for a saucy calendar!*

EXCLUSIVE!

Glamorous grannies raise eyebrows as well as cash!

And their fruity photos have proved so popular with the locals that the ladies have had to order a reprint.

Friends

"It was just a bit of fun, so we're amazed how popular it has become," said 68-year-old grandmother Doris Willis, who posed in the altogether with friends from her bowls club.

"We're none of us Spring chickens but we like to think we're game old birds."

Cheers

60-year-old Mavis Carlisle is chairwoman of the WI knitting circle, but didn't hesitate to pose without a stitch on when she heard about the project.

"Until the calendar came out, the only people who had seen me in my birthday suit were my husband and my doctor," said Mavis. "Now everybody in Fulchester has seen me in the pink! I'm on the February page with my legs wide open, masturbating two erect penises into my hair."

Seinfeld

And sales of the calendar look set to exceed the ladies' wildest dreams.

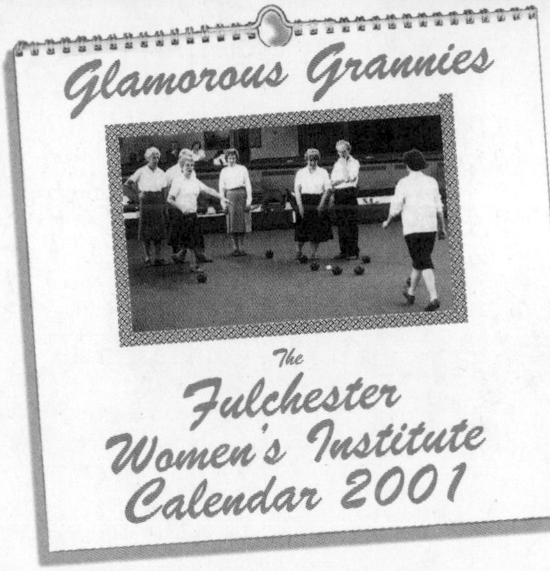

Glamorous Grannies
The Fulchester Women's Institute Calendar 2001

The Fulchester Women's Institute Calendar - a genteel cover, but the contents will raise a few eyebrows.

"We had 500 printed, and they sold out on the first day at the village fete," said Enid Marshall, who appears on the August picture performing fellatio on the chairman of the Parish Council and pulling her labia apart to expose her clitoris whilst her face and breasts are splashed with three men's ejaculate. "Now we're having another thousand printed, and it looks like they should sell out too."

Frasier

Local photographer Ernie Stewart is more used to taking pictures of local people's weddings, so when he was asked to snap the naughty pics for the calendar he was more than a little surprised.

Bugner

"It was certainly an eye-opener," said Ernie, who gave his services for free. "I think I was more embarassed than they were at first. But we got the pictures done, and I think it's turned out really well. I hope it raises lots of money."

Jackson

Publican Brian Dougal has even hung up a copy of the cheeky calendar behind his bar at the Dog & Duck. "I'm particularly looking forward to December, because that's the month my wife Noreen appears in a saucy snap taken on the steps of the cricket pavilion," he said.

Dellasandro

"She's urinating into the mouth of Mrs Preece from the flower shop, whilst Mr Williams the churchwarden felches his sperm from out of her anus."

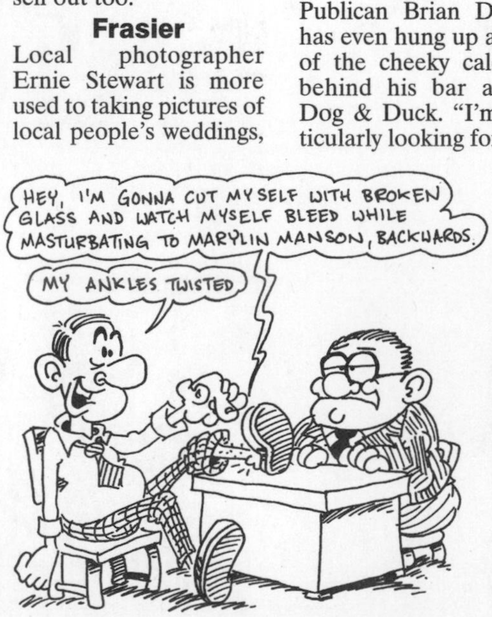

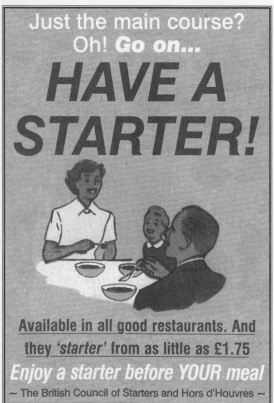

HEY, I'M GONNA CUT MYSELF WITH BROKEN GLASS AND WATCH MYSELF BLEED WHILE MASTURBATING TO MARYLIN MANSON, BACKWARDS.
MY ANKLES TWISTED.

FAMOUS PEOPLE ON THE TOILET

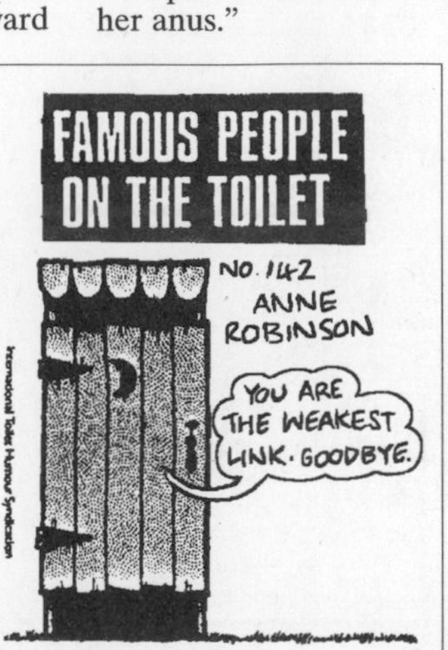

NO. 142
ANNE ROBINSON
YOU ARE THE WEAKEST LINK. GOODBYE.

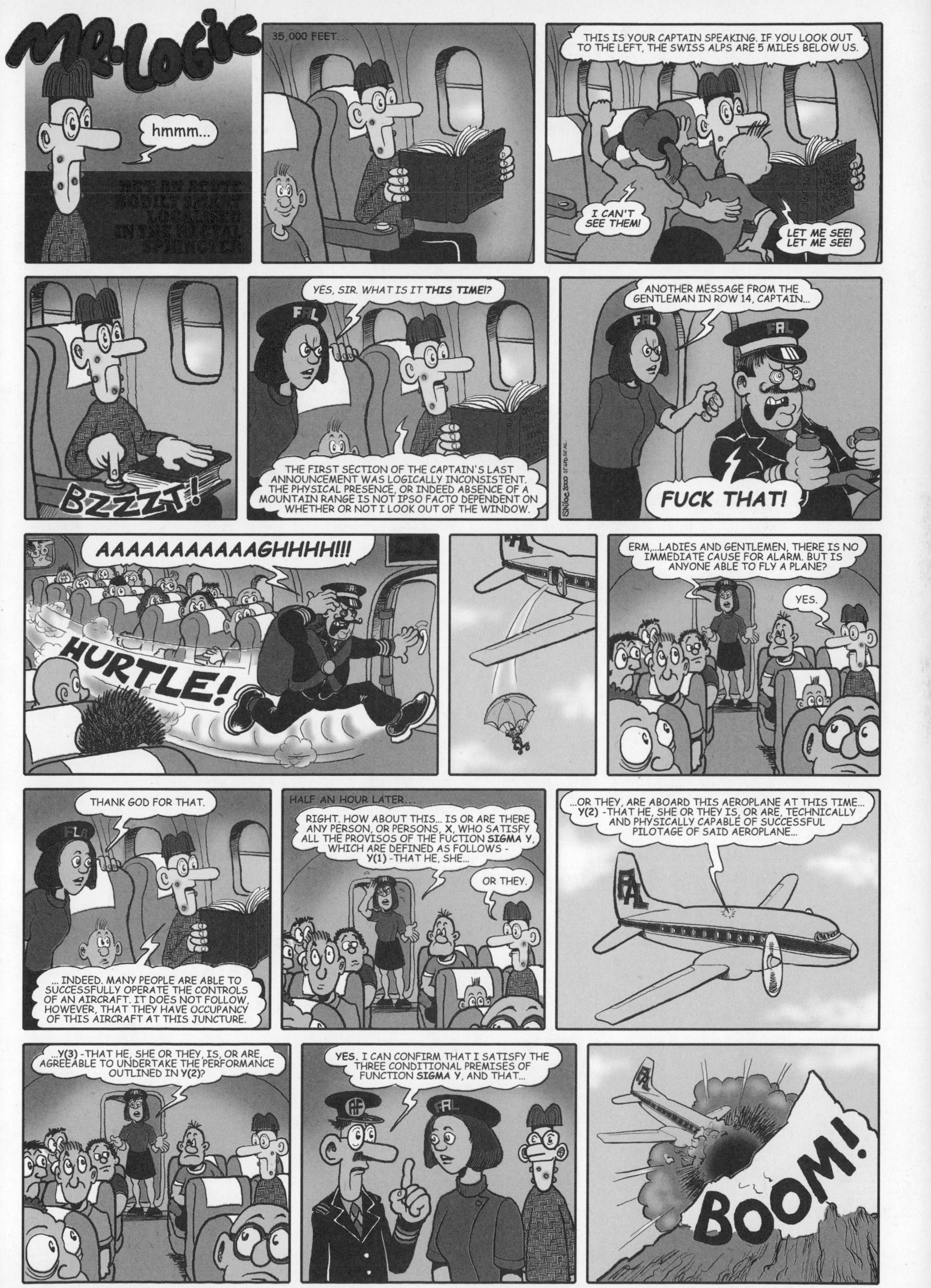
MR LOGIC
hmmm...
35,000 FEET...
THIS IS YOUR CAPTAIN SPEAKING. IF YOU LOOK OUT TO THE LEFT, THE SWISS ALPS ARE 5 MILES BELOW US.
I CAN'T SEE THEM!
LET ME SEE! LET ME SEE!
BZZZZT!
YES, SIR. WHAT IS IT THIS TIME!?
THE FIRST SECTION OF THE CAPTAIN'S LAST ANNOUNCEMENT WAS LOGICALLY INCONSISTENT. THE PHYSICAL PRESENCE, OR INDEED ABSENCE OF A MOUNTAIN RANGE IS NOT IPSO FACTO DEPENDENT ON WHETHER OR NOT I LOOK OUT OF THE WINDOW.
ANOTHER MESSAGE FROM THE GENTLEMAN IN ROW 14, CAPTAIN...
FUCK THAT!
AAAAAAAAAAAGHHHH!!!
HURTLE!
ERM,...LADIES AND GENTLEMEN, THERE IS NO IMMEDIATE CAUSE FOR ALARM. BUT IS ANYONE ABLE TO FLY A PLANE?
YES.
THANK GOD FOR THAT.
... INDEED. MANY PEOPLE ARE ABLE TO SUCCESSFULLY OPERATE THE CONTROLS OF AN AIRCRAFT. IT DOES NOT FOLLOW, HOWEVER, THAT THEY HAVE OCCUPANCY OF THIS AIRCRAFT AT THIS JUNCTURE.
HALF AN HOUR LATER...
RIGHT. HOW ABOUT THIS... IS OR ARE THERE ANY PERSON, OR PERSONS, X, WHO SATISFY ALL THE PROVISOS OF THE FUCTION SIGMA Y, WHICH ARE DEFINED AS FOLLOWS - Y(1) -THAT HE, SHE...
OR THEY.
...OR THEY, ARE ABOARD THIS AEROPLANE AT THIS TIME... Y(2) -THAT HE, SHE OR THEY IS, OR ARE, TECHNICALLY AND PHYSICALLY CAPABLE OF SUCCESSFUL PILOTAGE OF SAID AEROPLANE...
...Y(3) -THAT HE, SHE OR THEY, IS, OR ARE, AGREEABLE TO UNDERTAKE THE PERFORMANCE OUTLINED IN Y(2)?
YES. I CAN CONFIRM THAT I SATISFY THE THREE CONDITIONAL PREMISES OF FUNCTION SIGMA Y, AND THAT...
BOOM!

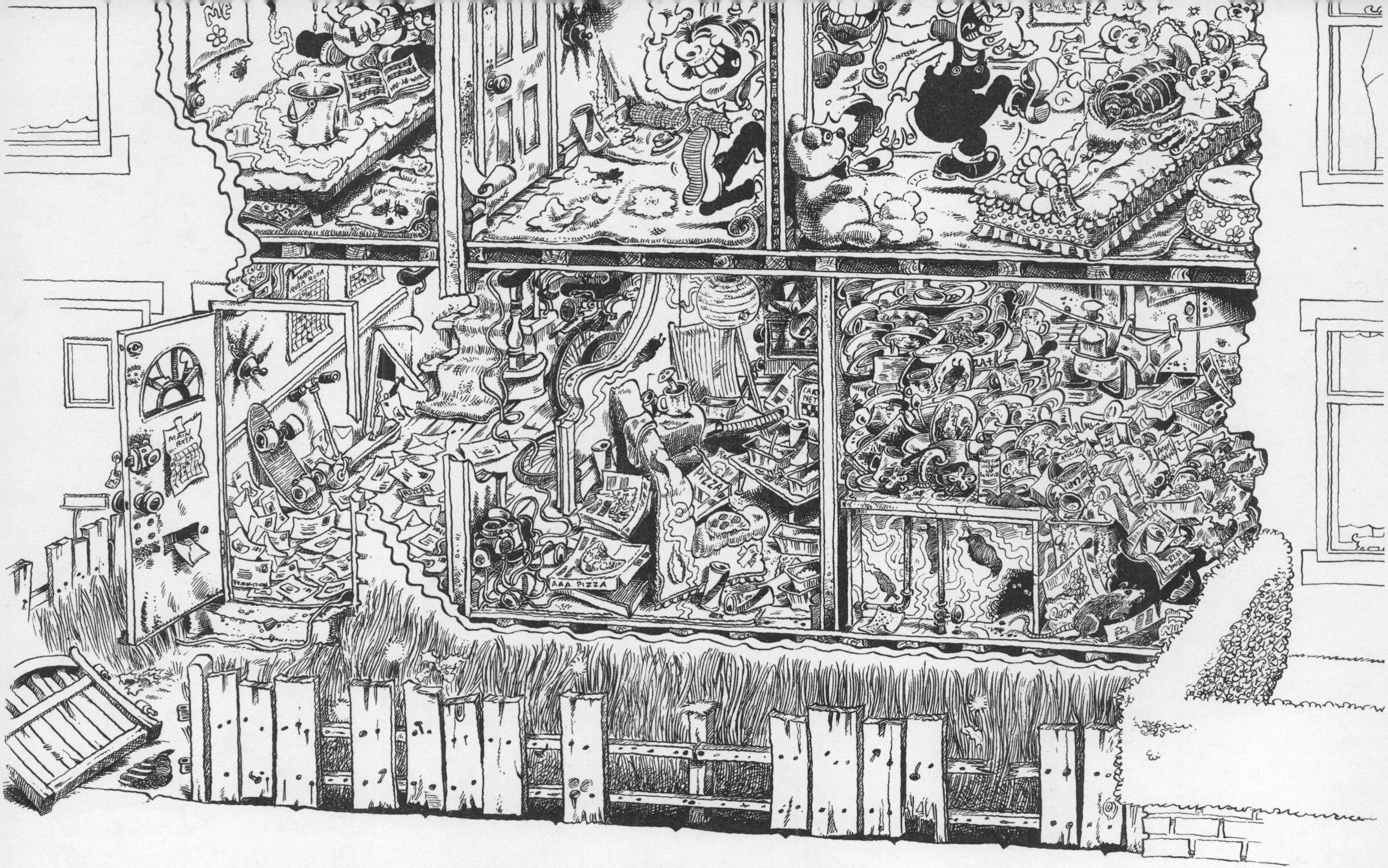
MAIN ROTA
AAA PIZZA
PIZZA

Balthazar the house Christian has hidden five packets of Rizlas to stop Wally 'skinning up' some 'squidgy black', which he 'scored' at Glastonbury and brought back up his arse. There's a million pounds to be won if you find them all and simultaneously buy a winning lottery ticket.

Where's Wally's Rizlas?

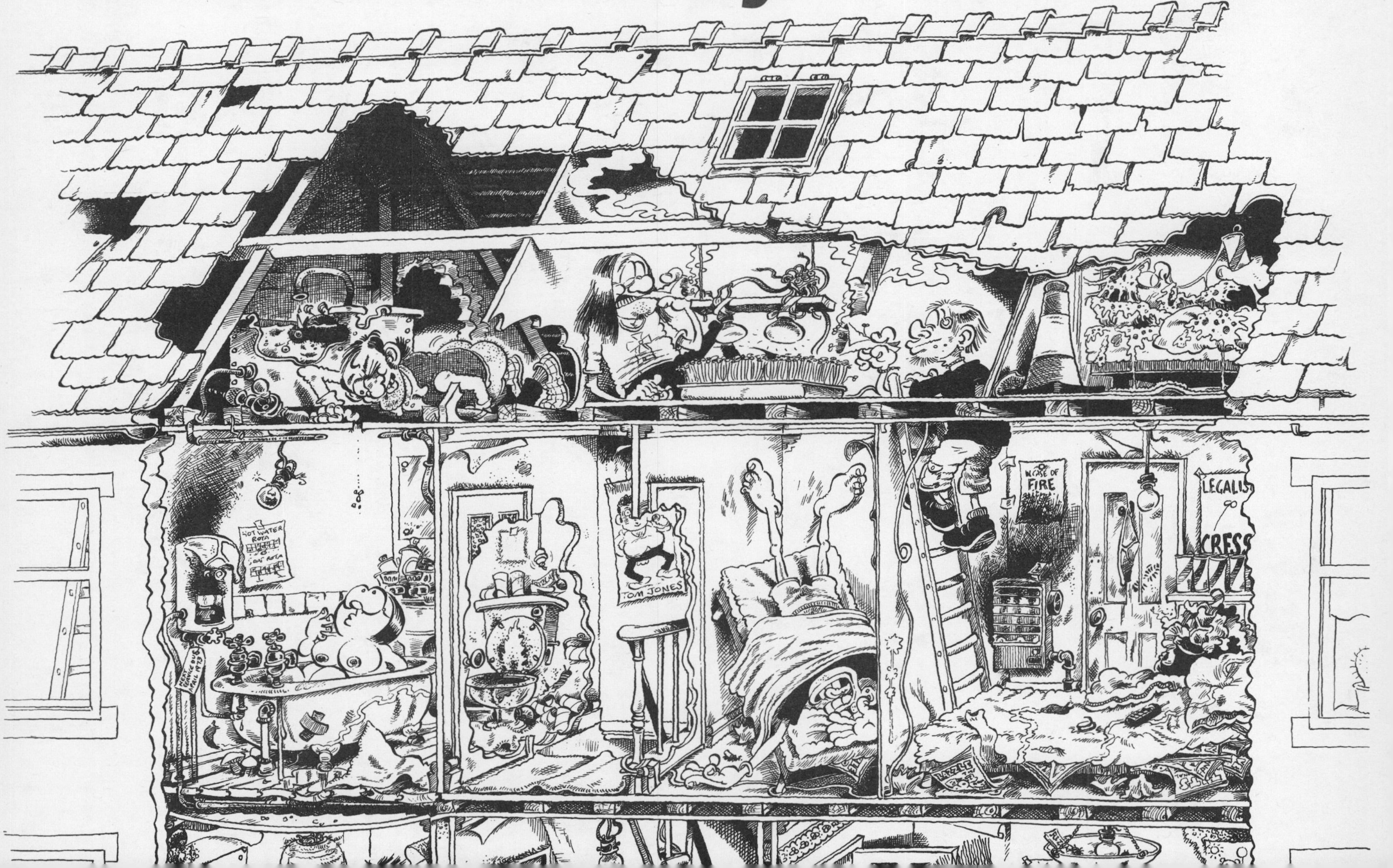
HOT WATER ROTA
SOAP ROTA
NEXT SERVICE DUE APRIL 1973
TOM JONES
IN CASE OF FIRE
LEGALIS
CRESS

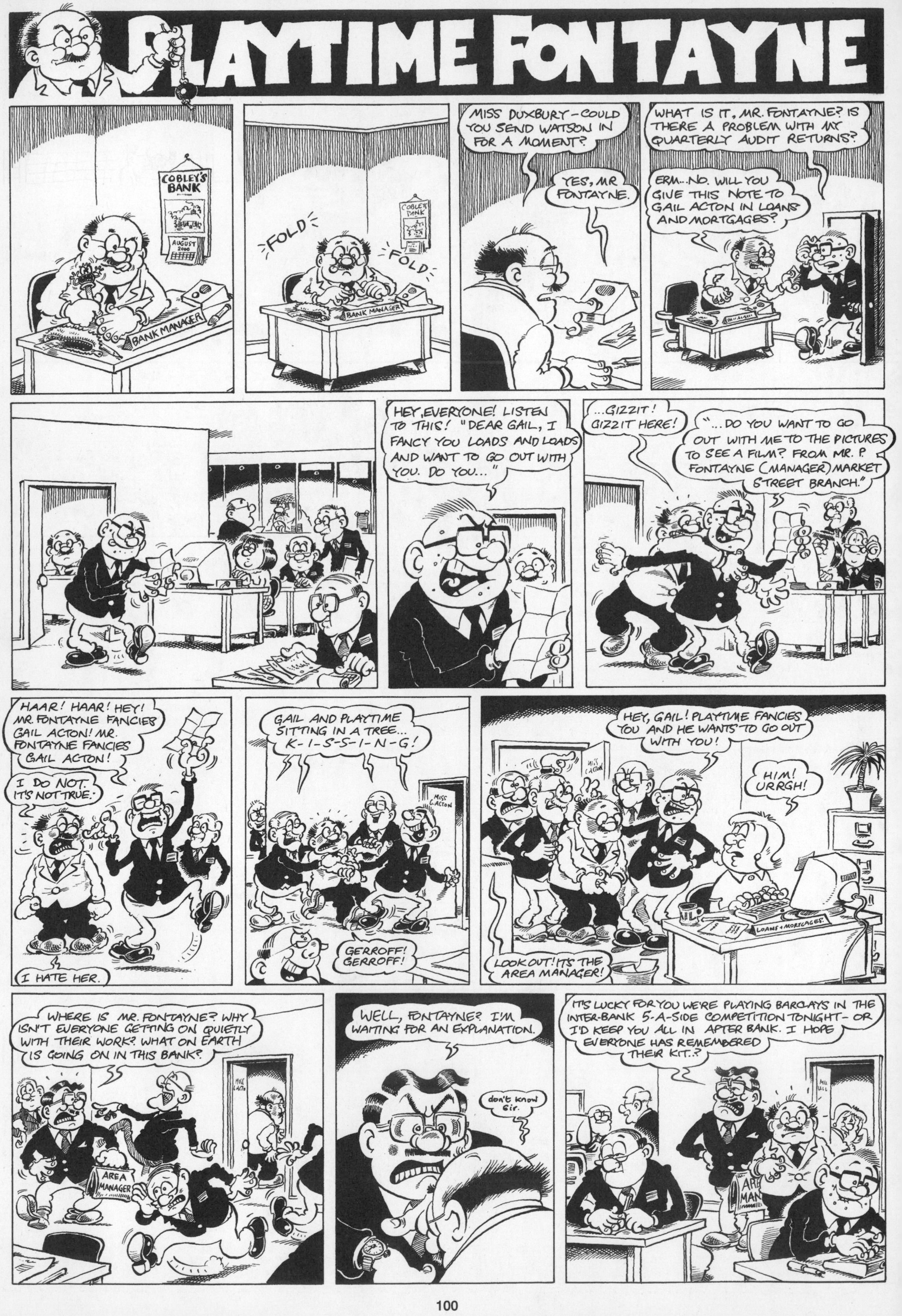
PLAYTIME FONTAYNE
COBLEY'S BANK
AUGUST 2000
BANK MANAGER
FOLD
FOLD
BANK MANAGER
MISS DUXBURY - COULD YOU SEND WATSON IN FOR A MOMENT?
YES, MR FONTAYNE.
WHAT IS IT, MR. FONTAYNE? IS THERE A PROBLEM WITH MY QUARTERLY AUDIT RETURNS?
ERM...NO. WILL YOU GIVE THIS NOTE TO GAIL ACTON IN LOANS AND MORTGAGES?
HEY, EVERYONE! LISTEN TO THIS! "DEAR GAIL, I FANCY YOU LOADS AND LOADS AND WANT TO GO OUT WITH YOU. DO YOU..."
...GIZZIT! GIZZIT HERE!
"...DO YOU WANT TO GO OUT WITH ME TO THE PICTURES TO SEE A FILM? FROM MR. P. FONTAYNE (MANAGER) MARKET STREET BRANCH."
HAAR! HAAR! HEY! MR. FONTAYNE FANCIES GAIL ACTON! MR. FONTAYNE FANCIES GAIL ACTON!
I DO NOT. IT'S NOT TRUE.
I HATE HER.
GAIL AND PLAYTIME SITTING IN A TREE... K-I-S-S-I-N-G!
MISS G. ACTON
GERROFF! GERROFF!
HEY, GAIL! PLAYTIME FANCIES YOU AND HE WANTS TO GO OUT WITH YOU!
HIM! URRGH!
LOANS + MORTGAGES
LOOK OUT! IT'S THE AREA MANAGER!
WHERE IS MR. FONTAYNE? WHY ISN'T EVERYONE GETTING ON QUIETLY WITH THEIR WORK? WHAT ON EARTH IS GOING ON IN THIS BANK?
AREA MANAGER
WELL, FONTAYNE? I'M WAITING FOR AN EXPLANATION.
don't know Sir.
IT'S LUCKY FOR YOU WE'RE PLAYING BARCLAYS IN THE INTER-BANK 5-A-SIDE COMPETITION TONIGHT - OR I'D KEEP YOU ALL IN AFTER BANK. I HOPE EVERYONE HAS REMEMBERED THEIR KIT..?

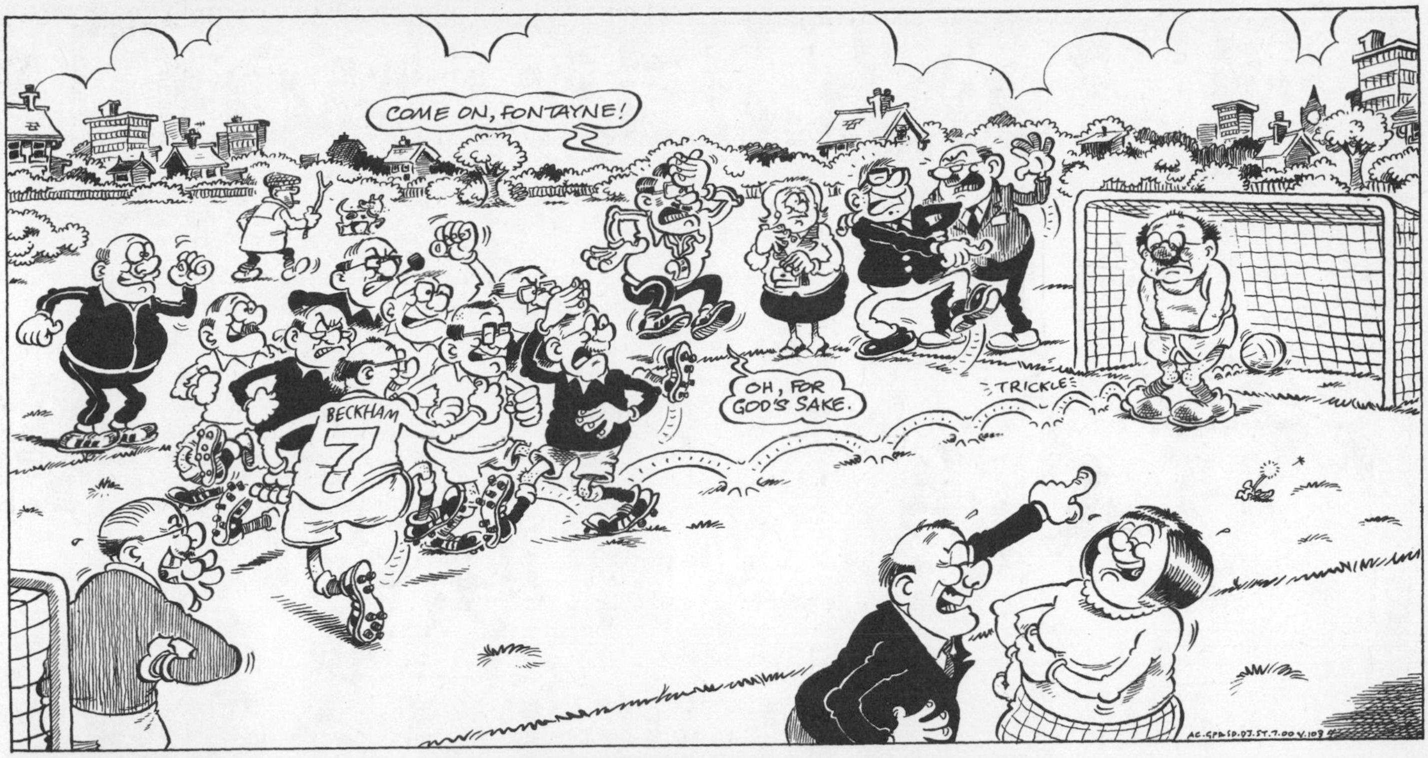
COME ON, FONTAYNE!
BECKHAM
7
OH, FOR GOD'S SAKE.
TRICKLE

NHS in CRISIS!

DESPITE government pledges to cut Health Service inefficiency, old people are waiting longer than ever to be murdered by their GPs, according to a report published yesterday.

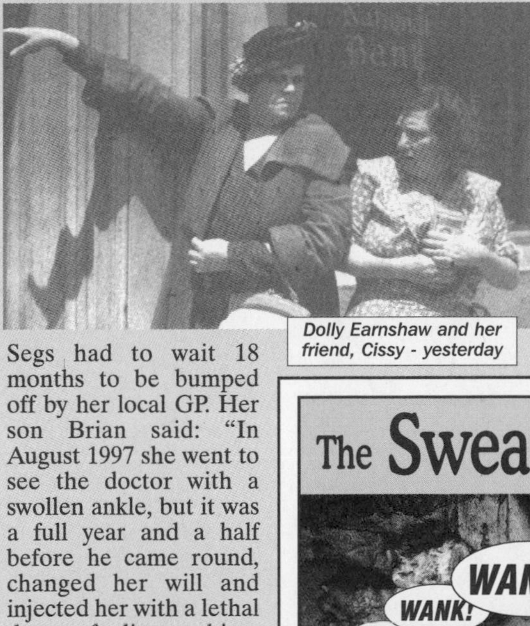
Dolly Earnshaw and her friend, Cissy - yesterday

Worst hit area in the country is Greater Manchester, where one pensioner recently died of natural causes after waiting over two years to be murdered by her family doctor. Many more have similar stories.

private

"I've been waiting six months to be smothered and robbed by my doctor," says 79-year old Dolly Earnshaw of Leeds. "But he kept on cancelling my appointments. In the end I decided to go private. They're going to do me in next Friday afternoon." The cost of Dolly's treatment will be around £3000, but the irony is it will probably be performed by the same doctor who was meant to murder her on the NHS.

corporal

"It's not what I paid my stamps for all those years. It's a ruddy disgrace, and that's swearing," she said.

Wealthy Merseyside grandmother Myrtle Segs had to wait 18 months to be bumped off by her local GP. Her son Brian said: "In August 1997 she went to see the doctor with a swollen ankle, but it was a full year and a half before he came round, changed her will and injected her with a lethal dose of diamorphine. It's a farce."

capital

We spoke to a junior doctor at a major London teaching hospital. "It's crazy," he told us. "I'm doing three or four 48-hour shifts every week, winning the trust of pensioners before killing them.

splendid

"With all the paperwork to be falsified, I don't know whether I'm coming or going. Frankly, it's only a matter of time before I make a mistake and leave an old codger alive."

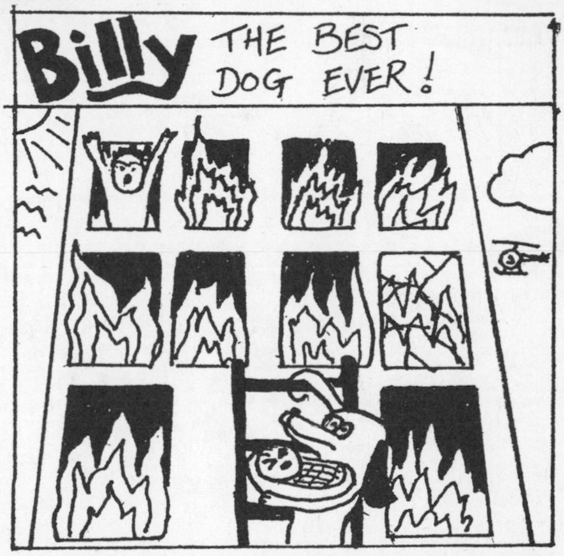
Billy THE BEST DOG EVER!

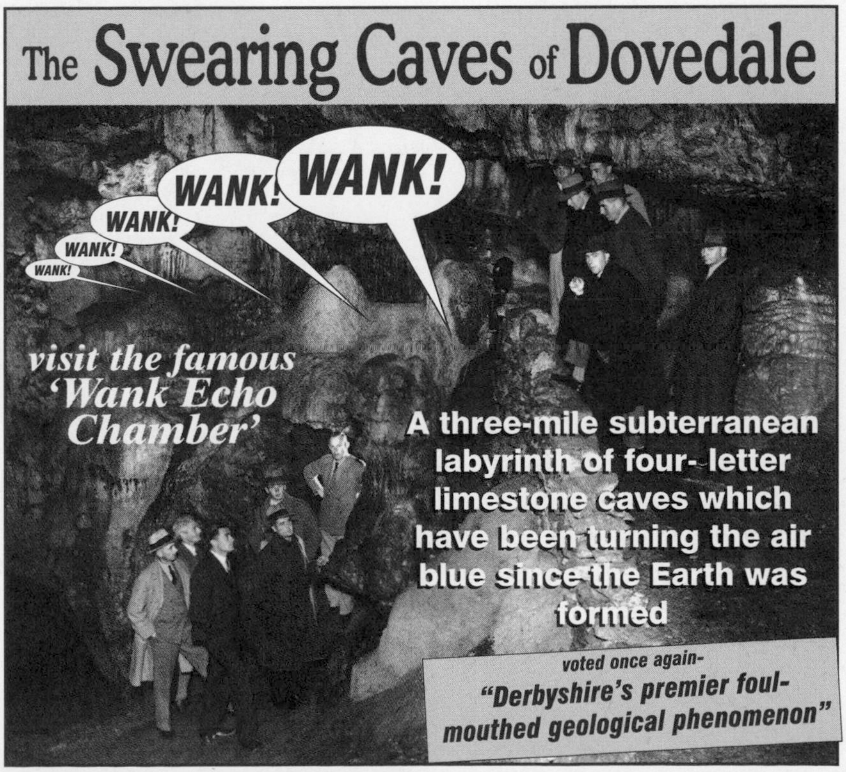
The Swearing Caves of Dovedale
WANK!
WANK!
WANK!
WANK!
WANK!
visit the famous 'Wank Echo Chamber'
A three-mile subterranean labyrinth of four- letter limestone caves which have been turning the air blue since the Earth was formed
voted once again-
"Derbyshire's premier foul-mouthed geological phenomenon"

Letterbocks

It's the page that sets out to climb Ben Nevis in trainers, has to be rescued and looks a twat on the news.

St★r Letter

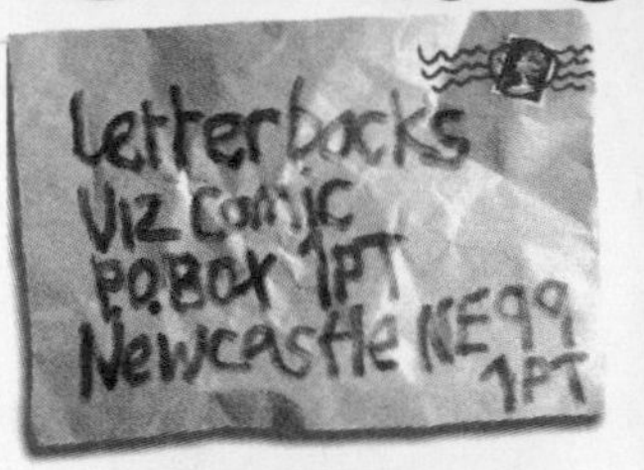
Letterbocks
Viz Comic
P.O.Box 1PT
Newcastle NE99 1PT

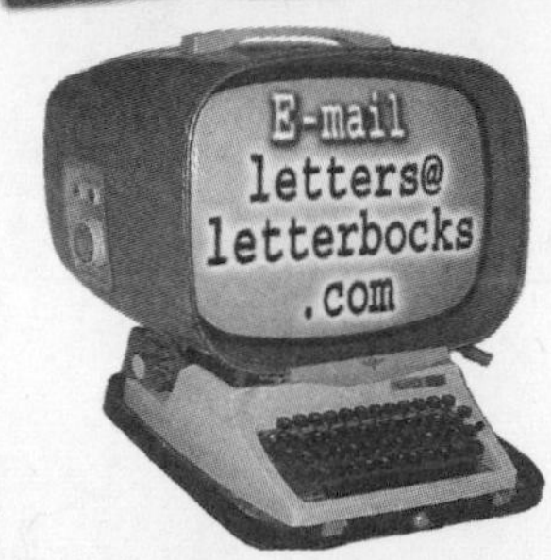
E-mail
letters@
letterbocks
.com

❑ These wind farms are ridiculous. As if this country doesn't have enough wind of its own without wasting electricity making more of it by running these big fans. It's a waste of the taxpayer's money.

Ben Cormack
Isle of Eigg

HGV licence to kill

❑ Since many lorry drivers have been off the roads due to the recent petrol crises, has anyone else noticed the dramatic decline in the number of women being murdered?

John Terry
Hebburn

❑ In response to your request for examples of sub-editors outwitting their bosses, here's a headline from the free rag METRO reporting on the Olympics.

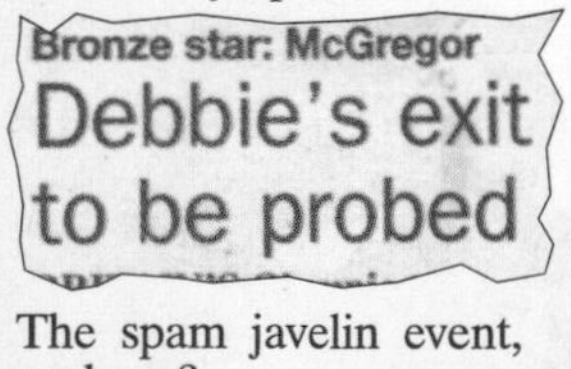
Bronze star: McGregor
Debbie's exit to be probed

The spam javelin event, perhaps?

J. Miller
London

**A £20 note is on its way to the chief sub-editor of Metro*

❑ I was awoken the other morning by a rattle at my letterbox. It was my son, Simon Rattle, the conductor of the Birmingham Symphony Orchestra, who had forgotten his keys.

Mrs. Rattle
Birmingham

❑ The other day, I rushed round to my neighbours' house to warn them of the kangaroo in their garden. Imagine how silly I felt when they explained it was just their greyhound having a shit.

Matthew Walker
Worcester

❑ I'm the drummer off the Teletubbies and I know that the purple one is bumming the green one. That's a fact.

Fat Al White
Wrenthorpe

❑ My car number plate is K236 LCL, but my postcode is AL60RE, which is amusingly similar to 'Al Gore', the

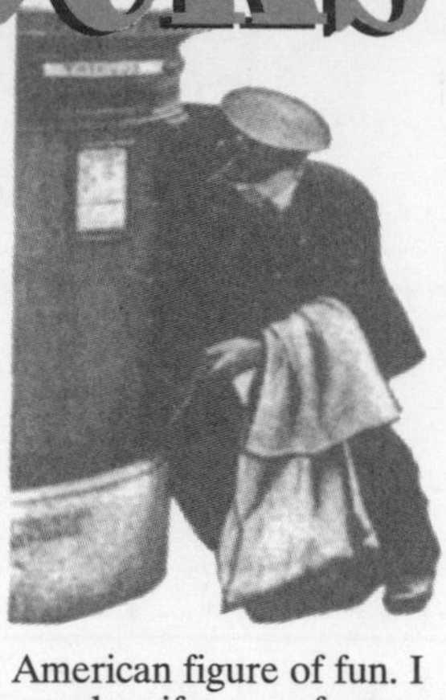

American figure of fun. I wonder if any of your readers would be interested in purchasing my postcode for use on their car.

D. Haslam
e-mail

Praise the landlord

❑ With alcohol-related crime rising and church attendance dropping, isn't it about time Tony Blair converted a few churches into pubs? I for one would be a lot less punchy if there were a few more pubs around that I wasn't barred from.

Guy
Nottingham

❑ With all the complaints about skyrocketing petrol prices and shortages, why don't we take a leaf out of the Americans' book and start running our cars on gas instead? It's cheaper and far more abundant. Come on British car scientists, don't let the Yanks get the jump on us.

Ian Davis
e-mail

Narrow minded

❑ In this age of low calorie food and drink, why don't boffins invent a low calorie petrol. The end result would be thinner vehicles enabling us to make three-lane motorways into five or six-lane ones, thus easing traffic congestion considerably. I think.

P. Welton
Stoke on Trent

❑ I am surprised to see that Supermarkets are already preparing for pancake day. I went to Tesco's yesterday and they already had flour and eggs in stock.

S. Drake
e-mail

The Big Match

❑ That old woman may not look much like the Queen Mother (issue 104), but she's a dead ringer for Big Ron Atkinson in a hat.

M.L. Edwards
e-mail

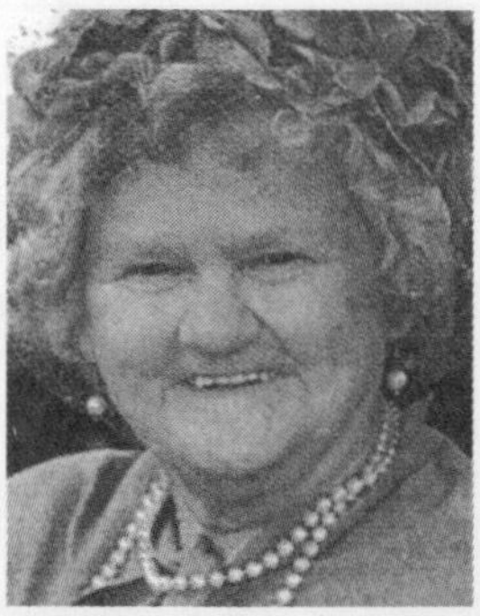

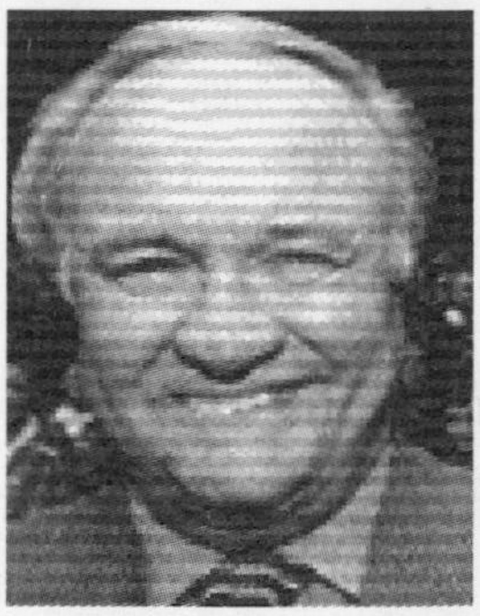

Smile, gentlemen please!

❑ In my efforts to assist in your quest for smiles lacking in sincerity, it would appear that in this picture of Cllr. Nigel Barron (below) from the Thurrock Gazette, I chanced upon a rare treat. But to find it in the very next column to one of Cllr Peter Maynard was nothing short of divine intervention.

Andy Slocombe, Grays

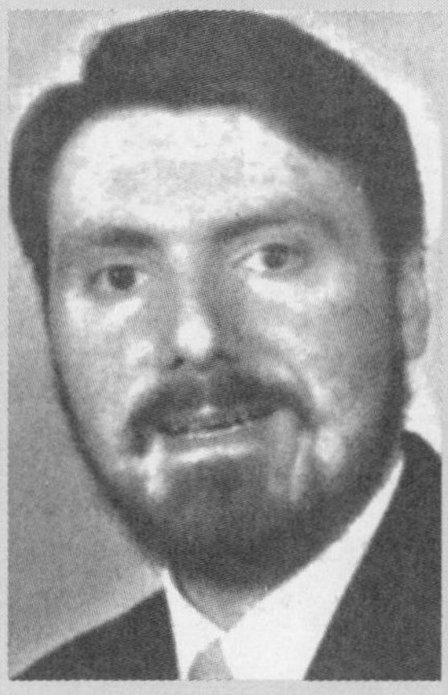

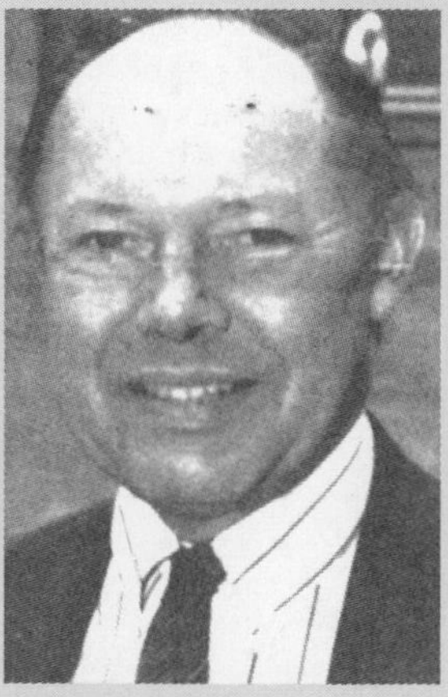

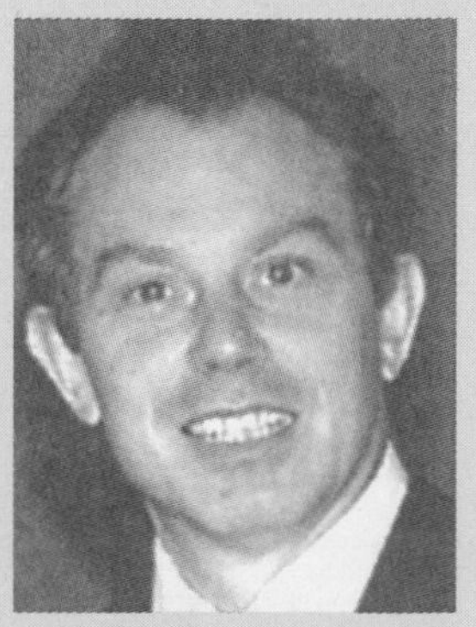

❑ On the subject of incincere smiles, I spotted this photo of Tony Blair, taken shortly after the petrol crisis. He may be kidding himself that it's a convincing grin, but you can't fuel us, Tony.

Dave Saunders
Cricklewood

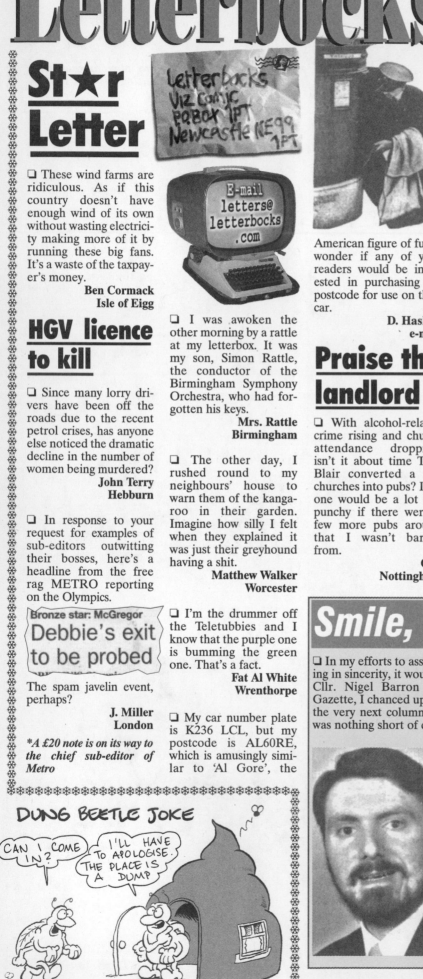

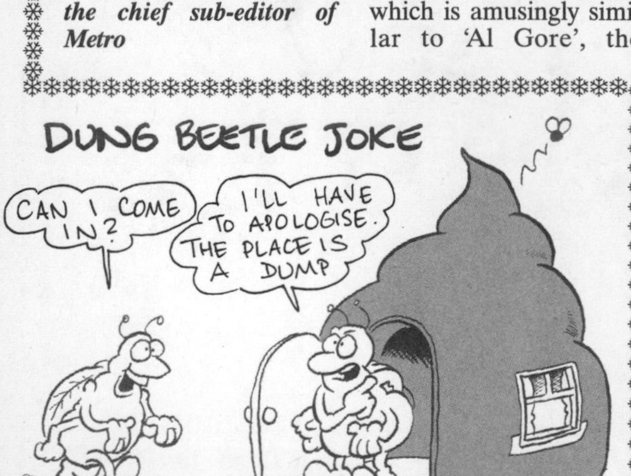
DUNG BEETLE JOKE
CAN I COME IN?
I'LL HAVE TO APOLOGISE. THE PLACE IS A DUMP

Celebrity Cunts

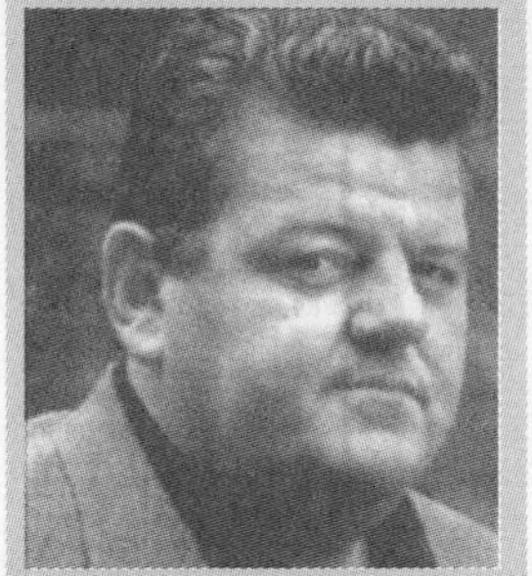

Shit's a Cracker

❑ I met Robbie Coltrane at a film award ceremony in Dublin a couple of months ago and he was a totally ignorant cunt when I tried to talk to him. All he was concerned with was shovelling pints of Guinness into his fat gob. And he's a much fatter pig in real life than he looks in the shit James Bond films.

Gary Byrnes
Dublin

❑ How dare the media interfere in the private life of Bruno Brookes? So what if he does or doesn't beat up his girlfriends, that's his own business.

Jerome Burns
e-mail

Family viewing

❑ What with the wonders of digital broadcasting, why don't we have a pay-per-view monarchy? That way, anyone with an abiding interest in their embarassingly irrelevant antics could voluntarily cough up their hard-earned cash to watch the chinless German inbreds piss about on horses to their hearts' content. Perhaps in return, they could get an exclusive share in the oft-referred to 'millions of pounds the royals bring into Britain', leaving the rest of us to enjoy the 21st century.

Craig Pert
e-mail

❑ I couldn't agree more with J. Beneaux when he slags off radio controlled cabs (issue 102). And those 'Self-Drive' vans are no better. I hired one last week and settled down for a nice kip. When I woke up four hours later I was still outside the hire centre. Of course the AA were useless as ever, and when they couldn't find anything wrong I ended up having to steer all the way while they towed me to Skelmersdale.

L. Maas
Carnbee

❑ As a lorry driver, I welcome the Chancellor's reduction of HGV excise duty, and the freezing of the tax on diesel until the year 2002. However, these measures still don't go far enough. We still have to pay the full rate of VAT on carpets we need to roll up our victims before disposing of their bodies in laybys.

Brian Watts
Leeds

Syntactical error

❑ As a professional drugs dealer working mainly in playgrounds and school gates, the "Just Say No" campaign presented no problems to me. I merely rephrased my questions, asking the kids if they wanted to not buy any drugs. My profits went through the roof.

H. Scorpion
Rhyll

❑ I'm fed up with people moaning about the recent floods and complaining that their councils did little to help. My dad was caught in a flood and he didn't just sit on his fat arse waiting for the council to bring him some sandbags. He got his finger out and built a bloody great boat and filled it with animals. Not bad for a six-hundred year old.

Japheth
Mount Ararat

❑ These so-called experts have got it wrong again, blaming the hole in the ozone layer for the recent floods. If they thought about it, what they should do is make the hole even bigger, allowing more sunlight through which would evaporate all the floodwater.

M. Cree
Dorchester

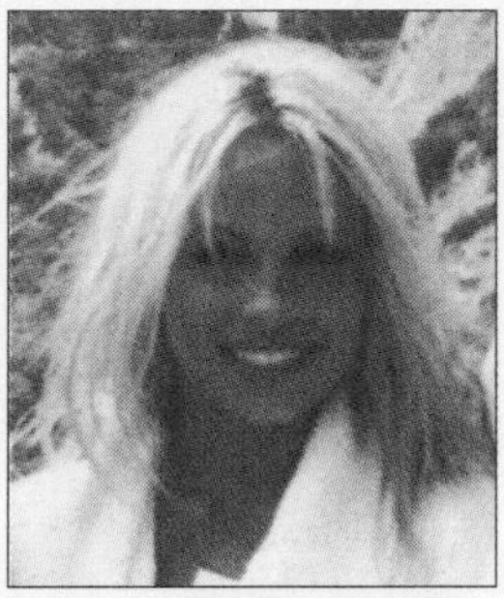

❑ In a recent interview, Pamela Anderson expressed her shock at having her 'Honeymoon video' stolen, and admits she has never seen it herself. Well if she wants to get in touch, she can borrow my copy, just as soon as all my mates have finished watching it.

John Pala
Darlington

❑ There's no pleasing some people. A couple of weeks ago the news was full of people moaning on about being flooded. These people would be the first to complain if they didn't have any water at all.

J. Lester
Derby

❑ I think the young leftie in the ad. department of the Newmarket Journal (below) ought to be rewarded for this one.

John Dolan
Ely

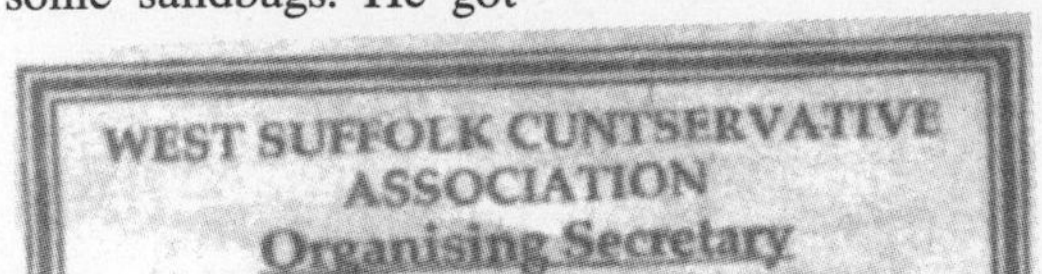

WEST SUFFOLK CUNTSERVATIVE ASSOCIATION
Organising Secretary
Full time (evening meetings)
Liaising with MP Officers, Councillors, Association members.
Help organise campaigning projects.
I.T. skills required.
Contact: P Merrick 01638 716177.

Top Tips

CAN'T remember the artist or title of a song stuck in your head? Simply record and release the song and wait to be sued for breach of copyright. The information you need will be on the writ.

Simon Sandall
Brisbane

COUNCIL highway departments. Save money erecting warning signs on dangerous bends. Simply sellotape a bunch of flowers to a nearby lamp post instead.

Adrian Webster
Macclesfield

SAVE money on electric toothbrushes by simply clamping a bottle brush into the chuck of a Black & Decker drill.

S. Grainger
Market Raisin

SERIAL killers. Make amends to the families of your murder victims by sending them a jar of Quality Street.

Craig Sullivan
Leeds

DADS. Force your son to play football only using his left foot by cutting the front off his right boot. In a few years time, when he's England's only left footed player, you can become his agent and retire.

G Coad
e-mail

MAKE your new neighbours immediately regret moving into their new home by introducing yourself as a 'senior resident of the street' and telling them that 'everyone round here likes things just the way they are.'

Guy
Nottingham

SPECTACLE wearers. Whilst having your morning shit, take a piece of loo paper, clean your glasses, and then wipe your arse. Hey presto, two uses for the one sheet of paper. NB. It must be done in that order.

Ian Thewlis
Leeds

Benson & Hedges
SANTA FAGS

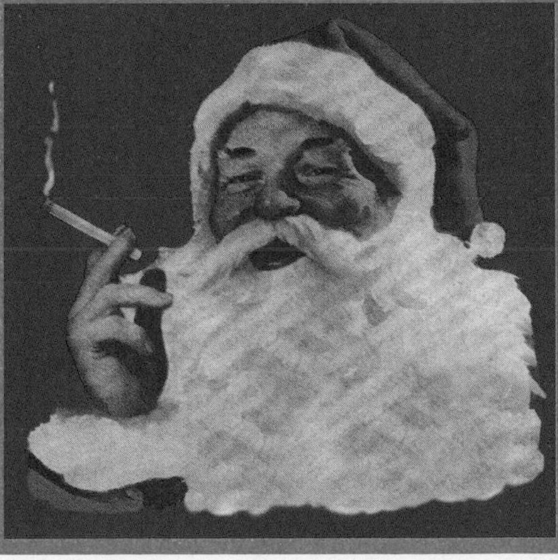

Government Health Warning
SMOKING MAY LEAD TO RUDDYING OF THE CHEEKS AND JOCULAR ROTUNDITY
6mg Tar 0.5mg Nicotine 4mg Mince Pies

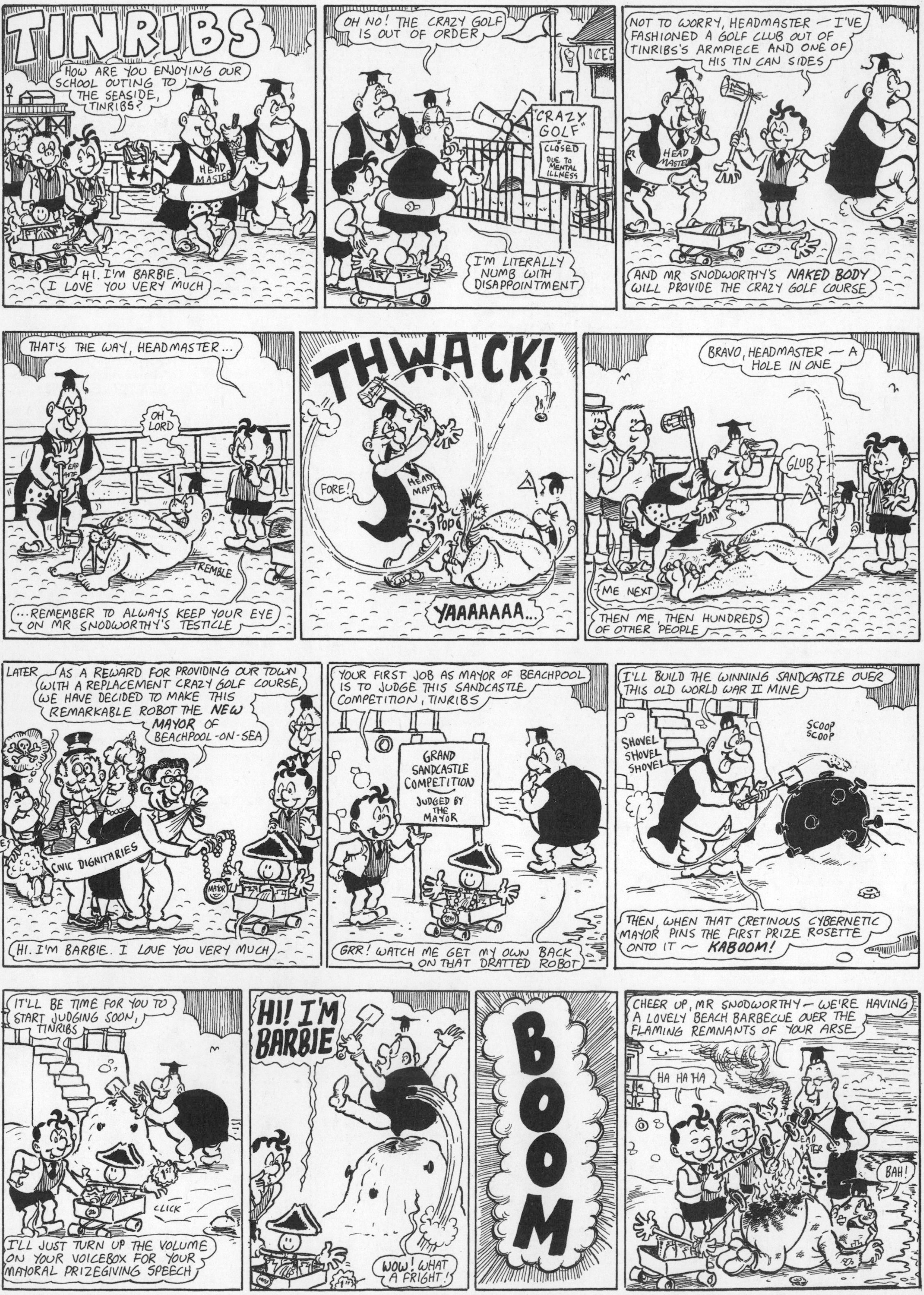
TINRIBS
HOW ARE YOU ENJOYING OUR SCHOOL OUTING TO THE SEASIDE, TINRIBS?
HEAD MASTER
HI. I'M BARBIE. I LOVE YOU VERY MUCH
OH NO! THE CRAZY GOLF IS OUT OF ORDER
ICES
"CRAZY GOLF" CLOSED DUE TO MENTAL ILLNESS
I'M LITERALLY NUMB WITH DISAPPOINTMENT
NOT TO WORRY, HEADMASTER — I'VE FASHIONED A GOLF CLUB OUT OF TINRIBS'S ARMPIECE AND ONE OF HIS TIN CAN SIDES
AND MR SNODWORTHY'S NAKED BODY WILL PROVIDE THE CRAZY GOLF COURSE
THAT'S THE WAY, HEADMASTER...
OH LORD
TREMBLE
...REMEMBER TO ALWAYS KEEP YOUR EYE ON MR SNODWORTHY'S TESTICLE
THWACK!
FORE!
POP
YAAAAAAA...
BRAVO, HEADMASTER — A HOLE IN ONE
GLUB
ME NEXT
THEN ME, THEN HUNDREDS OF OTHER PEOPLE
LATER
AS A REWARD FOR PROVIDING OUR TOWN WITH A REPLACEMENT CRAZY GOLF COURSE, WE HAVE DECIDED TO MAKE THIS REMARKABLE ROBOT THE NEW MAYOR OF BEACHPOOL-ON-SEA
ICE
CIVIC DIGNITARIES
MAYOR
HI. I'M BARBIE. I LOVE YOU VERY MUCH
YOUR FIRST JOB AS MAYOR OF BEACHPOOL IS TO JUDGE THIS SANDCASTLE COMPETITION, TINRIBS
GRAND SANDCASTLE COMPETITION JUDGED BY THE MAYOR
GRR! WATCH ME GET MY OWN BACK ON THAT DRATTED ROBOT
I'LL BUILD THE WINNING SANDCASTLE OVER THIS OLD WORLD WAR II MINE
SHOVEL SHOVEL SHOVEL
SCOOP SCOOP
THEN, WHEN THAT CRETINOUS CYBERNETIC MAYOR PINS THE FIRST PRIZE ROSETTE ONTO IT ~ KABOOM!
IT'LL BE TIME FOR YOU TO START JUDGING SOON, TINRIBS
CLICK
I'LL JUST TURN UP THE VOLUME ON YOUR VOICEBOX FOR YOUR MAYORAL PRIZEGIVING SPEECH
HI! I'M BARBIE
WOW! WHAT A FRIGHT!
BOOM
CHEER UP, MR SNODWORTHY — WE'RE HAVING A LOVELY BEACH BARBECUE OVER THE FLAMING REMNANTS OF YOUR ARSE
HA HA HA
HEAD MASTER
BAH!

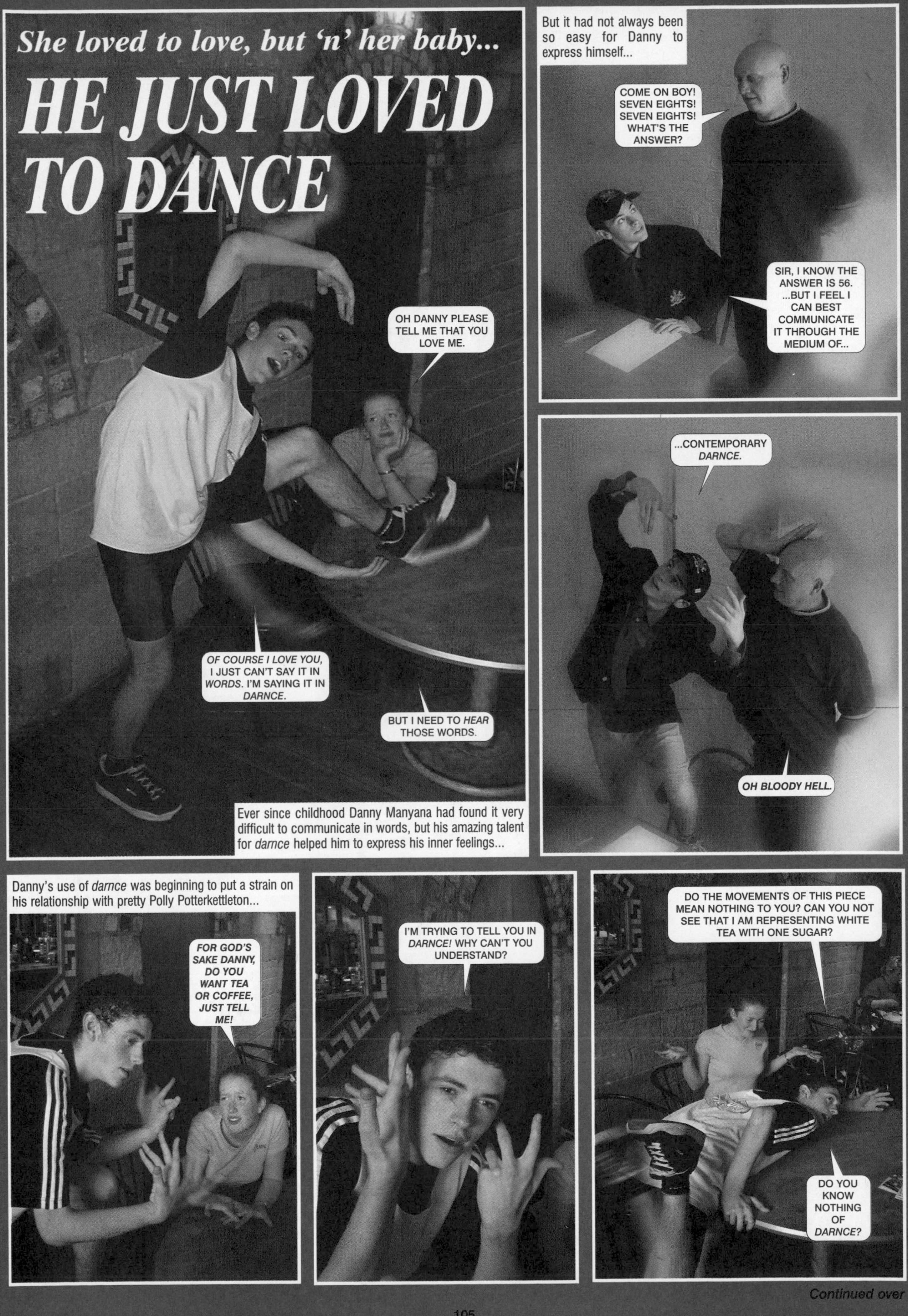
She loved to love, but 'n' her baby...
HE JUST LOVED TO DANCE
OH DANNY PLEASE TELL ME THAT YOU LOVE ME.
OF COURSE I LOVE YOU, I JUST CAN'T SAY IT IN WORDS. I'M SAYING IT IN DARNCE.
BUT I NEED TO HEAR THOSE WORDS.
Ever since childhood Danny Manyana had found it very difficult to communicate in words, but his amazing talent for darnce helped him to express his inner feelings...
But it had not always been so easy for Danny to express himself...
COME ON BOY! SEVEN EIGHTS! SEVEN EIGHTS! WHAT'S THE ANSWER?
SIR, I KNOW THE ANSWER IS 56. ...BUT I FEEL I CAN BEST COMMUNICATE IT THROUGH THE MEDIUM OF...
...CONTEMPORARY DARNCE.
OH BLOODY HELL.
Danny's use of darnce was beginning to put a strain on his relationship with pretty Polly Potterkettleton...
FOR GOD'S SAKE DANNY, DO YOU WANT TEA OR COFFEE, JUST TELL ME!
I'M TRYING TO TELL YOU IN DARNCE! WHY CAN'T YOU UNDERSTAND?
DO THE MOVEMENTS OF THIS PIECE MEAN NOTHING TO YOU? CAN YOU NOT SEE THAT I AM REPRESENTING WHITE TEA WITH ONE SUGAR?
DO YOU KNOW NOTHING OF DARNCE?

Continued over

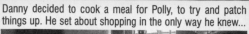

IF YOU CAN'T EVEN TELL ME YOU WANT A CUP OF TEA, YOU'RE NEVER GOING TO TELL ME YOU LOVE ME. I CAN'T TAKE IT ANY MORE...I'M,...I'M,...I'M,...
...I'M GOING FOR A WALK.
Danny decided to cook a meal for Polly, to try and patch things up. He set about shopping in the only way he knew...
WHAT DOES THAT MEAN THEN? MINCE IS IT?...BUT HOW MUCH?... HALF A POUND?
I THINK THE RAPID ARM MOVEMENTS REPRESENT THE BILLOWING OF A PLUMP PORK SAUSAGE...AND THE JERKY STEPS ARE SAYING THREE QUARTERS OF A POUND.
WELL I THINK HE'S TRYING TO SAY CHOPPED LIVER.
Outside...
Fulchester FAMILY BUTCHERS
THERE'S POLLY NOW. SHE'LL BE SO PLEASED WHEN SHE SEES WHAT I'VE BOUGHT FOR A ROMANTIC CANDLE-LIT DINNER TOGETHER.
OH NO, THAT CAR, SHE HASN'T SEEN IT! I MUST WARN HER!
Fulchester FAMILY BUTCHERS
OH NO!
CRUMP!
SORRY MATE. I DIDN'T SEE HER!
WHOLESALE & CATERING
OH POL! IF I HAD USED WORDS, PERHAPS YOU WOULD HAVE HEARD ME. THE MEDIUM OF *DARNCE* WAS JUST NOT SUITABLE IN THIS SITUATION.
A827 KL

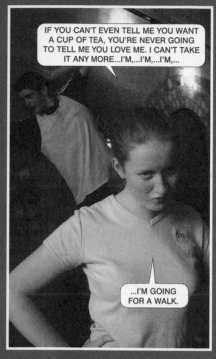

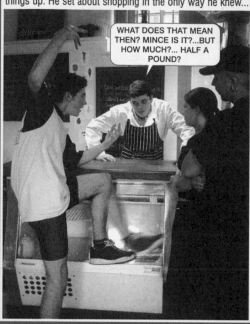

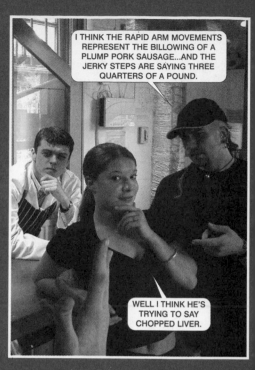

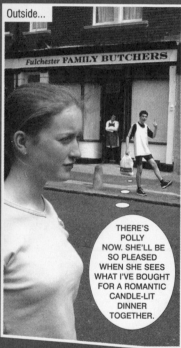

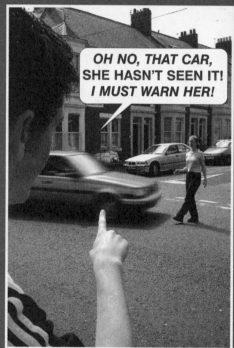

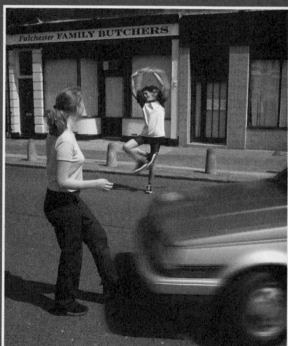

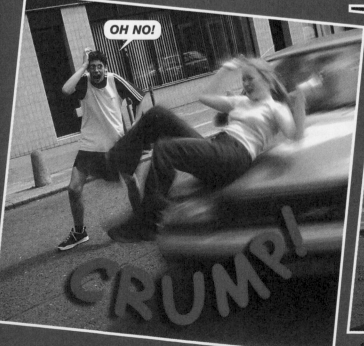

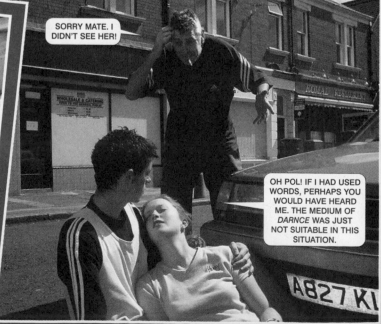

...I'VE LEARNED THE HARD WAY, I SHALL ALWAYS USE WORDS TO EXPRESS MYSELF FROM NOW ON...POLLY I WILL LOVE YOU UNTIL THE MOMENT YOU DIE.
OH DANNY...
...CROAK!
hmm... HELLO.
I FEEL ABSOLUTELY COMPELLED TO VOCALISE MY LUSTFUL DESIRES TO FONDLE YOUR AMPLE BREASTS AND ALL STUFF LIKE THAT.
OOOH, SOUNDS LUSH.

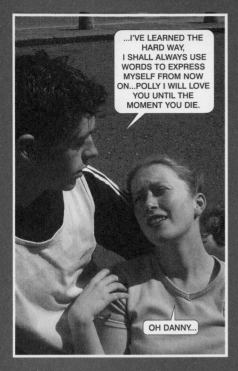

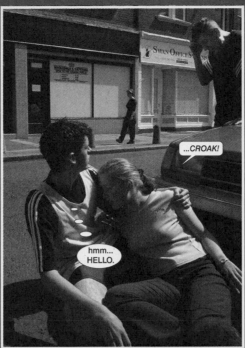

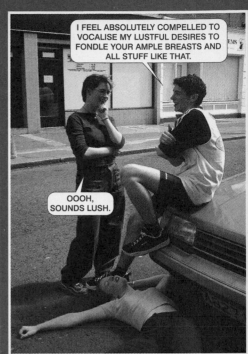

THE END

GREER of the YEAR

By our Germaine Greer Correspondent, Abdul Latif Lord of Harpole

COMEDY harridan Germaine Greer was yesterday crowned 'Greer of the Year' at a star-studded ceremony in central London.

It is the first time the feminist writer has been awarded the title. The presentation, made by last year's winner Ian Greer, professor of Obstetrics and Gynaecology at Glasgow Royal Infirmary, was followed by an informal press conference at the Grosvenor House Hotel. during which, Mrs Greer posed cheekily for photographers with her book 'Slip-Shod Sibyls: Recognition, Rejection and The Woman Poet'.

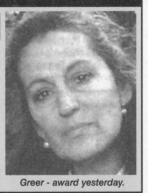

Greer - award yesterday.

Quakey Shakey!

LONG-DORMANT pop star Shakin' Stevens may be set to explode back into activity, according to seismologists who have been monitoring him.

The Welsh rocker, who topped the charts throughout the eighties with hits such as *Green Door, This Ole House* and *Marie Marie*, stopped shaking and became still in the early 90's, and has remained inactive for nearly a decade.

tremors

However, Stevens' concerned neighbours recently called in experts after they felt tremors which dislodged pictures from walls and caused pottery to rattle.

"It may be nothing, but it could be a warning that Shaky is becoming active again," said Professor Kid Chocolate of Swansea University's department of geophysics.

Stevens - shakin.

squirm

"If this shaking continues, there could be a devastating full scale eruption, with villages, towns and even cities laid waste under millions of tons of red hot lava."

Billy
THE BEST DOG EVER!
THE BIG ISSUE

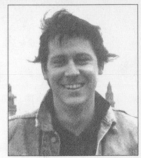

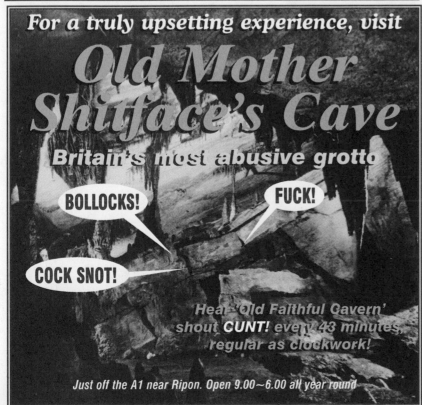

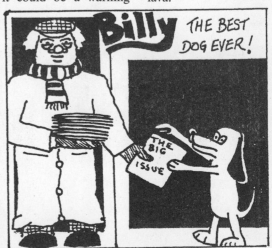

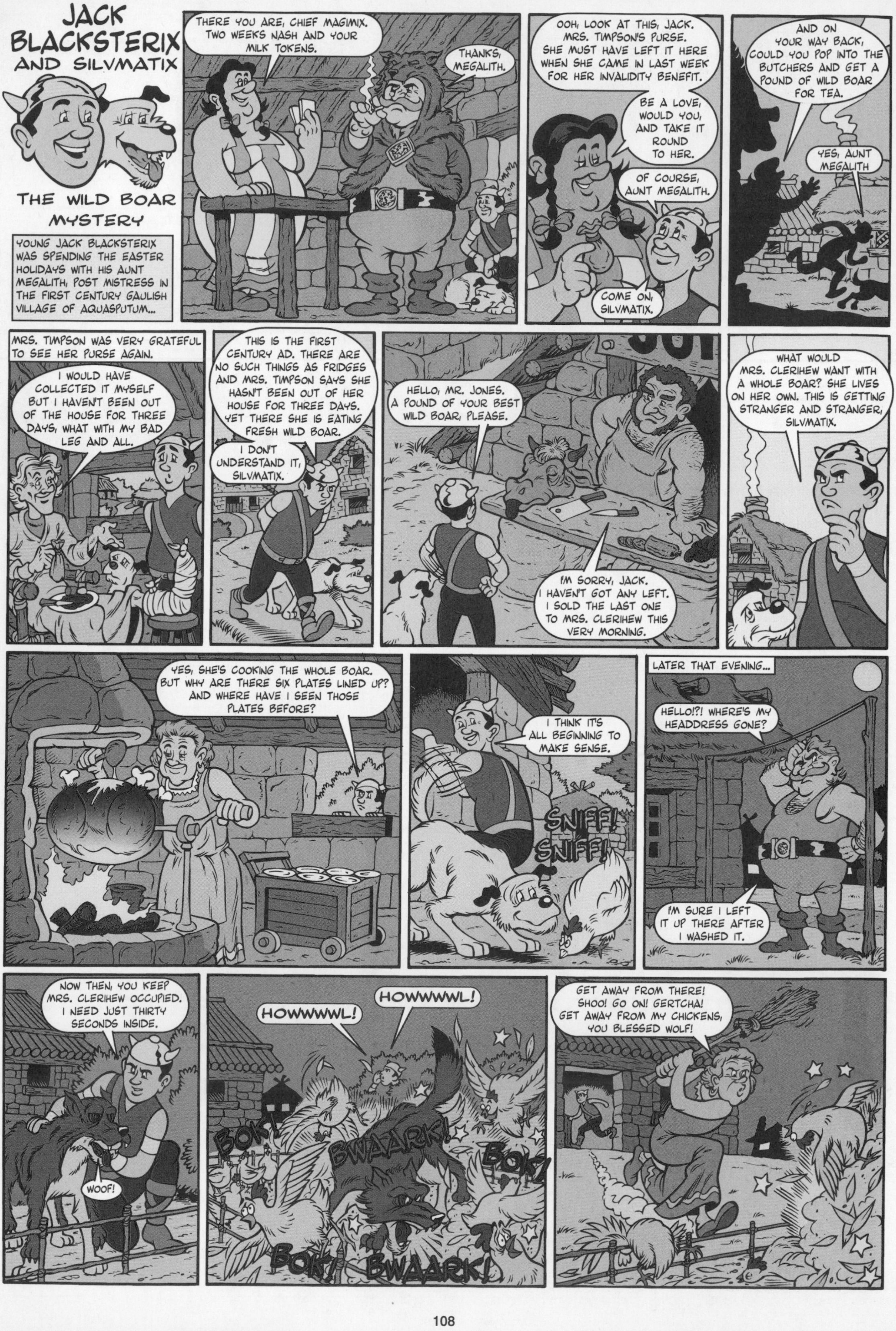
JACK BLACKSTERIX AND SILVMATIX
THE WILD BOAR MYSTERY
YOUNG JACK BLACKSTERIX WAS SPENDING THE EASTER HOLIDAYS WITH HIS AUNT MEGALITH, POST MISTRESS IN THE FIRST CENTURY GAULISH VILLAGE OF AQUASPUTUM...
THERE YOU ARE, CHIEF MAGIMIX. TWO WEEKS NASH AND YOUR MILK TOKENS.
THANKS, MEGALITH.
OOH, LOOK AT THIS, JACK. MRS. TIMPSON'S PURSE. SHE MUST HAVE LEFT IT HERE WHEN SHE CAME IN LAST WEEK FOR HER INVALIDITY BENEFIT.
BE A LOVE, WOULD YOU, AND TAKE IT ROUND TO HER.
OF COURSE, AUNT MEGALITH.
COME ON, SILVMATIX.
AND ON YOUR WAY BACK, COULD YOU POP INTO THE BUTCHERS AND GET A POUND OF WILD BOAR FOR TEA.
YES, AUNT MEGALITH
MRS. TIMPSON WAS VERY GRATEFUL TO SEE HER PURSE AGAIN.
I WOULD HAVE COLLECTED IT MYSELF BUT I HAVEN'T BEEN OUT OF THE HOUSE FOR THREE DAYS, WHAT WITH MY BAD LEG AND ALL.
THIS IS THE FIRST CENTURY AD. THERE ARE NO SUCH THINGS AS FRIDGES AND MRS. TIMPSON SAYS SHE HASN'T BEEN OUT OF HER HOUSE FOR THREE DAYS. YET THERE SHE IS EATING FRESH WILD BOAR.
I DON'T UNDERSTAND IT, SILVMATIX.
HELLO, MR. JONES. A POUND OF YOUR BEST WILD BOAR, PLEASE.
I'M SORRY, JACK. I HAVEN'T GOT ANY LEFT. I SOLD THE LAST ONE TO MRS. CLERIHEW THIS VERY MORNING.
WHAT WOULD MRS. CLERIHEW WANT WITH A WHOLE BOAR? SHE LIVES ON HER OWN. THIS IS GETTING STRANGER AND STRANGER, SILVMATIX.
YES, SHE'S COOKING THE WHOLE BOAR. BUT WHY ARE THERE SIX PLATES LINED UP? AND WHERE HAVE I SEEN THOSE PLATES BEFORE?
I THINK IT'S ALL BEGINNING TO MAKE SENSE.
SNIFF! SNIFF!
LATER THAT EVENING...
HELLO!?! WHERE'S MY HEADDRESS GONE?
I'M SURE I LEFT IT UP THERE AFTER I WASHED IT.
NOW THEN, YOU KEEP MRS. CLERIHEW OCCUPIED. I NEED JUST THIRTY SECONDS INSIDE.
WOOF!
HOWWWWL!
HOWWWWL!
BOK!
BWAARK!
BOK!
BOK!
BWAARK!
GET AWAY FROM THERE! SHOO! GO ON! GERTCHA! GET AWAY FROM MY CHICKENS, YOU BLESSED WOLF!

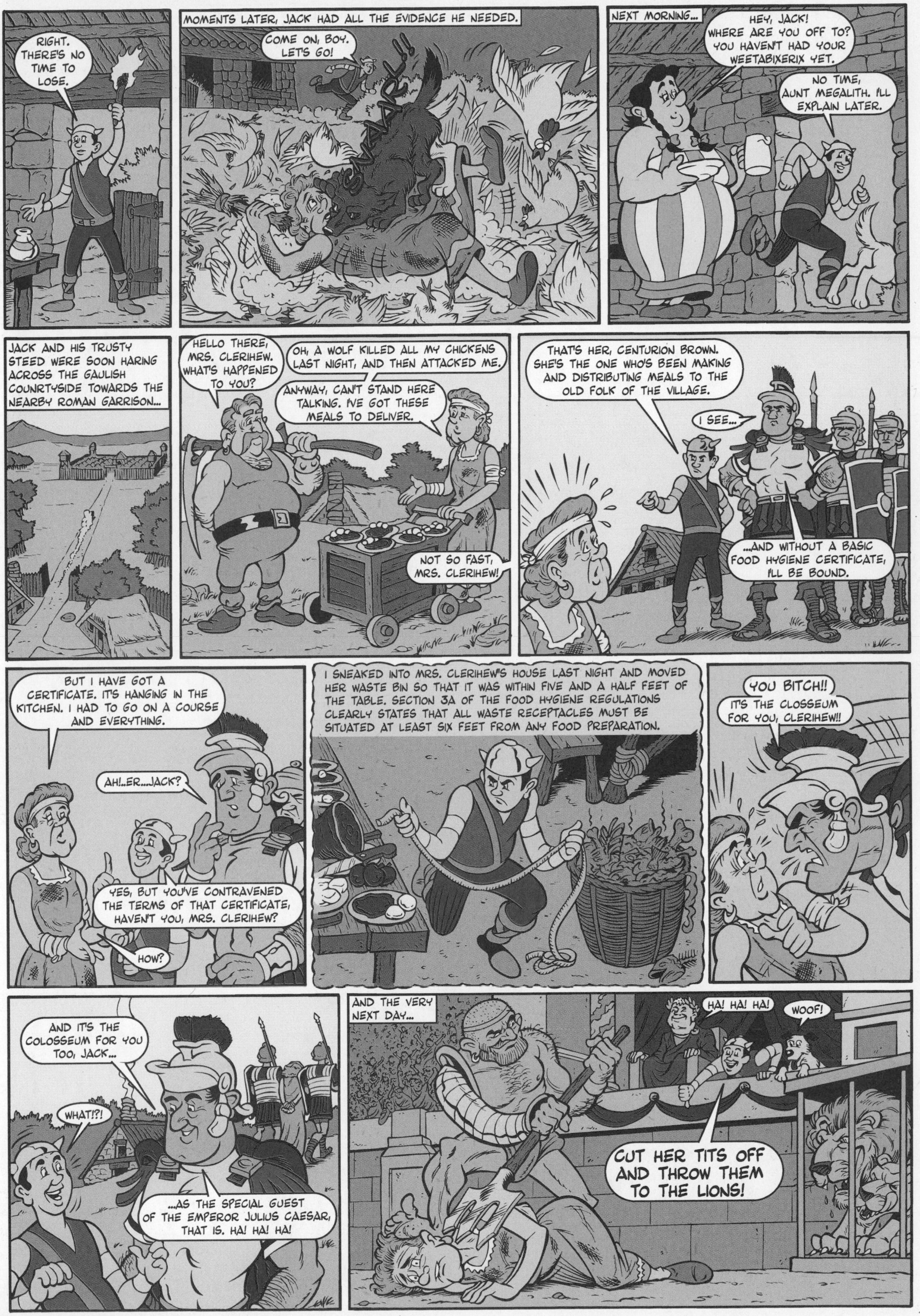
RIGHT. THERE'S NO TIME TO LOSE.
MOMENTS LATER, JACK HAD ALL THE EVIDENCE HE NEEDED.
COME ON, BOY. LET'S GO!
NEXT MORNING...
HEY, JACK! WHERE ARE YOU OFF TO? YOU HAVEN'T HAD YOUR WEETABIXERIX YET.
NO TIME, AUNT MEGALITH. I'LL EXPLAIN LATER.
JACK AND HIS TRUSTY STEED WERE SOON HARING ACROSS THE GAULISH COUNRTYSIDE TOWARDS THE NEARBY ROMAN GARRISON...
HELLO THERE, MRS. CLERIHEW. WHAT'S HAPPENED TO YOU?
OH, A WOLF KILLED ALL MY CHICKENS LAST NIGHT, AND THEN ATTACKED ME.
ANYWAY, CAN'T STAND HERE TALKING. I'VE GOT THESE MEALS TO DELIVER.
NOT SO FAST, MRS. CLERIHEW!
THAT'S HER, CENTURION BROWN. SHE'S THE ONE WHO'S BEEN MAKING AND DISTRIBUTING MEALS TO THE OLD FOLK OF THE VILLAGE.
I SEE...
...AND WITHOUT A BASIC FOOD HYGIENE CERTIFICATE, I'LL BE BOUND.
BUT I HAVE GOT A CERTIFICATE. IT'S HANGING IN THE KITCHEN. I HAD TO GO ON A COURSE AND EVERYTHING.
AH!..ER...JACK?
YES, BUT YOU'VE CONTRAVENED THE TERMS OF THAT CERTIFICATE, HAVEN'T YOU, MRS. CLERIHEW?
HOW?
I SNEAKED INTO MRS. CLERIHEW'S HOUSE LAST NIGHT AND MOVED HER WASTE BIN SO THAT IT WAS WITHIN FIVE AND A HALF FEET OF THE TABLE. SECTION 3A OF THE FOOD HYGIENE REGULATIONS CLEARLY STATES THAT ALL WASTE RECEPTACLES MUST BE SITUATED AT LEAST SIX FEET FROM ANY FOOD PREPARATION.
YOU BITCH!!
IT'S THE CLOSSEUM FOR YOU, CLERIHEW!!
AND IT'S THE COLOSSEUM FOR YOU TOO, JACK...
WHAT!?!
...AS THE SPECIAL GUEST OF THE EMPEROR JULIUS CAESAR, THAT IS. HA! HA! HA!
AND THE VERY NEXT DAY...
HA! HA! HA!
WOOF!
CUT HER TITS OFF AND THROW THEM TO THE LIONS!

Benson & Hedges
KRAUT FAGS

Government Health Warning

SMOKING KRAUT FAGS MAY CAUSE YOU TO INVADE POLAND

6mg Tar 0.5mg Nicotine 3mg Lederhosens

The Bat in the Hat!

Jay in a flap over titmice in his titfer

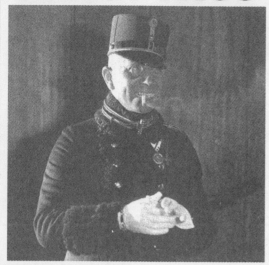

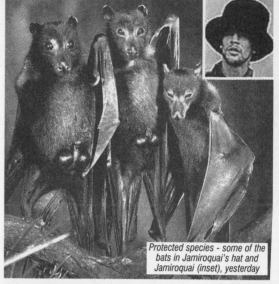

Protected species - some of the bats in Jamiroquai's hat and Jamiroquai (inset), yesterday

RUBBER-LEGGED pop star Jay Kay is steaming mad after being banned from driving... for 150 YEARS! And it's not for speeding or drink-driving. It's because he's got bats... *IN HIS HAT!*

The colony of over 1000 Pipistrel bats was discovered after Kay's common-law wife, ex-Big Breakfast babe Denise Van Outen was awoken in the early hours by loud, inaudible squeaking.

Sonar

Denise said: "I heard all sonar noise coming from Jamiroquoi's hat. I peeped inside with a torch and there was all these bats flying around inside eating moths."

Radar

The showbiz golden couple called in pest experts, but were dismayed to be told that as the furry sightless birds were a protected species, there was nothing they could do to get rid of them. On the contrary, if Kay disturbed them at all - he could be sent to *PRISON!*

"That was a real blow for Jay, because he can't fit into any of his Ferarris without taking his hat off," said Outen.

Hawkeye

And the future looks bleak for the funk-lite popster, for bat boffins have told him that a colony of Pipistrels can stay in the same place for up to 150 years - or even twice that.

Fanny's Batter bits

'Top Gun' heart-throb ***Tom Cruise*** *is recovering in his swanky Malibu Beach home after being bitten by a spider. The pint-size actor became ensnared in a sticky web whilst dusting a pelmet, and spent four terrifying hours fending off the hungry insect before being rescued by wife* ***Nicole Kidman****. Ironically Cruise, who lost an arm and a leg in the attack, recently gave almost a hundred billion dollars to spider charities.*

The BIRDMAN of ALKA~SELTZER

Tweet Tweet
Tweet tweet
Tweet Tweet Tweet
Tweet
PLINK! PLINK! FIZZZ...
Tweet
Tweet tweet
Tweet
Tweet
'ERE, BERT! WE'VE DUG A TUNNEL AND WE'RE BREAKING OUT TONIGHT. ARE YOU WITH US?
Tweet Tweet Tweet
Tweet
Tweet Tweet
Tweet
NO, I'M SORRY. I'D LOVE TO BUT I'VE GOT TERRIBLE HEARTBURN AGAIN IT'D GET MUCH WORSE IF I HAD TO CROUCH.
Tweet Tweet Tweet
Tweet Tweet Tweet Tweet Tweet
Tweet Tweet Tweet
Tweet Tweet
Tweet Tweet Tweet
Tweet Tweet Tweet
GLUG-GLUG-GLUG!
Tweet
Tweet
Tweet

Joe Dolce says...

SHUTTER-UPPA YA FACE!

WITH POLICE APPROVED
FACIAL SECURITY SHUTTERS

it's as easy as...

UNO... DUE...TRE!

"A face left-a unattended she is an open invitation to-a da thieves."

Joe Dolce MBE, former Deputy Chief Constable of Greater Manchester.

YOURS FOR ONLY **£599** **NO** HIDDEN EXTRAS

Product & Installation extra.

FREEFONE 0800 FACIAL SECURITY

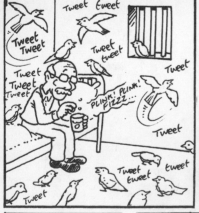

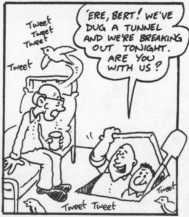

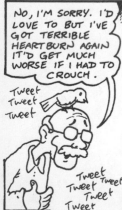

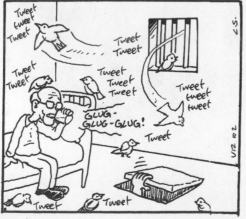

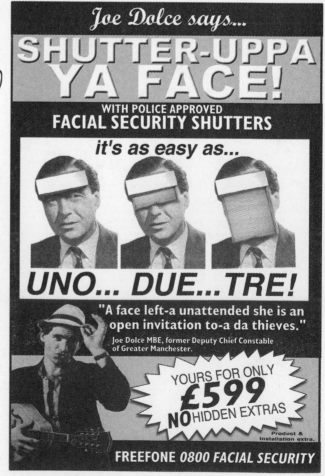

NORMAN the DOORMAN

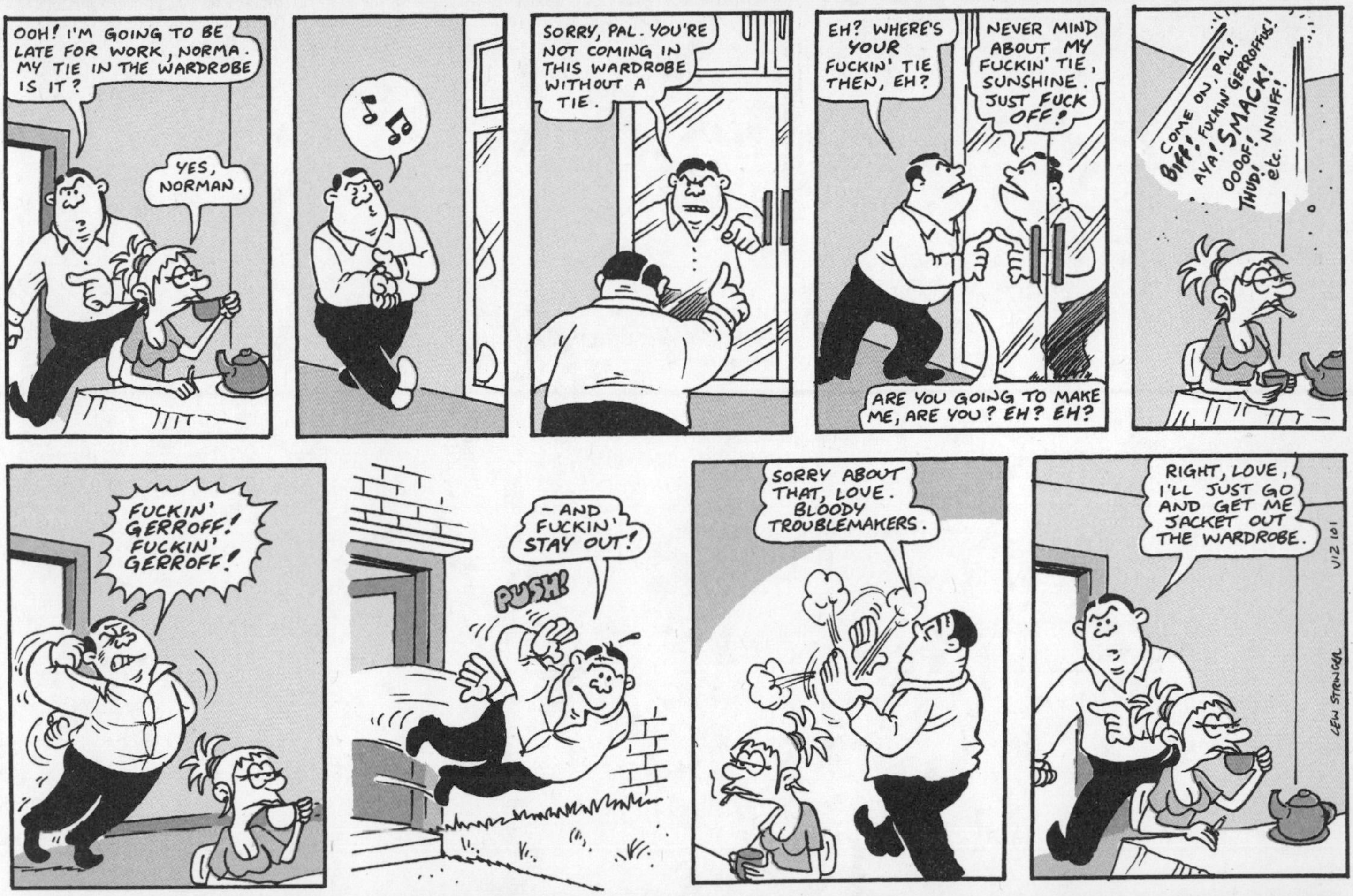

OOH! I'M GOING TO BE LATE FOR WORK, NORMA. MY TIE IN THE WARDROBE IS IT?
YES, NORMAN.
SORRY, PAL. YOU'RE NOT COMING IN THIS WARDROBE WITHOUT A TIE.
EH? WHERE'S YOUR FUCKIN' TIE THEN, EH?
NEVER MIND ABOUT MY FUCKIN' TIE, SUNSHINE. JUST FUCK OFF!
ARE YOU GOING TO MAKE ME, ARE YOU? EH? EH?
COME ON, PAL! BIFF! FUCKIN' GERROFFUS! AYA! SMACK! OOOOF! NNNFF! THUD! etc.
FUCKIN' GERROFF! FUCKIN' GERROFF!
PUSH!
– AND FUCKIN' STAY OUT!
SORRY ABOUT THAT, LOVE. BLOODY TROUBLEMAKERS.
RIGHT, LOVE, I'LL JUST GO AND GET ME JACKET OUT THE WARDROBE.
VIZ 101
LEW STRINGER

Save Our Scare Stories!

BARMY Brussels bureaucrats have poked their big Belgian conks into Britain's business again. Not content with banning bent bananas, swapping traditional pints for Froggie litres and insisting we take the Queen's head off our own coins, their latest potty scheme is to standardise the good old British *SCARE STORY*.

By our European Affairs Analyst
Billy 'Bulldog' Bigot

If Brussels get their way, from next April every tabloid newspaper article about European policy will have to contain a maximum of:

- 3 insulting references to Belgians, of which only 2 may alliterate.
- 2 references to the Blitz or Churchill.
- 1 reference to imaginary regulations concerning the straightness of bananas.
- 1 badly drawn cartoon of a bulldog or moustachioed frog wearing a beret.
- 1 'sound-bite' quote from either Michael Winner or Sir Teddy Taylor.

Brussels waves the rules at Britannia

"It's an absolute outrage. Britain has always led the world in tabloid scaremongery" said Southend MP, Sir Teddy Taylor, responding to our wildly exaggerated version of the facts.

Churchill

"If these Belgian bureau-crackpots think we're going to take this lying down, they can think again. Churchill didn't take it from them during the Blitz, and *we're* not going to take it now," he added.

Stannah

Millionaire film director Michael Winner was equally furious when we called him at his home at 3am. "It beggars belief!" he spluttered. "The French and the Germans would not put up with this nonsense, and neither should we. These Euro-prats are making a laughing stock of us."

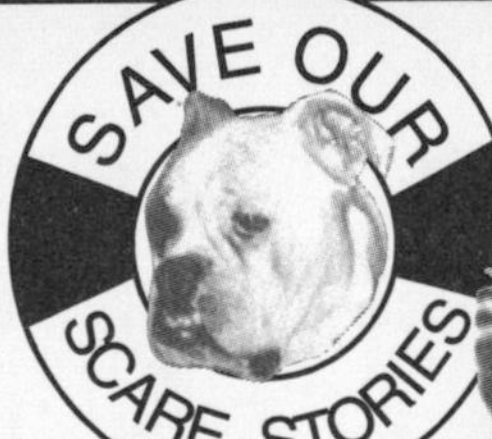

SAVE OUR SCARE STORIES

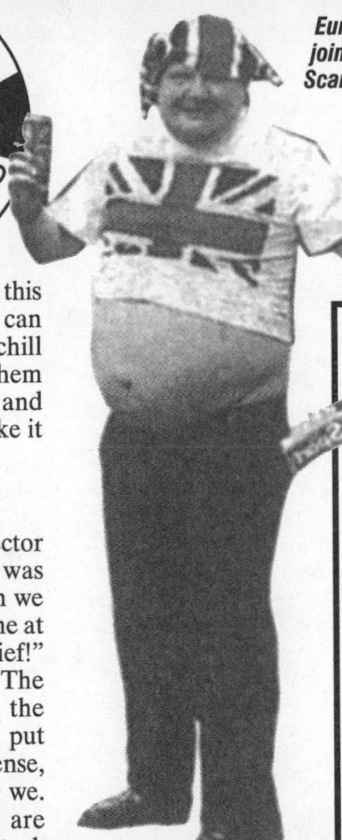

Euro-sceptic MP Sir Teddy Taylor joins the xenophibic Viz 'Save Our Scare Stories' campaign yesterday:

"Fuck them Belgians" he told us. "I'm giving up sprouts and Tintin books and I'm going to post a turd to Plastic Bertrand"

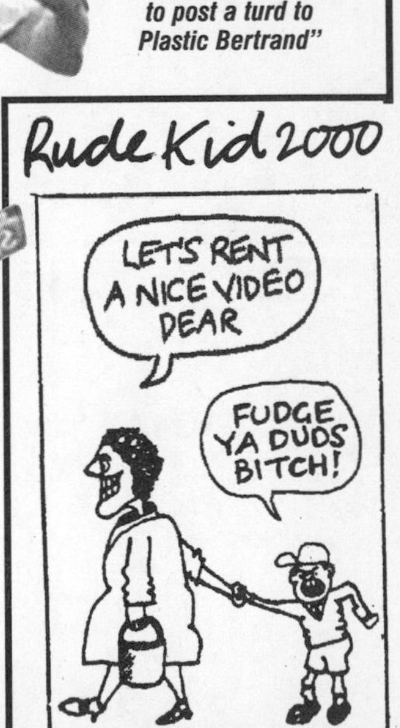

Rude Kid 2000
LET'S RENT A NICE VIDEO DEAR
FUDGE YA DUDS BITCH!

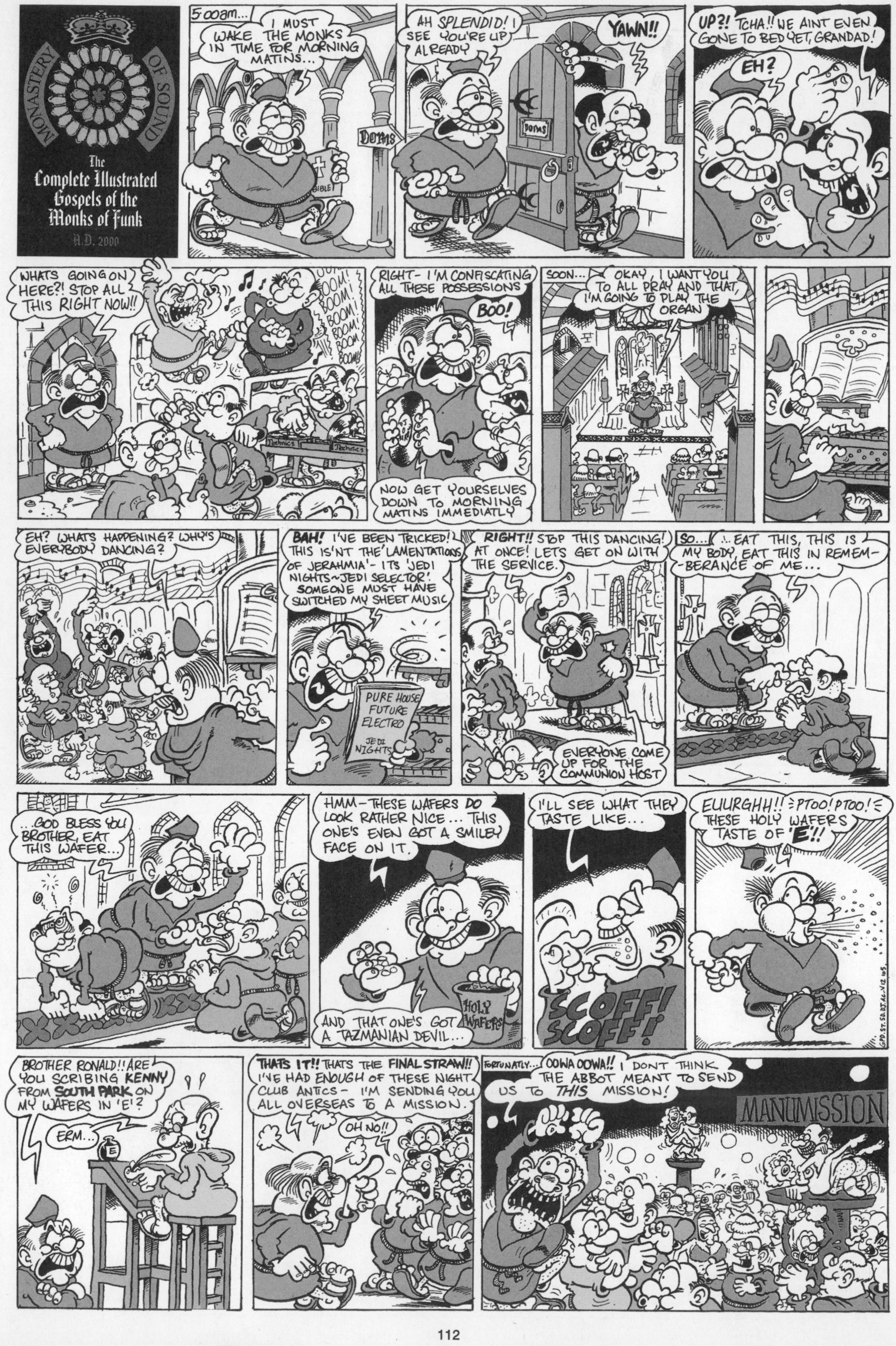
MONASTERY OF SOUND
The Complete Illustrated Gospels of the Monks of Funk
A.D. 2000
5:00am...
I MUST WAKE THE MONKS IN TIME FOR MORNING MATINS...
DORMS
BIBLE
AH SPLENDID! I SEE YOU'RE UP ALREADY
YAWN!!
DORMS
UP?! TCHA!! WE AINT EVEN GONE TO BED YET, GRANDAD!
EH?
WHATS GOING ON HERE?! STOP ALL THIS RIGHT NOW!!
BOOM! BOOM! BOOM! BOOM! BOOM! BOOM!
Technics
Technics
RIGHT - I'M CONFISCATING ALL THESE POSSESSIONS
BOO!
NOW GET YOURSELVES DOWN TO MORNING MATINS IMMEDIATLY
SOON...
OKAY, I WANT YOU TO ALL PRAY AND THAT, I'M GOING TO PLAY THE ORGAN
EH? WHATS HAPPENING? WHY'S EVERYBODY DANCING?
BAH! I'VE BEEN TRICKED! THIS IS'NT THE 'LAMENTATIONS OF JERAHMIA' - ITS 'JEDI NIGHTS~JEDI SELECTOR'. SOMEONE MUST HAVE SWITCHED MY SHEET MUSIC
PURE HOUSE FUTURE ELECTRO
JEDI NIGHTS
RIGHT!! STOP THIS DANCING! AT ONCE! LETS GET ON WITH THE SERVICE.
EVERYONE COME UP FOR THE COMMUNION HOST
SO...
...EAT THIS, THIS IS MY BODY, EAT THIS IN REMEMBERANCE OF ME...
...GOD BLESS YOU BROTHER, EAT THIS WAFER...
HMM - THESE WAFERS DO LOOK RATHER NICE... THIS ONE'S EVEN GOT A SMILEY FACE ON IT.
AND THAT ONE'S GOT A TAZMANIAN DEVIL...
HOLY WAFERS
I'LL SEE WHAT THEY TASTE LIKE...
SCOFF! SCOFF!
EUURGHH!! PTOO! PTOO! THESE HOLY WAFERS TASTE OF 'E'!!
BROTHER RONALD!! ARE YOU SCRIBING KENNY FROM SOUTH PARK ON MY WAFERS IN 'E'?
ERM...
E
THATS IT!! THATS THE FINAL STRAW!! I'VE HAD ENOUGH OF THESE NIGHT CLUB ANTICS - I'M SENDING YOU ALL OVERSEAS TO A MISSION.
OH NO!!
FORTUNATLY...
OOWA OOWA!! I DONT THINK THE ABBOT MEANT TO SEND US TO THIS MISSION!
MANUMISSION

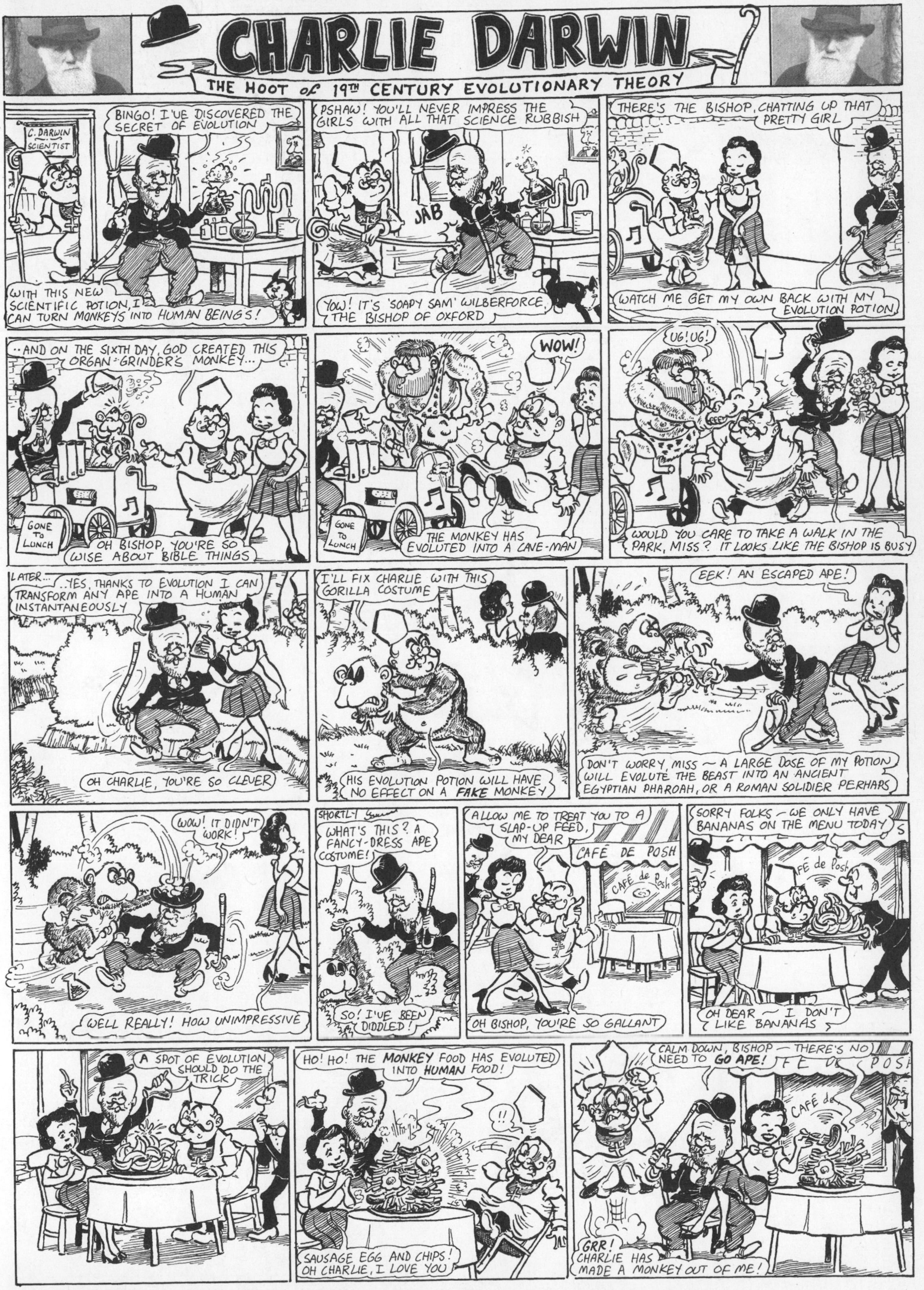
CHARLIE DARWIN
THE HOOT of 19TH CENTURY EVOLUTIONARY THEORY
C. DARWIN SCIENTIST
BINGO! I'VE DISCOVERED THE SECRET OF EVOLUTION
WITH THIS NEW SCIENTIFIC POTION, I CAN TURN MONKEYS INTO HUMAN BEINGS!
PSHAW! YOU'LL NEVER IMPRESS THE GIRLS WITH ALL THAT SCIENCE RUBBISH
JAB
YOW! IT'S 'SOAPY SAM' WILBERFORCE, THE BISHOP OF OXFORD
THERE'S THE BISHOP, CHATTING UP THAT PRETTY GIRL
WATCH ME GET MY OWN BACK WITH MY EVOLUTION POTION
..AND ON THE SIXTH DAY, GOD CREATED THIS ORGAN-GRINDER'S MONKEY...
GONE TO LUNCH
OH BISHOP, YOU'RE SO WISE ABOUT BIBLE THINGS
WOW!
GONE TO LUNCH
THE MONKEY HAS EVOLUTED INTO A CAVE-MAN
UG! UG!
WOULD YOU CARE TO TAKE A WALK IN THE PARK, MISS? IT LOOKS LIKE THE BISHOP IS BUSY
LATER...
..YES, THANKS TO EVOLUTION I CAN TRANSFORM ANY APE INTO A HUMAN INSTANTANEOUSLY
OH CHARLIE, YOU'RE SO CLEVER
I'LL FIX CHARLIE WITH THIS GORILLA COSTUME
HIS EVOLUTION POTION WILL HAVE NO EFFECT ON A FAKE MONKEY
EEK! AN ESCAPED APE!
DON'T WORRY, MISS ~ A LARGE DOSE OF MY POTION WILL EVOLUTE THE BEAST INTO AN ANCIENT EGYPTIAN PHAROAH, OR A ROMAN SOLIDIER PERHAPS
WOW! IT DIDN'T WORK!
WELL REALLY! HOW UNIMPRESSIVE
SHORTLY
WHAT'S THIS? A FANCY-DRESS APE COSTUME!
SO! I'VE BEEN DIDDLED!
ALLOW ME TO TREAT YOU TO A SLAP-UP FEED, MY DEAR
CAFÉ DE POSH
CAFÉ de Posh
OH BISHOP, YOU'RE SO GALLANT
SORRY FOLKS – WE ONLY HAVE BANANAS ON THE MENU TODAY
OH DEAR ~ I DON'T LIKE BANANAS
A SPOT OF EVOLUTION SHOULD DO THE TRICK
HO! HO! THE MONKEY FOOD HAS EVOLUTED INTO HUMAN FOOD!
!!
SAUSAGE EGG AND CHIPS! OH CHARLIE, I LOVE YOU
CALM DOWN, BISHOP – THERE'S NO NEED TO GO APE!
GRR! CHARLIE HAS MADE A MONKEY OUT OF ME!

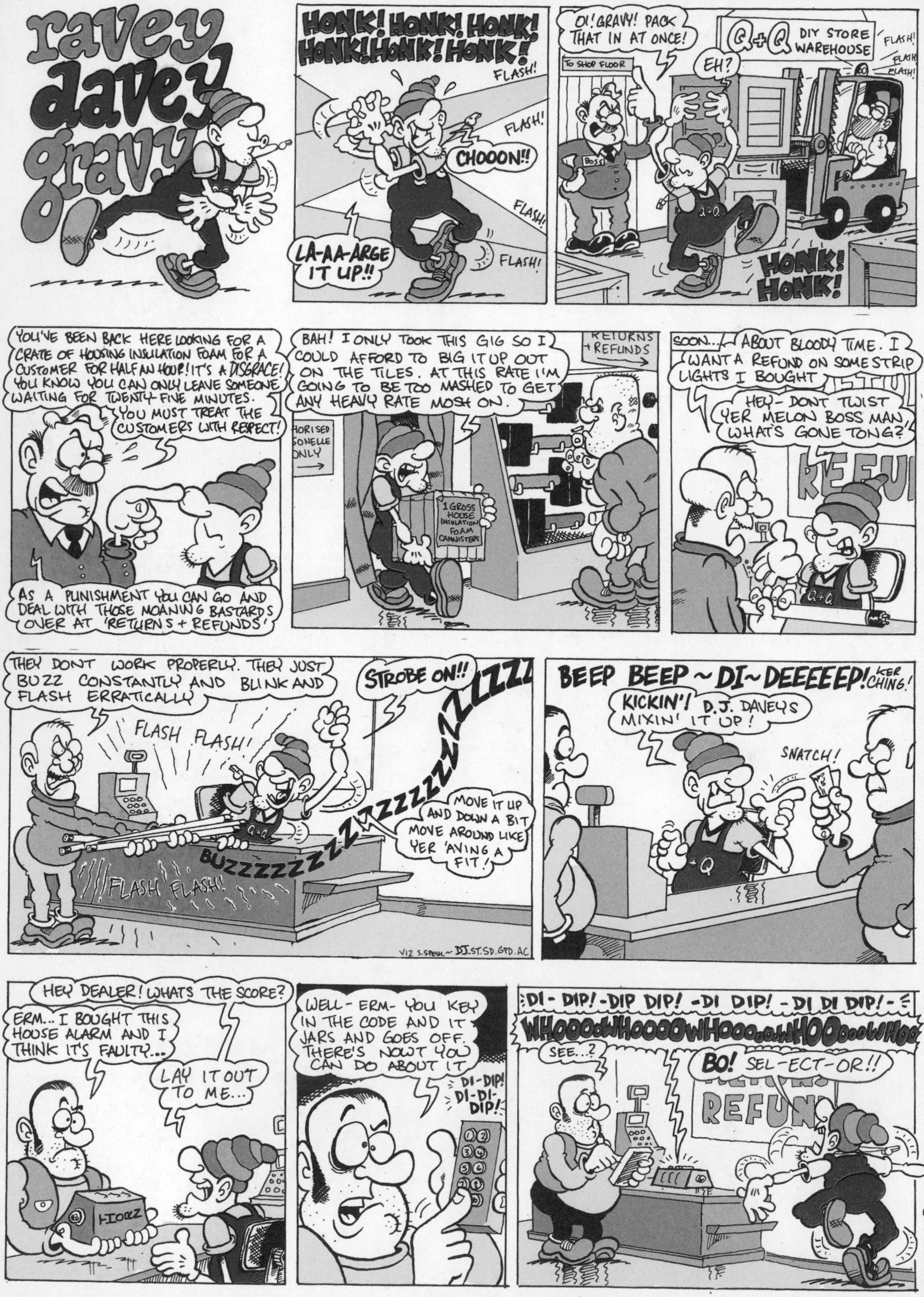
ravey davey gravy
HONK! HONK! HONK! HONK! HONK! HONK!
FLASH!
FLASH!
CHOOON!!
FLASH!
LA-AA-ARGE IT UP!!
FLASH!
OI! GRAVY! PACK THAT IN AT ONCE!
TO SHOP FLOOR
Q+Q DIY STORE WAREHOUSE
FLASH!
FLASH
FLASH!
EH?
BOSS
Q+Q
HONK! HONK!
YOU'VE BEEN BACK HERE LOOKING FOR A CRATE OF HOUSING INSULATION FOAM FOR A CUSTOMER FOR HALF AN HOUR! IT'S A DISGRACE! YOU KNOW YOU CAN ONLY LEAVE SOMEONE WAITING FOR TWENTY-FIVE MINUTES.
YOU MUST TREAT THE CUSTOMERS WITH RESPECT!
AS A PUNISHMENT YOU CAN GO AND DEAL WITH THOSE MOANING BASTARDS OVER AT 'RETURNS + REFUNDS'
BAH! I ONLY TOOK THIS GIG SO I COULD AFFORD TO BIG IT UP OUT ON THE TILES. AT THIS RATE I'M GOING TO BE TOO MASHED TO GET ANY HEAVY RATE MOSH ON.
RETURNS + REFUNDS
HORISED SONELLE ONLY
1 GROSS HOUSE INSULATION FOAM CANNISTERS
SOON...
ABOUT BLOODY TIME. I WANT A REFUND ON SOME STRIP LIGHTS I BOUGHT
HEY- DONT TWIST YER MELON BOSS MAN WHAT'S GONE TONG?
REFU
Q+Q
THEY DONT WORK PROPERLY. THEY JUST BUZZ CONSTANTLY AND BLINK AND FLASH ERRATICALLY
FLASH FLASH!
STROBE ON!!
ZZZZZZZZZZZZZ
MOVE IT UP AND DOWN A BIT MOVE AROUND LIKE YER 'AVING A FIT!
BUZZZZZZZZZ
FLASH FLASH!
V12 S.SPESH.~ DJ.ST.SD.GPD.AC
BEEP BEEP ~ DI ~ DEEEEEEP!
KER CHING!
KICKIN'! D.J. DAVEYS MIXIN' IT UP!
SNATCH!
HEY DEALER! WHATS THE SCORE?
ERM... I BOUGHT THIS HOUSE ALARM AND I THINK IT'S FAULTY...
LAY IT OUT TO ME...
WELL- ERM- YOU KEY IN THE CODE AND IT JARS AND GOES OFF. THERE'S NOWT YOU CAN DO ABOUT IT
DI-DIP! DI-DI-DIP!
DI - DIP! - DIP DIP! - DI DIP! - DI DI DIP! -
WHOOOOWHOOOOWHOOO...WHOO...WHOO
SEE...?
BO! SEL-ECT-OR!!
REFUN

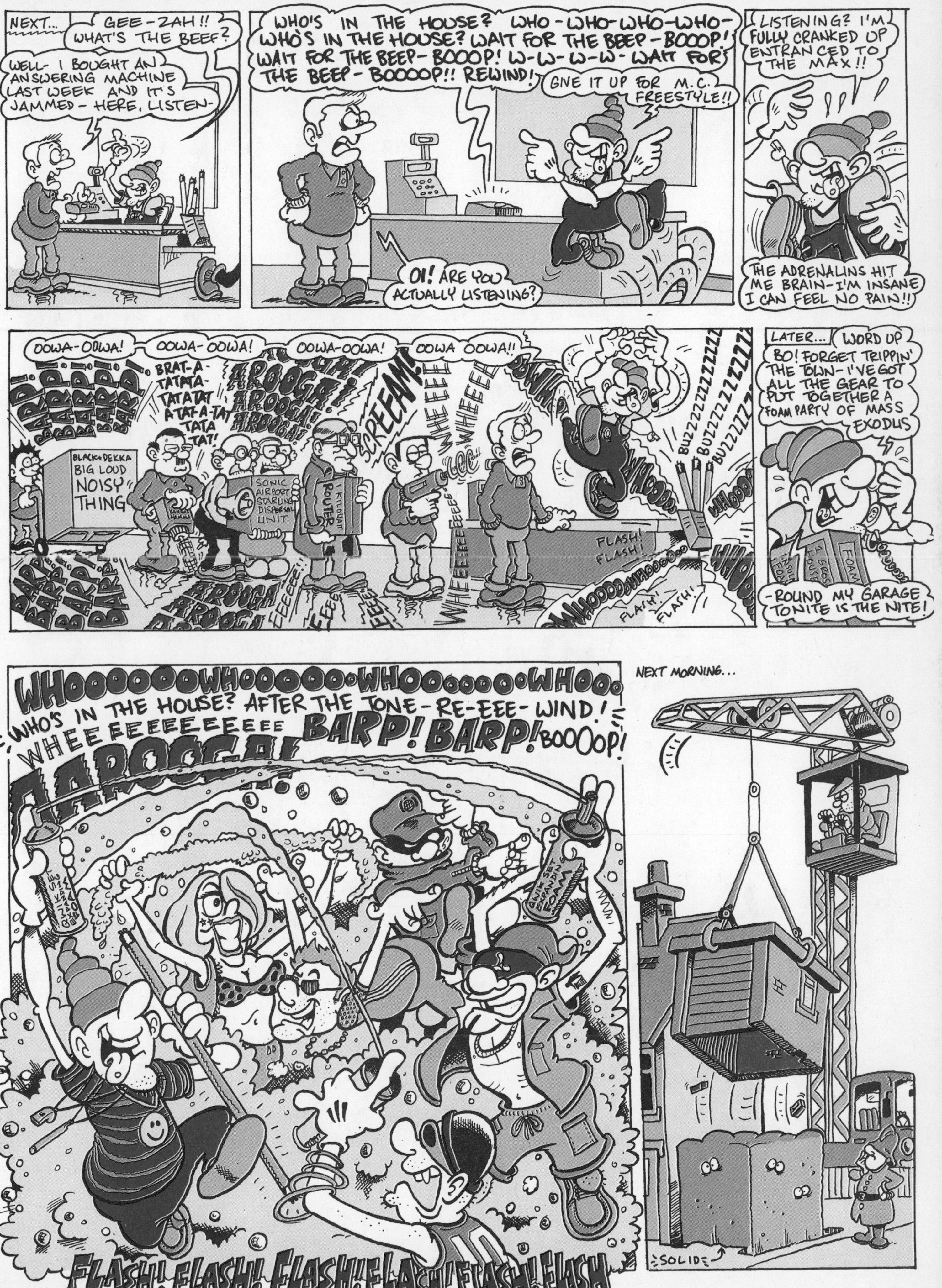
NEXT...
GEE-ZAH!! WHAT'S THE BEEF?
WELL- I BOUGHT AN ANSWERING MACHINE LAST WEEK AND IT'S JAMMED - HERE, LISTEN-
WHO'S IN THE HOUSE? WHO-WHO-WHO-WHO-WHO'S IN THE HOUSE? WAIT FOR THE BEEP-BOOOP! WAIT FOR THE BEEP-BOOOP! W-W-W-W-WAIT FOR THE BEEP-BOOOOP!! REWIND!
GIVE IT UP FOR M.C. FREESTYLE!!
OI! ARE YOU ACTUALLY LISTENING?
LISTENING? I'M FULLY CRANKED UP ENTRANCED TO THE MAX!!
THE ADRENALINS HIT ME BRAIN-I'M INSANE I CAN FEEL NO PAIN!!
OOWA-OOWA!
OOWA-OOWA!
OOWA-OOWA!
OOWA OOWA!!
BARP! BARP! BARP! BARP!
BRAT-A TATATA TATATAT A-TAT-A-TAT TATA TAT!
AROOGA! AROOGA! AROOGA!
SCREEAM!
WHEEEEE
BLACK+DEKKA BIG LOUD NOISY THING
SONIC AIRPORT STARLING DISPERSAL UNIT
1 KILOWATT ROUTER
BUZZZZZZZZZ BUZZZZZZZ BUZZZZZZ
FLASH! FLASH!
LATER...
WORD UP BO! FORGET TRIPPIN' THE TOWN- I'VE GOT ALL THE GEAR TO PUT TOGETHER A FOAM PARTY OF MASS EXODUS
-ROUND MY GARAGE TONITE IS THE NITE!
WHOOOOOOOWHOOOOOOOWHOOOOOOOOWHOOO
WHO'S IN THE HOUSE? AFTER THE TONE-RE-EEE-WIND!
WHEEEEEEEEEEEE BARP! BARP! BOOOOP!
AROOGA!
QWIK SET EXPANDING FOAM
FLASH! FLASH! FLASH! FLASH! FLASH! FLASH
NEXT MORNING...
SOLID

I've Been Ad

One of the nice things about being let into people's living rooms every night through the medium of television, is that the audience feel they actually know you. Over the years, a bond of trust develops. The best thing about this is that a celebrity can abuse this trust, endorsing any old shit in return for cash. And over the years I've endorsed more than my fair share of shit, both at home and abroad. Here's a few of my own favourites.

Walk upstairs after a skinful?...ME? FUCK OFF!

"I've got a WINSTON Stair Lift"

says Roger Mellie OBE, star of TV's 'Opportunity Cocks'

Call FREE *NOW!*
Dial 100 and ask for

FREEPHONE WINSTON

"Fuck what Raymond Baxter and Thora Hird say, all other stairlifts are a load of fucking shit"

Roger Mellie OBE

BRITISH MADE

"I got forty grand up front for this one. And a free stairlift. Though I must confess, I wasn't their first choice. My old pal Ollie Reed was already lined up for the gig, but fortunately he kicked the bucket and I was in like a rat up a fucking drain-pipe. One photo, one signature, one Ferrari. Ten minutes! Life doesn't come better than that."

"Here's yours truly doing his bit to help British exports. Some people might criticise me for doing this ad, but what these lefties don't understand is that I got paid 80 fucking grand in a suitcase. I can see that torture equipment might not be everyone's cup of tea, but the workmanship of the stuff was first rate."

La Estrella Británica famosa, Roger Mellie, ordenado principal de la televisión "Up Your Cunt" y "Fuck a Duck" del recomienda siempre el equipo de la tortura fabricado por

Anglo-Fulchester Light Engineering.

"Con un rango tan extensoa elegir de, el Anglo-Fulchester es su opción de una parada el dictador del crisol de la lata de hoy" exclaimas Roger.

Británicos fabricación!

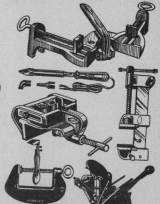

● Alojamientos de la mano.
● Grillos de la pierna.
● Bastones de mando de alto voltaje del control de la muchedumbre.
● Alicates del testículos.
● Vice del pene.
● Puntas de prueba anales eléctricas.

'Concesión de la Reina para las Exportaciones Barbáricas e Inhumanes' 1982

Oficinas Regionales - Chile, Beijing, Indonesia, la Arabia Saudita

TODO EL PAPELEO FALSIFICADO EN LA CONSULTA CON LA OFICINA NO NATIVA!!

116

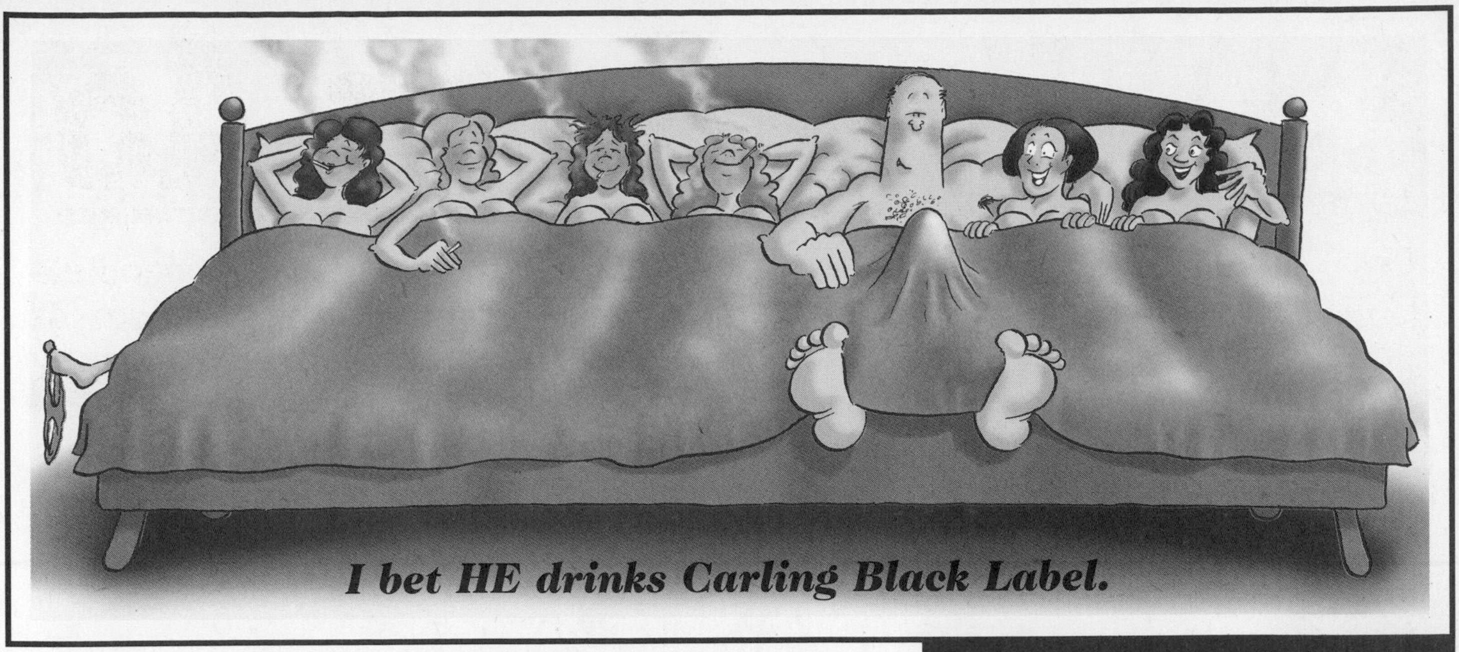
I bet HE drinks Carling Black Label.

"This was part of the famous lager campaign of the 80's. I was a bit nervous before the shoot because, to be honest, I'd only ever shagged five birds in a row before, (backstage at a Nolan Sisters concert) so I was entering unknown territory. But I rose to the occasion magnificently, though I say so myself. Then would you believe it, the clients lost their bottle and pulled the ad. But it paid for my third divorce so who gives a fuck."

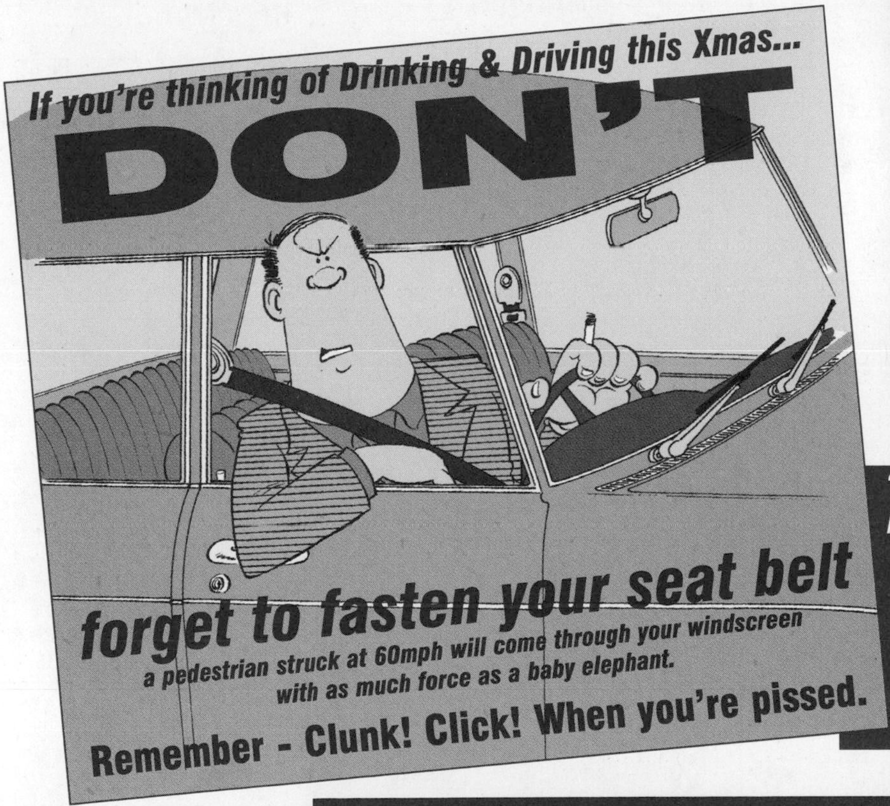
If you're thinking of Drinking & Driving this Xmas...
DON'T
forget to fasten your seat belt
a pedestrian struck at 60mph will come through your windscreen with as much force as a baby elephant.
Remember - Clunk! Click! When you're pissed.

"Like any celeb worth his salt, I get pulled for DD every year. Except for 1975, when I did this poster for the local fuzz. In return for me doing the ad, they agreed to look the other way when I drove out the pub car park, just like they do for the Chief Constable. Best Christmas I ever had."

"This is a very early advert from when I first shot to fame doing 'Last Turkey in the Shop' on Saturday Night at the London Palladium, filling in for Bruce Forsyth who'd had a bad curry and was shitting fizzy gravy in his dressing room. When I did the ad, they gave me a free sample, which I lent to Frank Muir. It fused during his vinegar strokes and gave the poor sod a 240v belt up his Jap's eye. Or was it Eamonn Andrews?"

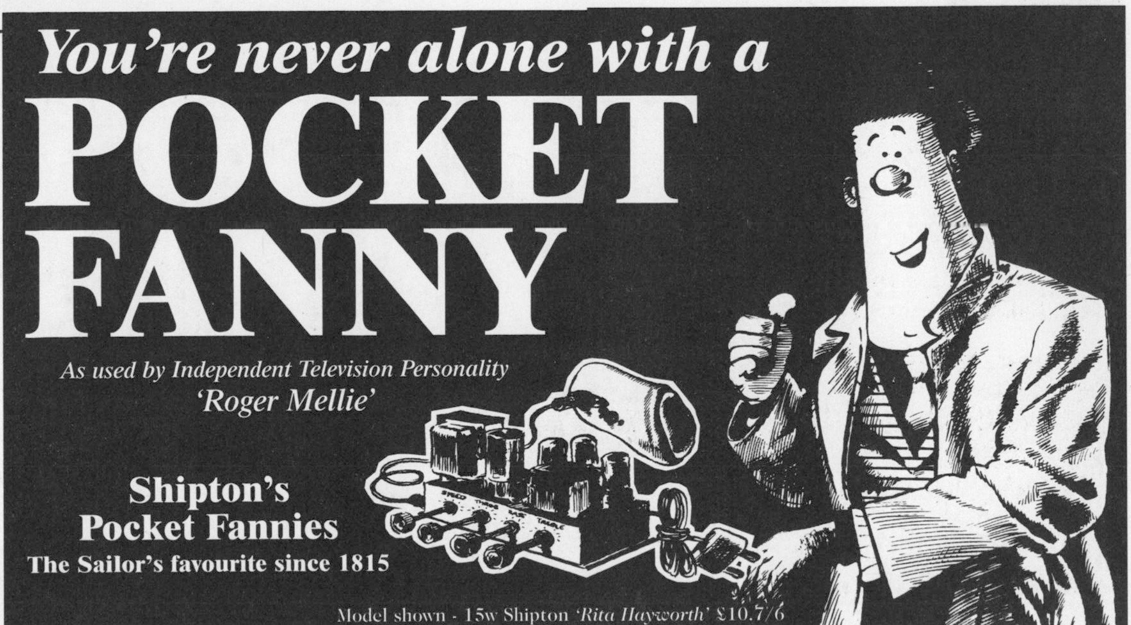
You're never alone with a
POCKET
FANNY
As used by Independent Television Personality
'Roger Mellie'
Shipton's
Pocket Fannies
The Sailor's favourite since 1815
Model shown - 15w Shipton 'Rita Hayworth' £10.7/6

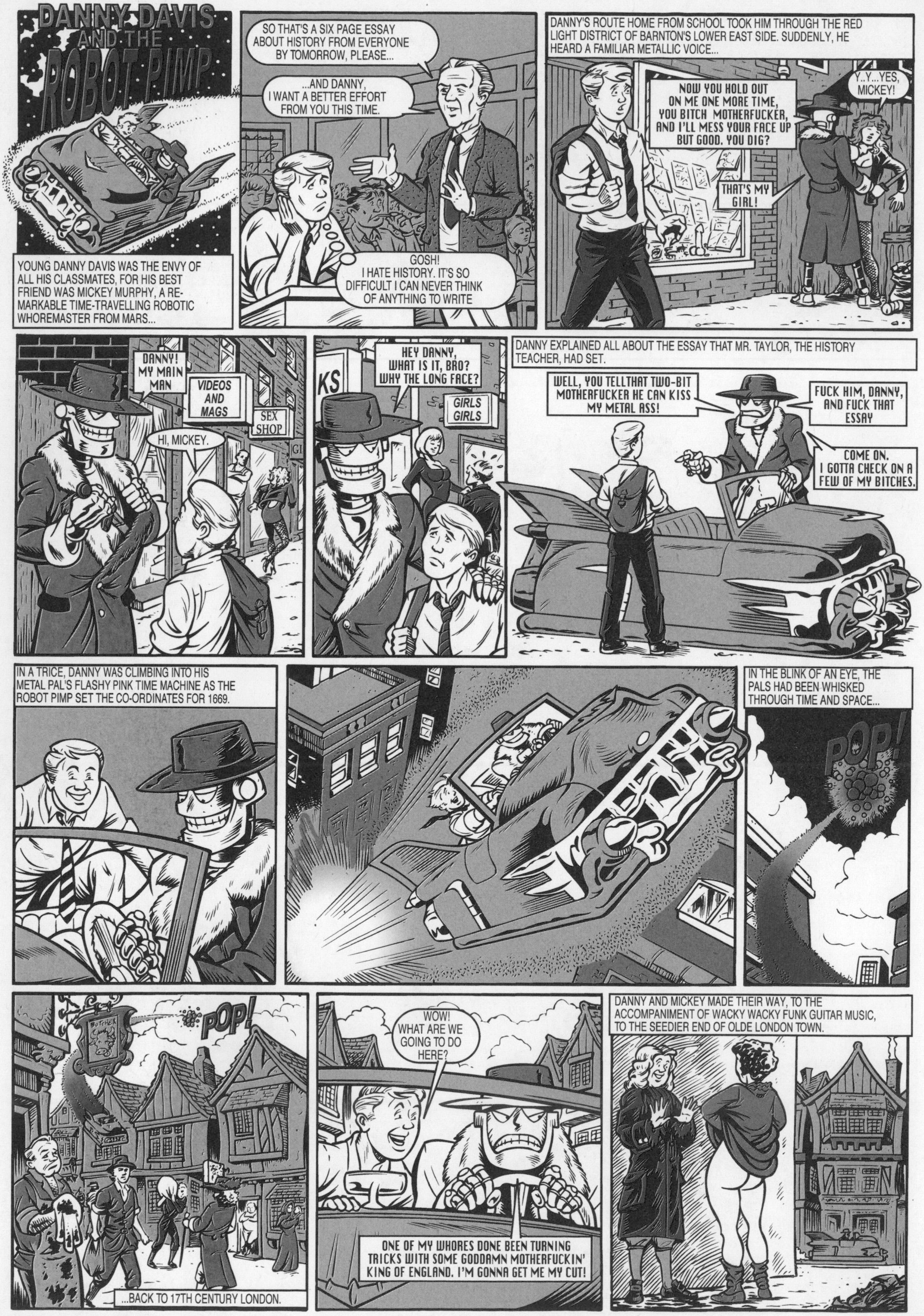
DANNY DAVIS AND THE ROBOT PIMP
YOUNG DANNY DAVIS WAS THE ENVY OF ALL HIS CLASSMATES, FOR HIS BEST FRIEND WAS MICKEY MURPHY, A REMARKABLE TIME-TRAVELLING ROBOTIC WHOREMASTER FROM MARS...
SO THAT'S A SIX PAGE ESSAY ABOUT HISTORY FROM EVERYONE BY TOMORROW, PLEASE...
...AND DANNY, I WANT A BETTER EFFORT FROM YOU THIS TIME.
GOSH! I HATE HISTORY. IT'S SO DIFFICULT I CAN NEVER THINK OF ANYTHING TO WRITE
DANNY'S ROUTE HOME FROM SCHOOL TOOK HIM THROUGH THE RED LIGHT DISTRICT OF BARNTON'S LOWER EAST SIDE. SUDDENLY, HE HEARD A FAMILIAR METALLIC VOICE...
NOW YOU HOLD OUT ON ME ONE MORE TIME, YOU BITCH MOTHERFUCKER, AND I'LL MESS YOUR FACE UP BUT GOOD. YOU DIG?
Y..Y...YES, MICKEY!
THAT'S MY GIRL!
DANNY! MY MAIN MAN
VIDEOS AND MAGS
SEX SHOP
HI, MICKEY.
HEY DANNY, WHAT IS IT, BRO? WHY THE LONG FACE?
GIRLS GIRLS
DANNY EXPLAINED ALL ABOUT THE ESSAY THAT MR. TAYLOR, THE HISTORY TEACHER, HAD SET.
WELL, YOU TELLTHAT TWO-BIT MOTHERFUCKER HE CAN KISS MY METAL ASS!
FUCK HIM, DANNY, AND FUCK THAT ESSAY
COME ON. I GOTTA CHECK ON A FEW OF MY BITCHES.
IN A TRICE, DANNY WAS CLIMBING INTO HIS METAL PAL'S FLASHY PINK TIME MACHINE AS THE ROBOT PIMP SET THE CO-ORDINATES FOR 1669.
IN THE BLINK OF AN EYE, THE PALS HAD BEEN WHISKED THROUGH TIME AND SPACE...
POP!
POP!
...BACK TO 17TH CENTURY LONDON.
WOW! WHAT ARE WE GOING TO DO HERE?
ONE OF MY WHORES DONE BEEN TURNING TRICKS WITH SOME GODDAMN MOTHERFUCKIN' KING OF ENGLAND. I'M GONNA GET ME MY CUT!
DANNY AND MICKEY MADE THEIR WAY, TO THE ACCOMPANIMENT OF WACKY WACKY FUNK GUITAR MUSIC, TO THE SEEDIER END OF OLDE LONDON TOWN.

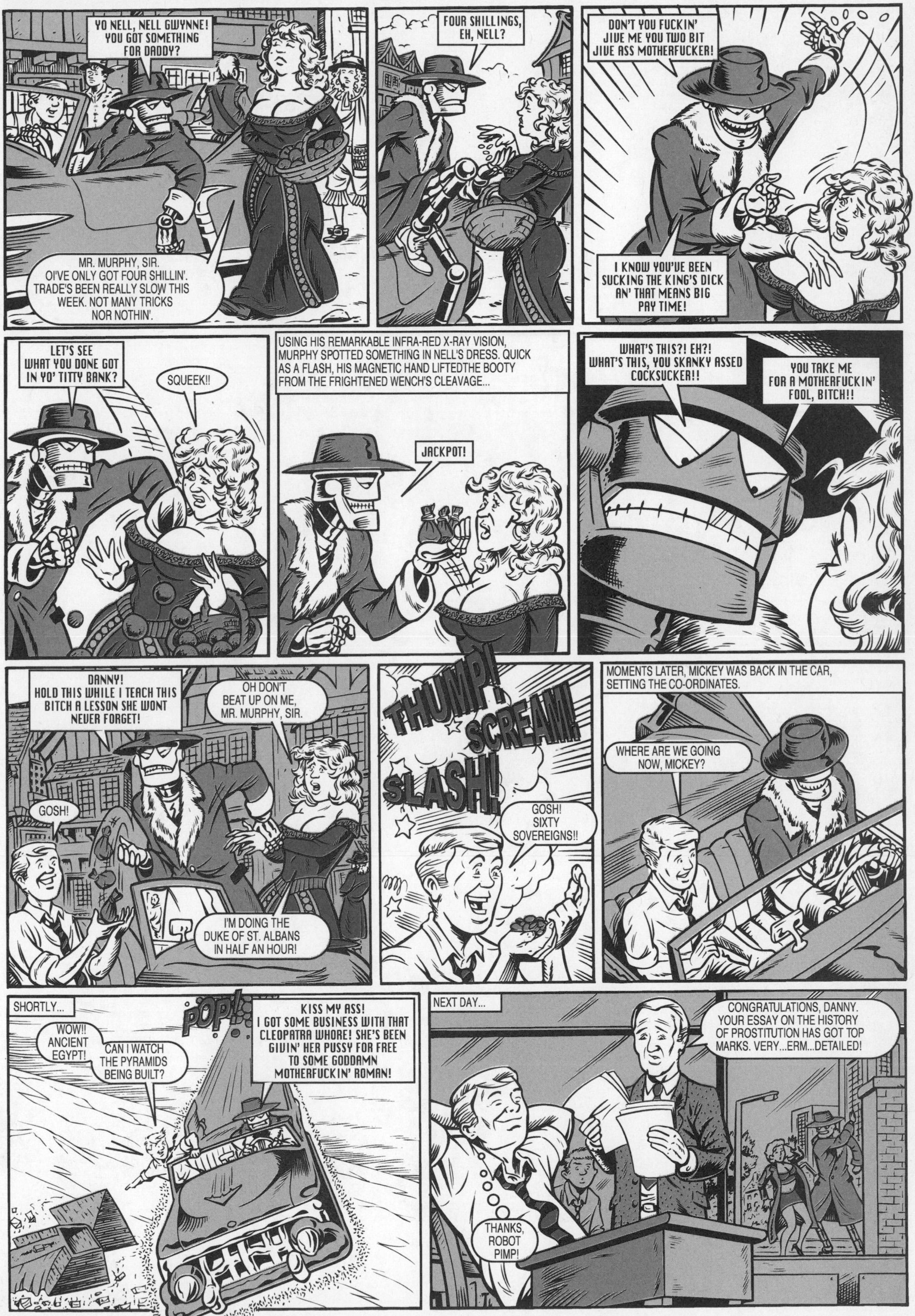
YO NELL, NELL GWYNNE! YOU GOT SOMETHING FOR DADDY?
MR. MURPHY, SIR. OI'VE ONLY GOT FOUR SHILLIN'. TRADE'S BEEN REALLY SLOW THIS WEEK. NOT MANY TRICKS NOR NOTHIN'.
FOUR SHILLINGS, EH, NELL?
DON'T YOU FUCKIN' JIVE ME YOU TWO BIT JIVE ASS MOTHERFUCKER!
I KNOW YOU'VE BEEN SUCKING THE KING'S DICK AN' THAT MEANS BIG PAY TIME!
LET'S SEE WHAT YOU DONE GOT IN YO' TITTY BANK?
SQUEEK!!
USING HIS REMARKABLE INFRA-RED X-RAY VISION, MURPHY SPOTTED SOMETHING IN NELL'S DRESS. QUICK AS A FLASH, HIS MAGNETIC HAND LIFTEDTHE BOOTY FROM THE FRIGHTENED WENCH'S CLEAVAGE...
JACKPOT!
WHAT'S THIS?! EH?! WHAT'S THIS, YOU SKANKY ASSED COCKSUCKER!!
YOU TAKE ME FOR A MOTHERFUCKIN' FOOL, BITCH!!
DANNY! HOLD THIS WHILE I TEACH THIS BITCH A LESSON SHE WONT NEVER FORGET!
OH DON'T BEAT UP ON ME, MR. MURPHY, SIR.
GOSH!
I'M DOING THE DUKE OF ST. ALBANS IN HALF AN HOUR!
THUMP! SCREAM! SLASH!
GOSH! SIXTY SOVEREIGNS!!
MOMENTS LATER, MICKEY WAS BACK IN THE CAR, SETTING THE CO-ORDINATES.
WHERE ARE WE GOING NOW, MICKEY?
SHORTLY...
WOW!! ANCIENT EGYPT!
CAN I WATCH THE PYRAMIDS BEING BUILT?
POP!
KISS MY ASS! I GOT SOME BUSINESS WITH THAT CLEOPATRA WHORE! SHE'S BEEN GIVIN' HER PUSSY FOR FREE TO SOME GODDAMN MOTHERFUCKIN' ROMAN!
NEXT DAY...
CONGRATULATIONS, DANNY. YOUR ESSAY ON THE HISTORY OF PROSTITUTION HAS GOT TOP MARKS. VERY...ERM...DETAILED!
THANKS, ROBOT PIMP!

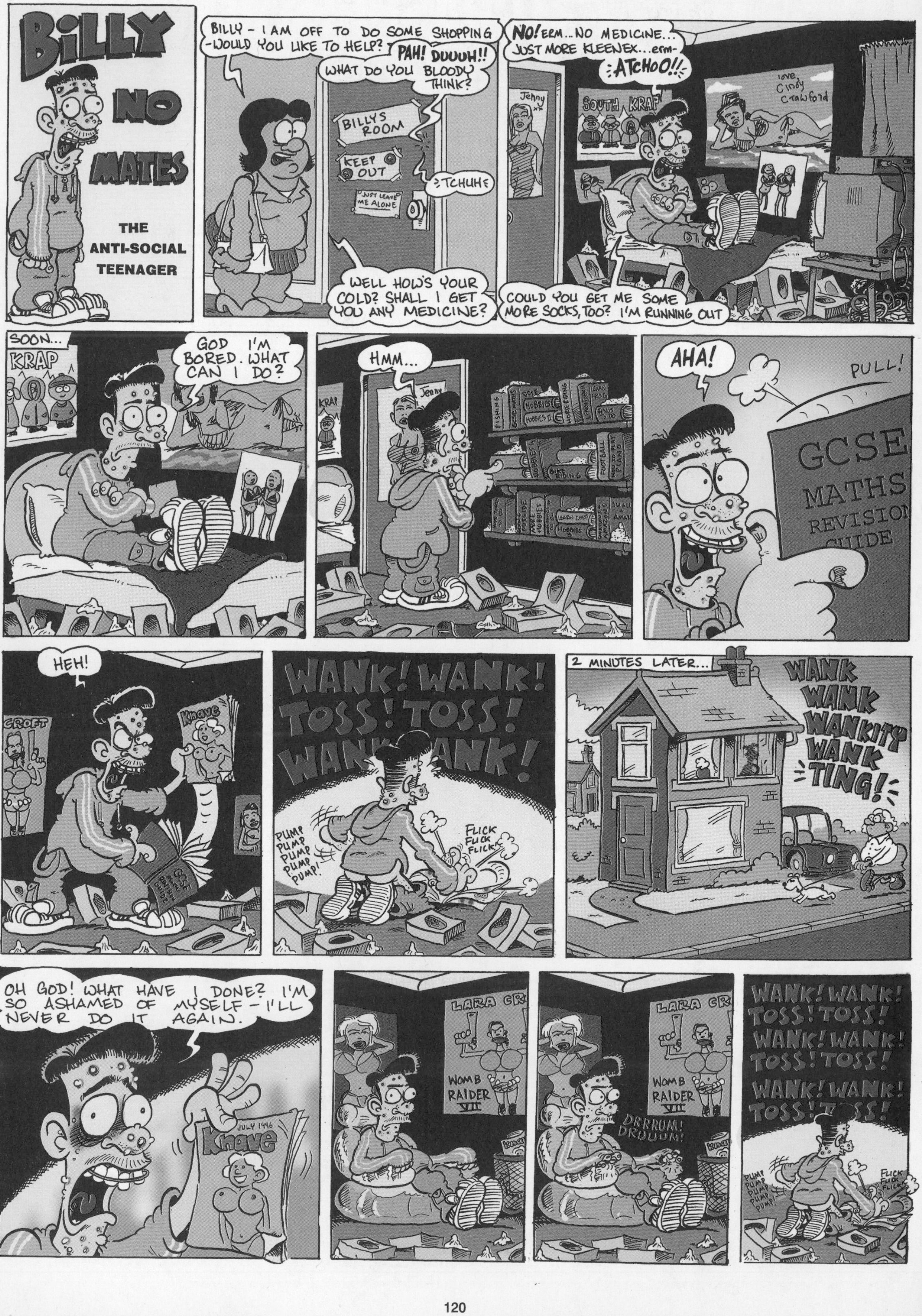
BILLY NO MATES
THE ANTI-SOCIAL TEENAGER
BILLY - I AM OFF TO DO SOME SHOPPING -WOULD YOU LIKE TO HELP?
PAH! DUUUH!! WHAT DO YOU BLOODY THINK?
BILLYS ROOM
KEEP OUT
JUST LEAVE ME ALONE
TCHUH
WELL HOW'S YOUR COLD? SHALL I GET YOU ANY MEDICINE?
NO! ERM... NO MEDICINE... JUST MORE KLEENEX... erm-
ATCHOO!!
SOUTH KRAP
Jenny
love Cindy Crawford
COULD YOU GET ME SOME MORE SOCKS, TOO? I'M RUNNING OUT
SOON...
KRAP
GOD I'M BORED. WHAT CAN I DO?
HMM...
Jenny
FOOTBALL
HOBBIES
AHA!
PULL!
GCSE MATHS REVISION GUIDE
HEH!
CROFT
Knave
GCSE
WANK! WANK! TOSS! TOSS! WANK! WANK!
PUMP PUMP PUMP PUMP PUMP!
FLICK FLICK FLICK!
2 MINUTES LATER...
WANK WANK WANKITY WANK TING!
OH GOD! WHAT HAVE I DONE? I'M SO ASHAMED OF MYSELF - I'LL NEVER DO IT AGAIN.
JULY 1996
Knave
LARA CR
WOMB RAIDER VII
LARA CR
WOMB RAIDER VII
DRRRUM! DRUUUM!
WANK! WANK! TOSS! TOSS! WANK! WANK! TOSS! TOSS! WANK! WANK! TOSS! TOSS!
PUMP PUMP PUMP PUMP!
FLICK FLICK FLICK

HOW with Fred Dinenage

Dear Fred... If a newsreader wanted to read the news dressed as a black and white minstrel, **HOW** would he go about making the change without anyone noticing?

Huw Edwards, London

Right, says Fred... The key to a successful transformation is careful planning and preparation. Firstly find out how much makeup you require to completely change yourself into a minstrel. Then, decide the number of news

Before | After

broadcasts over which you are going to spread it. Say, 300 programmes over the course of a year. Now divide the makeup into 300 equal portions. Simply apply one of the portions of makeup before you go on air each night. The differences from day to day will be imperceptible, but over the course of a year the full transformation will take place. And that's **HOW** you become a black and white minstrel without anyone noticing.

If you want to ask Fred **HOW** to do something, why not hang around in the car park at Southern Television until he comes out.

Fanny's Batter bits

Seventies all-in wrestler turned haulage contractor Kendo Nagasaki has been signed by Steven Speilberg to star in a $750 million Hollywood remake of 'Georgy Girl'. Nagasaki, who will pocket £120 for playing the title role made famous by Lynn Redgrave, has vowed to keep his trademark ninja-style mask on throughout the film.

CRASH! PAM! WALLOP!

Knocker-hungry Net-Nerds
Knicky Knacky Noo. Baywatch
Babe's Tits Down for 4 Hours

FILMING of hit US TV show VIP was thrown into chaos last night after so many internet surfers logged onto Pamela Anderson's cheeky 'sucking-off-her-

Showbiz Exclusive

husband-on-a-boat website' that her tits CRASHED! ~Reuters

John Cleese's Faulty Towers
No. 26. Ronan Point

EURGH! WHAT'S THAT?

THAT'S JUST WHAT THE DOCTOR ORDURED.

next week: The Leaning Tower of Pisa

For a **GREAT** day out, come to

DadLand
(formerly Chessington World of Uncles)

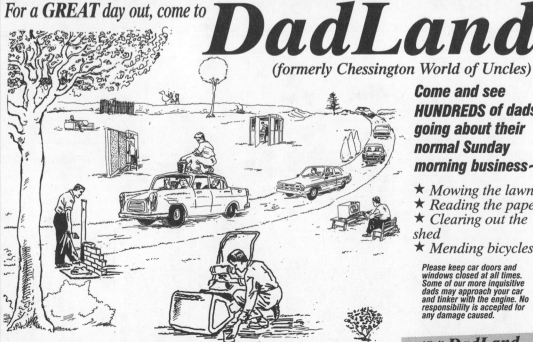

Come and see HUNDREDS of dads going about their normal Sunday morning business~

★ Mowing the lawn
★ Reading the paper
★ Clearing out the shed
★ Mending bicycles

Please keep car doors and windows closed at all times. Some of our more inquisitive dads may approach your car and tinker with the engine. No responsibility is accepted for any damage caused.

Visit *DadLand.*
It's a load of dads in a field
...and a whole lot more!

How to find us: Drive up the M4, then turn left. Go 60-odd miles and we're second on the right after the tree. Open Sundays 9.30~2.00. (Hilarious Dad's Dinner Party at 1.00. Watch the comical antics of the dads as they fight to carve the roast). Adults £1. Children and OAP's 50p. Family ticket (2 adults, 2 children) £3.

Ever fancied leaping out of an aeroplane and shattering your pelvis for charity?

Then JUMP TO IT!

Intensive one day courses culminating in a 35,000ft free-fall and compound fracture available throughout the country

"I jumped, broke both my legs and my back, and my physiotherapy bill is so far running at thirty-two grand and rising. And what's more I raised £4.50 for blind dogs." - Mrs.B, Essex.

Phone *100* and ask for Freephone 'I Want to Break my Pelvis'.

121

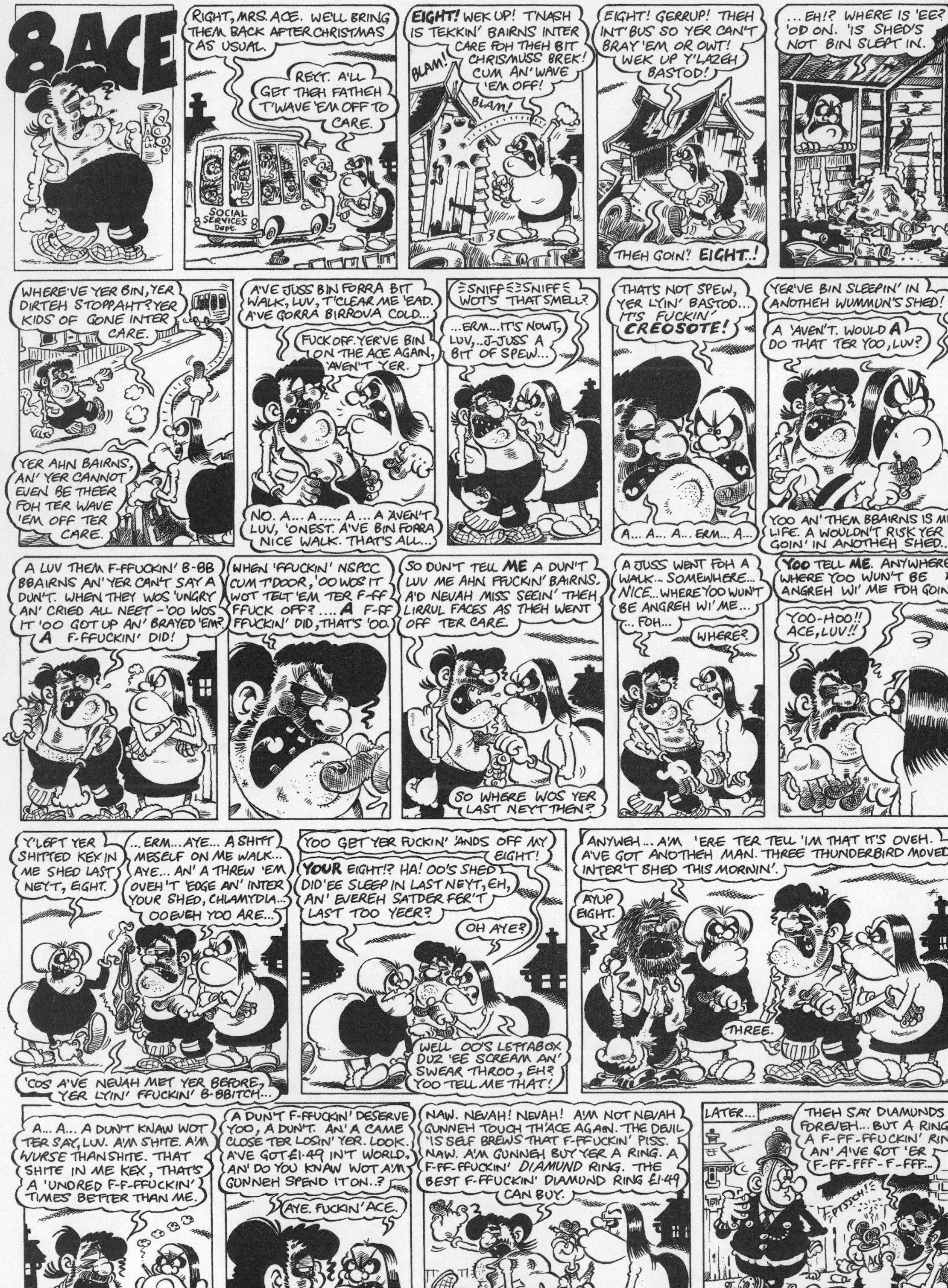
8 ACE
RIGHT, MRS. ACE. WE'LL BRING THEM BACK AFTER CHRISTMAS AS USUAL.
RECT. A'LL GET THEH FATHEH T'WAVE 'EM OFF TO CARE.
SOCIAL SERVICES DEPT.
EIGHT! WEK UP! T'NASH IS TEKKIN' BAIRNS INTER CARE FOH THEH BIT CHRISMUSS BREK! CUM AN' WAVE 'EM OFF!
BLAM!
BLAM!
EIGHT! GERRUP! THEH INT'BUS SO YER CAN'T BRAY 'EM OR OWT! WEK UP Y'LAZEH BASTOD!
THEH GOIN'! EIGHT..!
...EH!? WHERE IS 'EE? 'OD ON. 'IS SHED'S NOT BIN SLEPT IN.
WHERE'VE YER BIN, YER DIRTEH STOPPAHT? YER KIDS OF GONE INTER CARE.
YER AHN BAIRNS, AN' YER CANNOT EVEN BE THEER FOH TER WAVE 'EM OFF TER CARE.
A'VE JUSS BIN FORRA BIT WALK, LUV, T'CLEAR ME 'EAD. A'VE GORRA BIRROVA COLD...
FUCK OFF. YER'VE BIN ON THE ACE AGAIN, 'AVEN'T YER.
NO. A... A..... A... A 'AVEN'T LUV, 'ONEST. A'VE BIN FORRA NICE WALK. THAT'S ALL...
SNIFF SNIFF WOT'S THAT SMELL?
...ERM... IT'S NOWT, LUV, J-JUSS A BIT OF SPEW...
THAT'S NOT SPEW, YER LYIN' BASTOD... IT'S FUCKIN' CREOSOTE!
A... A... A... ERM... A...
YER'VE BIN SLEEPIN' IN ANOTHEH WUMMUN'S SHED!
A 'AVEN'T. WOULD A DO THAT TER YOO, LUV?
YOO AN' THEM BBAIRNS IS ME LIFE. A WOULDN'T RISK YER BY GOIN' IN ANOTHEH SHED...
A LUV THEM F-FFUCKIN' B-BB BBAIRNS AN' YER CAN'T SAY A DUN'T. WHEN THEY WOS 'UNGRY AN' CRIED ALL NEET - 'OO WOS IT 'OO GOT UP AN' BRAYED 'EM? A F-FFUCKIN' DID!
WHEN 'FFUCKIN' NSPCC CUM T'DOOR, 'OO WOS IT WOT TELT 'EM TER F-FF FFUCK OFF? .... A F-FF FFUCKIN' DID, THAT'S 'OO.
SO DUN'T TELL ME A DUN'T LUV ME AHN FFUCKIN' BAIRNS. A'D NEVAH MISS SEEIN' THEH LIRRUL FACES AS THEH WENT OFF TER CARE.
SO WHERE WOS YER LAST NEYT THEN?
A JUSS WENT FOH A WALK... SOMEWHERE... NICE... WHERE YOO WUN'T BE ANGREH WI' ME... ...FOH...
WHERE?
YOO TELL ME. ANYWHERE WHERE YOO WUN'T BE ANGREH WI' ME FOH GOIN'...
YOO-HOO!! ACE, LUV!!
Y'LEFT YER SHITTED KEX IN ME SHED LAST NEYT, EIGHT.
...ERM... AYE... A SHIT MESELF ON ME WALK... AYE... AN' A THREW 'EM OVEH 'T 'EDGE AN' INTER YOUR SHED, CHLAMYDIA... OOEVEH YOO ARE...
'COS A'VE NEVAH MET YER BEFORE, YER LYIN' FFUCKIN' B-BBITCH...
YOO GET YER FUCKIN' 'ANDS OFF MY EIGHT!
YOUR EIGHT!? HA! OO'S SHED DID'EE SLEEP IN LAST NEYT, EH, AN' EVEREH SATDER FER'T LAST TOO YEER?
OH AYE?
WELL OO'S LETTABOX DUZ 'EE SCREAM AN' SWEAR THROO, EH? YOO TELL ME THAT!
ANYWEH... A'M 'ERE TER TELL 'IM THAT IT'S OVEH. A'VE GOT ANOTHEH MAN. THREE THUNDERBIRD MOVED INTER'T SHED THIS MORNIN'.
AYUP EIGHT.
THREE.
A... A... A DUN'T KNAW WOT TER SAY, LUV. A'M SHITE. A'M WURSE THAN SHITE. THAT SHITE IN ME KEX, THAT'S A 'UNDRED F-F-FFUCKIN' TIMES BETTER THAN ME.
A DUN'T F-FFUCKIN' DESERVE YOO, A DUN'T. AN' A CAME CLOSE TER LOSIN' YER. LOOK. A'VE GOT £1·49 IN'T WORLD, AN' DO YOU KNAW WOT A'M GUNNEH SPEND IT ON..?
AYE. FUCKIN' ACE.
NAW. NEVAH! NEVAH! A'M NOT NEVAH GUNNEH TOUCH TH'ACE AGAIN. THE DEVIL 'IS SELF BREWS THAT F-FFUCKIN' PISS. NAW. A'M GUNNEH BUY YER A RING. A F-FF-FFUCKIN' DIAMUND RING. THE BEST F-FFUCKIN' DIAMUND RING £1·49 CAN BUY.
LATER...
THEH SAY DIAMUNDS IS FOREVEH... BUT A RING'S A F-FF-FFUCKIN' RING... AN' A'VE GOT 'ER F-FF-FFF-F-FFF...
F-PSSSCH!
F-FFUCKIN' EIGHT OF 'EM.

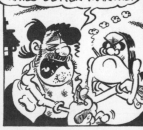

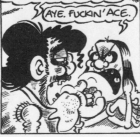

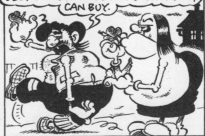

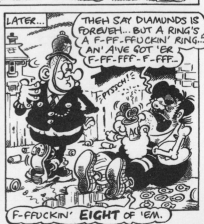

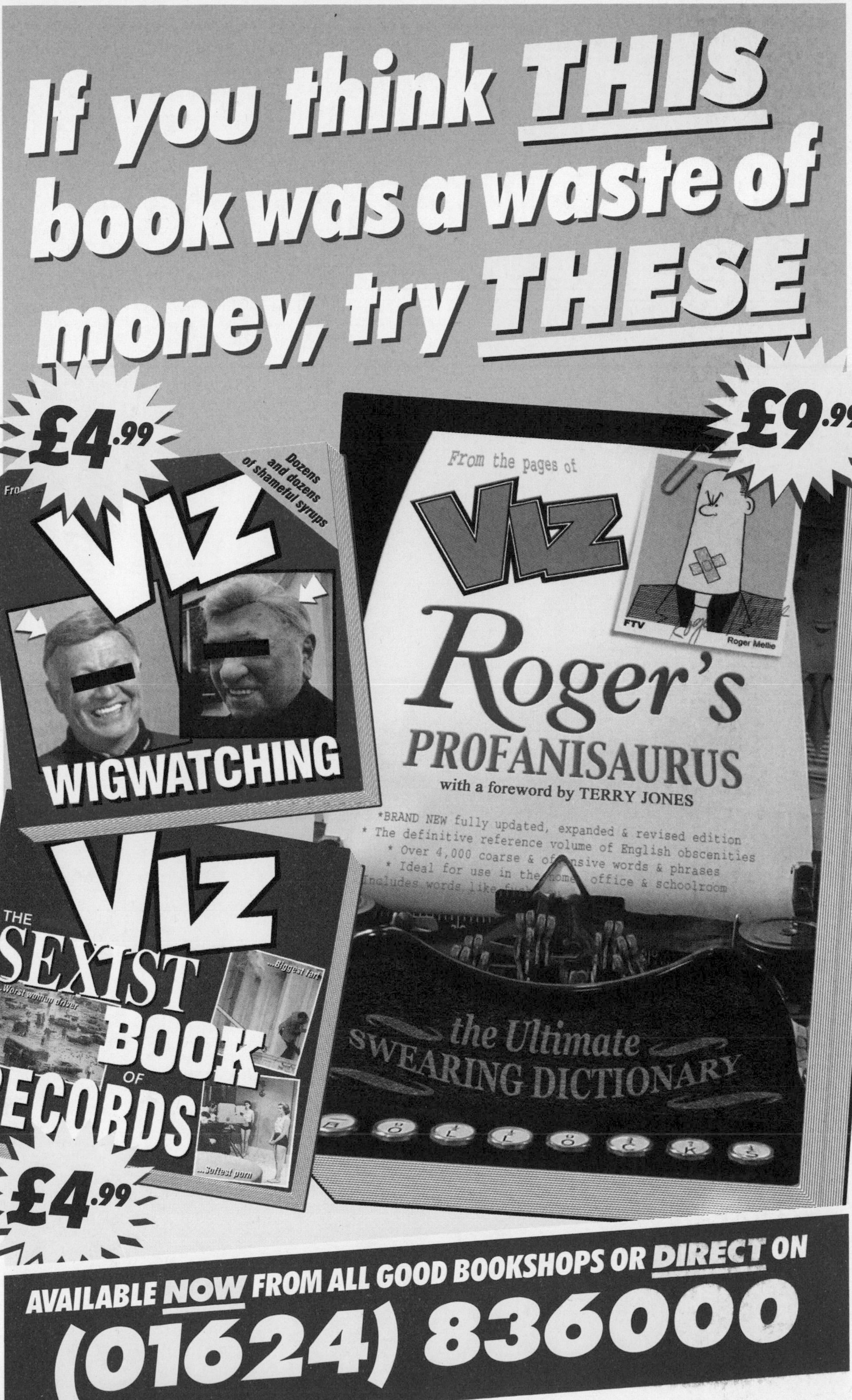

If you think THIS book was a waste of money, try THESE
£4.99
Dozens and dozens of shameful syrups
VIZ
WIGWATCHING
£9.99
From the pages of
VIZ
FTV
Roger Mellie
Roger's PROFANISAURUS
with a foreword by TERRY JONES
*BRAND NEW fully updated, expanded & revised edition
* The definitive reference volume of English obscenities
the Ultimate SWEARING DICTIONARY
VIZ
THE SEXIST BOOK OF RECORDS
...Worst woman driver
...Biggest fart
...Softest porn
£4.99
AVAILABLE NOW FROM ALL GOOD BOOKSHOPS OR DIRECT ON
(01624) 836000

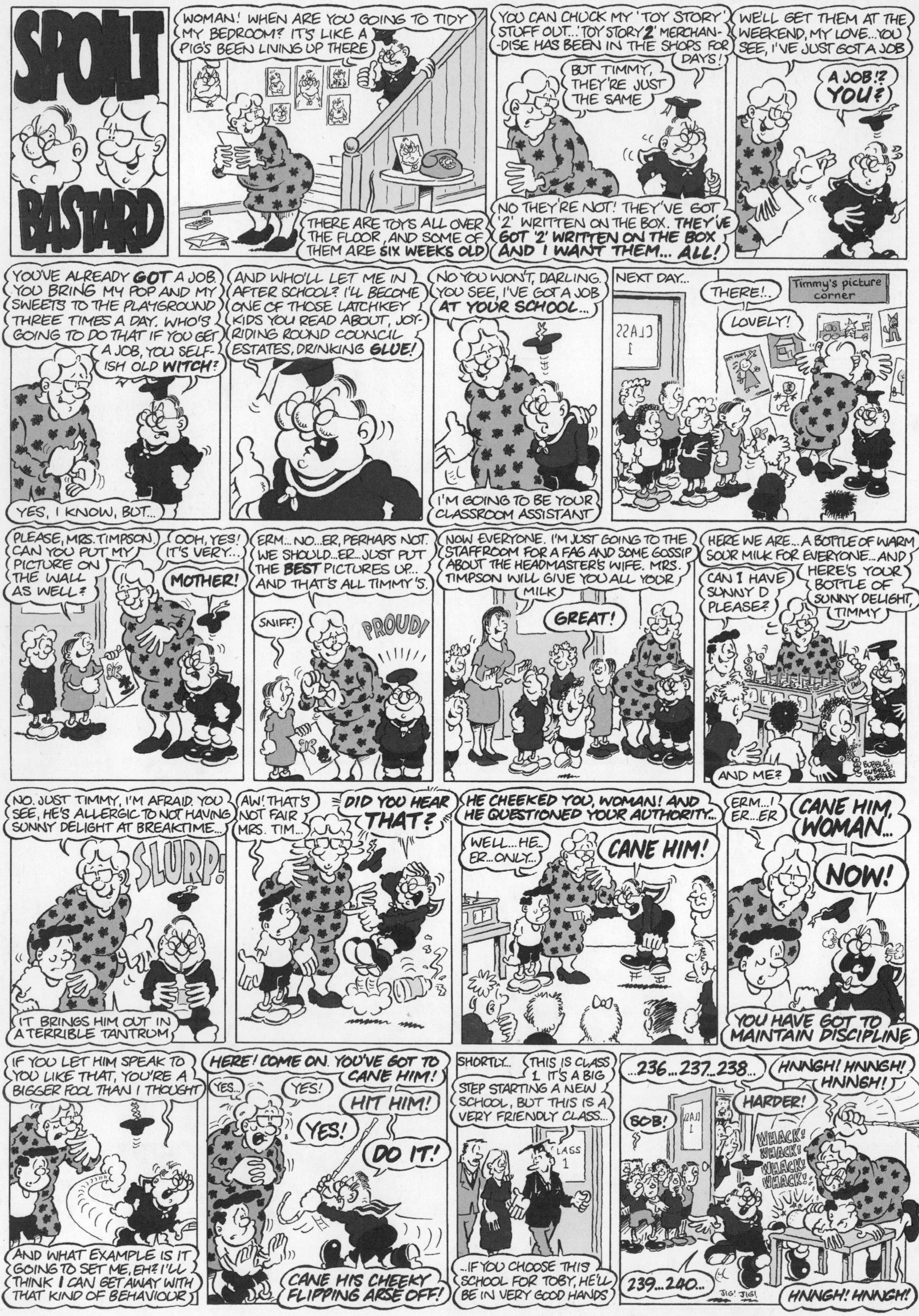
SPOILT BASTARD
WOMAN! WHEN ARE YOU GOING TO TIDY MY BEDROOM? IT'S LIKE A PIG'S BEEN LIVING UP THERE
THERE ARE TOYS ALL OVER THE FLOOR, AND SOME OF THEM ARE SIX WEEKS OLD
YOU CAN CHUCK MY 'TOY STORY' STUFF OUT... 'TOY STORY 2' MERCHAN--DISE HAS BEEN IN THE SHOPS FOR DAYS!
BUT TIMMY, THEY'RE JUST THE SAME
NO THEY'RE NOT! THEY'VE GOT '2' WRITTEN ON THE BOX. THEY'VE GOT '2' WRITTEN ON THE BOX AND I WANT THEM... ALL!
WE'LL GET THEM AT THE WEEKEND, MY LOVE... YOU SEE, I'VE JUST GOT A JOB
A JOB!? YOU?
YOU'VE ALREADY GOT A JOB. YOU BRING MY POP AND MY SWEETS TO THE PLAYGROUND THREE TIMES A DAY. WHO'S GOING TO DO THAT IF YOU GET A JOB, YOU SELF-ISH OLD WITCH?
YES, I KNOW, BUT...
AND WHO'LL LET ME IN AFTER SCHOOL? I'LL BECOME ONE OF THOSE LATCHKEY KIDS YOU READ ABOUT, JOY-RIDING ROUND COUNCIL ESTATES, DRINKING GLUE!
NO YOU WON'T, DARLING. YOU SEE, I'VE GOT A JOB AT YOUR SCHOOL...
I'M GOING TO BE YOUR CLASSROOM ASSISTANT
NEXT DAY...
CLASS 1
Timmy's picture corner
THERE!..
LOVELY!
PLEASE, MRS. TIMPSON, CAN YOU PUT MY PICTURE ON THE WALL AS WELL?
OOH, YES! IT'S VERY...
MOTHER!
ERM... NO... ER, PERHAPS NOT. WE SHOULD... ER... JUST PUT THE BEST PICTURES UP... AND THAT'S ALL TIMMY'S.
SNIFF!
PROUD!
NOW EVERYONE. I'M JUST GOING TO THE STAFFROOM FOR A FAG AND SOME GOSSIP ABOUT THE HEADMASTER'S WIFE. MRS. TIMPSON WILL GIVE YOU ALL YOUR MILK
GREAT!
HERE WE ARE... A BOTTLE OF WARM SOUR MILK FOR EVERYONE... AND
CAN I HAVE SUNNY D PLEASE?
HERE'S YOUR BOTTLE OF SUNNY DELIGHT, TIMMY
AND ME?
BUBBLE! BUBBLE! BUBBLE!
NO. JUST TIMMY, I'M AFRAID. YOU SEE, HE'S ALLERGIC TO NOT HAVING SUNNY DELIGHT AT BREAKTIME...
SLURP!
IT BRINGS HIM OUT IN A TERRIBLE TANTRUM
AW! THAT'S NOT FAIR MRS. TIM...
DID YOU HEAR THAT?
HE CHEEKED YOU, WOMAN! AND HE QUESTIONED YOUR AUTHORITY...
WELL... HE... ER... ONLY...
CANE HIM!
ERM...! ER... ER
CANE HIM, WOMAN...
NOW!
YOU HAVE GOT TO MAINTAIN DISCIPLINE
IF YOU LET HIM SPEAK TO YOU LIKE THAT, YOU'RE A BIGGER FOOL THAN I THOUGHT
AND WHAT EXAMPLE IS IT GOING TO SET ME, EH? I'LL THINK I CAN GET AWAY WITH THAT KIND OF BEHAVIOUR
HERE! COME ON. YOU'VE GOT TO CANE HIM!
YES...
YES!
HIT HIM!
YES!
DO IT!
CANE HIS CHEEKY FLIPPING ARSE OFF!
SHORTLY...
THIS IS CLASS 1. IT'S A BIG STEP STARTING A NEW SCHOOL, BUT THIS IS A VERY FRIENDLY CLASS...
CLASS 1
...IF YOU CHOOSE THIS SCHOOL FOR TOBY, HE'LL BE IN VERY GOOD HANDS
...236...237...238...
HNNGH! HNNGH! HNNGH!
SOB!
HARDER!
WHACK! WHACK! WHACK! WHACK!
239...240...
JIG! JIG!
HNNGH! HNNGH!

MY KIND OF DAY **Fuck a Duck** Weekdays BBC1

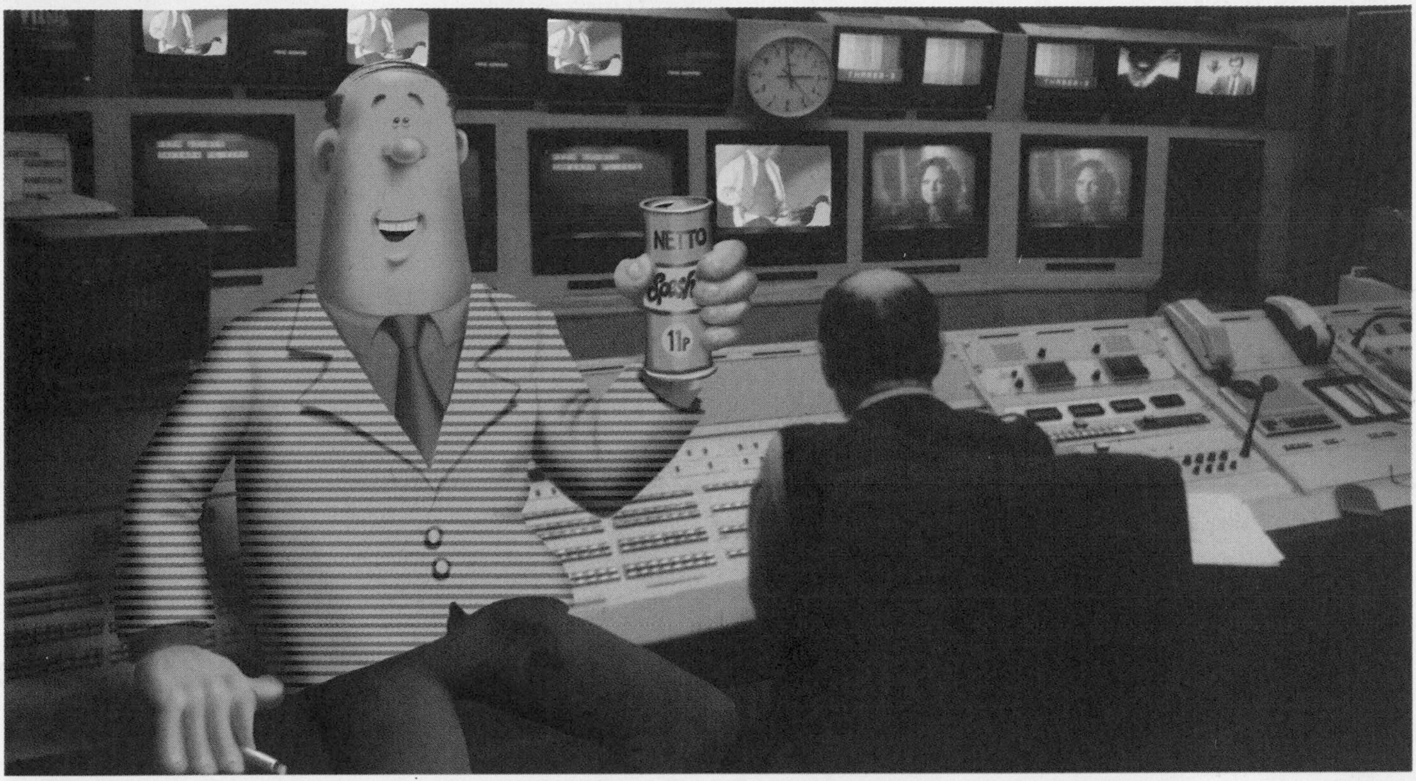
NETTO
11p

In the editing suite of FTV studios where Roger's show *Fuck a Duck* is recorded. "I'm a professional. I don't do rehearsals."

Roger Mellie

It's hard to believe it's 35 years since my first broadcast as a cub reporter on the News with Robert Dougall. After all that time you'd think that my routine would be pretty well established by now. Let me tell you, it's not!

Following my wife's death last year I seem to be busier than ever sorting out the formalities. There seems to be no end of red tape involved at such a difficult time. Only last night I was up until the early hours with my lawyer, trying to block an exhumation order from the local CID. But life goes on.

I'm tremendously happy with my new partner, Candy *(Candy Wonderbra- an 18-year-old researcher at Mellie's production company)*. She moved in shortly after my wife's death. Our relationship was purely platonic at first. She helped me to cope with all those complex feelings of loss, bereavement and isolation. However almost imperceptibly we found ourselves being drawn together, and by the time forensics had taken the body out of the bedroom, I had already given her one on the kitchen table. She's all a man could want - she's a wonderful cook, doesn't mind pushing the hoover about, and has absolutely no gag reflex.

I'm tremendously excited about my new gameshow *(Fuck a Duck - weekdays 9.30 am BBC1)*. It's a bit like Catchphrase, but with general knowledge questions. You get fifty quid for every one you get right. If you get three in a row we bring out the ducks and then it really starts getting interesting. The animal rights protesters have been up in arms but it's just a bit of fun.

Rehearsals start at 10 a.m. but I've never been much of a morning person, so I tend to get out of bed some time in the early afternoon. There's an awful lot of standing around in studios doing fuck all involved in television, and at my time of life I can do without it. Anyway, I'm a professional, I don't need to rehearse. The public like the occasional ad-lib or fluffed line. That bit where the elephant shat all over Val Singleton - was that scripted? Was it bollocks. Same when they carried Norman Tebbit out of that hotel in his jim-jams. Completely off the cuff - and it made great television.

I get to the studio round about 5.20. Shooting starts at 5.30, so there's time for a swift couple or three with Bob Holness in the bar before I go on. Half an hour later, the show's in the can and I'm back propping up the bar. Once the Six O'clock News is finished, Moira Stuart comes sprinting in for a drink and a go on the bandit. You could set your watch by her. I don't hang around much after then. After eight pints of Bass she's on the karaoke doing Unchained Melody, and it's time to leave.

Me and a few friends, (Alex Higgins, George Best and Chris Quinten) have just opened a restaurant in Stoke Newington, so I might pop in there for a few drinks before dinner. We've got a sort of nazi monkey theme, with the waitresses in gorilla costumes and swastika armbands. It's early days yet, and things are still a bit slow but we've all sunk a lot of money into this project so it's got to be a success.

I eat out most nights, but on my rare nights in it's not unknown for me to knock up a little something in the kitchen. I cook a mean Pasta 'n' Sauce, which I wash down with two or three bottles of sherry, before heading out to the pub.

In my younger days I used to drink and drive without a second thought, but following my big accident *(Mellie ran over and killed a bus queue in 1986)* I am much more aware of how precious my licence is. These days if I've had a skinful, I drive very slowly and close to the kerb.

The pubs chuck out at half eleven, but the night is still young as far as I'm concerned. I head for my favourite club, an exclusive lap-dancing establishment in Acton, where I might stay until two or three in the morning. I've been down all the usual showbiz paths - sports cars, houses, drugs - but in a business where you can make ten grand cash for opening some poxy supermarket, I don't know any better way of spending money than stuffing it down some fat-titted bird's knickers.

One of the things I most regret is not having any kids. At least, none that I have access to. That's why I take very seriously my responsibilities as godfather to my producer Tom's young son *(Tom jnr - aged 8)*. I try to pop round there five or six nights a week for a snack, a bit of a drink and to use his toilet on my way back from Acton. I've been working with Tom now for fifteen years or more, and I've recently begun to notice how tired and stressed he's looking. I've seen the showbiz lifestyle do that to a lot of people around me. But I give him that same bit of advice that Robert Dougall gave me on the night of my first broadcast all those years ago: "It's not fucking brain surgery, Roger. It's just telly. Bollocks to it. Bollocks to everything."

Roger Mellie was talking to Parsley d'Lion.
Next week: Rostrum cameraman Ken Morse.

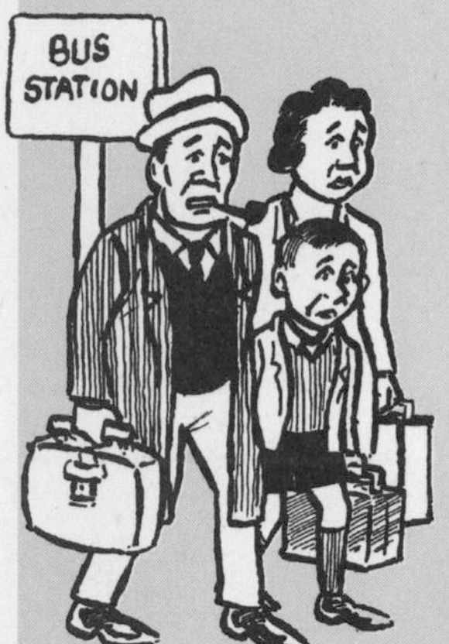
BUS
STATION

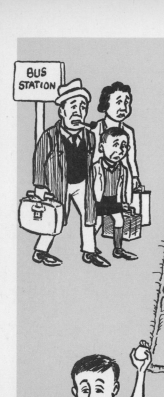

Ready, Skeggy, GO!

SKEGO

THE SKEGNESS

Saturday morning
You arrive in Skegness after sitting in traffic for two hours breathing in the fumes of your sister's travel sick. **Miss a turn.**

Saturday afternoon
You arrive at your B+B but the landlady will not allow you in until 7.00pm. **Miss 2 turns** whilst you sit on the beach with your suitcases.

Saturday evening
Give up and
GO HOME

Saturday night
You settle down to watch Starsky and Hutch in the guest house, but a poncy family with glasses insist on watching BBC2. **Miss two turns** as the night drags.

Sunday morning
Typhoon Daisy hits th
Lincolnshire coast an
police warn everyone
stay indoors. Your gue
house landlady insists y
leave by 10 am as it is t
rules. **Miss 2 turns** as y
sit all day in your
fogged-up car.

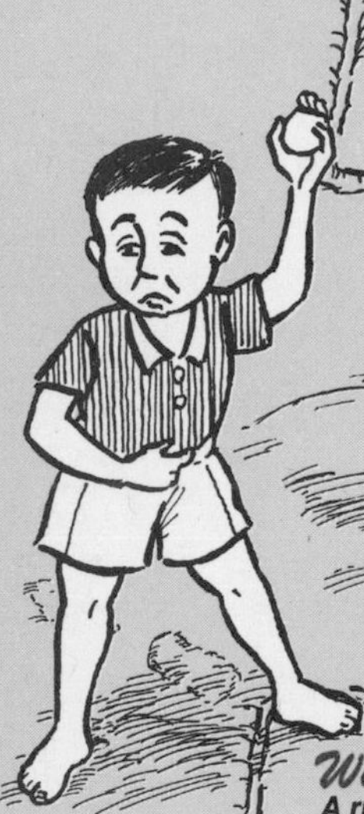

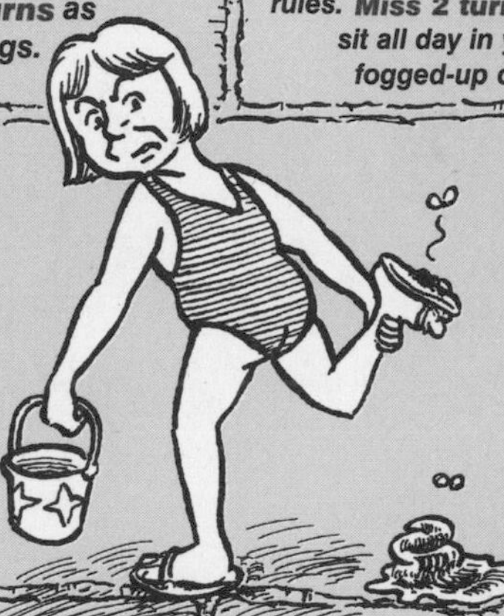

Tuesday night
It is pitch dark and y
are still looking for t
keys. Your dad keep
rooting through his p
ets and swearing. **M
forward one squa**

Wednesday morning
You return the next morning to look for the keys.
Have another go.

Wednesday afternoon
Give up and
GO HOME

Wednesday evening
A rumour goes round the town that a jellyfish has been washed up on the shore. You rush to the beach to throw stones at it.
Have another go.

Wednesday night
It's pissing with rain, so you wander into Woolworth's and have your picture taken in the photo booth wearing a kagoul.
Have another turn.

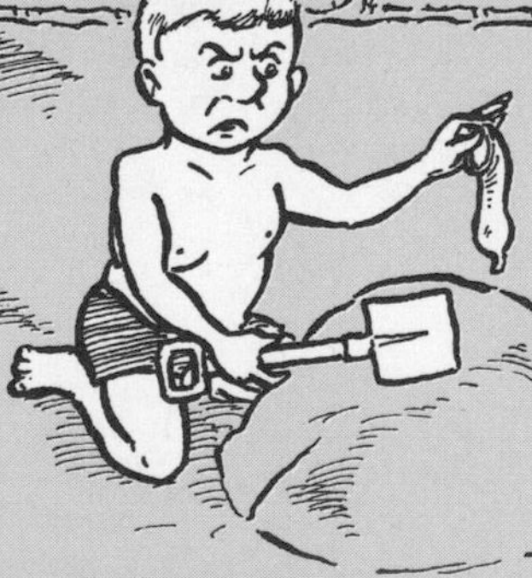

Thursday morning
You cut your instep on your spade and spend an hour trying to get an elastoplast to stick to your wet, sandy foot.
Move forward one square.

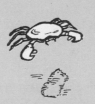

Thursday afternoon
You decide to sit on the beach all day. At the end of the day you look at your watch and it's only actually been ten minutes.
Miss a turn.

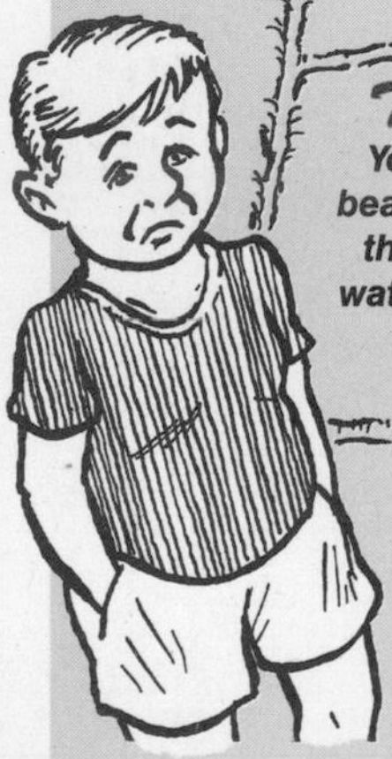

Thursday evening
A small ornament, a porcelain lady in a crinoline dress, has been broken and everyone is ordered to pack up and leave your guest house. **Miss 2 turns** whilst you walk the streets with your luggage looking for alternative accommodation.

Thursday night
You settle down to watch Top of the Pops, but the family in glasses turn the TV off to discuss some of the inventions they have just seen on Tomorrows World.
Go back 2 squares.

Friday morning
It's a sweltering hot day a
you decide to take a dip in
sea, but you only manage
seconds before you hobb
back to the beach, your f
crippled with cold.
Miss a turn.

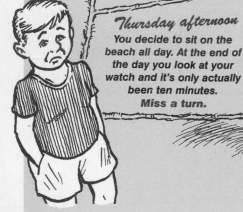